Lecture Notes in Computer Science

Vol. 1: GI-Gesellschaft für Informatik e.V. 3. Jahrestagung, Hamburg, 8.–10. Oktober 1973. Herausgegeben im Auftrag der Gesellschaft für Informatik von W. Brauer. XI, 508 Seiten. 1973.

Vol. 2: GI-Gesellschaft für Informatik e.V. 1. Fachtagung über Automatentheorie und Formale Sprachen, Bonn, 9.–12. Juli 1973. Herausgegeben im Auftrag der Gesellschaft für Informatik von K.-H. Böhling und K. Indermark. VII, 322 Seiten. 1973.

Vol. 3: 5th Conference on Optimization Techniques, Part I. (Series: I.F.I.P. TC7 Optimization Conferences.) Edited by R. Conti and A. Ruberti. XIII, 565 pages. 1973.

Vol. 4: 5th Conference on Optimization Techniques, Part II. (Series: I.F.I.P. TC7 Optimization Conferences.) Edited by R. Conti and A. Ruberti. XIII, 389 pages. 1973.

Vol. 5: International Symposium on Theoretical Programming. Edited by A. Ershov and V. A. Nepomniaschy. VI, 407 pages. 1974.

Vol. 6: B. T. Smith, J. M. Boyle, J. J. Dongarra, B. S. Garbow, Y. Ikebe, V. C. Klema, and C. B. Moler, Matrix Eigensystem Routines – EISPACK Guide. XI, 551 pages. 2nd Edition 1974. 1976.

Vol. 7: 3. Fachtagung über Programmiersprachen, Kiel, 5.–7. März 1974. Herausgegeben von B. Schlender und W. Frielinghaus. VI, 225 Seiten. 1974.

Vol. 8: GI-NTG Fachtagung über Struktur und Betrieb von Rechensystemen, Braunschweig, 20.–22. März 1974. Herausgegeben im Auftrag der GI und der NTG von H.-O. Leilich. VI, 340 Seiten. 1974.

Vol. 9: GI-BIFOA Internationale Fachtagung: Informationszentren in Wirtschaft und Verwaltung. Köln, 17./18. Sept. 1973. Herausgegeben im Auftrag der GI und dem BIFOA von P. Schmitz. VI, 259 Seiten. 1974.

Vol. 10: Computing Methods in Applied Sciences and Engineering, Part 1. International Symposium, Versailles, December 17–21, 1973. Edited by R. Glowinski and J. L. Lions. X, 497 pages. 1974.

Vol. 11: Computing Methods in Applied Sciences and Engineering, Part 2. International Symposium, Versailles, December 17–21, 1973. Edited by R. Glowinski and J. L. Lions. X, 434 pages. 1974.

Vol. 12: GFK-GI-GMR Fachtagung Prozessrechner 1974. Karlsruhe, 10.–11. Juni 1974. Herausgegeben von G. Krüger und R. Friehmelt. XI, 620 Seiten. 1974.

Vol. 13: Rechnerstrukturen und Betriebsprogrammierung, Erlangen, 1974. (GI-Gesellschaft für Informatik e.V.) Herausgegeben von W. Händler und P. P. Spies. VII, 333 Seiten. 1974.

Vol. 14: Automata, Languages and Programming – 2nd Colloquium, University of Saarbrücken, July 29–August 2, 1974. Edited by J. Loeckx. VIII, 611 pages. 1974.

Vol. 15: L Systems. Edited by A. Salomaa and G. Rozenberg. VI, 338 pages. 1974.

Vol. 16: Operating Systems, International Symposium, Rocquencourt 1974. Edited by E. Gelenbe and C. Kaiser. VIII, 310 pages. 1974.

Vol. 17: Rechner-Gestützter Unterricht RGU '74, Fachtagung, Hamburg, 12.–14. August 1974, ACU-Arbeitskreis Computer-Unterstützter Unterricht. Herausgegeben im Auftrag der GI von K. Brunnstein, K. Haefner und W. Händler. X, 417 Seiten. 1974.

Vol. 18: K. Jensen and N. E. Wirth, PASCAL – User Manual and Report. VII, 170 pages. Corrected Reprint of the 2nd Edition 1976.

Vol. 19: Programming Symposium. Proceedings 1974. V, 425 pages. 1974.

Vol. 20: J. Engelfriet, Simple Program Schemes and Formal Languages. VII, 254 pages. 1974.

Vol. 21: Compiler Construction, An Advanced Course. Edited by F. L. Bauer and J. Eickel. XIV. 621 pages. 1974.

Vol. 22: Formal Aspects of Cognitive Processes. Proceedings 1972. Edited by T. Storer and D. Winter. V, 214 pages. 1975.

Vol. 23: Programming Methodology. 4th Informatik Symposium, IBM Germany Wildbad, September 25–27, 1974. Edited by C. E. Hackl. VI, 501 pages. 1975.

Vol. 24: Parallel Processing. Proceedings 1974. Edited by T. Feng. VI, 433 pages. 1975.

Vol. 25: Category Theory Applied to Computation and Control. Proceedings 1974. Edited by E. G. Manes. X, 245 pages. 1975.

Vol. 26: GI-4. Jahrestagung, Berlin, 9.–12. Oktober 1974. Herausgegeben im Auftrag der GI von D. Siefkes. IX, 748 Seiten. 1975.

Vol. 27: Optimization Techniques. IFIP Technical Conference. Novosibirsk, July 1–7, 1974. (Series: I.F.I.P. TC7 Optimization Conferences.) Edited by G. I. Marchuk. VIII, 507 pages. 1975.

Vol. 28: Mathematical Foundations of Computer Science. 3rd Symposium at Jadwisin near Warsaw, June 17–22, 1974. Edited by A. Blikle. VII, 484 pages. 1975.

Vol. 29: Interval Mathematics. Procedings 1975. Edited by K. Nickel. VI, 331 pages. 1975.

Vol. 30: Software Engineering. An Advanced Course. Edited by F. L. Bauer. (Formerly published 1973 as Lecture Notes in Economics and Mathematical Systems, Vol. 81) XII, 545 pages. 1975.

Vol. 31: S. H. Fuller, Analysis of Drum and Disk Storage Units. IX, 283 pages. 1975.

Vol. 32: Mathematical Foundations of Computer Science 1975. Proceedings 1975. Edited by J. Bečvář. X, 476 pages. 1975.

Vol. 33: Automata Theory and Formal Languages, Kaiserslautern, May 20–23, 1975. Edited by H. Brakhage on behalf of GI. VIII, 292 Seiten. 1975.

Vol. 34: GI – 5. Jahrestagung, Dortmund 8.–10. Oktober 1975. Herausgegeben im Auftrag der GI von J. Mühlbacher. X, 755 Seiten. 1975.

Vol. 35: W. Everling, Exercises in Computer Systems Analysis. (Formerly published 1972 as Lecture Notes in Economics and Mathematical Systems, Vol. 65) VIII, 184 pages. 1975.

Vol. 36: S. A. Greibach, Theory of Program Structures: Schemes, Semantics, Verification. XV, 364 pages. 1975.

Vol. 37: C. Böhm, λ-Calculus and Computer Science Theory. Proceedings 1975. XII, 370 pages. 1975.

Vol. 38: P. Branquart, J.-P. Cardinael, J. Lewi, J.-P. Delescaille, M. Vanbegin. An Optimized Translation Process and Its Application to ALGOL 68. IX, 334 pages. 1976.

Vol. 39: Data Base Systems. Proceedings 1975. Edited by H. Hasselmeier and W. Spruth. VI, 386 pages. 1976.

Vol. 40: Optimization Techniques. Modeling and Optimization in the Service of Man. Part 1. Proceedings 1975. Edited by J. Cea. XIV, 854 pages. 1976.

Vol. 41: Optimization Techniques. Modeling and Optimization in the Service of Man. Part 2. Proceedings 1975. Edited by J. Cea. XIII, 852 pages. 1976.

Vol. 42: James E. Donahue, Complementary Definitions of Programming Language Semantics. VII, 172 pages. 1976.

Vol. 43: E. Specker und V. Strassen, Komplexität von Entscheidungsproblemen. Ein Seminar. V, 217 Seiten. 1976.

Vol. 44: ECI Conference 1976. Proceedings 1976. Edited by K. Samelson. VIII, 322 pages. 1976.

Vol. 45: Mathematical Foundations of Computer Science 1976. Proceedings 1976. Edited by A. Mazurkiewicz. XI, 601 pages. 1976.

Vol. 46: Language Hierarchies and Interfaces. Edited by F. L. Bauer and K. Samelson. X, 428 pages. 1976.

Vol. 47: Methods of Algorithmic Language Implementation. Edited by A. Ershov and C. H. A. Koster. VIII, 351 pages. 1977.

Vol. 48: Theoretical Computer Science, Darmstadt, March 1977. Edited by H. Tzschach, H. Waldschmidt and H. K.-G. Walter on behalf of GI. VIII, 418 pages. 1977.

Lecture Notes in Computer Science

Edited by G. Goos and J. Hartmanis

61

The Vienna Development Method: The Meta-Language

Edited by
D. Bjørner and C. B. Jones

Springer-Verlag
Berlin Heidelberg New York 1978

Editors

Dines Bjørner
Department of Computer Science
Building 343 and 344
Technical University of Denmark
DK-2800 Lyngby

Cliff B. Jones
IBM International Education Centre
Chaussee de Bruxelles 135
B-1310 La Hulpe

Library of Congress Cataloging in Publication Data
Main entry under title:

The Vienna development method.

    (Lecture notes in computer science ; 61)
    Bibliography: p.
    Includes index.
    1. Programming languages (Electronic computers)--
Addresses, essays, lectures. I. Bjørner, Dines.
II. Jones, Cliff B., 1944-   III. Title: Meta-
language. IV. Series.
QA76.7.V53   001.6'424   78-7232

AMS Subject Classifications (1970): 68-02, 68 A 05, 68 A 30
CR Subject Classifications (1974):

ISBN 3-540-08766-4 Springer-Verlag Berlin Heidelberg New York
ISBN 0-387-08766-4 Springer-Verlag New York Heidelberg Berlin

© by Springer-Verlag Berlin Heidelberg 1978
Printed in Germany

Printing and binding: Beltz Offsetdruck, Hemsbach/Bergstr.
2145/3140-5432

CONTENTS

Introduction   V

Acknowledgements   XVII

Addresses of All Authors   XIX

ON THE FORMALIZATION OF PROGRAMMING LANGUAGES:
   EARLY HISTORY AND MAIN APPROACHES   1
Peter Lucas

PROGRAMMING IN THE META-LANGUAGE: A TUTORIAL   24
Dines Bjørner

THE META-LANGUAGE: A REFERENCE MANUAL   218
Cliff B.Jones

DENOTATIONAL SEMANTICS OF GOTO: AN EXIT FORMULATION
   AND ITS RELATION TO CONTINUATIONS   278
Cliff B.Jones

A FORMAL DEFINITION OF ALGOL 60 AS DESCRIBED
   IN THE 1975 MODIFIED REPORT   305
Wolfgang Henhapl & Cliff B.Jones

SOFTWARE ABSTRACTION PRINCIPLES:
-- Tutorial Examples of: An Operating System
   Command Language Specification, and a PL/I-like
   On-Condition Language Definition   337
Dines Bjørner

References & Bibliography   375

All papers lists their CONTENTS at their very beginning.

INTRODUCTION

The purpose of this volume is to provide a summary of a body of work
which has reached a relatively stable state. The work is, however, far
from complete (in the sense - even - that the authors whose work is
presented here feel that they have satisfactory solutions to the problems they set out to solve.) Notwithstanding their own recognition of
difficulties and shortcomings in the current presentation, the authors
hope that what has been achieved may be of use to others. Furthermore,
a summary of the results of any significant effort may be hoped to
stimulate the work of researchworkers.

The purpose of this introduction is, of course, to introduce the volume. Firstly an outline is provided of the so-called "Vienna Development Method" and some motivation offered of the meta-language which is
the part of the method of concern in this volume. Following this a review is provided of other work done in the Vienna Laboratory, in order
to put what is presented here in context.

Vienna Development Method

Before entering into the description itself, it is perhaps worth spend-
ing a few moments on the name itself in the hope to avoid a misunder-
standing which could arise. The earlier work of the Vienna laboratory
developed a meta-language for definitions which became known as the
"Vienna Definition Language" (*VDL*). The relationship between the work
presented in this volume and the *VDL* is discussed below. Of course,
the earlier meta-language had a large influence on the later one. But
even here there is a sharp difference between the two (technically,
VDL was designed for writing operational definitions whilst the meta-
language used in *VDM* is intended for the presentation of denotational
definitions). Moreover, as the name suggests, the Vienna Development
Method (abbreviated to *VDM* in this volume) is much more than just a
meta-language.

Turning now to the content of *VDM*. The "method" is meant to be a systematic approach to the development of large computer software systems.
Strictly, there is nothing which restricts the application to software
but no attempts have been made to use the approach on hardware design.
The key proposals are simple and by no means unique to *VDM*. As indicated in *fig. 1*, the first objective in getting any complex system

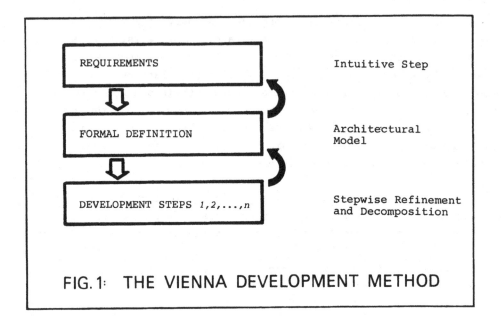

FIG. 1: THE VIENNA DEVELOPMENT METHOD

under control is the construction of a formal definition of the required function. This specification is a reference point for the subsequent development. For a large system there will follow a sequence
of development steps. The downward pointing arrows are suggestive of
a time sequence. Because it is often necessary to 'think ahead' in a
design process, it is more accurate to view the arrows as showing the
relationships between the final stages of the documentation. Thus, a
reader may understand the design of a system in a strictly top-down
way although this is an idealization of the actual (iterative) design
process.

The backward links in *fig.* *1* relate to another key point of *VDM*. At
each stage of development a justification is provided. Just as the
overall process begins with a specification, each intermediate development step can be viewed as presenting a solution to a specification
(all that distinguishes the last 'implementation' phase is that instead
of generating new specifications, all of the required units are avàil-
able). The aim of a justification is to document why the proposed solution. is believed to fulfil its specification. Such justifications
can be presented at different levels of formality. But without entering here into a discussion of what level might be chosen in various cir-

cumstances, it should be clear that justifications documented during the development process are likely to be both much more intuitive and of more use in early detection of design errors than any attempt to construct a proof for a complete system after construction.

Decomposition and correctness arguments are two key points: a third is the use of abstraction to handle complexity. In the papers in this volume it will be made clear how a specification can be viewed as an abstract model of the system to be specified. Such an abstract model will make extensive use of abstract data objects (see Bjørner 78b): it is the choice of appropriate abstractions which can make a short and readable formal specification. The use of abstract objects during the development process and their refinement to objects which are representable in the eventual realization is discussed in Bjørner 77a, Jones 77a.

Whilst *VDM* was first envisaged for languages and the development of their processors, the definition methods have subsequently been applied to other "systems" - see Hansal 76, Nilsson 76, Madsen 77.

The Meta-Language

Having employed an internal name ("Vienna Development Method") for the first part of the title of this volume, the anonymous sub-title may cause some surprise. In fact there is an internal name ("Meta-IV") for the meta-language used in *VDM* so its omission can be guessed to have strong grounds. The point is that in defining and developing systems a number of concepts have been used; it has of course been necessary to use a notation to manipulate the concepts. It is, however, the concepts which are important not the particular concrete syntax used for expressions realizing these concepts. It was felt by the authors that making wide use of a name for the meta-language might focus attention on the wrong issues and so it has been avoided. Furthermore, it should be made clear that the meta-language is not "closed" in that (well defined) extensions can be made without fear of a 'standards committee'.

The need for a meta-language should be clear. Decomposition has been shown to be a part of *VDM* and this only makes sence if something is written about each stage of development. If something is to be written it must use some language. In view of the systematic approach being taken

to development and, in particular, the use of justifications, it should
be obvious that a formal notation is required. Given that abstract objects are required, choosing established notation (e.g. for sets) would
appear to be wise. Surprisingly, the decision to use 'standard' mathematical notation for standard things has actually caused some people
to object! The clue is a concern, which is unfounded, that the use of
notation from a branch of mathematics implies that a deep knowledge
thereof is required.

Another influence on the meta-language has been programming languages.
Just as choosing understood mathematical objects can aid the reader,
the use of sequencing constructs from programming languages (e.g. *if
then else*) can enhance the readability of a definition. Of course, all
such constructs employed must themselves be precisely defined - this
is tackled in Jones 78a.

The major inpetus towards denotational semantics has come from Oxford
University. There is, however, a striking difference in the appearance
of definitions created by Oxford or Vienna. This subject is returned
to later in the volume but it is important to remember the objectives
of the different groups in order to avoid (erroneously) seeking a "correct" choice. The Oxford group have been interested in the foundations
of their meta-language and its use on examples small enough to facilitate complete proofs; the Vienna group was forced to take a more engineering approach when faced with languages like PL/I.

Several things have been deliberately excluded from this volume. Firstly the subject of concrete syntax is well-documented elsewhere (e.g.
Uzgalis 77) and thus, whilst an important part of a system definition, it is
ignored. Secondly, there is no formal description of methods for defining parallelism. Thirdly the relationship to other methods is only
discussed by P. Lucas: this is not a comment on the other authors' views
of, for example, axiomatic definitions.

Relation to Earlier Vienna Work

The purpose of this section is to identify the main differences between
the work presented in this volume and that done earlier in the Vienna
Laboratory. For this objective a complete historical view would be unnecessarily long and is not attempted. (This section fits, logically,
into the introduction, but the reader who is unfamiliar with the material will find it more beneficial to first read both the more general
historical review - Lucas 78 - and one of the descriptions of the current meta-language - Bjørner 78b or Jones 78a.)

In order to have precise names for the two phases that are to be compared, "VDL" and "VDM" will be used. "Vienna Definition Language"
(VDL) was a term coined and used most widely in North America and identifies the language definition notation developed and used in the Vienna Laboratory during the 1960's. The Vienna Development Method (VDM)
has been described above. It owes much to the earlier work but differs
in some inportant technical respects: these differences and their mo-
tivations are the subject here.

We begin by briefly reviewing some of the important documents relating
to the earlier work. The Vienna group had constructed a compiler for
ALGOL 60 and following this work was asked to undertake a formal definition of the PL/I language. The acknowledged basis of this work was
the papers McCarthy 63a, Landin 64, Landin 65, Elgot 64 and the Baden
TC2 conference of 1964 (see Steel 66 - especially McCarthy 66). The
first "tentative steps" towards a style for "Universal Language Description" (ULD) are recorded in Bandat 65. It is worth quoting the
objective as described by P. Lucas:

> "The result may serve as a vehicle for language design groups,
> implementation groups, and as a useful background for educated
> and sophisticated programmers. ... It should be possible to for-
> mulate and prove statements about the object language."

The first version of the PL/I definition did not cover the complete
language when printed in 1966. The 1968 version 2 was essentially complete and became an internal control and reference tool for the e-
volving language. This evolution led to the requirement for a third
version and subsequent (extensive) revisions. It is interesting to
review the structure of this third version:

Compile Time Facilities   Fleck 69
Concrete Syntax   Urschler 69a
Translation Concrete to Abstract Urschler 69b
Abstract Syntax and Interpreter Walk 69
Informal Introduction   Alber 69

The *VDL* notation is a means of describing abstract interpreters (see Lucas 78 for definition of this approach.) A very general view was taken of objects and their manipulation (cf. the "μ" function) and the control component was made part of the state of the interpreter. This meant that extremely "flexible" interpreters could be constructed which may have been one of the reasons why *VDL* was quickly adopted by a number of groups both in and outside IBM. To give just a few references: Lauer 68, Zimmermann 69, Lee 72, Moser 70a (this is one of several attempts to use the meta-language for the descriptions of "systems").

The best overview of the *VDL* work is probably still Lucas 69 along with Bekic 70b on the subject of storage models. Other reviews are available in Wegner 72 and Ollengren 75. (Although this section is not a full historical survey it would be remiss not to mention the guidance provided by H. Zemanek - see, for example, Zemanek 66).

Rather than listing the users of *VDL* it will be more germane to consider how such definitions were used in the justification of implementations of defined languages. Just as with the work on program development, the initial work concentrated on proofs: once this basis was laid, attention was turned to systematic development methods. Realizing his earlier (quoted) hopes P. Lucas was able to demonstrate the use of a *VDL* definition in proving an implementation correct in Lucas 68. A considerable amount of work in this direction was then undertaken and is reviewed in Jones 71. Much of this work was made more difficult than one felt was necessary by the "flexibility" of the abstract interpreters which could be written using *VDL*. In particular the ability to explicitly change the control meant that inductive proofs over the structure of (abstract) programs were not, in general, valid; and the inclusion of objects like the environment in a "Grand State" complicated proofs. Although the proofs in Jones 71 avoided the former problem, the latter led to some of the longest proofs in the paper. The attempts to use *VDL* definitions as a basis for systematic development of implementations was, then, providing indications that a change of definition style might be worthwhile.

Other important questions were being raised on the style of definition.
Of great importance were the observations in Bekič 70a that a more
"Mathematical" style could avoid much unnecessary detail. One of the
problems which had caused the use of the control in *VDL* was providing
a model for goto statements. An alternative "exit approach" had been
described in Henhapl 70a. A "functional" definition of ALGOL 60 used
this approach in Allen 72. Furthermore, this definition had used a
"small state" in that the environment was made a separate argument to
the defining functions. This definition is <u>not</u>, however, "mathematical"
("denotational") and is unnecessarily complicated by the avoidance of
combinators for frequently recurring patterns. (Other work on the question of "style" had, of course, been pursued – see, for example, Lauer
71, Hoare 69, Hoare 74).

The "denotational" approach is characterized in Lucas 78. The work of
the Oxford group is well documented in Scott 71, Mosses 74, Stoy 74
(the most readable account) and Milne 76.

Towards the end of 1972 the Vienna group again turned their attention
to the problem of systematically developing a compiler from a language
definition. The overall approach adopted has been termed the "Vienna
Development Method". Based on the above comments it should be no surprise that a "denotational" approach was adopted for the definition itself. (Using, however, the exit approach rather than "continuations" –
see Jones 78b). This change was, in fact, less drastic than some authors choose to suggest. It is possible to read a denotational definition as an abstract interpreter. However, there is a denotational
"rule" which requires that the denotations of compound objects should
depend only on the denotations of their components: this rule leads
one to the construction of definitions which are much clearer and easier
to reason about. In fact the change from operational to denotational
style was further masked by a preservation of an overall Vienna "flavour". This flavour comes from the choice of appropriate abstractions
for source and semantic objects and a writing style which aims at readability rather than conciseness.

The meta-language actually adopted ("Meta-IV") is used to define major
portions of PL/I (as given in ECMA 74 – interestingly a "formal" standards document written as an abstract interpreter) in Bekič 74. The project went on to consider how this definition would be used to construct
a compiler. An indication of the interface problem which results from

using a typical "product oriented" front-end, is shown in Weissenböck 75. A concern is often expressed as to how one can check that a formal definition captures one's intuitive notion of a language. Since the latter is inherently informal, the short answer is that one can not so do. But certain consistency conditions can be established and this is the subject of Izbicki 75. Although the project was not pursued to the stage of a running compiler, the overall method used is described in Jones 76a.

Again the meta-language developed for the *VDM* phase has been used by a number of other groups. The only significant IBM publication is Hansal 76 which is interesting because it addresses the problem of relational data bases. Externally, Nilsson 76 and many working documents of the Technical University of Denmark have used "Meta-IV" (see also Bjørner 77b).

There are still a number of open issues. The problem of defining arbitrary merging and/or parallelism was tackled in Bekic 74 but the technique used has not yet been defined in a satisfactorily "Mathematical" way - see Bekic 71 and Milner 73. Another area of future research is outlined in Mosses 77. In the general view of making definitions more abstract, the rôle of the environment is questioned in Jones 70.

On the Definition of PL/I

Bekič 74 contains a definition of most of the non-I/O parts of PL/I as described in ECMA 74. (Some of the input-output statements were defined by W. Pachl, but the work is not published). The ALGOL 60 definition in this volume (Henhapl 78) has benefited from that work and exhibits many of the formulations used earlier. There are, unfortunately, minor notational differences to be faced in reading the earlier work. The significant differences, however, derive from the extra "richness" of PL/I and the main aspects of the relevant formulations are reviewed here. (Again, this section should be skipped at first reading).

As mentioned above, some attempt was made in Bekič 74 to cover the problem of arbitrary order. In particular the order of access to variables anywhere within expressions is not constrained. The "," combinator was introduced to tackle this problem.

Because PL/I offers a larger set of ways of building aggregates than
is available in ALGOL 60, a more implicit model of storage is used.
Furthermore, the normal way of governing the lifetime of variables in
ALGOL 60 becomes one of four ways available in PL/I: this normal way
is called *AUTOMATIC*; the "own" variables of ALGOL 60 correspond roughly to *STATIC*; in addition PL/I offers *BASED* and *DEFINED* storage classes.
With *BASED* variables explicit allocation statements must be executed
and there is no automatic freeing. There are a number of expressions
involved such as references to pointer variables and the main interest
is in showing when, in what environment and with what exception conditions (see below) these various expressions are evaluated.

As well as parameters of type *ENTRY* (i.e. procedure) and *LABEL*, PL/I
permits variables of these types. Furthermore, their use is not statically constrained, as is the case in ALGOL 68, to prevent attempted
access to entities local to a block after the lifetime of that block.
Therefore, the problem of checking for "past activations" had to be
tackled in the PL/I definition.

Perhaps the most interesting extension is the use of "ON conditions"
and "condition built-in-functions/pseudo-variables". ON statements
ca be modelled as assignments to *ENTRY* variables (notice they are dynamically, not lexicographically, inherited). The effect of encounter-
ing a condition (whether *SIGNAL*led or implicitly raised) can be modelled by a call of the procedure which is currently assigned to the appropriate variable. The pseudo-variables used for investigating and
returning values from these procedures behave like global variables.

For further details on the PL/I model, the reader is referred to the
"annotation" section of Bekić 74.

The Structure of this Volume

The papers of this volume can be grouped in four categories.

(I) The first paper:

    On the Formalization of Programming Languages: Early History &
    Main Approaches

by Peter Lucas sets the stage. It discusses the main approaches to language definition, the intrinsic aspects of the problem area and their origins. As such the paper provides a frame for the remainder of the volume.

(II) The next two papers:

Programming in the Meta-Language: A Tutorial

by Dines Bjørner, and:

The Meta-Language: A Reference Manual

by Cliff B. Jones give complementary descriptions of the meta-language. The tutorial is a partly informal introduction to, partly comprehensive primer for, the meta-language. The reference manual gives precise semantics definitions of the more important meta-language constructs. The tutorial is primarily aimed at persons new to formal definitions, but with some background in (ALGOL-like) programming. The reference manual, in contrast, is primarily aimed at people, familiar with the basic ideas of denotational semantics, who wishes to understand the meta-language. Comprehension of the tutorial is otherwise a sufficient prerequisite for any other paper of this volume. The tutorial describes constructs not formally covered by the reference manual. Any such construct can, however, be simply reduced to simple combinations of constructs formally covered by the reference manual. It is in this sense we say that the language described in the tutorial is 'larger' than that defined by the reference manual.

(III) The fourth paper:

Denotational Semantics of Goto: An Exit Formulation and its Relation to Continuations

by Cliff B. Jones, brings focus on a major factor distinguishing the Oxford, Scott-Strachey, School of expressing Denotational Semantics, from the current Vienna School. As such the paper contributes to a deeper understanding of the *VDM* meta-language by analyzing one of its combinators, the *exit* construct.

(IV) The last group of papers exhibits actual abstractions:

A Formal Definition of ALGOL 60 as Described in the 1975 Modified Report

by Wolfgang Henhapl & Cliff B. Jones presents the latest in a number of ALGOL 60 definitions. Over its only 32 pages of text and formulae it demonstrates, we believe, the power of the abstractional techniques used, and the meta-language tool described earlier, by giving a very readable and neat denotational semantics definition. The last paper of the volume:

Software Abstraction Principles: Tutorial Examples of an Operating System Command Language Specification and a PL/I-like On-Condition Language Definition.

by Dines Bjørner summarizes a number of complementing & contrasting abstract modeling techniques. The first example is chosen to indicate the applicability of the software abstraction ideas to other than conventional programming languages; the second in order to illustrate various state modeling techniques & also the unusual On-Condition Language construct.

The volume ends with a unified bibliography recording the literature referred to in the various papers.

ACKNOWLEDGEMENTS

The editors of this volume gratefully acknowledge the Computer Science Department of The Technical University of Denmark and the European Systems Research Institute of the IBM Corporation for their kind support, enabling us to prepare this volume.

The editors are especially happy to thank the co-authors: Wolfgang Hanhapl & Peter Lucas, for their much appreciated contributions.

These latter actually stretches back over the many years the authors were members of the IBM Vienna Laboratory. To all of our colleagues, some of them still there, goes our most sincerely felt appreciation for the seemingly never-ending source of inspiration they represent.

Very special, deep and fond thanks goes to Prof. Heinz Zemanek for having created such unique working environments; and to Dr. Hans Bekic for his unwavering high standards which kept us straight.

Finally all co-authors join the editors in expressing their indebtness for the expert and untiring assistance of Mrs. Annie Rasmussen and Mrs. Jytte Søllested.

Dines Bjørner & Cliff B. Jones

Montpellier, France

January, 1978

ADDRESSES OF ALL AUTHORS

Dines Bjørner
Department of Computer Science
Buildings 343-344
Technical University of Denmark
DK-2800 Lyngby
Denmark

Wolfgang Henhapl
Institut für Informatik
Technische Hochschule Darmstadt
Steubenplatz 12
D-61 Darmstadt
Germany

Cliff B. Jones
    on assignment to:
IBM European Systems Research Institute
Chaussée de Bruxelles 135
B-1310 La Hulpe
Belgium
    from:
IBM Laboratory Vienna
IBM Haus
Obere Donaustrasse 2
A-1020 Vienna II
Austria

Peter Lucas
IBM Laboratory
IBM Haus
Obere Donaustrasse 2
A-1020 Vienna II
Austria

ON THE FORMALIZATION OF PROGRAMMING LANGUAGES: EARLY HISTORY AND MAIN APPROACHES

Peter Lucas

Abstract:

The paper discusses the nature of the subject, and summarizes its origins. The main approaches and their interrelationships are discussed. The author's view on the long and short range objectives is presented.

CONTENTS

1. On the Significance of the Area   3

2. Historical Background   6

3. Basic Methodological Approaches   10
    3.1 Abstract Syntax   10
    3.2 Mathematical Semantics   11
    3.3 Operational Semantics   15
    3.4 Axiomatic Approach   18

4. Challenges   21-23

1. ON THE SIGNIFICANCE OF THE AREA

Computer systems can be viewed as machines capable of interpreting
languages; they accept and understand declarative sentences, obey imperative sentences and answer questions, all within the framework of
those languages for which the systems were built. A computer system
accomplishes its tasks on the basis of a prescription of these tasks,
i.e. on the basis of a program expressed in some programming language.

There is no inherent disparity between human languages (including natural language and the artificial languages of science) and languages
used to talk to computers. Thus there is no need to apologize for "an-
thropomorphisms" in the above point of view; in fact our only way to
talk scientifically about the relation of humans to their natural languages is in terms of computer notions (or so it seems to me).

By viewing computers as language interpreting machines it becomes quite
apparent that the analysis of programming (and human) languages is
bound to be a central theme of Computer Science.

Part of the fascination of the subject is of course related to its in-
timate connection to human language, i.e. the mechanisms we study mirror
in some way at least part of our own internal mechanisms.

Although there is no inherent disparity between human language and computer language, there is at present a huge gap between what we can
achieve by human conversation and our communication with machines. A
little further analysis will indicate the nature of the gap.

First we consider the structural aspect of language, i.e. how phrases
are composed of words and sentences are built from phrases, commmonly
called "syntax". There are efficient and precise methods to define the
syntax of a language and algorithms to compose and decompose sentences
according to such definitions. The problem is more or less solved. Yes,
computer language usually have a simpler and more regular syntax than
natural languages (as even some scientific notations) and there are
technical problems yet to be solved. Yet, it seems to me, there is not
much of a gap.

Second, there is the aspect of meaning, or "semantics" as it is usually
called. Now we get into more subtle problems. Let me restrict the discussion, for the time being, to the objects we can talk about in the

various languages(rather than considering what we can say about them).
Programming languages in the strict sense talk invariably about rather
abstract objects such as numbers, truth-values, character strings and
the like. Certainly, the major programming languages in use do not let
us talk about tables, chairs or people, not even about physical dimensions of numbers such as: hours, pounds or feet. The commercial languages do not know about the distinction of dollars and francs, and
scientific languages do not know about time and space. There have been
some attempts to include those notions or a device that makes it possible to define these notions within a language, e.g. the class concept in SIMULA and PASCAL and the investigations around abstract data
types. If we extend the notion of programming language to include query
languages and database languages we may observe a tendency in the indicated direction. Yet, there is a gap. Artificial Intelligence has
experimented for some time with languages that can be used to talk about
objects other than numbers etc.; we should probably look a lot more frequently accross the fence.

Definition methods concerning semantic, and even more so, mechanical ways
to use semantic definitions are much less understood than in the case
of the syntactic aspect.

Thirdly, there is the aspect of language understanding; I hesitate to
call this "pragmatics" since the latter term has been used for too
many things.

Suppose I ride on a train with a friend. The friend observes: "The
windows are wet"[1] . The statement is presumably structured according
to the english grammar and has a certain meaning. However, I would
probably not just analyze the sentence and determine its meaning, and
leave it at that. Most likely I would react by looking at a window, observe that there are drops, conclude that it is raining, prepare my um-
brella so that I don't get wet and ruin my coat when I get off the
train, etc.,. To draw all these conclusions and act accordingly I need

----

(1) It would not make any difference to the following argument if my
    learned friend had used META-IV and passed a note saying: "wet
    (windows)". That is to say, I do not discuss the distinction be-
    tween natural language and standard (formal) notation but the dis-
    tinction of the human and computer use of the statement irrespec-
    tive of the form.

to use a lot of knowledge about the physical world in general and about
my specific environment. It is in this area of language understanding,
where I see the bigger gap between our interaction with the computer
as opposed to humans. What is lacking in the machine are models of the
external world and general mechanisms to draw conclusions and trigger
actions. Again Artificial Intelligence and natural language research
have been concerned with the problem. Yet, this has not had any practical influence on e.g. commercial applications. With the increase
in computer power it might very well be worth looking over the fence.

With the preceding paragraphs I wanted to put the present subject into
a much larger context than is usual. Thank God, there is more to programming languages than procedures, assignment and goto's (or no gotos).

The rest of the paper is a lot less ambitious and remains more or less
within the traditional concepts of programming languages. It presents
my subjective perception of the various origins of the methods of semantic definitions. Each of the three main approaches are then summa-
rized. The paper concludes by outlining some more short range objectives.

2. HISTORICAL BACKGROUND

The theory of programming languages, the related formal definition
techniques in particular, has roots in - and is related to - several
other disciplines such as linguistics, formal logic and certain mathematical disciplines. In fact, the terms "syntax" and "semantics" and
with these terms the distinction between the respective aspects of
language, have been introduced by the american philosopher Charles Morris [Morris 38, Zemanek 66]. He developed a science of signs which
he called semiotics. Semiotics, according to Morris, is subdivided into three distinct fields: syntax, semantics, and pragmatics. In his
book on Signs, Language, and Behavior [Morris 55] Morris defines:

"pragmatics - deals with the origin, uses and effects of signs within
    the behavior in which they occur;

semantics - deals with the signification of signs in all modes of sig-
    nifying;

syntax - deals with the combination of signs without regard for their
    specific significations or their relation to the behaviour in which
    they occur."

The clear distinciton between syntax and semantics, first applied to
a programming language in the ALGOL 60 report [Naur 63], has turned
out to be tremendously useful. There have been several not so successful attempts to carry the notion of pragmatics into the theory of programming languages (see e.g. San Dimas Conference [ACM 65]). We may
start the history of formal definition methods for programming languages
with the year 1959 when J. Backus proposed a scheme for the syntactic
definition of ALGOL 60 [Backus 59]. This scheme (a generative grammar)
was then actually used in the ALGOL 60 report; the related notation is
known as BNF (for Backus Normal Form or Backus Naur Form). BNF, or
variations thereof, have been used in many instances; it has stimulated
theoretical research as well as practical schemes for compiler production (both automatic and non-automatic). Roughly speaking, BNF grammars
coincide with the class of context free grammars of Chomsky [Chomsky
59]; it is worth mentioning that Chomsky divides his grammatical for-
malisms in an attempt to obtain a basis for the syntax of the English
language. Much research has been devoted to the study of subtypes and
extended types of BNF grammars; the latter in support of the desire to capture more syntactic properties of the language to be
defined; the former, i.e. the study of subtypes is usually motivated

by the wish to guarantee properties which permit fast syntax recognition and analysis algorithms. The subject of formal syntax definition, and the related computational problems and methods, have found their way into textbooks and computer science curricula; in fact, the larger part of compiler writing courses is usually spent on syntax problems.

At least since the ALGOL 60 report, the lack of rigorous definition methods for the semantics of programming languages was widely recognized; furthermore, the success of formal syntax definitions invited similar attempts for the semantic aspects of programming languages, yet, the problem turned out to be of an obstinate nature. To date, there is no satisfactory solution, at least none that enjoys the consensus of the computing community.

The instructions of machine languages are defined by the behaviour of the respective machine upon execution of these instructions. The associated manuals usually describe first what constitutes the state of the specific machine (e.g. content of main storage, content of registers, etc.) and then for each instruction and any given state the successor state after execution of the instruction to be defined. Hence, for a programmer, the most direct way to define a programming language is in terms of an interpreting machine; only that, for higher level languages, we must abstract from particularities of hardware machines and inplementation details and use a suitable hypothetical machine instead. E.W. Dijkstra formulated the situation in 1962 [Dijkstra 62] as follows: "A machine defines (by its very structure) a language, viz. its input language; conversely, the semantic definition of a langauge specifies a machine that understands it"[1].

The classic paper that has triggered a large volume of follow-on work is by McCarthy [McCarthy 63]. The paper outlines a basis for a theory of computation; more important for our subject, it establishes the main goals and motivation: methods to achieve correctness of programs in general and of compilers in particular; rigorous language definitions constitute a subgoal. The schema for language definitions proposed by McCarthy contains a number of novel subjects. Firstly, a complete se-

----

(1) it would be unfair to include this quotation and not say that Prof. E.W. Dijkstra would probably no longer defend this position, and rather tend to be a proponent of the direction described under "Axiomatic Approach" in this paper.

paration of notational issues, i.e. the representation of phrases by linear character strings, from the definition of the essential syntactic structure of a language. The latter definition is called Abstract Syntax. It is, at least for complicated languages, much more concise than the concrete syntax. Thus, a semantic definition on the basis of an abstract syntax becomes independent of notational details and is also more concise. Secondly, state vectors are introduced as the bases of the semantic definitions proper, i.e. the meaning of an instruction or statement is defined as a state transition. The paper shows in principle the task of proving compilers correct. The basic scheme of language definitions has been elaborated in many instances during the past decade, e.g. by the earlier work of the Vienna Laboratory on PL/I [Lucas 69] and the proposed ECMA-ANSI standard [ECMA 74].

Another successful direction of research was initiated by P. Landin [Landin 64,65], using the lambda-calculus [Church 41] as the fundamental basis. He revealed that certain concepts of ALGOL 60 (and similar languages) can be viewed as syntactic variations (syntactic sugar) of the lambda-calculus. The inherently imperative concepts, assignment and transfer of control, were captured by introducing new primitives into the lambda-calculus; the extended base is defined by the so-called SECD machine, a hypothetical machine whose state consists of 4 components: Storage, Environment, Control and Dump. The machine state has more structure than the state vectors of McCarthy, because the machine had to reflect more complicated concepts (blocks, local names) than McCarthy's original simple example was intended to.

In 1964 [Strachey 66] C. Strachey argued that, with the introduction of a few basic concepts, it was possible to describe even the imperative parts of a programming language in terms of the lambda-calculus. With the referenced paper, C. Strachey initiated a development that led to an explication of programming languages known as mathematical or denotational semantics. The fundamental mathematical basis for the latter development was contributed by D. Scott in 1970 [Scott 70]. The joint paper, by D. Scott and C. Strachey [Scott 71] offers a description method and its application to essential language concepts based upon the indicated research.

Research on axiom systems and proof theory suitable as a base for correctness proofs of programs was initiated by R. Floyd [Floyd 67], with a simple flow diagram language. C.A.R. Hoare [Hoare 69,71], extended and refined the results to apply to constructs of higher level languages.

The area has been the most actively pursued, including expreriments in automatic program verification.

There are several pioneering research efforts, which do not so evidently fall into the categories introduced above. Among the very early results on semantics published is A. van Wijngaarden's "Generalized ALGOL" [van Wijngaarden 62]. De Bakker [de Bakker 69] discovered that the schema proposed by A. van Wijngaarden can be viewed as a generalized Markov Algorithm. A. Carraciolo   Forinó 66] also used Markov Algorithms as the starting point for the formalization of programming language semantics.

For anyone familiar with syntax directed compilers it is tempting to apply similar ideas to the definition of semantics. A definition method on this basis is due to D. Knuth: Semantics of Context Free Languages [Knuth 68]. In some way or another, a formal definition of the semantics of a language invariably specifies a relation between any phrase of the language and some mathematical object called the denotation of the phrase. D. Knuth provides a convenient scheme that allows the specification of functions over the phrases of a language assuming that the phrase structure of the language is given by a production system.

Most research so far has been devoted to the definition and analysis of existing languages (or concepts found in existing languages). Yet, formal semantics could be a most valuable intellectual tool for the design of novel programming concepts (or synonymously: novel programming language constructs). There are rare instances of such applications of formal semantics (e.g. [Dennis 75, Henderson 75]).

3. BASIC METHODOLOGICAL APPROACHES

3.1 Abstract Syntax

The notion of abtract syntax is of considerable value for practical definitions of notationally complicated languages. There exist several methodological variations, which all achieve the same objective: to abstract from semantically irrelevant notational detail and reduce the syntax to define the essence of the linguistic forms only.

For illustration consider the following examples. Let v be the category of variables and e be the category of expressions. Several notational variants are in use to denote assignment statements e.g.:

    v = e
    v := e
    e → v

The semantically essential structure common to these notations is: That there is a syntactic category called assignment statement, and that an assignment statement has two components, a variable and an expression.

An abstract syntax may define an expression to be either an elementary expression (variable, constant, etc.,) or a binary operation consisting of an operator, a first operand, and a second operand (the definition of expressions may have several other alternatives); operands are again expressions.

As a concrete syntax, meant to define character strings, such a definition would be hopelessly insufficient and ambiguous, e.g. we would not know whether to parse $x+y*z$ into:

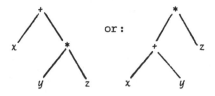

Thus the concrete syntax has to introduce punctuation marks such as parentheses, and, in the example of expressions, precedence rules of operators to avoid ambiguities. However, the definition of expressions given above is perfectly usable as an abstract syntax definition.

It can be regarded as a definition of parsing trees, hence the ambiguity problem is completely avoided. Thus there are advantages gained even in the case where only one language is considered: representational details are suppressed and each phrase is given a kind of normal form.

For practical cases, such as PL/I, the number of rules necessary to define an abstract syntax is much smaller than for the corresponding concrete syntax; hence we have obtained a more concise basis for the semantic definition. The price we pay is an additional part for the formalization of a language, which establishes the relation between the concrete and the abstract syntax.

3.2 Mathematical Semantics

The semantics of a given language is formalized by associating a suitable mathematical object (set, function, etc.) with each phrase of the language; the phrase is said to denote the associated object; the object is called the denotation of the phrase. Furthermore, to gain a view which is referentially transparent, of the language to be defined, denotations of composite phrases shall be defined solely in terms of the denotations of the subphrases. The major problem in establishing the mathematical semantics for a given language is to find suitable mathematical objects, that can serve as the denotations.

Using the notation introduced by D. Scott and C. Strachey we will write $I[p]$ for the denotation of a phrase p[1]. To indicate the various phrases to be discussed, we will use an ALGOL like and otherwise obvious notation, e.g. $I[x:=x-1]$ is the denotation of the assignment statement $x:=x-1$.

----

(1) for small examples, like those introduced in this paper, it is better to abstain from using abstract syntax and META-IV functions. For larger examples (e.g. PL/I), the notational conventions used here would lead to considerable difficulties.

The further elaboration of the subject will go through a series of programming language concepts in increasing order of complexity. Take
first a simple language with a fixed set of variables (id), expressions
(e) without side effects, assignments statements ($id:=e$) and compound
statements ($s1;s2$). If we were to construct a definitional interpreter,
we would certainly introduce a state vector (á lá McCarthy). Although
we do not wish to specify particular ways to compute the effect of executing programs and their parts, we still have to characterize the
overall effect of this execution. Therefore we introduce state vectors
σ, which are (usually) partial functions from variable names ID into
the set of values, VAL, which a variable may assume, i.e.

$$\sigma: ID \xrightarrow{\sim} VAL.$$

Let Σ be the set of all possible states. The kinds of denotations that
occur in the example language can now be chosen as follows:

$$I[e] : \Sigma \xrightarrow{\sim} VAL$$
$$I[st] : \Sigma \xrightarrow{\sim} \Sigma$$

i.e. the denotations of expressions are functions from states into values and the denotations of statements are functions from states to states.

Assuming that $I[e]$ has been defined elsewhere, the definition of assignment and compound statement according to the philosophy of mathematical semantics read:

$$I[id:=e](\sigma) = assign(\sigma,id,I[e](\sigma))$$
$$\text{where: } assign(\sigma,id,val) = \sigma', \quad \sigma'(x) = \begin{cases} val \text{ for } x=id \\ \sigma(x) \text{ for } x \neq id \end{cases}$$

$$I[s1;s2] = I[s2] \cdot I[s1] \qquad \text{... functional composition}$$

Note that denotations of composite phrases are given in terms of denotations of immediate subphrases and that we have avoided introducing
a statement counter. For each additional language feature we may have
to revise the definition of states, introduce new ways to compose denotations or even design new kinds of mathematical objects.

As a first complication we introduce a loop statement of the form:
$while$ e do s, say. We assume that e returns a truth value and intui-

tively expect that the denotation of the loop statement can be defined
as:

$$I[\underline{while}\ e\ \underline{do}\ s](\sigma)) \ = \ \begin{cases} I[\underline{while}\ e\ \underline{do}\ s](I[s](\sigma)) & \text{if} \quad I[e](\sigma) \\ \sigma & \text{if} \sim I[e](\sigma) \end{cases}$$

Evidently, the definition is of the form $f=F(f)$, with $f=I[\underline{while}\ e\ \underline{do}\ s]$,
i.e. f is defined as the fixed point of F. Before this definition can
be accepted as meaningful, one has to ask whether such a fixed point
always exists and whether it is unique. The existence can be asserted
under appropriate mathematical restrictions (introducing concepts of
monotonicity and continuity); there will in general be more than one
fixed point satisfying the equation. Thus an additional rule has to be
introduced which makes the defined object unique (the "smallest" fixed
point under a suitably defined ordering relation). This is not the
place to elaborate the issue at length and the reader must be referred
to the respective literature.

However, it should by now be evident that we are led into deep mathematical issues, and this at a stage where, from a programming language
point of view, we have only introduced the most primitive language constructs. At this point, it seems that we have to contemplate the potential uses of a semantic definition. The author suggests to distinguish
between the foundation of the subject matter and more practical problems like the description of real-life programming languages for compiler writers. Like the foundations of mathematics on the one hand and
applied mathematics on the other, these two fields are not unrelated
but are distinct. If we accept the program of mathematical semantics,
the steps we have tried to indicate follow, and the difficulties observed above are inevitable. On the other hand, it seems unrealistic
and in fact unnecessary to require that each compiler writer be fluent
in modern algebra. Rather, one would expect that the foundations are
used to justify, once and for all, useful practical methods which in
turn can be applied directly by the practitioner (not everybody who
applies Fourier Analysis need to be a specialist in the foundations of
mathematics).

Next we introduce expressions with side effect, i.e. evaluation of an
expression returns a value and changes the state. Consequently, we
change the type of object an expression denotes to:

$$I[e] \ : \quad \Sigma \ \tilde{\rightarrow} \ \Sigma \ VAL$$

The definition of assignment and loops are to be changed accordingly. A further important concept in most programming languages is that of local names, i.e. names which are declared for a specific textual scope of a program. The syntactic category is called block and takes the form: _begin dcl id; st end_.

Since the same name may now be used in different blocks for different purposes we have to introduce some device in the definition which enables us to distinguish the different uses of a name. One usually introduces an auxiliary object called environment, _env_, which is a function from names (variable names in the present example) to so called locations; the state then maps location into values. Thus a state σ is now a function of type $\sigma: LOC \underset{m}{\to} VAL$, where LOC is a set of primitive objects called locations; the auxiliary object _env_ is of type $env: ID \underset{m}{\to} LOC$.

In order to interpret a given phrase we always have to have an environment which associates the names occurring in the phrase with locations. The mathematical types of the denotations have to be revised:

$$I[e] : ENV \overset{\sim}{\to} (\Sigma \overset{\sim}{\to} \Sigma \ VAL)$$

i.e. $I[e]$ when applied to an environment yields a function which transforms a state and returns a value.

$$I[\underline{begin} \ \underline{dcl} \ \underline{id;s} \ \underline{end}] : ENV \overset{\sim}{\to} (\Sigma \overset{\sim}{\to} \Sigma)$$

The types of the denotations of the other constructs are designed similarly. The denotation of blocks, the new construct, is defined as:

$$I[\underline{begin} \ \underline{dcl} \ \underline{id;s} \ \underline{end}](env)(\sigma) = I[s](env')(\sigma') \ | \ restrict \ to \ \underline{dom} \ of \ \sigma$$

where $\sigma'(x) = \begin{cases} \Omega \ if \ x = loc \\ \sigma(x) \ otherwise \end{cases}$ $env'(x) = \begin{cases} loc \ if \ x = id \\ env(x) \ otherwise \end{cases}$

where: loc is some $loc \in LOC$ not in $\underline{dom}$ of σ

The last features to be discussed in this section are procedure declarations and parameter passing. What should the denotation of a procedure (in the sense of ALGOL or PL/I) be? According to the philosophy of mathematical semantics it is of type:

$$ENV \to ((A1 \ ... \ Ah) \overset{\sim}{\to} (\Sigma \overset{\sim}{\to} \Sigma))$$

i.e. given arguments $a1,a2,...,an$, and env to interpret the global identifiers occurring in the procedure, the procedure is simply a state to
state transition function. Some higher level programming languages permit procedures to be passed as arguments in particular a procedure can
be passed as an argument to itself. In contrast, the type of a function
is usually considered distinct from its range of arguments and value
range to avoid the well-known paradoxes. The establishment of a type
free theory of functions which provides the appropriate domain of denotations for procedures is a major achievement of D. Scott [Scott 70].
Apart from those language constructs which none of the methods has so
far addressed, there are several problems which have as yet no known
solution in the framework of mathematical semantics; in particular parallel and quasi-parallel execution (tasking, unspecified order of execution). Condition handling in PL/I; labels and goto's have been formulated, however, the models do not closely correspond to the intuitive
concept of the construct. With parallel processing, it seems referential transparency cannot be achieved as long as denotations of statements merely reflect the initial state / result state relation. There
are two sizable language definitions in this style. Firstly, a definition of ALGOL 60 [Mosses 74]. Secondly a recent definition of a subset
of PL/I [Bekič 74].

There is an exellent tutorial on the subject by J. Stoy [Stoy 74].

3.3 Operational Semantics

The semantics of a programming language can be defined via a hypothetical machine which interprets the programs of that language; such methods have been called "operational", or "constructive". The latter
term is, however, misleading, because the specification of hypothetical machines may contain non-constructive elements, such as quantifiers,
implicit definitions and infinite objects. The term "definitional interpreter" is sometimes used instead of "hypothetical machine".

By machine we understand a structure consisting of a set of states, two
subsets thereof: the initial states and the end states, a state transition function and a function which maps programs and their input data
into initial states; also usually not given explicitly, there should
be a function which takes end states as arguments and yields that part of

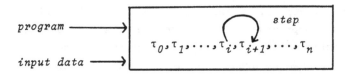

τ_0 ... initial state τ_n ... end state
$step$ ... state transition function $\tau_0, \ldots, \tau_n$ ... computation

an end state which is the result of the program. Since most higher
level languages are such that the program remains constant, i.e. is
not modified, during its interpretation, one could also keep the program separate and only include a statement counter to the currently
executed statement within the state itself. The definition of the step
function, if properly done, will reflect the syntactic structure of
the language, such that we cannot only relate an entire program to a
computation, but also subphrases of the program to sections of the
computation, i.e. we may ask what a specific subphrase in a given context means. In languages, like e.g. PL/I, where the order of operations
is not entirely fixed, the defining hypothetical machine is non-deterministic, i.e. the $step$ function will, in general, yield a set of possible successor states and a program will thus be related to a set of
computations.

To illustrate the differences (and similarities) between mathematical
semantics and operational methods consider the following example:

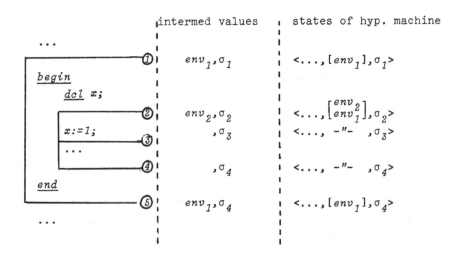

The example program part is a block with one declaration and a compound statement as the executable part. In order to elaborate this program part, given a mathematical definition, we would have to compute the intermediate states and environments shown in column one of the above table. The sequence of intermediate values almost represents the computaion of a hypothetical machine. The previously introduced concept of a machine requires that each state of a computation only depends upon its immediate predecessor state. Consequently, in order to have the environment available at point (5) of the computation it has to be remembered, i.e. contained in the states (2), (3) and (4). This is accomplished by an environment stack as shown in the second column of the above table; the stack is part of the state of the hypothetical machine.

The example shows that the state has to be extended in order to get from the mathematical semantics to a corresponding hypothetical machine; we have to construct a "grand state" as it is sometimes called. At the same time the discussed step indicates how one could get from a language definition, in a systematic fashion to the related implementation. More precisely, what remains to be done is to find a finite representation of the grand states in terms of data and storage structure of the target machine and the machine code which simulates the given transformation on the grand state.

In the relevant literature there exist various examples relating language definition to implementaions (e.g. [McCarthy 67]). A comprehensive elaboration of this subject would be of great tutorial and practical value and would in fact complement the existing material on the subject of syntax definition and parsing, which, in contrast, is well understood. (Books on compiler writing have usually a lot to say on the syntactic part of the question and very little on semantics, object time organization and code generation.) The step from the syntax definition to the respective parser can be automatic. We are far from that stage on the semantic side of the problem.

The method has been applied to several large languages; in fact the proposed ECMA/ANSI PL/1 standard [ECMA 74] has been formulated using an operational definition. The method is the only one presently known, which is capable of covering the currently existing language constructs.

There is a tutorial on the subject by A. Ollongren [Ollongren 75], and several summaries, e.g. an in depth evaluation by J.C. Reynolds [Reynolds 72]

3.4 Axiomatic Approach

The essential semantics of a programming language is defined by a collection of axioms and rules of inference, which permits the proof of properties of programs, in particular that a given program is correct, i.e. realizes a specified input/output relation. Of course, one can prove assertions about programs using either a mathematical or operational definition and ordinary mathematical reasoning. In fact, the axioms and rules of inference can be regarded as theorems within the framework of mathematical semantics.

However, the objective of the axiomatic method is a fomal system which permits to establish proofs using the uninterpreted program text only, i.e. without referring to denotations of the program or program parts. Whenever we talk about denotations in this section, then this is for explanatory purposes and is not part of the axiomatic system.

The problem of correctness proofs of programs is usually split into two subproblems; the first is conditional correctness, i.e. correctness under the assumption that the execution of the program terminates, and secondly, the termination of the program. Until further notice this section deals with conditional correctness.

To illustrate the approach we will refer to the simplest language level of section 3.2, i.e. a fixed set of variables, assignment statement and compound statement. The notation and particular axioms of the example are due to C.A.R. Hoare. The basic new piece of notation are propositions of the form:

$p1\{st\}p2$

where $p1$ and $p2$ are propositions referring to variables of the program, and st is a statement. The intuitive meaning of the new form is: if $p1$ is true before the execution of st and the execution of st terminates, then $p2$ is true after the execution of st. $p1$ is called precondition, $p2$ is the so-called postcondition or consequence.

As example for axioms and rules of inference we take the assignment statement and the compound statement. The axiom (more precisely the axiom schema) for the assignment statement reads:

$p_e^x\{x:=e\}p$ where p_e^x means: replace all occurences of x in p by e.

In fact, p_e^x is the weakest possible precondition given p and vice versa given p_e^x as the precondition p is the strongest possible consequence; i.e. the schema captures all there is to know about the assignment statement. A specific instance of the schema would e.g. be:

$0<x+1$ $\{x:=x+1\}$ $0<x$

Note that in order to use the schema it is not necessary to refer to the denotation of "$x:=x+1$". The definition of the compound statement takes the form of a rule of inference and reads:

IF $p1\{st_1\}p2$ AND $p2\{st_2\}p3$
    THEN $p1\{st_1;st_2\}p3$

For a full language definition there will in general be an axiom per primitive statement and a rule of inference per composite statement; in addition, there are some general rules which have not been exemplified in this section.

The structure of the proofs reflects the syntactic structure of the program text, as one would hope.

There is a simple relation between the discussed axiomatic approach and a corresponding definition á lá mathematical semantics. As already mentioned the axioms and rules of inference can be interpreted as theorems within mathematical semantics. In particular we interpret the new propositional form, $p1\{st\}p2$ as follows. Assume for the moment that $p1$ and $p2$ are expressions that are also valid expressions in the programming language, denoting truth values.

$p1\{st\}p2$ $=$ $I[p1](\sigma) \supset I[p2](I[st](\sigma))$
                for all σ for which $I[st]$ is defined, i.e.
                                        st terminates.

The various axioms and rules of inference may now be rewritten according to the above interpretation and proven with respect to the definitions of mathematical semantics (see [Manna 72]).

Neither the generation of the proof nor solving the termination problem can be completely mechanical, since both are in general undecidable. However, there is hope that for frequently occurring program structures the problems can be solved effectively by algorithms. Proposals to solve the termination problem frequently rely on an indirect proof, in particular on finding a quantity which decreases as the computation proceeds, but cannot decrease indefinitely.

The subject of axiomatic definitions and program verification has stimulated widespread research activities due to the intellectually pleasing content but also because of its potential economic value. The belief in the latter is based on the vision that, ultimately, the extremely cost-intensive program testing and so-called program maintenance can be replaced by systematic program design and verification, possibly to some extent automated.

There are many examples of correctness proofs of specific programs (see [London 70]) and several automated verification aids (e.g. [King 75]). The existing examples are mostly small programs for more or less complicated mathematical problems. Some of the algorithms published in the respective section of the CACM are certified by proofs. An attempt to axiomatize a full language, PASCAL, has been undertaken by Hoare and Wirth [Hoare 73] resulting in the definition of at least a large subset.

Intimately connected to axiom systems for programming languages is the issue of programming style and development methodology. The essence of structured programming is, in the light of the presented research, the recommendation to use only language constructs which have simple axioms (this excludes e.g. the general form of gotos, although restricted forms may well lead to simple correctness arguments). As it turns out, the process of developing a program is intimately connected to the generation of the corresponding correctness proof. Thus we may expect guidance how to develop programs rather than merely learn how to prove ready made programs correct.

Yet, there is an enormous gap between current programming practice and the complexity of the software being produced on the one hand, and the vision and capabilities of the systematic techniques described. The proper discussion of the dilemma needs a larger context than has been given in this section and will therefore be deferred to the next section.

4. CHALLENGES

In accordance with the intent of the entire paper, the scope of this
section excludes topics considered to belong to the theory of computation. With this restriction in mind we may certainly say that the definition of programming language semantics is not an end in itself;
consequently, the discussion of future directions cannot be isolated
from the intended applications of semantic definitions, i.e. precise
definition of real life languages, compiler development, program development and language design.

There are two topics we want to clearly separate to avoid a frequent
confusion: Firstly, the semantic analysis and formal definition of existing programming languages; secondly, the design of novel, useful
language constructs.

Current programming languages are a compromise between the desire to
provide the most comfortable and elegant language for the human user
and the aim to construct efficient implementations on given systems
with known compiler technology. Furthermore, the more intensely used
languages undergo an evolution over the years to support new system
functions. These languages were not designed with the aim to make
formal correctness proofs easy nor were they designed to fit most com-
fortably into the framework of mathematical semantics. However, it
would be a mistake to conclude that these languages are no longer
worth the attention of computer science. In view of the heavy invest-
ment by users as well as manufacturers it is not likely that the current
programming languages will change radically in the near future. Thus
the carriers of new programming style will be, at least for some time,
current languages. The initial motivation of formal semantics, precise
definition to achieve portability, is still valid; there is as yet no
semantic analysis of COBOL (the most widely used programming language).
A comparative language study on the semantics level would be quite valuable [Strachey 73]. Finally, there is no comprehensive representation
of the existing implementation techniques related to formalized semantic concepts.

Whereas BNF, or slight variations thereof, are widely accepted as a
means to define a concrete syntax, there is no such widespread consensus for any of the semantic description schemes.

Next I wish to offer a top down argument to justify the major long range goals of the present subject. Firstly, we can observe that over the past two decades the speed and storage capacity of computers have been increased exponentially roughly at a rate of about 40 percent a year. This trend has been balanced by a similar decrease of cost per operation and per storage unit (i.e. bit or byte). Similarly the size of systemcode (operating system, compilers, etc.) has increased exponentially as well. However, in this case no balancing trend of decreasing cost per line of code can be observed. Furthermore, we will not only have to master greater quantity but larger complexity as well. We conclude that software production is or soon will be the bottleneck for the use of computers.

There are three general research directions promising to improve the situation:

1. Advance Automatic Programming
2. Remove Testing in favor of Correctness Proofs
3. Advance Modular Programming

By the first research area we mean to extrapolate the development of higher level languages by introducing more abstract datatypes (such as e.g. sets) and their associated operations, relax restrictions in current languages and introduce more powerful control structures; the intent is, of course, to automate part of the production process; in short, follow the trends suggested under the term "very high level language". Topics one and two are intimately connected. As J. Schwartz [Schwartz 75] observes, it is much easier to prove the correctness on an abstract level rather than on the level of detailed representations. If the abstract program can be compiled, the task of the programmer is completed, provided the compiler has been proven as well. Thus the step from the abstract algorithm to its ultimate representation in machine form is proven once and for all by a compiler proof. The author believes that research in correctness proof must therefore be investigated hand in hand with the development of very high level languages. Even under the assumption that the level of programming languages can be raised, correctness proofs will remain sufficiently complicated to warrant machine assistance in the form of proof generators and checkers. Although the latter subject has been considerably advanced over the last decade, it has not yet reached the stage of applicability in practical programming. Various subgoals may be envisaged, e.g. conversational systems like EFFIGY [King 75] which offer a combination of generalized testing by symbolic execution and some assistance for generating proofs.

A notorious problem in designing large pieces of software is modularity. It is rarely the case that existing modules can be used to build new systems without major trimming, if at all. As J. Dennis [Dennis 75] observes, the success of modular programming not only depends on how modules are written, but also on the characteristics of the linguistic level at which these modules are expressed. This conjecture is supported by a detailed analysis of some high level languages in [Dennis 75]. Modules are usually expressed by procedures, subroutines or programs (depending on the specific languages used). In short, we have to look for constructs other than procedures (etc.) and the related traditional ways to compose procedures into larger units, in order to achieve the desired modularity.

After this detour we now return to the subject proper and ask what the relevance of formal semantics with these issues is. Firstly, axiomatic semantics provides the proof theory for program correctness proofs, and thus is also the basis for the mechanical aids in this area. It is rather difficult to propose useful axioms and rules of inference without having an interpreted system first, such as provided by a mathematical or operational system. However, this is a controversial issue.

In search for new language constructs (such as a useful notion of module), formal semantics ought to provide the framework for formulating the problem and for stating and justifying solutions [Strachey 73]. So far most research in formal semantics has been concerned with constructs as found in traditional languages. Here is a piece of language, what does it mean, was the question in the light of the discussed software problems. We should start from the other end, i.e. construct novel denotations and associate a name after we are satisfied with their properties.

PROGRAMMING IN THE META-LANGUAGE: A TUTORIAL

Dines Bjørner

Abstract:

This paper provides an informal introduction to the
"art" of abstractly specifying software architectures
using the *VDM* meta-language*. A formal treatment of
the semantics, as well as a BNF-like concrete syntax,
of a large subset of the meta-language is given in
[Jones 78a] following this paper.

* *colloquially known as:* *META-IV*

CONTENTS

Part I: Prelude   31

  0. Introduction   32
     Example 0   34

  1. Overview of Meta-Language   43
    1.1 Abstract Data Types   43
    1.2 Combinators: Statements and Structured Expressions   44
    1.3 Abstract Syntax   46
    1.4 Logic   46
      -- Quantified Expressions   47
    1.5 Descriptor Expressions   47
    1.6 Undefined & Erroneous Situations   47
    1.7 User-Defined Identifiers   48
    1.8 Structure of Tutorial   50

Part II: Domains, Objects & Operations   51

  2. *SET*s   52
     Example 1   52
    2.1 Defining Domains of *SET* Objects   54
     Example 2-3   54
    2.2 Representing Instances of *SET* Objects 55
      2.2.1 Explicit Enumeration   55
        The Empty Set   55
      2.2.2 Implicit Enumeration   55
      Examples 4-5-6   56
    2.3 *SET* Operations   56
     Example 7   58
    2.4 *SET*-oriented Combinators   59
     Example 8   60
    2.5 Further Examples (9,10)   61,63

3. *TUPLE*s   65

Example 11   65

3.1 Defining Domains of *TUPLE* Objects   67

    Example 12   67

3.2 Representing Instances of *TUPLE* Objects   68

    3.2.1 Explicit Enumeration   68

        The Empty Tuple   69

    3.2.2 Implicit Enumeration -- Pt.1   69

        Example 13   69

    3.2.3 Element Ordering   70

    3.2.4 Implicit Enumeration -- Pt.2   71

    Examples 14-15   72

3.3 *TUPLE* Operations   73

    Examples 16-17   74

3.4 *TUPLE*-oriented Combinators   75

    Example 18   76

4. *MAP*s   77

Example 19   77

4.1 Defining Domains of *MAP* Objects   81

    Example 20   81

    Defining *MAP* Domains -- Cont'd.   82

    Example 21   82

    Defining *MAP* Domains -- Cont'd.   82

    Example 22   83

    Defining *MAP* Domains -- Term'd.   83

    Example 23   83

4.2 Representing Instances of *MAP* Objects   84

    4.2.1 Explicit Enumeration   84

        The Empty Map   85

        Example 24   85

    4.2.2 Implicit Enumeration   86

        Example 25   87

    4.2.3 A Note on Scopes   88

        Example 26   88

4.3 *MAP* Operations   90

    Example 27   91

4.4 *MAP*-oriented Combinators   93

    Example 28   93

4.5 Further Examples   93
    Introductory Example Cont'd -- 29   93
    Another Example -- 30   96
    A Last Example -- 31   99

5. *TREE*s   102
   Examples 32-33   102
   5.1 Defining Domains of *TREE* Objects   104
       Example 34   105
       5.1.1 Tree Constructor Axioms   105
       Examples 35-36   106
   5.2 Representing Instances of *TREE* Objects   108
   5.3 *TREE* Operations: Selector Functions   109
       Explicitly Defined Selector Function Names   109
       Implicitly Defined Selector Function Names   110
       Example 37   110
       Non-Unique Selector Function Name Convention   110
       Example 38   111

6. *FUNCTION*s   113
   Examples 39-40   114
   6.1 Defining Domains of *FunCTion* Objects   115
       Example 41   115
   6.2 Representing Instances of *FunCTion* Objects   116
       Functional Abstraction   117
       λ-Expressions   118
       Free- & Bound Variables -- Scope   121
       Application   122
       Definition vs. Application   123
       The γ Operator   123
   6.3 *FunCTion* Operations   125
       Example 42   125

7. ABSTRACT SYNTAX   128
   Example 43   128
   7.1 Domains of Abstract Objects   129
       Syntactic & Semantic Domains   130
       Domain Definitions & Compositions   131
           Definitions/Rules   132
           Compositions/Domain Expressions   132
           Domain Operators   132
           The Scope Delimiting (...) Operator   134
           Infix Operator Commutativity & Associativity   134
           Examples 44-45-46   134
       Semantics of the | Operator   135
       Constructing Disjoint Domains   136

7.2 Abstract Syntaxes & Rules	137
Context Constraint	137,139
is-Function	137
Example 47	138
Semantics of Abstract Syntaxes	139
Example 48	140
7.3 Abstract Syntax-oriented Combinators	141
The McCarthy Conditional Clause	141
The Cases Conditional Clause	141
Example 49	141
Part III Combinators	144
8. Variables	145
Example 50	145
8.1 Declarations & The State	146
Example 51	147
8.2 Variable References	148
Prelude	148
8.3 Assignment	149
Example 52	149
8.4 Derived References	152
Sub-References to *TUPLE* Elements	153
Sub-References to *MAP* Range Elements	153
Sub-References to Sub-"*TREE*"s	154
Discussion	154
9. Structured Clauses	155
9.1 Overview	155
Conditional Clauses	155
Iterative Clauses	156
Examples -- 53	156
9.2 Detailed Syntax & Semantics	157
9.2.1 *If-then-else* Conditional	157
Schema	157
Meaning	157
Programming Notes	157
9.2.2 McCarthy Conditional	158
Schema	158
Meaning	159
Programming Note	159

9.2.3 The *Cases* Conditional   160
    Schema   160
    Programming Note   160
    Meaning   161
    Name Binding & Scope   161
  Example 54   163
   Abstract Syntax   163
   Semantic Functions   164
9.2.4 The Ordered, Iterative *For-To-Do* Statement   165
    Schema   165
    Programming Note   165
    The Controlled Variable   165
    Name Binding & Scope   165
    Meaning   165
    Example 55   166
    Further Examples 56-57   168
9.2.5 The Unordered, *For-All* & Parallel Statements 169
    The *For-All* Statement   169
      Schema   169
      The Controlled Variable   169
      Name Binding & Scope   169
      Meaning   170
    The Parallel Statement   170
      Schema   170
      Meaning   170
    Examples 58-59   170
9.2.6 The *While-Do* Statement   171
    Schema   171
    Programming Note   172
    Meaning   172
    Examples: 172-173
      Example 60   172
      Example 61   173
10. Blocks   174
  Reference to Block Examples   174
  The Block Concept   175
  10.1 *let* Constructs   176
    The Syntactic *let* Construct   176
    The Semantic *let* Construct   176
    let Construct Variants   176
    Composite Object *let* Decompositions   177
    Simultaneous & Recursive *let* Definitions   178
    Notational Conventions   179

10.2 Pure & Impure Expressions   180

10.3 The ";" Combinator   181

10.4 Compound Statements & Statement Sequences   182

10.5 Statement- & Expression Blocks   182

10.6 *Return*   183

11. *EXIT*s   184

Example 62   184

11.1 The *EXIT* Mechanisms   187

11.2 Pragmatics & Semantics of the *EXIT* Mechanism   189

    Scope Rules   190

    Some Equivalence Transformations 191

11.3 Examples: No. 63   192

          No. 64 194

Part IV: Abstract Models   197

12. Function Definitions & Abstract Models   198

Example   198

12.1 The Syntax of Function Definitions   198

    Example 65   199

    Example 66   200

    Schönfinckeling/Currying   201

        Formal Examples 201

    Formal Parameter Syntactic Transformations 202

12.2 The Semantics of Function Definitions

    - & Abstract Models   203

    Scope & Binding   203

    General   203

    Examples   203

    A Note on Input/Output   204

Part V: Miscellaneae   204

13. *ELEM*entary Data Types   205

13.1 Rational *NUM*bers   206

    Programming Note: Numbers & Numerals 207

13.2 *BOOL*eans & Logic Expressions   207

    Predicate Expressions   207

    Examples   208

    Comments   208

13.3 *QUOT*ations   209
    Example 67   209
13.4 *TOKEN*s   210
    Example 68   211

Part VI: Postlude   212

Annotated Index to Examples   213-217

PART I: PRELUDE

Section 0 frames the subject, and gives an extensively annotated exam=
ple. This example illustrates many of the important aspects of the me=
ta-language. The particular abstraction choices made are, however, not
commented upon, nor explicitly singled out.

Section 1 forms an overview of the various meta-language constructs.
Although this primer is almost 200 pages (long), the meta-language, as
it transpires from section 1, is not 'big'! Certain meta-language no=
tions are considered so common, or simple, that they are not treated
beyond section 1. We think here, in particular on sections 1.5 - 1.7.

0. INTRODUCTION

This tutorial teaches you the meta-language. The primary aim is to render you fluent in the notation and its meaning, both as a reader and as a writer. That is: both as a user of software architectures abstractly specified by other people, and as a producer of such documents oneself. The secondary aim is to make you use the meta-language as per its intentions, i.e. in good style. We wish that you be able to produce suitable software abstractions. Thus we emphasize giving a rather complete, yet informal coverage of the syntax & semantics of the meta-language. We refrain however, from presenting a comprehensive introduction to the kind of abstraction principles and techniques which the meta-language is especially designed to facilitate and express. The tutorial contains an extensive set of examples. A careful study of these is intended to give you a rather complete overview of the fundamentals of abstract modeling -- as we see this activity. See also [Bjørner 78c].

The meta-language, as already mentioned in the introduction to this volume, evolved in the course of documenting a readable, denotational semantics of a PL/I subset [Bekič 74]. It has subsequently, in addition to denotational semantics definitions of other languages, been applied to similarly abstracted, formal definitions of relational data base systems [Hansal 76, Nilsson 76], components of operating systems and their command & (job) control languages [Bjørner 78c, Madsen 77], as well as more applications oriented software. These all exemplify, or imply, large complexes of software, with many, and intricate facilities. Individual examples of this tutorial, will, however, also illustrate applications to basic algorithmic functions .

The examples of this tutorial can be grouped according to either of two criteria: free-standing examples (illustrating an isolated software concept); versus examples strung together over several sections (usually illustrating systems software). The latter can (furthermore) be grouped according to the kind of systems software being abstracted. The following is a reference guide to these: *

Programming Language Constructs:
Examples: 30-34, 36-38, 40, 42-43, 47, 49-62, 64-68.

(Most of these examples are mere transcriptions and annotations of parts of the mini-language definition of appendix III [Jones 78a].)

----

* See pages 213-217 for a complete, annotated index to all examples.

File System Concepts
   Examples: 3-8, 12-13, 17-18, 20-25, 27-28, 35.
(Operating or File System) Catalogues/Directories
   Examples: 19, 29, 63.

Usually major sections will start with a large example illustrating all
the main notions introduced by the section. The examples interspersed
in the text outlining the individual language constructs are usually
far simpler than the more encompassing introductory example. Finally,
many sections are trailed by yet additional, larger examples. If you
find difficulties in comprehending the introductory examples you may
wish to skip these intially. If you find difficulty in understanding
the interspersed examples this tutorial will have failed!

(We mention, in passing, that no examples will be given of concurrent
system architectures: the subject meta-language was not designed to
cater for this [sadly neglected] area.) Finally some examples will be
of a rather formal, or schematized nature; not illustrating 'practical'
notions, but paraphrasing principal, or 'theoretical', aspects of the
meta-language.

We stress here, as was stressed in the introduction to this volume, that
the meta-language is to be used, not for solving algorithmic problems
(on a computer), but for specifying, in an implementation-independent
way, the architecture (or models) of software. Instead of using inform-
mal English mixed with technical jargon, we offer you a very-high-level
'programming' language. We do not offer an interpreter or compiler for
this meta-language. And we have absolutely no intention of ever wasting
our time trying to mechanize this meta-language. We wish, as we have
done in the past, and as we intend to continue doing in the future, to
further develop the notation and to express notions in ways for which
no mechanical interpreter system can ever be provided. Given a terse
and readable abstract model of some software item, and as e.g. expressed
in this meta-language, we see it as the foremost and almost solely distinguishing task of programming to carefully turn the abstraction, in
stages of, at most semi-automated, development, into an efficient realization. Once such an implementation has been reached we let the entire,
possibly annotated, documentation: the abstract model, as well as all
intermediate development stages, serve as the only documentation of the
realized software.

To give you a flavor of the meta-language, but not really the kind of
software we primarily intend it aimed at, we now give you a rather comprehensive example.

Example 0

We will present this example completely formally: first the abstract
model, then the annotations. Other than these annotations, which represent a mere reading of the formulae, we do not here explain the formulae. Thus the example is brought to give you, from the very start, a
capsule view of core aspects of the meta-language; as well as an idea
about what a model is: its parts, their purpose and interrelations.

Semantic Domains

1   *GROCER*   :: *SHELVES STORE CASH CATALOGUE*
2   *SHELVES*   = $Wno \underset{m}{\rightarrow} N_1$
3   *STORE*   = $Wno \underset{m}{\rightarrow} N_1$
4   *CASH*   = N_0
5   *CATALOGUE*   = $Wno \underset{m}{\rightarrow} Description$
6   *Description*   :: *Price Minimum Maximum Size*
7   *Price*   = N_1
8   *Minimum*   = N_1
9   *Maximum*   = N_1
10   *Size*   = N_1

-- annotations:

The model is concerned with rather self-contained fragments of a grocery: its inventory, cash and catalogue subsystem. The model describes a
domain of such groceries and exemplifies a few of the manipulations that
groceries are subject to: customer purchases, and inventory/cash control.

The reader is, throughout this primer, well-adviced in reading the annotations with a finger following the formulae and trying, otherwise, to
establish the connection!

1   A grocery is here selectively abstracted by abstractions of its
        shelves and store, i.e. inventory, its cash register, and its
        catalogue.

2   The shelves display a finite, non-zero number of items of a
        finite variety of merchandise. Merchandise presently being ab-
        stracted by ware number codes.

3   In the store-room is similarly kept a finite, non-zero number of boxed quantities of items of a finite selection of wares.

4   The cash register is simply abstracted by the cash it contains.

5   The grocers' catalogue lists a description of each sort of merchandise.

6   Such a description here consists of the unit (item) sales price; the minimum and maximum (lower- & upper-bound) numbers of items, of the described merchandise, which ought, respectively may be placed on the shelves; and finally the size of a stored box, measured in terms of the number of merchandise items it contains.

7   Prices are measured in integer (positive number) units of currency.

etc..

Comments

The above description 'read' the formulae as describing a grocery. The formulae, in fact, defines a whole domain (i.e. class) of such.

The formulae (1-10), and (12-15) below, constitute an abstract syntax (abstract syntaxes). Each line (1, 2, ..., 10) is an abstract syntax rule. The rules all have their left-hand sides being identifiers. The right-hand sides are so-called domain-expressions.

The described domains are said to constitute the semantic domains. Semantic domains are "what the whole thing is about". Syntactic domains, described below in formulae 12-14, are (just the) objects which denote manipulations of semantic objects.

Well-Formedness Constraints

11.0 $is\text{-}wf\text{-}GROCER(mk\text{-}GROCER(shelves,\ store,\ cash,\ catalogue))=$
.1 $(\underline{dom}\ store \subseteq \underline{dom}\ shelves \subseteq \underline{dom}\ catalogue)$
.2 $\wedge(\forall wno \in \underline{dom}\ catalogue)$
.3 $(\underline{let}\ mk\text{-}Description(price,min,max,size) = catalogue(wno)\ \underline{in}$
.4 $(0 \leq size \leq max - min)$
.5 $\wedge((wno \in \underline{dom}\ shelves)$
.6 $\supset(\underline{let}\ items = shelves(wno)\ \underline{in}$
.7 $((wno \in \underline{dom}\ store) \rightarrow (min \leq items \leq max),$
.8 $T \qquad\qquad\qquad \rightarrow\ items \leq max)))$

-- annotations :

The domain descriptions captured the essence of how we abstractly view
groceries, but the defined domains contain objects, i.e. groceries,
which do not satisfy natural constraints:

11.0   For a grocery (which consists of shelves, a store room, the cash
register, and a catalogue) to be well-formed, the following constraints must be satisfied:

11.1   There cannot be merchandise in the store room which is not also
displayed on the shelves; and any merchandise on the shelves
must be described in the catalogue. Furthermore:

11.2   For each type of merchandise described in the catalogue,

11.3   look-up the price, minimum & maximum shelf-, and box size quantities for that ware in the catalogue:

11.4   Now the maximum must be higher than or equal to the minimum, and
their difference (in that order) must be lower than or equal to
the box size. (This is a pragmatic constraint. It permits the
update of shelves with the full contents of boxes, without viola-
ting (min, max) constraints.)

11.5   If, in addition, the ware is also, actually displayed on a shelf,
then :

11.6   Let us call the number of items of that ware on the shelves for
items. Now:

11.   If the ware additionally is further stored in the back room, then
the number of items on the shelves must actually fall between the

minimum, lower and maximum, upper bounds; otherwise

11.8   there can be no more items on the shelves than is maximally permitted.

Comment:

The *is-wf-* function is defined relative to some named domain, here the
class of all *GROCER*ies. In the fóllowing we shall understand by *GROCER*
the class of those objects which satisfy the predicate (11). In fact,
any manipulation, i.e. any transformation of, or process on, a grocery,
shall leave us a(nother) grocery also satisfying the well-formedness
constraint. Thus the predicate (11) is also seen as forming a major
part of the invariant according to which we 'program' our manipulations -- whether on the abstract, or concrete level.

Syntactic Domains

12   *Transaction* =   *Purchase | Control | ...*
13   *Purchase*   ::   *Wno*$^+$
14   *Control*   ::   *Wno-set*
15   ...

-- annotations:

The grocer sees a customer purchase, his own daily check on the availa-
bility of certain wares, etc., as transactions. These are operations on
the grocery. Syntactically speaking:

12   A transaction is either a customer purchase, a clerk control, or
       something else - presently undefined!

13   A customer purchase is presented at the check-out counter as a
       sequence of not necessarily distinct wares. In this sequence
       groups of items of the same kind need not occur together.

14   A store clerk control consists of a set of distinct ware types
       (for which their inventory amounts are asked).

<u>Comment</u>:

Observe that only the last parenthesized phrase above invoked semantic
notions. That is: we have totally separated syntactic descriptions from
those of their semantics.

<u>Dynamic Consistency Constraints</u>

```
16.0   is-well-formed-purchase(purchase, grocery) =
  .1       (let mk-Purchase(wl)                    = purchase
  .2           mk-GROCER(shelves, , , )            = grocery in
  .3        let mini-shelf = make-shelf(wl)([]) in
  .4        (dom mini-shelf ⊆ dom shelves)
  .5       ∧(∀wno ∈ dom mini-shelf)
  .6           (mini-shelf(wno) ≤ shelves(wno)))
```


-- <u>annotations</u> :

The customer can select merchandise only from the shelves, and in
quantities bounded by what is displayed:

16.0   For the combination: a purchase and a grocery to be consistent,
       we must therefore require that

16.1   the ware list of which the purchase is made up, and

16.2   the shelves (from which the wares <u>were</u> selected) satisfy the
       constraints given in lines 16.4-16.6.

16.3   To express those constraints let us compute for each ware type,
       in the purchase, the number of times it occurs in the purchase.
       Since this corresponds, in the way we abstracted shelves, to an
       object of *SHELVES*, we call it *mini-shelf*. That is: *mini-shelf*
       displays, as do   shelves, a functional association between ware
       codes and numbers of (*shelves, mini-shelf*) items of that ware.
       The function *make-shelf*, which takes the ware-list of the pur-
       chase and computes this association, is activated with an empty
       shelf. The function definition is given below (17).

       Now to the constraints themselves:

16.4   The kind of wares purchased must form a (not necessarily proper)
       subset of the merchandise displayed on the shelves.

And:

16.5   For each ware purchased

16.6   the number of items purchased must be less than or equal to the
        number of wares of that kind on the shelves.

Comment

The abstraction given is not as elegant and transparent as we would
have hoped. Thus we find the introduction of the *make-shelf* auxiliary
function somewhat of a resort to an operational description of the constraint.

Auxiliary Function

17.0   *make-shelf(wl)(shelf)=*
   .1   *if* wl = <>
   .2   *then* shelf
   .3   *else* (*let* wno = *hd* wl *in*
   .4   *let* shelf' = ((wno ∈ *dom* shelf)
   .5   → shelf+[wno→(shelf(wno)+1)],
   .6   T→ shelfU[wno→1]) *in*
   .7   *make-shelf(tl wl)(shelf'))*

        type: Wno$^+$ → (SHELVES → SHELVES)

-- annotations :

The function takes, as arguments, a tuple (or list) of wares and a
shelf (really: an object of *SHELVES*) and yields, as result, a *SHELVES*
object. The *type* clause expresses this. The form after the *type* colon
is a so-called domain expression. The function is recursively defined,
cf. line 17.7. It performs its function by treating each item (*wno*) in
the ware list separately: 17.3-17.6. That is: by 'chopping' off the list
from its front, or *head*, leaving treatment of the rest, i.e. *tail*, of
the list, till another recursion (17.7), passing it the shelves object
(*shelf'*) so far computed. Thus:

17.1   If the (*tail* of the) ware list is the null tuple,

17.2   then the accumulated *shelf* computed up till now is delivered

17.3 Otherwise: Let us call the first item of the remaining ware list for *wno*.

17.4 And then update the *shelf* so far computed. If the item under inspection (being "tallied") has already occurred in the ware list,

17.5 then the updated *shelf* has one added to the number of items, of the same kind, so far purchased.

17.6 Otherwise, this is a first occurrence of this particular ware, and the *shelf* is augmented by the initialization of its tally count to *1*.

Semantic Functions

18.0   *Elab-Purchase(mk-Purchase(wl), grocer)=*
.1   *if* $wl = <>$
.2   *then grocer*
.3   *else (let mk-GROCER(shs,sto,cash,cat)* = *grocer,*
.4   *mk-Description(p,min,max,size)* = *cat(hd wl),*
.5   *wno*   = *hd wl*   *in*
.6   *let cash'* = *cash+p,*
.7   *(shs',sto')* =
.8   *(let items = shs(wno),*
.9   *stored*= *((wno* $\in$ *dom sto)* → *sto(wno),*
.10 T → *0) in*
.11   *if ((items=min)∧(stored>0))*
.12   *then*
.13   *(shs + [wno→items-1+size],*
.14   *((stored=1)* → *sto\\{wno},*
.15 T → *sto+[wno→stored-1]))*
.16   *else*
.17   *(((items=1)* → *shs\\{wno },*
.18 T → *shs+[wno→items-1]),*
.19   *sto)) in*
.20   *Elab-Purchase (mk-Purchase(tl wl),*
.21   *mk-GROCER(shs',sto',cash',cat)))*
     type: Purchase GROCER $\overset{\sim}{\rightarrow}$ *GROCER*

-- annotations:

To purchase a ware is to take a grocery store and deliver another. In the resulting grocery store the shelf count for the purchased ware (wno) is diminished by 1 (18.13 & 18.18), and if the shelf display goes under minimum **and** there are supplies stored (18.11) then the shelf is replenished by *size* items (18.13). To the cash register is added the purchase price of the ware (18.6).

The *Purchase Elaboration*, as did the above auxiliary function, works by updating the grocery store, once completely for each item in the purchase (18.3-18.19). That is:

18.1   If the purchase has been completely serviced,

18.2   then the result is the 'input' grocery.

18.17 If the shelf display of the purchased ware would go to zero, cognizance of this ware is deleted from the shelf. Likewise:

18.14 If by replenishing the shelves from the store the supplies go to zero, this ware is deleted from the store room.

18.20 The rest of the purchase is elaborated.

18.21 with the updated grocery.

$$...$$

19.0 $Elab\text{-}Control(mk\text{-}Control(wno), grocer) =$
       $Tabulate(wno, grocer)([\,])$

      <u>type</u>: $Control\ GROCER\ \rightarrow\ (wno\ \underset{m}{\rightarrow}\ N_0)$

-- <u>annotations</u> :

To control the grocery for the quantities available of each of a given set of ware categories is to tabulate these, starting with an empty table.

The tabulate function is auxiliary. The resulting table associates to each ware category the possibly zero quantity on hand, on the shelves as well as in the supply.

Auxiliary Function

```
20.0   Tabulate(wnos,grocer)(table)=
  .1       if wnos={}
  .2          then table
  .3          else (let mk-GROCER(shs,sto, ,cat) = grocer,
  .4                   wno ∈ wnos in
  .5             let items = ((wno ∈ dom shs) → shs(wno),
  .6                           T               → 0),
  .7                 stored= ((wno ∈ dom sto) → sto(wno),
  .8                           T               → 0),
  .9                 size  = s-Size(cat(wno)) in
  .10            let sum   = items + (stored*size)  in
  .11                Tabulate(wnos\{wno},grocer)(table∪[wno→sum])))
```

$$type:\ Wno\text{-}set\ GROCER \to ((Wno \xrightarrow{m} N_0) \to (Wno \xrightarrow{m} N_0))$$

-- annotations :

are left to the reader!

1. OVERVIEW OF META-LANGUAGE

In this section we briefly survey the meta-language. The overview   of
sections 1.1-1.3 emphasizes only syntactic aspects. The aim of sections
1.1-1.3 is to give you a rather comprehensive feeling for the composition and extent of the meta-language.

1.1 Abstract Data Types

The elementary data types (except for booleans) of the meta-language
are not fixed. For a suggestion of suitable base types we refer to
section 13.

The composite, very-high level abstraction-facilitating, data types are:

Sets:

Domains:	$A\text{-}set$
Constructors	$\{...\}$
Operations	$\cup$, $\cap$, $\diagdown$, $\subseteq$, $\subset$, $\in$, $card$, $power$, $=$, $\neq$

Tuples:

Domains:	A^*, A^+
Constructors:	$<...>$
Operations:	hd, tl, len, ind, $elems$, $\frown$, $[.]$, $conc$, $=$, $\neq$

Maps:

Domains:	$A \xrightarrow{m} B$
Constructors:	$[..\rightarrow..]$
Operations:	dom, rng, $(.)$, $\cup$, $+$, $\diagdown$, $\overset{\bullet}{}$, $=$, $\neq$

Functions:

Domains:	$A{\rightarrow}B$, $A\widetilde{\rightarrow}B$
Constructors:	$\lambda...\bullet...$
Operations:	$(.)$

<u>Trees</u>:

Domains:	$A \ :: \ B_1 \ B_2 \ \dots \ B_n, \ \ (C_1 \ C_2 \ \dots \ C_n)$
Constructors:	$mk\text{-}A, \ mk, \ (\dots)$
Operations:	$s\text{-}B_i, \ =, \ \neq$

The 'domains' lines above exemplify the expression of domains of objects of the subject type. A, B, B_i and C_i are given (or defined) domains. The constructors hint at the following typical object construction expressions:

$$\{a_1, a_2, \dots, a_n\}, \qquad\qquad \{ \ F(d) \ | \ P(d) \ \},$$

$$<a_1, a_2, \dots, a_n>, \qquad\qquad < F(i) \ | \ P(i) \ \wedge \ m \leq i \leq n >$$

$$[a_1 \rightarrow b_1, a_2 \rightarrow b_2, \dots, a_n \rightarrow b_n], \qquad [\ F(o) \ \rightarrow \ G(o) \ | \ P(o)]$$

representing respectively explicit & implicit set, tuple and map object denoting expressions. Also:

$$\lambda id.clause$$

abstracts the meta-language expression or statement *clause* into the function of *id* that *clause* is. Finally:

$$mk\text{-}A(b_1, b_2, \dots, b_n), \quad mk(c_1, c_2, \dots, c_n) \ \text{and} \ (c_1, c_2, \dots, c_n)$$

denote trees.

1.2 <u>Combinators</u>: <u>Statements</u> <u>and</u> <u>Structured</u> <u>Expressions</u>

Declaration:	<u>dcl</u> *Var* := *expr* <u>type</u> D,
Assignment:	*Var* := *expr*,
Identity:	<u>I</u> (null statement)
Contents **expressions**:	<u>c</u> *Var*
Conditional Clauses:	<u>if</u> *expr* <u>then</u> *clause*$_1$ <u>else</u> *clause*$_2$

$$(expr_1 \ \rightarrow \ clause_1,$$
$$expr_2 \ \rightarrow \ clause_2,$$
$$\dots$$
$$expr_n \ \rightarrow \ clause_n)$$

is the classical McCarthy conditional clause, with:

$\underline{cases}\ expr_0:$
$\quad (expr_1 \rightarrow clause_1,$
$\quad\ expr_2 \rightarrow clause_2,$
$\quad\ \ldots$
$\quad\ expr_n \rightarrow clause_n)$

being a variant of the Hoare/Wirth cases clause.

$\underline{while}\ expr\ \underline{do}\ stmt,$

$\underline{for}\ \underline{all}\ id\ \in\ set\ \underline{do}\ stmt,$ 　　　　　　　　and:

$\underline{for}\ i\ =\ m\ \underline{to}\ n\ \underline{do}\ stmt$

are the (conventional) iteration statements. Compound statements use the semicolon operator: $(stmt_1;\ stmt_2;\ldots;\ stmt_n)$ -- where $stmt$ are statements. Statement- & expression blocks may occur anywhere a statement, respectively expression, may occur:

$(\underline{let}\ def = expr\ \underline{in}\ clause),$

and:

$(\underline{let}\ def : expr;\ clause)$

illustrate the two block forms: the former basically of the applicative kind, the latter of the imperative kind.

Function definitions are written:

$fid(id_1, id_2, \ldots, id_n) =$
$\quad clause$
$\quad \underline{type}:\quad D_1\ D_2\ \ldots\ D_n\ \rightarrow\ D$

-- or in some such form. The language has no gotos, but provides both imperative and applicative variants of a phrase-structured, block-oriented, un-labelled $\underline{exit}$ mechanism:

$(\underline{trap}\ \underline{exit}(id)\ \underline{with}\ F(id)\ \underline{in}\ clause)$

and:

$(\underline{tixe}\ [\ G(o)\ \rightarrow\ F(o)\ |\ P(o)\ ]\ \underline{in}\ clause)$

with:

exit, exit(expr)

being the exit causing constructs.

1.3 Abstract Syntax

Abstract syntaxes are used in defining named domains of objects:

$$
\begin{array}{llll}
A_0 & = & B_1 \mid B_2 \mid \ldots \mid B_n & \text{union} \\
A_1 & = & B\text{-}set & \text{sets} \\
A_2 & = & B^* & \text{tuples} \\
A_3 & = & B^+ & \text{tuples} \\
A_4 & = & B \underset{m}{\rightarrow} C & \text{maps} \\
A_5 & = & B \rightarrow C & \text{functions} \\
A_6 & = & B \overset{\sim}{\rightarrow} C & \text{partial functions} \\
A_7 & :: & B_1 \; B_2 \; \ldots \; B_n & \text{trees}
\end{array}
$$

are typical rules. Objects, *o*, in the domains defined by some such rule satisfy:

$$is\text{-}A_i(o) .$$

1.4 Logic

Only one elementary data type is assumed:

BOOL

consisting of the two truth valued objects:

true, false

to which the following non-commutative operations apply:

$\wedge, \vee, \supset$ (and, or, implication)

as well as:

$\sim, \equiv$ (negation, identity).

Quantified Expressions

Predicates asserting truth properties:

(1) $(\forall o \in set)(P(o))$
(2) $(\exists o \in set)(P(o))$
(3) $(\exists! \ o \in set)(P(o))$

read as follows:

(1) for all objects [in the set] the predicate (P) holds.

(2) there exists an object [in the set] for which the predicate (P) holds.

(3) there exists a unique object [in the set] for which the predicate (P) holds.

1.5 Descriptor Expression

This subsection will be the only place in which the descriptor expression is treated.

$(\iota o)(P(o)), \quad (\Delta o)(P(o))$

ι (iota) and Δ (delta) are offered as alternate forms of representing the descriptor operator. The forms above denote (and read):

the unique object satisfying the predicate (P).

1.6 Undefined & Erroneous Situations

The form:

undefined

is offered as a notation expressing some further unspecified undefined object. Applying operations outside their domain is (likewise) said to yield undefined results. Similarly for descriptor expressions.

The form:

error

is offered as a notation for stating situations for which there are no
clear definitions.

In this primer we consistently use _undefined_ to denote undefined (non-
state) objects, i.e. in basically applicative contexts. We consistently
use _error_ to denote undefined state transitions, i.e. in basically
imperative contexts. Thus we consider _undefined_ to be an expression;
error, a statement!

1.7 User-Defined Identifiers

The meta-language sets no spelling standard for identifiers naming objects (defined functions, variables, parameters, etc.) or domains (as
in abstract syntaxes).

The following outlines the conventions basically followed in this primer.

Identifiers are either single Greek letters or sequences of one or more
Roman letters and Arabic digits. Identifiers might contain proper infix
hyphens, and possibly be decorated with (simple) subscripts (digits and
letters) and/or single, double, triple, ..., (superscript) primes.

The choice between Greek letters and other identifier forms is basically
governed by these informal, enumerative rules:

(So-called) State Domain Names:	Σ, or Ξ
State Object Names:	σ, respectively ξ
(So-called) Environment Domain Names:	_ENV_
Environment Object Names:	_env_, or ρ
(So-called) Continuation Domain Names	_C_
Continuation Object Names:	θ

The criterium on when to use upper and lower case letters is basically
this:

(So-called) Semantic Domain Names:

  Sequences of one or usually more UPPER CASE LETTERS, possibly
  trailed by a digit.

(So-called) Syntactic Domain Names:

> UPPER case letter followed by one or more lower case letters, possibly trailed by a digit.

Object Names:

> Lower case counterparts of corresponding domain names, usually amounting to prefixes of such, and quite often decorated.

Assignable Variable Names:

> -- in this primer usually written in *script* and underlined with tildes. When variable is global, first letter is upper case; otherwise lower-case.

Other conventions are:

Function Names:

> Elaboration functions primarily applicable to objects of domain Xyz have names:

elab-Xyz	(for imperatively stated) respectively:
E-Xyz	for (applicatively expressed) elaboration functions;
int-Xyz	(for imperatively stated) respectively:
I-Xyz	for (applicatively expressed) interpretation functions;
eval-Xyz	(for imperatively stated) respectively:
V-Xyz	for (applicatively expressed) evaluation functions.

(Elaboration is a term comprising both interpretation and evaluation. Interpretation implies elaboration of constructs basically for the sake of their side-effects. Evaluation implies elaboration of constructs basically for the sake of values explicitly yielded.)

Other Function Names:

> Let A be some domain name, then

$$is-A, \quad s-A, \quad mk-A, \quad is-wf-A,$$

> are reserved names. $is-A$ was explained in section 1.3. $s-A$ and $mk-A$ in 1.1. $is-wf-A$ is to be the name for any static context

condition predicate function applicable to all A objects and
yielding *true* only for those A objects one actually intends
the definition of A to cover! s-A and mk-A may not actually
be defined by some abstract syntax. The above reservation
then intends to prevent confusion.

1.8 Structure of Tutorial

The structure of this primer is as follows.

In part II we cover data types: sets, tuples, maps, trees, functions
and the notion of abstract syntax. Respectively sections 2,3,4,5,6 & 7.
The language features covered enable us to express domains, objects
and primitive operations on these -- in particular operator/operand
expressions. Examples of earlier sections will necessarily employ meta-
language notions only formally introduced in later sections. Insofar
as this is the case we rely on your good-will and patience, attempting,
on our behalf, however, to keep such uses to a reasonable minimum.

In part III we cover language constructs such as variables: their declaration, assignment and contents access; structure expressions and statements; blocks, and the *exit* mechanism. With these meta-language features
we are now able to express composite transformations, respectively state
compound processes, on objects, respectively state variables. The examples of this part take on a flavor distinct from that of the examples of
part II. There the examples were explicitly tied to the individual subjects being covered. Explicit examples using the constructs formally
introduced in part III are given already in part II. Instead the examples of part III tend to be rather more comprehensive, illustrating several
aspects of abstract modeling simultaneously.

In part IV we wrap up the story on function definitions and abstract
models.

This part is not comprehensive. It relies on the subject being already,
albeit partially covered in parts II & III. Part V ties up loose ends
concerning elementary data types.

. . .

In addition to the above contents survey we advise the reader to carefully study the contents listing in order to ascertain the logical
structure of this primer.

PART II   DOMAINS, OBJECTS & OPERATIONS

Function definitions describe transformations on data objects. As such
the defined functions apply to a domain of objects and yield objects
of the range. The specific transformation is expressed, in terms of
forms (constructors) denoting objects, operators and structured combinators denoting operations on objects.

The above paragraph serves the purpose of delineating the three cor-
nerstones of this part: the story on meta-language means of defining
domains of objects, representing constructed objects and operations on
objects. Most sections will be structured accordingly. These will have
basically three subsections. One will outline and exemplify how domains are defined, i.e. represented by means of so-called logical
type- (or, as we shall prefer to call them, domain) expressions.
Another will outline and exemplify how instances of objects of the
domain are constructed. Finally a third will outline and exemplify
expressions formed around operators denoting operations on objects.
This last is split into two subsections: one on primitive operations,
the other on combinators.

Each section dealing with a composite abstract data type will be introduced by   examples   whose purpose is to capture the essence
of the objects under discussion, thus motivating you right   into the
rather formally structured parts. And each section will be concluded
with larger examples.

In bringing examples we intend to illustrate basic principles of abstract modeling using the meta-language. The examples take care to use
the meta-language in "good style".

[In this way you will also be introduced to representational- & operational abstraction; to applicative- & imperative programming; and,
in a few places, to configurational- & hierarchical abstraction.]

2 _SET_s

Example 1:

The situation which we wish to abstractly define is perhaps rather
'childish'. We are given a set of classes, each class consisting of a
set of students. Let students be abstracted by their school registra-
tion code. Let the domain of all such codes be _Student_. Then:

$$Class = Student\text{-}set$$

is an abstract syntax rule whose left-hand side is an identifier, and
whose right-hand side is a domain expression. It describes a class as
being a set of (distinct) students. The equation gives the name _Class_
to a domain, and this domain is defined, by _Student-set_, to be the domain of finite subsets of _Student_.

Let suitably decorated s's and c's denote respectively students and
classes, i.e.:

$$is\text{-}Student(s)$$
$$is\text{-}Class(c)$$

Now:

$$\{s_1, s_2, \ldots, s_n\}$$

is a set constructor expression. It denotes a class.

To test whether a given student, s, attends a given class, c, we write:

$$s \in c$$

-- which we read: s is a member of c. If s is not a member of c, then
the expression is _false_, otherwise _true_. If we call the function that
tests class recordings for _is-in-class_ then:

$$is\text{-}in\text{-}class(s,c) = s \in c$$

is a function definition. To compute the students attending two classes,
c_1 and c_2, we write:

$$c1 \cap c2$$

-- which we read: the intersection of c_1 and c_2, i.e.: the set of students common to both c_1 and c_2. If no students attend both c_1 and c_2, then:

$$c_1 \cap c_2 = \{\}$$

their intersection is empty. The students following either c_1 or c_2 or both is denoted by:

$$c_1 \cup c_2$$

-- which we read: the union of c_1 and c_2. To record that a class, c, is diminished by the departure of a student, s, we write:

$$c \smallsetminus \{s\} \qquad \text{or} \qquad c - \{s\}$$

-- which we read as: the complement of s with respect to $\{s\}$, or -- which might be more to your liking -- the set c subtracted $\{s\}$. We use the notation $\smallsetminus$ and - interchangeably, although not in this primer, where $\smallsetminus$ is preferred. To record that a class, c, is augmented by the entry of a student, s, we write:

$$c \cup \{s\}$$

The number of students in a class is:

$$\underline{card\ c}$$

-- for cardinality.

2.1 <u>Defining</u> <u>Domains</u> <u>of</u> <u>*SET*</u> <u>Objects</u>

Let *A* be the name of a class of objects i.e. a domain. To define the class of objects which are finite sets of *A* objects (i.e. finite subsets of *A*), we use the domain expression operator *-set: A-set*.

<u>Example</u> <u>2</u>:

The domain whose objects are finite sets of integers, i.e. finite subsets of *INTG*, is definable as:

    INTG-set

Call this domain *IS*. Then:

    IS = INTG-set

is an abstract syntax rule formally defining this name. Then the domain whose objects are finite sets of (potentially overlapping) finite sets of integers is definable as:

    IS-set, or: *(INTG-set)-set*

<u>Example</u> <u>3</u>:

Let *R* represent the domain whose objects are abstractions of what, in a file system, is otherwise thought of as records. If files of such a system are, or can be, unordered, finite collections of distinct records, then:

R-set

is an abstraction of the class of files. The domain *R-set*, if *R* is an infinite class, is also infinite -- its objects are, however, all finite sets. The form *R-set* is a domain expression.

The file system thus modeled may seem a bit contrived. That is: you may never wish to design such a system. Note that at this stage the system has no notion of sequential files or keyed records. The examples, when expanded in subsequent sections will, however, appear more 'realistic'.

2.2   Representing Instances of *SET* Objects

2.2.1 Explicit Enumeration

Given distinct objects a_1, a_2, ..., a_n which are all *A* objects, the expression:

$$\{a_1, a_2, \ldots, a_n\}$$

is said to be an explicit enumeration of a set, which denotes an object of *A-set*.

Empty Set

-- is denoted by:

$$\{\}$$

2.2.2 Implicit Enumeration

Given a function $F: D \to A$, where *D* denotes some logical type (i.e. an arbitrary domain); and a predicate $P: D \to BOOL$, the expression:

$$\{F(d) \mid P(d)\}$$

is said to be an implicit set enumeration, and then denotes an object
of *A-set*. Since *A* could be any logical type expression the above describes how arbitrary sets may be represented. The implicit set constructor expression can be read as: The set of objects $F(d)$ such that
the predicate $P(d)$ holds. Thus we read | as 'such that!

Examples 4-5-6:

The constructor expression:

$$\{\{1,3,5,7,9\},\{2,5,11,13,15\},\ldots,\{\},\ldots\{2,1,8\}\}$$

denotes an object in *(INTG-set)-set* whose element sets, in this example,
are not disjoint.

...

Let r_1, r_2, ..., r_n denote distinct objects of *R*, i.e. be abstractions
of records, then:

$$\{r_1,r_2,\ldots,r_n\}$$

is (an abstraction of) a file, i.e. an object in *R-set*.

Let $F_\hbar$ be a total function from records into records, i.e.:
type: $F_\hbar$: $R \to R$, and let f denote a file, e.g. the above, then:

$$\{ F_\hbar(r) \mid r \in f \}$$

denotes a file derived from f having each of the records of f processed
by $F_\hbar$.

2.3 *SET* Operations:

The following special *SET* operations are defined:

∪   union
∩   intersection
╲,-   complement, difference, subtraction   (two forms provided)
⊂   proper subset
⊆   subset
power powerset
∈   membership
card cardinality
union distributed union

Each of these will now be individually and quite informally explained.

It is assumed below that *set, set1, set2* denote sets and *setsets* a set of sets.

set1∪set2   denotes the set of those objects which are either in *set1*, or in *set2*, or in both.

set1∩set2   denotes the set of objects which are both in *set1* and *set2*.

set1╲set2   denotes the set of objects which are in *set1* but not in *set2*.

set1⊂set2   denotes (the *BOOL*ean truth value) *true* if all members of *set1* are in *set2* and there is at least one member of *set2* not in *set1*, otherwise *false*.

set1⊆set2   denotes (the *BOOL*ean truth value) *true* if all members of *set1* are in *set2*, otherwise *false*.

power set   denotes the set of all finite subsets of *set*.

obj∈set   denotes (the *BOOL*ean truth value) *true* if the object denoted by *obj* is a member of *set*, otherwise *false*.

card set   denotes the (*N*atural) number of members of *set*. Read as *card*inality.

union setsets denotes the set consisting of all the objects of all the sets being elements of *setsets*.

The set operations applied to anything other that sets are _undefined_.

Let f denote a file, i.e. be in $R\text{-}set$; let r and r_i denote records
(i.e. both be in R). The operator-operand expressions and constructs:

(1)	$f \cup \{r\}$
(2)	$f \smallsetminus \{r\}$
(3)	$r \in f$
(4)	$\underline{card}\ f$
(5)	$(f \smallsetminus \{r\}) \cup \{F_h(r)\}$
(6)	$\underline{let}\ r_i \in f$
(7)	$\underline{let}\ r_i \in f\ \underline{be\ s.t.}\ P(r)$

express typical set manipulations. These pure expressions could be
used to provide a model of the following typical operations on files:
(1) writing a (most likely new) record to a file; (2) deleting a record -- most likely, but necessarily, contained in a file -- from that
file; (3) asking whether a given record is in a file; (4) asking for
the number of records in a file; (5) updating a record in a file to a
new record, i.e. replacing it -- with the possibility that it might
not already be in the file, in which case (1~5); (6) reading an arbitrary record from a file assumed not to be empty; and (7) reading an almost arbitrary record, namely one further satisfying the property expressed by the predicate function P.

Let $f1$ and $f2$ denote files, i.e. both be in $R\text{-}set$, then:

(8)	$f1 \cap f2$
(9)	$f1 \subseteq f2$
(10)	$f1 \subset f2$
(11)	$f1 = f2$
(12)	$f1 \neq f2$

might be reasonable abstractions of the following, slightly hypothetical, operations among files: (8) collecting, into a file, the records common to two files; (9) asking whether all records of one file
are contained in another file; (10) -- and, in addition to (9) --
asking whether some records of the latter are not in the former; (11)
asking whether two files are identical; or (12) different!

The expression:

(13) $f1 \cup f2$

is a generalization of (1), in that {r} there denotes a singleton
file, i.e. a file of exactly one record. (13) can be understood as
the merge of the records of two files. The type of the object denoted
by (13) is a file.

2.4 *SET*-oriented Combinators

The following combinators are applicable to *SET* objects:

> *let* *obj* $\in$ *Set*
> *let* *obj* $\in$ *Set* *be* *s.t.* P(obj)

which you have already seen applications of, and:

> *for all* *obj* $\in$ *set* *do* S(obj)

The *let* clauses occur in expression- or statement blocks:

> (*let* obj $\in$ Set ... *in*
> C(obj))

where C represents either an expression or a statement. The *for all*
clause is a statement, and so must S be.

For the general meaning of *let* clauses we refer to section 10.1. The
specific *let* clauses shown above bind the identifier *obj* to an arbitrary, etc., member of the set, or domain, *Set*, anywhere in C where
obj occurs free.

Note that *Set* in *let* clauses may either be an expression denoting a
finite set; or a domain-expression, potentially denoting infinite sets.

In the *for-all* statement *set* must however be restricted to denote a
finite set, in particular: the expression: *set* must not be a domain
expression.

The meaning of the *for-all* clause is given here, but more systematically repeated in section 9.2.5. Let *set* denote the finite set whose
n objects we may arbitrarily name: $id_1, id_2, \ldots, id_n$, where no id_j is
free in $S(id)$; then:

$$//\{S(id_1), S(id_2), \ldots, S(id_n)\}$$

is a sufficient transliteration of the *for-all* statement into a quasi-
parallel 'compound' statement, each of whose statements, $S(id)$, arises
from $S(obj)$ by replacing all free occurrences of *obj* in $S(obj)$ by *id*.
For the meaning of compound statements rely on your intuition, or look
it up in section 10.4. Since the set element naming was arbitrary one
can permute the above statements arbitrarily.

Example 8:

The constructor expression:

$$\{ F_h(r) \mid r \in f \}$$

is an applicative expression -- provided F_h does not rely on any state
component. An imperative analogue can be achieved by means of the
for-all statement:

> *dcl* *file* := {} *type* R-set
> (*for all* $r \in f$ *do*
>   *file* := *c file* ∪ $\{F_h(r)\}$;
> *c file*)

The above can be seen to be a process-oriented abstraction of parts
of a file manipulation system architecture. The global variable *file*
is initialized to the empty file, {}, of no records; and fixed to
contain only finite sets of distinct records *(type R-set)*. File now
denotes a constant reference, to an *R-set* object, i.e. an object in
ref R-set; with *c file* denoting the dynamic contents at that reference, i.e. value of the file variable.

2.5 Further Examples

To sharpen your understanding of set manipulations we now bring
further examples.

Example 9:

The problem which we wish to abstractly define is that of recording
equivalence classes. A set (e.g. *sas*) consisting of disjoint sets
(e.g. *as1, as2,..., asn*) of (e.g. *A*) objects is said to define (or,
which is the same, to 'realize') an equivalence relation. In fact we
call the member sets (*as1,...*) for equivalence classes. The set of
equivalence classes thus is a partitioning of the union of all the
(A) objects of the equivalence classes. Given one partitioning and
an *(A)* object, supposed to be a member of an equivalence class, we
wish to inquire whether it is indeed in some equivalence class of that
partitioning. (We call the predicate which tests for this *isRecorded*.)
As another subproblem we wish, given a partitioning and two 'recorded'
(A-) objects, (*a1,a2*) to generate a new partitioning as follows: If
the two *A* objects are recorded in the same equivalence class, then
the result partitioning is the same as the argument partitioning. If
the two *A* objects are recorded in distinct equivalence classes, then
the result partitioning is as the argument partitioning except for
the collapse (union) into one memberset of the two sets of which *a1*
and *a2* are respective members. (We call the new equivalence class
generator function for *enter*).

1        $EQ = B\text{-}set$
          $B = A\text{-}set$

   i.e.:

          $EQ = (A\text{-}set)\text{-}set$

2        $is\text{-}wf\text{-}EQ(sas)=$
.1 $(\forall as1, as2 \in sas)(as1 \neq as2 \supset as1 \cap as2 = \{\})$

3        $isRecorded(a, sas)=$ $isRecorded(a, sas)=$
.1 $(a \in \underline{union}\ sas)$ $(\exists as \in sas)(a \in as)$

where we gave two versions of $isRecorded$.

4        $enter((a1, a2), sas)=$
.1 $\{as \mid as \in sas \land \{a1, a2\} \cap as = \{\}\}$
.2 $\cup\ \{\ as1 \cup as2 \mid (as1 \in sas) \land (a1 \in as1) \land (as2 \in sas) \land (a2 \in as2)\}$

5        $equiv((a1, a2), sas)=$
.1 $(\exists as \in sas)(a1 \in as \land a2 \in as)$

     $\underline{type:}$ $is\text{-}wf\text{-}EQ:$ EQ $\rightarrow$ $BOOL$
          $isRecorded:$ A EQ $\rightarrow$ $BOOL$
          $enter:$ $(A\ A)\ EQ$ $\overset{\sim}{\rightarrow}$ EQ
          $equiv:$ $(A\ A)\ EQ$ $\rightarrow$ $BOOL$

== annotations:

1. EQ names a domain of objects. These are finite sets of B objects,
   with the latter being finite sets of A objects -- hence an EQ object
   is a set of sets of A objects.

2. For such a set to be a partitioning, i.e. to be well-formed as per the
   intentions of defining the domain EQ, no two distinct members (of
   sas) may have any A objects in common; or, which is the same, all
   membersets must be disjoint.

3. For an A object, a, to be recorded, shall mean that the object (a)
   is in some memberset, i.e. (3.3) that there is a memberset, as, of
   which it is an element.

4. The two lines (4.1 & 4.2) express what was stipulated above: the result partitioning is as the argument partitionings (4.1), except
   (4.2) -- etc.

The _type_ clauses of the functions define the set of the input arguments,
to the left of the arrows, and those of the results, to the right of the
arrows. The arrows express that the defined functions are (indeed) (possibly partial ($\tilde{\rightarrow}$)) functions -- from the argument domains into the result domains.

Example 10:

As in the previous example, we deal with objects:

$$S = (A\text{-}set)\text{-}set$$

-- but now not subject to any restrictions. To check whether an S object,
sas, is a partitioning we apply:

$$isDecomposed(sas)=$$
$$(\forall as1,as2\in sas)(as1\neq as2 \supset as1\cap as2=\{\})$$

type: $S \rightarrow BOOL$

To decompose an S object, sas, into the coarsest, i.e. smallest, having
fewest elements, partioning of sas, we apply $decompose(sas)$.

A possibly incomplete definition of a coarsest partitioning, given a
set, sas, of potentially overlapping sets, goes as follows: Let sas' be
the result of $decompose(sas)$. For all $a1$ and $a2$ that are members of
member-sets of sas, $a1$ and $a2$ are in the same member-set of sas' if-and-
only-if (iff) for any subset, $\{as1,as2,...,asn\}$ of sas, $a1$ is in all asi,
for $i\in\{1:n\}$, iff $a2$ is in all asi (for $i\in\{1:n\}$); and only such a's are
in member-sets of sas' which are similarly in sas, i.e.: _union_ sas =
union sas' .

Sometimes a picture is worth quite a few words:

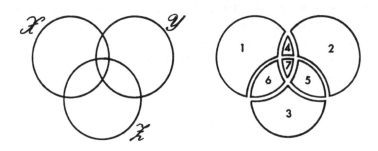

To the left is some *sas* ({X,Y,Z}), to the right is its corresponding *sas'*: the digits 1-7 index the corresponding forms in the right-hand side expression below:

$$decompose(\{X,Y,Z\}) = \{X \setminus (Y \cup Z), Y \setminus (X \cup Z), Z \setminus (Y \cup X),$$
$$(X \cap Y) \setminus Z, (Y \cap Z) \setminus X, (X \cap Z) \setminus Y,$$
$$X \cap Y \cap Z\}$$

Here is a formal definition of the function:

$$decompose(sas)=$$
$$\underline{if}\ (\exists as1, as2 \in sas)((as1 \neq as2) \wedge ((as1 \cap as2) \neq \{\}))$$
$$\underline{then}\ (\underline{let}\ as1, as2 \in sas\ \underline{be}\ \underline{s.t.}\ as1 \cap as2 \neq \{\};$$
$$decompose(\{as1 \setminus as2, as2 \setminus as1, as1 \cap as2\} \cup sas \setminus \{as1, as2\}))$$
$$\underline{else}\ sas$$
$$\underline{type}:\ S \rightarrow S$$

3. _TUPLEs_

Example 11:

The problem with which we wish to illustrate, before going into a
more systematic coverage, the meta-language abstract data type of
TUPLEs, is perhaps not a very abstract one. We are to compute the
first k rows of the PASCAL triangle; informally:

$$
\begin{array}{ccccccc}
 & & & 1 & & & \\
 & & 1 & & 1 & & \\
 & 1 & & 2 & & 1 & \\
 1 & & 3 & & 3 & & 1 \\
1 & & 4 & & 6 & & 4 & & 1 \\
1 & & 5 & & 10 & & 10 & & 5 & & 1
\end{array}
$$

etc.. So we define two functions: one computing the i'th row; another
putting the first k rows together. The second function invokes the
first.

$$\underline{type}: row: N_1 \rightarrow N_1^+$$
$$\underline{type}: tri: N_1 \rightarrow N_1^{++}$$

row takes a positive, non-zero integer, i.e. a natural number larger
then _1_, and produces a tuple of such numbers; _tri_ takes a non-zero
natural number and produces a tuple of as many tuples of natural numbers. N_1^+ stands for the domain of tuples of natural numbers; N_1^{++}
for tuples of tuples of these numbers. An implicit way of specifying
row and _tri_ would e.g. define their _pre_- and _post_-conditions, i.e.
the conditions that input (alone) must satisfy, respectively the conditions that input and output (together) must satisfy:

$$\underline{type}: pre\text{-}row: N_1 \rightarrow BOOL$$
$$\underline{type}: post\text{-}row: N_1 \; N_1^+ \rightarrow BOOL$$

$$\underline{type}: pre\text{-}tri: N_1 \rightarrow BOOL$$
$$\underline{type}: post\text{-}tri: N_1 \; N_1^{++} \rightarrow BOOL$$

In particular:

      pre-row(i) = <u>true</u>

      post-row(i,r)=
               <u>cases</u> i: (1 → *(r = <1>),*
                      2 → *(r = <1,1>),*
                      T → *(<u>let</u> rim1 = row(i-1) <u>in</u>*
                              (<u>l</u> r = i) ∧ (r[1]= 1 = r[<u>l</u> r]) ∧
                              (∀j ∈ {2:<u>l</u> r-1})
                                      (r[j] = rim1[j-1]+rim1[j])))

      pre-tri(k) = <u>true</u>

      post-tri(k,rr)=
          (<u>l</u> rr = k)
          ∧(∀i ∈ {1:k})(rr[i] = row(i))

In the notation of the meta-language, *tri(6)* would be presented as:

      <<1>,<1,1>,<1,2,1>,<1,3,3,1>,<1,4,6,4,1>,<1,5,10,10,5,1>>

Giving the above implicit definitions of *row* and *tri* almost amounts
to giving their explicit counterpart. Instead of doing this, let us
"read" the *pre-* and *post-*'s:

The *pre* of *row* is always <u>true</u> (for *i>0*). The *post* of *row* says: if
i=1 then the resulting row *r* is just the tuple of length *1* whose only
member is a *1*. If *i=2* then *r* is a 2-tuple both of whose elements are
1's. In general, the length of *r* is *i*, its first and last elements
are both *1*'s, and, for *i>2*, the elements of *r*, i.e. of *row(i)*, are
related to elements of *row(i-1)* as follows: let *j* be any index into
r exclusive of the first and last, then the *j*'th element of *r* is the
sum of the *j-1*'st and *j*'th elements of *row(i-1)*.

The computation specified below computes *tri(k)* by imperative means:

$$(\underline{dcl} \; \underline{Tri} \; := \; <<1>,<1,1>> \; \underline{type} \; N_1^{++},$$
$$\underline{Rowi} \; := \; <1> \qquad \underline{type} \; N_1^{+};$$
$$\underline{for} \; i=2 \; \underline{to} \; k \; \underline{do}$$
$$(\underline{let} \; rim1 \; : \; (\underline{c} \; \underline{Tri})[i-1];$$
$$\underline{for} \; j=2 \; \underline{to} \; \underline{len} \; rim1 \; \underline{do}$$
$$\underline{Rowi} \; := \; (\underline{c} \; \underline{Rowi}){\frown}<rim1[j-1]+rim1[j]>;$$
$$\underline{Rowi} \; := \; (\underline{c} \; \underline{Rowi}){\frown}<1>;$$
$$\underline{Tri} \; := \; (\underline{c} \; \underline{Tri}){\frown}<\underline{c} \; \underline{Rowi}>);$$
$$\underline{return}(\underline{c} \; \underline{Tri}))$$

3.1 Defining Domains of *TUPLE* Objects

Let A be the name of a class of objects. To define the class of objects
all of whose members are finite length tuples whose elements are A objects we use either of the domain expression operators: $*$ or $+$.

A^* denotes the infinite domain of finite *length* tuples all of
whose *elements* are in A. The 0-length tuple, $<>$, is in $A*$
-- for any $A!$

A^+ denotes the infinite domain of finite non-zero length *TUP-
LE*s, all of whose *elements* are in A. Thus $<>$ is not in A^+.

Example 12:

Let G denote a class of objects, i.e. a domain, abstracting the fields
of a record, with records consisting now of a finite number of such
ordered fields, then:

$$G^*$$

is a domain expression abstracting the class of records. Call this R,
i.e.:

$$R \; = \; G^*$$

Now let files be ordered, finite length sequences of one or more records. Then:

$$R^+ \text{ or } (G*)^+$$

are equivalent domain expressions abstracting the class of files. In the
latter expression, the parentheses are solely used for grouping --
you could, of course, omit parentheses here: G^{*+}. If you so wish you
can likewise name the file domain:

$$Ft = R^+$$

In this example we did not retain the view that files consisted of
collections of distinct, unordered records. Had we done so:

$$Fs = R\text{-set}$$
$$R = G*$$

or:

$$Fs = (G*)\text{-set, or: } Fs = G*\text{-set}$$

would have been applicable abstractions.

3.2 Representing Instances of *TUPLE* Objects

3.2.1 Explicit Enumeration

Given not necessarily distinct objects a_1, a_2, ..., a_n which are all
in A, the expression:

$$<a_1, a_2, \ldots, a_n>$$

denotes an n-tuple, i.e. an object of, or in: A^*, A^+ (for $n>0$).

Empty Tuple

-- is denoted by:

<>

3.2.2. Implicit Enumeration - Part 1

Given a function $F: INTG \rightarrow D$ the expression:

$$< F(i) \mid 1 \leq i \leq n >$$

denotes an n tuple -- as above! So does:

$$< F(i) \mid i \in \{1:n\} >, \qquad\qquad \text{and}$$

$$< G(d) \mid i \in \{m:m+n-1\} >, \qquad\qquad \text{etcetera,}$$

where $G: D \rightarrow A$. Thus we shall not be too particular about the form of the "type-building" predicate as long as it is clear, to the readers of your formulae, what the size, i.e. *length*, of your tuple will be. Since $G(d)$ is independent of i the n tuple consists of identical $G(d)$ elements.

Examples 13:

Let g_1, g_2, ..., g_m, and g_{ij} for varying i,j denote fields of a record, i.e. all objects in G, then :

$$<g_1, g_2, \ldots, g_m>,$$

$$<<g_{11}, g_{12}, \ldots, g_{1x}>, <g_{21}, g_{22}, \ldots, g_{2y}>, \ldots, <g_{n1}, g_{n2}, \ldots, g_{nz}>>$$

are constructor expressions denoting objects in G^*, respectively R^+
That is: abstractions of (instances of) records, respectively files!

Let F_g, $F_\hbar$ be total functions from fields to fields, respectively
records to records, i.e.: _type:_ F_g: $G \rightarrow G$, _type:_ $F_\hbar$: $R \rightarrow R$;
and let f,r denote a file, respectively a record; then:

$$< F_g(r[i]) \mid 1 \leq i \leq l\, r >$$
$$< F_\hbar(f[j]) \mid 1 \leq j \leq l\, f >$$

denotes a record, respectively a file, derived from r, respectively
f, having all its fields, respectively records, processed -- in any
order -- by F_g, respectively $F_\hbar$. Although to be dealt with more
systematically below $r[i]$ denotes the i'th field of record r, with
$l\, r$ denoting the length, in terms of not necessarily distinct,
fields, of record r.

3.2.3 Element Ordering

Sets are unordered collections of objects. Tuple elements are ordered.
In:

$$<a_1, a_2, \ldots, a_n>$$

a_1 is the _1_st element, a_2 the _2_nd,..., and a_n the nth element. In:

$$< F(i) \mid i \in \{m : m+n-1\}>$$

the _1_st element is $F(m)$, the _2_nd element is $F(m+1)$,..., and $F(m+k)$
for $0 \leq k \leq n-1$ is the $k+1$-st element. In:

$$< G(d) \mid i \in \{m : m+n-1\}>$$

all elements are alike, and are $G(d)$ -- with n of them!

By:

$$< obj \mid obj \in set >$$

we mean a _card set_ tuple of all distinct members of the assumed
finite set set -- occurring in arbitrary order.

In general the form of an implicit tuple building constructor expression is:

$$< F(i) \mid O(i) \wedge P(i) >$$

where $O(i)$ is an ordering predicate indicating, mainly through the
natural ordering of integers i, the order of those elements $F(i)$, for i,
for which the more general predicate $P(i)$ holds:

3.2.4 Implicit Enumeration - Part 2:

Let P: _INTG_ $\rightarrow$ _BOOL_ be a (total function) predicate then the expression:

$$< F(i) \mid i \in intgset \wedge P(i) >$$

denotes an l tuple :

$$< F(i_1), F(i_2), \ldots, F(i_l) >$$

where :

$$\{i_1, i_2, \ldots, i_l\} \subseteq intgset$$
$$\wedge \quad i_1 < i_2 < \ldots < i_l$$
$$\wedge \quad P(i_1) \wedge P(i_2) \wedge \ldots \wedge P(i_l)$$
$$\wedge \quad (\sim \exists i \in intgset \setminus \{i_1, i_2, \ldots, i_l\})(P(i))$$

In words: The ordering of the resulting tuple elements follow the
natural ordering of the _INTe_Gers. The _length_ of the tuple will be
the _cardinality_ of that subset of the finite integer set, _intgset_,
for which P is satisfied.

Example 14-15:

Although not illustrative of abstraction techniques, as we intend them, the following examples might help drive home the idea of implicit tuple constructions:

(1) Let *fib* denote the so-called fibonacci function, *type*: $fib: N_0 \rightarrow N_1$ where N_0, N_1 denote the sets of natural numbers larger than or equal to 0, respectively 1. In particular think of: $fib(0)=1$, $fib(1)=1$, with $fib(i)$ for $i \geq 1$ being $fib(i-2)+fib(i-1)$. Then:

$$< fib(i) \mid (m \leq i \leq n) \wedge \underline{odd} \; fib(i) >$$

denotes a tuple of those of the *m*'th, *m+1*'st,..., up to, and including the *n*'th fibonacci number provided these are not even numbers, and $m, n \geq 0$. For $m=3$ and $n=11$ you would get:

$$<3,5,13,21,55,89>$$

i.e. the tuple of the 3rd, 4th, 6th, 7th, 9th and 10'th fibonacci number.

The type of the above expressions is: N_1^*

(2) The following pure expression constructs the pascal triangle between rows *1* and *k*:

$$
\begin{aligned}
< row(i) \mid & \; 1 \leq i \leq k \\
\wedge & \; \underline{cases} \; i \\
& (1 \;\rightarrow\; row(i) = <1>, \\
& \;\; 2 \;\rightarrow\; row(i) = <1,1>, \\
& \;\; T \;\rightarrow\; row(i) = <1> \\
& \qquad\qquad \sim< (row(i-1))[j]+ \\
& \qquad\qquad\quad (row(i-1))[j+1] \\
& \qquad\qquad \mid 1 \leq j \leq \underline{len} \; row(i-1))> \\
& \qquad \sim<1>) >
\end{aligned}
$$

You are invited to compare this formulation with the impure expression-block given as the last item of example 11 above.

3.3 *TUPLE* Operations

The following special *TUPLE* operations are provided:

	[pairwise] concatenation,
h, hd	head,
t, tl	tail, (two forms provided)
l, len	length,
elems	elements,
ind	indices,
[*i*], (*i*)	index, selection, (two forms provided)
conc	distributive concatenation (of tuple of tuples),
+	replace.

Each of these operators will now be individually, and quite informally explained. It is assumed below that *tuple, tuple1, tuple2*
denoted *TUPLE*s and *tuplelist* a *TUPLE* of *TUPLE*s.

tuple1⌢tuple2 denotes the *TUPLE* whose first *l tuple1* elements are those of *tuple1* in the given
order; whose last *l tuple2* elements are those
of *tuple2*, and in that order; and whose length
is exactly the sum of the lengths of *tuple1*
and *tuple2*.

h tuple denotes the *1st* element of *tuple*. Taking the
head of an empty tuple is *undefined*.

t tuple denotes the *tuple* of all but the first element of *tuple* and otherwise in the same order
as the elements of *tuple*. Taking the tail of
an empty tuple is *undefined*.

l tuple denotes the length of the tuple, i.e. the *Num-*
ber of not necessarily distinct elements of
tuple.

elems tuple denotes the *SET* of elements contained in the
tuple.

ind _tuple_	denotes the _SET_ of _Natural_ numbers which are the indices of _tuple_.
tuple[_i_]	denotes the _i_th element of _tuple_ provided _i_ is a _Natural_ number larger than _0_ and less than or equal to the length of _tuple_.
conc _tuplelist_	denotes the _TUPLE_ of elements of the tuples which are the immediate elements of _tuplelist_ and in the order otherwise given in the unravelled or de-bracketed, element tuples.
tuple+[_i→o_]	denotes the tuple which is as _tuple_ -- only the _i_th object is not _tuple_[_i_] but _o_. If _1>i>l_ _tuple_ the expression is _undefined_.

This last operation is (presently) only defined for a right operand singleton map (in $\acute{N}_1 \xrightarrow[m]{} OBJ$).

The tuple operations applied to objects other than tuples are _undefined_.

Examples 16-17:

Let _VAL_ denote the class of values obtained during, i.e. as a result of partial, evaluations of expressions of some language, and let _STACK_ be an abstraction of stacks of these values.

$$STACK = VAL*$$

can then be considered a not too abstract, yet sufficiently implementation-independent, model of the domain of stacks. Let _stk∈STACK_, _v∈VAL_   then:

(1)	<_v_>~_st_
(2)	_h_ _st_, _hd_ _st_
(3)	_t_ _st_, _tl_ _st_
(4)	<>

are correspondingly reasonable abstractions of the following typical
operations on or facts about stacks: (1) pushing a new object "on
top" of, or into the stack; (2) reading the top of the stack; (3)
the resulting stack after a pop operation -- with (4) not abstracting any operation but only brought here to exemplify the empty, un-
used stack .

$$\cdots$$

Reverting now to our examples around file systems, let possibly
suitably decorated f, r and g denote files, records and fields respectively, i.e. objects in F, R and G, then the expressions:

(5)	$f \triangleleft \langle r \rangle$	$r \triangleleft \langle g \rangle$
(6)	$\underline{h} f, \quad \underline{hd} f$	$\underline{h} r, \quad \underline{hd} r$
(7)	$f[i]$	$r[j]$
(8)	$f1 \triangleleft f2$	$r1 \triangleleft r2$
(9)	$f + [i \rightarrow r]$	$r + [j \rightarrow g]$
(10)	$\underline{conc} f$	
(11)	$\underline{l} f, \quad \underline{len} f$	$\underline{l} r, \quad \underline{len} r$

are reasonable abstractions of the following typical operations on
files (left column) [and records (right column)]: (5) writing a record [field] to a sequential, even serial file [record]; (6) & (7)
reading the first, respectively the i'th record [j'th field] of a
file [record]; (8) chaining two files [records] together to form a
new file [record]; (9) updating the i'th record [j'th field] of a
file [record]; (10) chaining all the records of a file together to
form a record (!); and (11) inquiring about the current size of a file
[record] in terms of its number of records [fields].

3.4 *TUPLE*-oriented Combinators

The following combinator:

$$\underline{for}\ i = m\ \underline{to}\ n\ \underline{do}\ S(i)$$

is provided for the imperative handling of primarily lists of objects.
In particular, let t denote a tuple, then:

$$\underline{for}\ i=1\ \underline{to}\ \underline{len}\ t\ \underline{do}\ S(t[i])$$

is a typical statement. The integer valued bounds m and n must be statically determined. S is any statement. See the doubly nested example of a use of the above iterative statement given as the last item of example 11.

The meaning is given by the transcription:

$$S(m);\ S(m+1);...;\ S(n)$$

where $S(j)$ arises from $S(i)$ by substituting all free occurrences of i in $S(i)$ by j. Since j is a constant no collision with other free variables in $S(i)$ will occur.

Example 18:

The constructor expression:

$$< F_{\hbar}(f[i])\ |\ 1 \leq i \leq \underline{len}\ f >$$

is an applicative expression -- provided $F_{\hbar}$ does not rely on any state component. An imperative analog can be achieved by means of the $\underline{for}$-$\underline{to}$-$\underline{do}$ linearly iterative loop statement:

$$\underline{dcl}\ file := <>\ \underline{type}\ R*$$
$$(\underline{for}\ i=1\ \underline{to}\ \underline{len}\ f\ \underline{do}$$
$$file := (c\ file) \sim < F_{\hbar}(f[i])>;$$
$$c\ file)$$

The above can be seen to be a process-oriented abstraction of parts of a file handling system specification. The global variable $file$ is initialized to the null tuple, $<>$, of no records; and fixed to contain only finite length sequences of not necessarily distinct records ($\underline{type}\ R*$). $file$ now denotes a constant reference to an $R*$ object, i.e. an object of $\underline{ref}\ R*$; with $c\ file$ denoting the dynamic contents at that reference.

4 MAPs

Example 19:

As a prelude to a systematic treatment of the subject of maps we are
in this introductory example going to illustrate the abstraction of
what could be an operating system directory in terms of recursively
nested maps. In this, perhaps hypothetical operating system users
are partially ordered, i.e. hierarchically structured -- and this is
reflected in the design of the directory. With each user is associated
a qualified name consisting of an ordered sequence of zero one or
more resource identifiers. The overall system directory is a directory and a directory consists of a finite non-empty set of uniquely identified resources. A resource is e.g. either a line printer, a
card reader, a display terminal, a file identifier or it is a directory.

Abstractly modeling we write:

1      $DIR = Rid \underset{m}{\rightarrow} RES$
2      $RES = LP \mid CR \mid DT \mid Fid \mid DIR \mid \ldots$

The resource- and file-identifiers are considered to be further un-
analyzed, e.g. elementary, objects:

$Rid = \ldots, \quad Fid = \ldots$

We also do not have here bother to specify what line printers, card
readers and display terminals are:

$LP = \ldots, \quad CR = \ldots, \quad DT = \ldots$

The above two equations (1,2) are examples of abstract syntax rules.
The first defines the domain of finite domain maps from resource
identifiers to resources, and names it DIR; the latter defines the
domain of resources to be the union ($\mid$) domain of the domains listed
to the right, i.e. in the definiens. Thus a particular resource, i.e.
an object of the domain RES, is either an object in LP (i.e. a line
printer), or -- etc.

If by suitably decorated lower case letter sequences analogous to the above domain names we mean to identify objects of respective classes, then the following is an expression of the meta-language denoting an object in DIR, i.e. an abstract "snapshot" of a directory:

$$[rid_1 \rightarrow lp_1,$$
$$rid_2 \rightarrow fid_2,$$
$$rid_3 \rightarrow [rid_4 \rightarrow cr_4,$$
$$\quad rid_5 \rightarrow dt_5,$$
$$\quad rid_6 \rightarrow [rid_7 \rightarrow lp_7,$$
$$\quad\quad rid_8 \rightarrow [rid_9 \rightarrow cr_9],$$
$$\quad\quad rid_{10} \rightarrow fid_{10}]],$$
$$rid_{11} \rightarrow fid_{11},$$
$$rid_{12} \rightarrow [rid_{13} \rightarrow dt_{13}]]$$

which we could informally picture:

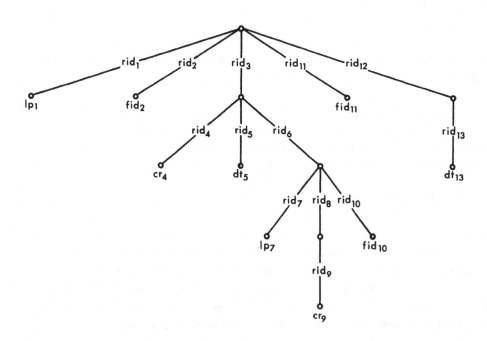

In the above hierarchical structure the labeling of edges (by rids) is usually understood to void any 'meaning' you may think that the left-to-right ordering of edges have.

Observe how, from the system-directory the qualified name $<rid_3,rid_6,rid_7>$ designates lp_7. Qualified names designating directories are: $<>$, $<rid_3>$, $<rid_{12}>$, $<rid_3,rid_6>$, $<rid_3,rid_6,rid_8>$, and these are the names associated with users.

Resources associated with existing users may be allocated or freed: Let $sys\text{-}dir$ stand for the system directory, qn for a name known to designate a direcotry in $sys\text{-}dir$, and let rid and res denote respectively the name by which the resource res is to be known in the directory designated by qn. The following function, when invoked by: $catalog(sys\text{-}dir,qn,rid,res)$ accomplishes this:

3.0 $catalog(dir,q,id,r)=$

.1   _if_ $q=<>$

.2   _then_ $dir \cup [id{\rightarrow}r]$

.3   _else_ $dir + [\underline{h}\,q{\rightarrow}catalog(dir(\underline{h}\,q),\underline{t}\,q,id,r)]$

          type: $DIR\ Rid^*\ Rid\ RES\ \overset{\sim}{\rightarrow}\ DIR$

The reader is encouraged to apply this function to the above example.

The line: "$dir \cup [id{\rightarrow}r]$" reads: "join, or merge, as a new entry, the association of id to r, to the map dir". The last line reads: "$\underline{h}\,q$, which is an Rid, designates a directory, $dir(\underline{h}\,q)$, embedded in dir. Replace this directory, $dir(\underline{h}\,q)$, with the one -- $catalog(dir(\underline{h}\,q),\underline{t}\,q,id,r)$ -- obtained by cataloging the resource r named id in the subdirectory of $dir(\underline{h}\,q)$ designated by $\underline{t}\,q$!".

Now it may be that the original qn did not designate a directory in $sys\text{-}dir$. Then the above function would go awry. So here is an improved version:

```
4.0   catalog(dir,q,id,r)=
 .1      if q=<>
 .2         then if id ∈ dom dir
 .3                 then error
 .4                 else dir ∪ [id→r]
 .5         else if h q ~∈ dom dir
 .6                 then error
 .7                 else (let res = dir(h q) in
 .8                         if ~is-DIR(res)
 .9                             then error
 .10                            else dir + [h q→catalog(res,t q,id,r)])
```

This function also makes sure that is is not already used in the
directory designated by q . Thus _dom dir_ denotes the domain, i.e.
the set of resource identifiers used in _dir_. Observe finally that
since a qualified name might designate either nonsense or a resource,
res, other than a directory, i.e. a _DIR_, we test, _is-DIR_, that _res_
is indeed a directory.

Further experiments with the above abstraction will be exhibited in
section 4.5.

4.1 Defining Domains of *MAP* Objects

Let A, B, A_i and B_j (for $i = 1,2,\ldots,n$ and $j = 1,2,\ldots,l$) be class
names. To define the class of objects which are finite domain maps
from (subsets of) A, respectively A_i, into B, respectively B_j, we
use the domain expression operator $\underset{m}{\rightarrow}$:

$$A \underset{m}{\rightarrow} B, \qquad A_i \underset{m}{\rightarrow} B_j$$

Examples 20:

Let our file system now come of age! Let the file system consist of
a set of uniquely named files; and let each file consist of a set of
uniquely keyed records, i.e. the file may have its records randomly
accessed by key. Let file names, keys and records presently be further
unspecified. Then:

$$Key \underset{m}{\rightarrow} REC$$

is a domain expression suitably abstracting our notion of files,
provided *Key* & *REC* denote the domains of keys and records. If you
wish to name this file domain, by e.g. *FILE*, then:

$$FILE = Key \underset{m}{\rightarrow} REC$$

is an example of an abstract syntax rule which lets *FILE* denote what
$Key \underset{m}{\rightarrow} REC$ denotes! Now:

$$Fid \underset{m}{\rightarrow} FILE$$

or equally well:

$$Fid \underset{m}{\rightarrow} (Key \underset{m}{\rightarrow} REC)$$

are domain expressions both suitable abstracting our ideas about the
file system and files, again provided *Fid* denotes the domain of file
names.

4.1.1 Defining *MAP* Domains -- Continued

Then the logical type expression:

$$(A_1 | A_2 | \ldots | A_n) \xrightarrow{m} (B_1 | B_2 | \ldots | B_l) \qquad l \gtrless n$$

denotes the class of objects whose members are finite domain maps
from (subset of) the union class of A_1, A_2, ..., and A_n objects into
the union class of B_1, B_2, ..., and B_l objects.

Example 21:

Now define keys and records to be either integers or characterstrings,
respectively finite, non-zero length sequences of either integers or
characterstrings -- presently with no constraints. Then, if *INTG* and
QUOT⁺ are suitable abstractions of integers and characterstrings respectively, we have that:

$$(INTG | QUOT^+) \xrightarrow{m} (INTG^+ | QUOT^{++})$$

is a domain expression which defines any one file to contain both
integers and characterstrings in its domain, i.e. as its keys; and
sequences of both of these in its co-domain or range, i.e. as its
records. Thus e.g. a given file may map *3* into <*A*,*X*,*H*>, <*P*> into
<*2*,*4*,*9*,*11*>, *5* into <*3*,*5*,*7*>, and <*Y*,*Z*> into <*I*,*J*>.

4.1.2 Defining *MAP* Domains -- Continued

The logical type expression:

$$(A_1 \xrightarrow{m} B_1) \underline{\cup} (A_2 \xrightarrow{m} B_2) \underline{\cup} \ldots \ldots \underline{\cup} (A_k \xrightarrow{m} B_k)$$

denotes the class of objects whose members are finite domain maps as
above but with the restriction that A_1 objects, if at all mapped,
i.e. in the domain, are mapped into B_1 objects, A_2 objects (...)
into B_2 objects, ..., and A_k objects into B_k objects. We read the
$\underline{\cup}$ *MAP* domain operator as a 'merge'-, rather than (as we did for |)
an 'either'-, union operation.

Example 22:

If we wish to constrain integer keys to map into integer field records, and characterstrings keys into records whose fields are characterstrings, then:

$$(INTG \xrightarrow[m]{} INTG^+) \quad \underline{\cup} \quad (QUOT^+ \xrightarrow[m]{} QUOT^{++})$$

is a domain expression of the right kind for specifying the above!

Defining _MAP_ Domains -- Terminated

The logical type expression:

$$(A_1 \xrightarrow[m]{} B_1) \quad | \quad (A_2 \xrightarrow[m]{} B_2) \quad | \quad \dots \quad | \quad (A_k \xrightarrow[m]{} B_k)$$

denotes a class of objects whose members are finite domain, partial
maps from A_1 into B_1, or A_2 into $B_2, \dots$, or A_k into B_k. Thus a given
member is either an $A_1 \xrightarrow[m]{} B_1$ object, or an $A_2 \xrightarrow[m]{} B_2$ object,..., or an
$A_k \xrightarrow[m]{} B_k$ object.

Example 23:

If finally any one file should not mix integers and characterstrings
in its key domain or record co-domain, then:

$$(INTG \xrightarrow[m]{} INTG^+) \quad | \quad (INTG \xrightarrow[m]{} QUOT^{++}) |$$
$$(QUOT^+ \xrightarrow[m]{} QUOT^{++}) \quad | \quad (QUOT^+ \xrightarrow{} INTG^+)$$

is a domain expression guaranteeing this! Note that the domain expression:

$$(INTG | QUOT^+) \xrightarrow[m]{} (INTG | QUOT^+)^+$$

permits any one record to have some fields being integers, others
being characterstrings. If that is your ideas about records, this is
a way in which you can so express it!

Note:

A map or a function from subsets of A into B is said to be a partial map, respectively partial function. It is quite common to deal with partial maps.

Programming Note:

Defining a class of functions using the $\underset{m}{\rightarrow}$ operator shall express that such objects have their graph, i.e. argument-value associations, computed when defined. This is in contrast to using the $\rightarrow$ and $\overset{\sim}{\rightarrow}$ operators whose use in defining total and partial functions shall express that the objects are implicitly defined through some λ-expressions-like device, about which it can be said that the graph of the denoted function is not computed when defined -- in fact: is never computed -- and where, in addition, the function domain(s) may be infinite. For the story on such functions see section 5.

4.2 Representing Instances of *MAP* Objects

4.2.1 Explicit Enumeration

Let a_1, a_2, ..., a_d be distinct A objects, a_{i1}, a_{i2}, ..., a_{id} be distinct A_i objects, b_1, b_2, ..., b_d be not necessarily distinct B objects, and b_{j1}, b_{j2}, ..., b_{jd} be not necessarily distinct B_j objects, then the constructor expressions:

$$[a_1 \rightarrow b_1, a_2 \rightarrow b_2, \ldots, a_d \rightarrow b_d]$$
$$[a_{i1} \rightarrow b_{j1}, a_{i2} \rightarrow b_{j2}, \ldots, a_{id} \rightarrow b_{jd}]$$

and :

denote maps from (subsets of) A into B, respectively (subsets of) A_i into B_j, i.e. in: $A \underset{m}{\rightarrow} B$, respectively $A_i \underset{m}{\rightarrow} B_j$. The constructor expression:

$$[a_{11} \to b_{11}, a_{12} \to b_{12}, \ldots, a_{1m_2} \to b_{1m_1},$$
$$a_{21} \to b_{21}, a_{22} \to b_{22}, \ldots, a_{2m_2} \to b_{2m_2},$$
$$\ldots$$
$$a_{k1} \to b_{k1}, a_{k2} \to b_{k2}, \ldots, a_{km_k} \to b_{km_k}]$$

denotes a map in:

$$(A_1 \underset{m}{\to} B_1) \; \underline{\cup} \; (A_2 \underset{m}{\to} B_2) \; \underline{\cup} \; \ldots \; \underline{\cup} \; (A_k \underset{m}{\to} B_k)$$

assuming of course that $a_{ij} \in A_i$, $b_{ij} \in B_i$ that is: that first subscripting index, i, binds to domain A_i respectively B_i. And:

$$[a_{x1} \to b_{y1}, a_{x2} \to b_{y2}, \ldots, a_{xm} \to b_{ym}]$$

denotes a map in:

$$(A_1 | A_2 | \ldots . A_n) \; \underset{m}{\to} \; (B_1 | B_2 | \ldots | B_l)$$

provided:

$$a_{xi} \in (A_1 | A_2 | \ldots | A_n) \text{ and } b_{yj} \in (B_1 | B_2 | \ldots | B_l).$$

Empty Map:

-- is denoted by:

[]

Example 24:

Let fid_1, fid_2, ..., fid_l denote, i.e. be abstractions of, distinct file names; let k_{ij} etc. denote, i.e. be abstractions of keys distinct for fixed i's; and let r_{ij} etc. denote, i.e. be abstractions of not necessarily distinct records. Then:

$$[fid_1 \rightarrow [k_{11} \rightarrow r_{11}, k_{12} \rightarrow r_{12}, \ldots, k_{1n_1} \rightarrow r_{1n_1}],$$
$$fid_2 \rightarrow [k_{21} \rightarrow r_{21}, k_{22} \rightarrow r_{22}, \ldots, k_{2n_2} \rightarrow r_{2n_2}],$$
$$\ldots$$
$$fid_l \rightarrow [k_{l1} \rightarrow r_{l1} \; k_{l2} \rightarrow r_{l2}, \ldots, k_{ln_m} \rightarrow r_{ln_l}]]$$

is a schematized (...) snapshot of an object in $Fid \underset{m}{\rightarrow} (Key \underset{m}{\rightarrow} REC)$, provided $fid_i \in Fid$, $k_{ij} \in Key$ and $r_{ij} \in REC$.

If $Key = INTG$ and $REC = QUOT^{++}$ then:

$$[3 \rightarrow <<\underline{A},\underline{Z},\underline{B}>, <\underline{Y},\underline{C}>, <\underline{X},\underline{D},\underline{W},\underline{E}>>,$$
$$5 \rightarrow <<\underline{V}>>,$$
$$7 \rightarrow <<\underline{F},\underline{U},\underline{G},\underline{T},\underline{H}>, <\underline{S}>>]$$

represents a file of three records, with keys $3, 5$ and 7; etc. Whereas keys of any one file need be distinct, records or any two keys of respectively distinctly names files need not be distinct:

$$[fid_\alpha \rightarrow [2 \rightarrow <3,4,5>, 3 \rightarrow <3,4,5>],$$
$$fid_\beta \rightarrow [3 \rightarrow <3,4,5>, 2 \rightarrow <3,4,5>]];$$

in fact, as the above example of a snapshot of a small file system shows, distinctly named files need themselves not be distinct.

4.2.2 Implicit Enumeration

Let F: $D_d \overset{\sim}{\rightarrow} A$ and G: $D_r \overset{\sim}{\rightarrow} B$ denote partial functions, then:

$$[\; F(d) \rightarrow G(r) \; | \; P(d,r) \;]$$

is a map constructor expression denoting a map in $A \underset{m}{\rightarrow} B$. P is assumed to be a predicate: $P: \; D_d \; D_r \; \rightarrow \; BOOL$.

Let F_i, F_{1n}, G_j, $G_{1\ell}$ denote partial functions:

$$F_i: \quad D_d \overset{\sim}{\to} A_i,$$
$$F_{1n}: \quad D_d \overset{\sim}{\to} (A_1|A_2|\ldots|A_n),$$
$$G_j: \quad D_r \overset{\sim}{\to} B_j \qquad\qquad \text{and:}$$
$$G_{1\ell}: \quad D_r \overset{\sim}{\to} (B_1|B_2|\ldots|B_\ell)$$

for $i=1,2,\ldots,n$ and $j=1,2,\ldots,\ell$. The expressions:

$$[F_i(d) \to G_j(r) \mid P(d,r)], \qquad \text{and:}$$
$$[F_{1n} \to G_{1\ell}(r) \mid P(d,r)]$$

denote maps from (subsets of) respectively A_i into B_j, and $(A_1|A_2|\ldots|A_n)$ into $(B_1|B_2|\ldots|B_\ell)$.

The expression:

$$[F_1(d) \to G_1(r) \mid P_1(d,r)]$$
$$\cup[F_2(d) \to G_2(r) \mid P_2(d,r)]$$
$$\cdots$$
$$\cdots$$
$$\cup[F_k(d) \to G_k(r) \mid P_k(d,r)]$$

where P_i are predicates, as above, denotes a map in:

$$(A_1 \vec{m} B_1) \;\underline{\cup}\; (A_2 \vec{m} B_2) \;\underline{\cup}\; \cdots \;\underline{\cup}\; (A_k \vec{m} B_k) .$$

Example 25:

Let F_n, F_b denote total (for simplicity: pure, applicative) functions from records into records, respectively files into files. Let s denote a file system, f some file, r some record; and, foregoing the next subsection (2.3.3) on operations, let $\underline{dom}\ s$ and $\underline{dom}\ f$ denote the set of filenames, respectively the set of keys, of the file-system -- respectively of a file. Then:

$$[\ fid \to F_b(s(fid)) \mid fid \in \underline{dom}\ s]$$
$$[\ k \quad \to F_n(f(k)) \quad \mid k \quad \in \underline{dom}\ f]$$

and:

$$[\ fid \to [\ k \to F_n((s(fid))(k)) \mid k \in \underline{dom}\ s(fid)] \mid fid \in \underline{dom}\ s\ ]$$

denotes a file system, a file, and a file system. The former file
system is derived from a given file system, s, by transforming each
of its files; the latter by transforming each of its records individually. The file is derived from a given file, f, by transforming
each of its records. Thus the above three implicit map constructor
expressions may be reasonable abstractions of various file 'processing' programs. Observe how randomness of record and file 'positions'
or 'accessing' is preserved by the unorderedness of 'fetching' files
(fid) respectively records (k, $f(k)$,....), for transformation.

4.2.3 A Note on Scopes

We have now seen three distinct meta-language constructs for implicit object constructions:

$$\{ \ F_{h}(r) \ \mid \ r \epsilon f \ \}$$
$$< F_{h}(f[i]) \ \mid \ 1 \leq i \leq lf \ >$$
$$[\ k \rightarrow F_{h}(f(k)) \ \mid \ k \in \underline{dom} \ f \ ]$$

In all three, F_{h} and f were quantities defined outside these expressions; and r, i and k respectively, were bound variables, being de-
fined and bound to the right of the builder combinator: |, and with
a scope extending to the closest embracing pair of { & }, < & >,
respectively [&]. The scope of these bound variables follow rules
analog to those in ordinary programming languages: thus they extend
to inner, i.e. nested expressions, including { }, < > and [ ] based
constructor expressions -- unless redefined in such inner forms, a
practice which certainly can and should be avoided! The last file
system building expression of the previous example section illustrates
the doubly nested use of bound variables. So does:

Example 26:

Let:

$$A \xrightarrow[m]{} (B \xrightarrow[m]{} C)$$
$$(A \ B) \xrightarrow[m]{} C$$

be domain expressions where we do not presently bother about A, B and C. Then: for suitably decorated, and occasionally distinct, $a \in A$, $b \in B$ and $c \in C$:

$$[\; a1 \to [b11 \to c11, b12 \to c12],$$
$$\quad a2 \to [b21 \to c21, b22 \to c22, b23 \to c23] \;]$$

and ŧ

$$[\; (a1, b11) \to c11, (a1, b12) \to c12,$$
$$\quad (a2, b21) \to c21, (a2, b22) \to c22, (a2, b23) \to c23]$$

are examples of somehow 'equivalently' denoting expressions in that functions can be defined which converts between their objects.

Let, for ease of reference, the first domain be named X, the second Y:

$$X \; = \; A \xrightarrow{m} (B \xrightarrow{m} C)$$
$$Y \; = \; (A \; B) \xrightarrow{m} C$$

then:

$convxy(x)=$
    $[(a,b) \to c \; | \; a \in \underline{dom} \; x \; \land \; b \in \underline{dom}(x(a)) \; \land \; c=(x(a))(b) \;]$

$convyx(y)=$
    $[\; a \to [b \to c \; | \; (a',b) \in \underline{dom} \; y \; \land \; a'=a \; \land \; c=y(a,b)] \; | \; (a, \;) \in \underline{dom} \; y \;]$

where:

$\underline{type}: \; convxy: \quad X \to Y$
$\underline{type}: \; convyx: \quad Y \to X$

In fact the two functions are each others inverses.

4.3 _MAP_ Operations

The following special _MAP_ operations are provided:

U	merge,
+	override,
(...)	apply,
⟍	restrict with,
		restrict to,
dom	domain,
rng	range,
	composition

Each of these operators will now be individually, and quite informally explained:

map1Umap2   denotes a _MAP_ provided the domains of _map1_ and _map2_
are disjoint, otherwise _undefined_. The denoted _map_
maps domain elements of _map1_ into the same range elements as does _map1_, and domain elements of _map2_ into
the same range elements as does _map2_, and maps nothing
else.

map1+map2   denotes the _MAP_ which maps domain elements of _map2_
into the same range elements as does _map2_, and maps
those domain elements of _map1_ which are not in the
domain of _map2_ into the same range elements as does
map1, and maps nothing else.

map(a)   denotes the range _OBJ_ect into which _map_ maps _a_. If _a_
is not in the domain of _map_ the operation is _undefined_.

map⟍wset   denotes the _MAP_ which maps those domain elements of
map which are not in the set _wset_ into the same range
elements as does _map_, and maps nothing else.

$map \mid tset$ denotes the *MAP* which map those domain elements of *map* which are also in *tset* into the same range elements as does *map*, and maps nothing else.

$\underline{dom}\ map$ denotes the set of objects which are domain elements of *map*.

$\underline{rng}\ map$ denotes the *SET* of *OBJ*ects which are the range elements of *map*.

$map1 \cdot map2$ denotes a *MAP* provided the range of *map2* is included, i.e. contained ($\subseteq$) in the domain of *map1*, otherwise the operation is *undefined*. The denoted map maps into those range elements of *map1* which are mapped to by the domain elements of *map1*, mapped into, as range elements of *map2* from domain elements of *map2*. More formally, and in this case certainly more concisely:

$$(map1 \cdot map2)(d) = \underline{if}\ d \in \underline{dom}\ map2$$
$$\underline{then}\ \underline{if}\ map2(d) \in \underline{dom}\ map1$$
$$\underline{then}\ map1(map2(d))$$
$$\underline{else}\ \underline{undefined}$$
$$\underline{else}\ \underline{undefined}$$

Example 27:

Let s, id, f, r and k stand for abstractions of file systems, file names, files, records and keys, then:

(1) $s \cup [id \rightarrow f]$ $f \cup [k \rightarrow r]$

(2) $s + [id \rightarrow f]$ $f + [k \rightarrow r]$

(3) $s \setminus \{id\}$ $f \setminus \{k\}$

(4) $s(id)$ $f(k)$

(5) $id \in \underline{dom}\ s$ $k \in \underline{dom}\ f$

(6) $f \in \underline{rng}\ s$ $r \in \underline{rng}\ f$

may be reasonable abstractions of the following typical operations
on file systems (left column) [and files (right column)]: (1) writing
an entirely new file [record] into the file system [a file] -- in the
sense of its name [key] not hitherto being one of a file [record] in
the system [file]; (2) updating an entire file [a single record] of
the system [a file]; (3) deleting an entire file [record] named id
[keyed with k] from the system [a file]; (4) reading an entire file
[a record]; (5) asking whether a file of a given name [a record with
a given key] is in the system [a file]; and (6) inquiring whether a
given file (i.e. its 'value', not name) [record ('value', not key)]
is in the system [a file].

Let suitably decorated id's and k's denote file names, respectively
keys. Then:

(7) $\qquad s \mid \{id_1, id_2, \ldots, id_n\} \qquad\qquad f \mid \{k_1, k_2, \ldots, k_m\}$

seems to be an acceptable abstraction for the operation of restricting
the files of a system to those of the indicated names -- i.e. deleting
all other! [respectively deleting all those file records whose keys
are different from k_i $(1 \leq i \leq m)$].

Combining the above operations:

(1') $\qquad s + [\ id \to s(id) \cup [k \to r]\ ]$
(2') $\qquad s + [\ id \to s(id) + [k \to r]\ ]$
(3') $\qquad s + [\ id \to (s(id) \smallsetminus \{r\}\ ]$
(4') $\qquad (s(id))(k)$
(5') $\qquad k \in \underline{dom}(s(id))$
(6') $\qquad r \in \underline{rng}(s(id))$
(7') $\qquad s + [\ id \to ((s(id)) \mid \{k_1, k_2, \ldots, k_n\})\ ]$

we get the right column equivalents, on a file system.

4.4 _MAP_-oriented Combinators

The same combinator: the _for-all-do_ statement, as was defined for processing sets, is available for processes on maps, e.g.:

$$\underline{for}\ \underline{all}\ d \in \underline{dom}\ map\ \underline{do}\ S(map(d))$$

Example 28:

We give the imperative variant of the last of the three implicit, applicative map constructions shown in the example 25.

$$\underline{dcl}\ system := [\ ]\ \underline{type}\ (Fid \xrightarrow{m} (Key \xrightarrow{m} REC)),$$
$$file := [\ ]\ \underline{type}\ (Key \xrightarrow{m} REC);$$
$$(\underline{for}\ \underline{all}\ fid \in \underline{dom}\ s\ \underline{do}$$
$$(file := [\ ];$$
$$\underline{for}\ \underline{all}\ k \in \underline{dom}\ s(fid)\ \underline{do}$$
$$file := (c\ file)\ \cup\ [\ k \rightarrow F_h\ ((s(fid))(k))\ ];$$
$$system := (c\ system)\ \cup\ [\ fid \rightarrow (c\ file)\ ]))$$

4.5 Further Examples

Example 29:

The introductory example of this section is now continued. We are now interested in defining a number of auxiliary functions applicable to the operating system directory. A function for catalogueing new entries, i.e. new resources, has already been shown. The dual function of uncatalogueing e.g. takes a directory and a non-null resource name and deletes the designated resource -- i.e. returns a directory in which the resource name is no longer a valid name:

```
1.0       uncatalog(dir,q)=
 .1          cases q:
 .2            (<id> → dir\{id}
 .3             T   → dir + [ h q → uncatalog(dir(h q),t q) ] )
             type:  DIR Rid⁺ → DIR
```

Provided q indeed does designate some resource in dir! When such is
the case we can show that:

$$uncatalog(catalog(dir,q,id,r),q\mathtt{\sim}<id>) = dir$$

A function for testing whether a non-null resource name, q, does indeed designate something meaningfull in a directory, dir, is e.g.
the following:

```
2         isvalidrn(dir,q) = q ∈ resnms(dir)
             type:  DIR Rid⁺ → BOOL
```

where:

```
3.0       resnms(dir)=
 .1          { <rid>⌢rn | rid ∈ dom dir
 .2                     ∧ (is-DIR(dir(rid)) → rn∈resnms(dir(rid)),
 .3                          T                → rn = <>) }
             type:  DIR → Rid⁺-set
```

another function would be:

```
4.0       isrnok(dir,q)=
 .1          (h q ∈ dom dir)
 .2          ∧(cases t q:
 .3             (<> → true,
 .4              T  → isrnok(dir(h q),t q)))
             type:  DIR Rid⁺ → BOOL
```

where we rely on the non-commutativeness, in the meta-language, of
the boolean ∧ and ∨ operators. A function for retrieving a resource
given its name could e.g. be expressed:

$$5.0 \quad retrieve(dir,q)=$$
$$.1 \quad \underline{cases} \; q:$$
$$.2 \quad (<id> \; \rightarrow \; dir(id),$$
$$.3 \quad T \quad \rightarrow \; retrieve(dir(\underline{h}\,q),\underline{t}\,q))$$

$$\underline{type}: \quad DIR \; Rid^{+} \quad \rightarrow \quad RES$$

The domain expression $Rid \xrightarrow{m} RES$ also defines the void map, [],
from no resource identifiers to no resources, as part of its domain.
In some of the above function definitions we have tacitly assumed
that no (embedded) directory was empty. A predicate function for
testing this well-formedness criteria not expressed by the domain
expressions might e.g. look like:

$$6.0 \quad is\text{-}wf\text{-}DIR_{O}(dir)=$$
$$.1 \quad (dir \neq [])$$
$$.2 \quad \wedge(\forall rid \in \underline{dom}\,dir)$$
$$.3 \quad (is\text{-}DIR(dir(rid)) \; \supset \; is\text{-}wf\text{-}DIR_{O}(dir(rid)))$$

$$\underline{type}: \quad DIR \rightarrow BOOL$$

File identifiers are part of the directory. If we e.g. impose that
no two distinct resource names, via designated file identifiers,
"point" to identical files, then the above $is\text{-}wf\text{-}DIR_{O}$ must be augmented:

$$7.0 \quad is\text{-}wf\text{-}DIR(dir)=$$
$$.1 \quad is\text{-}wf\text{-}DIR_{O}(ir)$$
$$.2 \quad \wedge(\forall rn_{1},rn_{2} \in resnms(dir))$$
$$.3 \quad ((rn_{1} \neq rn_{2})$$
$$.4 \quad \supset(((is\text{-}Fid(retrieve(dir,rn_{1}))\wedge is\text{-}Fid(retrieve(dir,rn_{2})))$$
$$.5 \quad \supset(retrieve(dir,rn_{1}) \neq retrieve(dir,rn_{2})))))$$

Another Example, 30:

In this example we shall motivate the modeling of the scope-binding and variable concepts of block- & procedure-oriented programming languages by means of so-called environments, respectively abstract stores. In subsequent examples, (31,40,42,61), we shall then illustrate the semantics modeling of procedures and blocks of such languages. The introduction, into our realm of abstract modeling concepts, of environments and stores will now be argued in a few, short, illustrative, but not really complete steps. The notation used in the following for some arbitrary, realistic source languages notions of begin-end blocks and variable declarations and use has been deliberately chosen to coincide with the meta-languages notation for the same constructs. These will, however, not be formally introduced till section 10.

The form:

$$(\underline{dcl} \ v \ := \ expr \ \underline{type} \ D;$$
$$C(\ldots))$$

is taken to represent some source languages block construct (with "(" equalling $\underline{begin}$, and ")" the $\underline{end}$). In the semantics of this source language v, which itself is an identifier, is to denote something constant. In fact: in this source-, as well as in our meta-, language, the denotation of identifiers is constant over their scope, i.e. does not change! The constant denotation of v over the above block, i.e. its defining scope, is, rather concretely speaking, taken to be the location (or: address) of the storage cell in which are to be held values, $\underline{c}v$, of the variable v. Thus, if by LOC, we denote the abstract domain of storage locations, and by OBJ, the values which can be held in those locations, then the domain of storages can be abstracted as:

$$LOC \xrightarrow[m]{} OBJ$$

We choose $\xrightarrow[m]{}$ since there will, at any point of execution of our source programs, only be a finite number of active variables, i.e. of allocated storage cells. Thus we abstract storages as unique associations, maps from locations to their values.

To keep track of the location that variable identifiers denote we introduce, speaking concrete again, a table, henceforth called an environment, in which is recorded the associations of variable names to their locations.

$$Id \xrightarrow[m]{} LOC$$

where e.g. $v \in Id$. Again the association is functional, and again the functional recordings are finite. Before argueing why we do not direct-ly model storages as:

$$Id \xrightarrow[m]{} OBJ$$

let us first see that we do indeed need the full use of the meta-lan-guage *MAP* concept, i.e. of the *MAP* operations. Simultaneously we exem-plify 'snapshots' of environments, ρ, and stores, σ. The example is that of one simple block, containing the declaration of the variable named i, nested in an outer block, also containing the declaration of a identi-cally named variable.

The environment immediately prior to outer block elaboration is ρ_0 and the state is σ_0. These are not detailed. Obeying the 'first' declaration results in the elaborator claiming a new, fresh storage cell for i, let us call its location li_1. Thus:

$$\sigma_1 \quad = \quad \sigma_0 \ \cup \ [li_1 \rightarrow o_1]$$

with:

$$\rho_1 \quad = \quad \rho_0 \ + \ [i \rightarrow li_1]$$

Thus we use ∪ as an abstraction of the storage allocation operation -- ∪ since li_1 is new, i.e. not in the <u>dom</u>ain of σ_0: $li_1 \not\in \underline{dom}\,\sigma_0$! But we use + as an abstraction of the environment 'update' action -- i may namely be already recorded in ρ_0. Observe that we do "fall back" to ρ_0 when "falling through" this, the outer, block. Similarly:

$$\sigma_1' \quad = \quad \sigma_0' \cup [li_1 \to o_1']$$

where the ' on σ_0 shall indicate that variables outside this block may have had their values updated. Also i may have been updated (o_1')! And:

$$\rho_2 \quad = \quad \rho_1 + [i \to li_2] \quad = \quad \rho_0 + [i \to li_2]$$
$$\sigma_2 \quad = \quad \sigma_1' \cup [li_2 \to o_2] \quad = \quad \sigma_0' \cup [li_1 \to o_1', li_2 \to o_2]$$

That is: the storage claimed for the inner blocks' i is also fresh, not clashing with the storage for the outer blocks' i.

Observe how environments, e.g. ρ_1, remain constant in the outer block.

$$\sigma_2' \quad = \quad \sigma_0'' \cup [li_1 \to o_1'', li_2 \to o_2']$$
$$\sigma_1'' \quad = \quad \sigma_2' \setminus \{li_2\} \quad = \quad \sigma_0'' \cup [li_1 \to o_1'']$$
$$\sigma_1''' \quad = \quad \sigma_0''' \cup [li_1 \to o_1''']$$
$$\sigma_0' \quad = \quad \sigma_1''' \setminus \{li_1\} \quad = \quad \sigma_0'''$$

Thus freeing, or deallocation of storage for declared variables follow the block structure, i.e.: is performed as part of the block epilogue. The *MAP* operator abstracting deallocation is: ∖.

We now turn to a brief justification for the use of <u>both</u> environments and stores. The above example of nested blocks redefining variable names is not a sufficiently convincing example. Static renaming of e.g. the inner i to e.g. j would permit modeling stores as $Id \xrightarrow{m} OBJ$. If, however, any block was [part of] a recursively defined procedure static renaming would not solve the problem of nested activations' i denoting distinct locations -- which are the semantics we normally expect!

In example 31 and onwards we use *ENV* and sometimes Σ as follows:

$$ENV = Id \xrightarrow{m} LOC$$
$$\Sigma = LOC \xrightarrow{m} OBJ$$

Finally, as a last example, we show the modeling of variable referencing, value access and of assignment.

For the elaborator 'state' (ρ,σ) elaboration of some $v \in \underline{dom}\,\rho$ is modeled ($\blacktriangle$) as:

$$v \qquad \blacktriangle \qquad \rho(v)$$

Accessing the contents of a variable v:

$$\underline{c}\ v \qquad \blacktriangle \qquad \sigma(\rho(v))$$

and assigning the object (value) o to variable v changes the state σ to:

$$v := o \qquad \blacktriangle \qquad \sigma + [\rho(v) \rightarrow o].$$

A Last Example, 31:

The variables of some source language are either of scalar or array type with all array objects being scalars. Variable references, however, are to scalars only, i.e. not to arrays or array-slices thereof.

The syntactic domains of variable declarations of a block can be modeled as a map from variable name identifiers to their type:

1      $Block$ $::$ $(Id \xrightarrow{m} Type) \ldots Stmt^*$

with :

2      $Type$ $::$ $Scalar\text{-}type\ [Expr^+]$

i.e. with types having an optional [...] array upper bounds expression list, $Expr^+$. If the optional part is absent, i.e. $\underline{nil}$, the variable is a scalar.

The corresponding semantic domain of storages can be modeled as a map from scalar locations to scalar values.

3   STG $=$ $(Bool\text{-}loc \xrightarrow{m} Bool) \; \underline{\cup} \; (Int\text{-}loc \xrightarrow{m} Intg)$

where:

4        $Bool$ $=$ $BOOL \; | \; \underline{undefined}$
5        $Intg$ $=$ $INTG \; | \; \underline{undefined}$

Environments keep track of variable name associations:

6   ENV $=$ $Id \xrightarrow{m} LOC$

with :

7   LOC $= Scalar\text{-}Loc \; | \; Array\text{-}Loc$
8        $Array\text{-}Loc \; = (N_1^+ \xleftrightarrow{m} Int\text{-}Loc) \; \cup \; (N_1^+ \xleftrightarrow{m} Bool\text{-}Loc)$
9        $Scalar\text{-}Loc = Int\text{-}Loc \; | \; Bool\text{-}Loc$

with the constraint that the integer index lists of any given array location forms a 'rectangle':

10.0 $(\forall l \in Array\text{-}Loc)$
  .1 $(\exists il \in N_1^+)(\underline{dom} \; l = rectangle(il))$

where we informally explain rectangle:

11.0 $rectangle(<ub_1, ub_2, \ldots, ub_n>) =$
  .1 $\{ \; <i_1, i_2, \ldots, i_n> \; | \; i_k \in \{1:ub_k\} \; \wedge \; 1 \leq k \leq n \; \}.$

The il 'picked' is (to be) the tuple, whose length corresponds to the array-dimension, and whose k'th element (ub_k) is the upper-bound index for the k'th dimension, all of whose lower-bounds are 1!

A particular storage is modeled (here) as a global meta-variable, $\underset{\sim}{STG}$:

12       $\underline{dcl} \; \underset{\sim}{STG} := [] \; \underline{type} \; STG$

In the block prologue (.1-.2) locations of block declared variables are (automatically) allocated, and these are likewise freed (.4-.8) in the block epilogue:

```
13      int-Block(mk-Block(dcls,...,stl))(ρ)=
.1          (let ρ' : ρ + [id → get-loc(dcls(id))(ρ)
.2                          | id ∈ dom dcls ];
.3          int-Stmt-list(stl)(ρ');
.4          let locs  = { ρ'(id) | id ∈ dom dcls } in
.5          let slocs = { l | ((l∈locs) ∧ is-Scalar-Loc(l))
.6                              v((l ∈ rng al) ∧ (al ∈ locs) ∧
.7                                      is-Array-Loc(al))} in
.8          STG := c STG ∖ slocs)
```

with:

```
14.0        get-loc(mk-Type(sctp,bdl)) (ρ)=
.1              if bdl=nil
.2                  then
.3                      (let l ∈ Scalar-Loc be s.t. (l~∈ dom cSTG)∧
.4                                          l-tp-match(sctp,l);
.5                      STG := c STG ∪ [l→undefined];
.6                      return(l))
.7                  else
.8                      (let ebdl : < eval-Expr(bdl[i])(ρ) | 1 ≤ i ≤ len bdl>;
.9                      if (∃i ∈ {1:len ebdl})(ebdl[i]<1)
.10                         then error
.11                         else
.12                             (let l ∈ Array-Loc be s.t.
.13                                     ((scl ∈ rng l)⊃ l-tp-match(sctp,scl))
.14                                     ∧(dom l = rectangle(ebdl))
.15                                     ∧((rng l ∩ dom c STG) = {});
.16                             STG := c STG ∪ [ scl→undefined | scl ∈ rng l];
.17                             return(l)))
```

and

```
15.0        l-tp-match(tp,l) = ((tp=BOOL) → is-Bool-Loc(l),
.1                              (tp=INT)  → is-Int-Loc(l))
```

Assuming that the state, Σ, is describable as:

```
16          Σ  =   STG →ₘ STG
```

(i.e. Σ is a one-point (STG) map), the type of the above functions are:

$$\underline{type:} \quad int\text{-}Block: \quad Block \overset{\sim}{\to} (ENV \overset{\sim}{\to} (\Sigma \overset{\sim}{\to} \Sigma))$$
$$get\text{-}Loc: \quad Type \overset{\sim}{\to} (ENV \overset{\sim}{\to} (\Sigma \overset{\sim}{\to} (\Sigma \ LOC)))$$
$$rectangle: \quad N_1^+ \quad \to (N_1^+)\text{-}set$$

5. TREEs

Examples 32-33:

Blocks of some source language consists of three distinct parts: an unordered set of *variable* declarations, an unordered set of distinctly named *proc*edures and an ordered sequence of one or more *statements*.

$$(Var\text{-}set \quad Id \underset{m}{\to} Proc \quad Stmt^+)$$

The above is a domain expressions. If *Var* denotes the domain of variable identifiers, *Id* that of procedure identifiers, *Proc* the domain of procedures and *Stmt* the domain of statements; then the above domain expression abstracts a <u>nameless</u> domain of blocks. These are <u>trees</u>, whose first subcomponents are sets of variable names, second subcomponents are maps from identifiers to procedures, and whose last subcomponents are tuples of statements.

If suitably decorated v's, id's, p's and s's stand for *variables, procedure names, procedures,* and *statements,* then:

$$mk(\{v_1, v_2, \ldots, v_v\}, [id_1 \to p_1, id_2 \to p_2, \ldots, id_p \to p_p], <s_1, s_2, \ldots, s_s>)$$

and:

$$(\{v_1, v_2, \ldots, v_v\}, [id_1 \to p_1, id_2 \to p_2, \ldots, id_p \to p_p], <s_1, s_2, \ldots, s_s>)$$

(the latter constructor expression having dropped the nameless constructor function, mk) represent the way we write down such composite objects. If b is a block, or more precisely, if b is an object in the domain specified above, then the following meta-language combinators:

$$\underline{let} \ mk(vs, pm, sl) = b;$$
$$\underline{let} \ (vs, pm, sl) = b;$$

provide means of decomposing nameless tree structured objects, here modelling blocks, into their proper constituents -- here the set of variables, vs; the map from procedure names to procedures, pm; and the statement list, sl.

The domain expression:

$$(s\text{-}vars\text{:}Var\text{-}set \quad s\text{-}procm\text{:}(Id \underset{m}{\to} Proc) \quad s\text{-}stmtl\text{:}Stmt^+)$$

(with inner $(,)$'s, around $Id \underset{m}{\to} Proc$, used only as syntactic delimiter) defines the same domain as above, but in addition defines three selector functions, here arbitrarily named: $s\text{-}vars$, $s\text{-}procm$, $s\text{-}stmtl$. Now:

$$\underline{let} \; vs = s\text{-}vars(b),$$
$$pm = s\text{-}procm(b),$$
$$sl = s\text{-}stmtl(b);$$

has the same effect as the previous decomposition combinators. In other words, if $vs \in Var\text{-}set$, $pm \in Id \underset{m}{\to} Proc$, $sl \in Stmt^+$, then:

$$s\text{-}vars(mk(vs,pm,sl)) = vs,$$
$$s\text{-}procm(mk(vs,pm,sl)) = pm,$$
$$s\text{-}stmtl(mk(vs,pm,sl)) = sl.$$

$$\cdots$$

We can give a name to the above block domain, e.g. $Block$:

$$Block \quad :: \quad Var\text{-}set \quad Id \underset{m}{\to} Proc \quad Stmt^+$$

-- note the dropping of $(,)$'s! With vs, pm and sl as before:

$$mk\text{-}Block(vs,pm,sl)$$

would $\underline{now}$ have to be our way of writing down instances of blocks. The trees denoted by $Block$ are now named $(Block)$. Also here we could introduce selectors:

$$Block \quad :: \quad s\text{-}vars\text{:}Var\text{-}set \quad s\text{-}procm\text{:}(Id \xrightarrow{m} Proc) \quad s\text{-}stmtl\text{:}Stmt^+$$

(where the $(,)$'s, around $Id \xrightarrow{m} Proc$, again are used as syntactic delimiters). And again:

$$s\text{-}vars(mk\text{-}Block(vs,\ldots,\ldots)) \quad = vs$$

etc.. A benefit derived from naming the class of constructed tree
objects, here $Block$, is that any object can be tested for membership of the named domain:

$$is\text{-}Block(b)$$

is _true_ provided b is the result of some $mk\text{-}Block(vs,pm,sl)$ -- for
any applicable vs, pm and sl.

5.1   Defining Domains of _TREE_ Objects

Two means of defining domains of tree objects exist in the meta-
language:

(1)   Named: Using the abstract syntax rule definition symbol
              $::$ to separate definiens from definiendum:

$$D \quad :: \quad D_1 \; D_2 \; \ldots \; D_n$$

(2)   Anonymous: Using the domain expressions operator $(\ldots)$,

$$(D_1 \; D_2 \; \ldots \; D_n)$$

The former defines named or root labelled trees:

(1) $\{ \; mk\text{-}D(d_1,d_2,\ldots,d_n) \; | \; is\text{-}D_i(d_i) \text{ for all } i \; \}$

The latter defines unnamed trees:

(2) $\{ \; mk(d_1,d_2,\ldots,d_n) \; | \; is\text{-}D_i(d_i) \text{ for all } i \; \}$

or, dropping the mk:

$$\{\ (d_1, d_2, \ldots, d_n)\ |\ is\text{-}D_i(d_i)\ \underline{for}\ \underline{all}\ i\ \}.$$

Example 34:

Statements of a source language are either assignment statements, while-do statements or if-then statements:

$$
\begin{array}{lll}
Stmt & = & Asgn\ |\ While\ |\ IfThen \\
Asgn & :: & Id\ Expr \\
While & :: & Expr\ Stmt \\
IfThen & :: & Expr\ Stmt
\end{array}
$$

Observe how the two last domains:

$$\{\ mk\text{-}While(e,s)\ |\ is\text{-}Expr(e) \wedge is\text{-}Stmt(s)\ \}$$
$$\{\ mk\text{-}IfThen(e,s)\ |\ is\text{-}Expr(e) \wedge is\text{-}Stmt(s)\ \}$$

are disjoint -- simply because the names of their object *make* functions, *mk-While* and *mk-IfThen*, are distinct:

5.1.1   Tree Constructor Axioms

For any two D' and D'' identifiers being definienses of tree constructing abstract syntax rules:

$$
\begin{array}{lll}
D' & :: & A_1\ A_2\ \ldots\ A_m \\
D'' & :: & B_1\ B_2\ \ldots\ B_n
\end{array}
$$

objects:

$$
\begin{array}{l}
mk\text{-}D'(a_1, a_2, \ldots, a_m), \\
mk\text{-}D''(b_1, b_2, \ldots, b_n)
\end{array}
$$

are identical if and only if (iff):

D' is the same identifier as D'';

$m = n$;

$a_i = b_i$ for all i,

        i.e. if A_i is the same identifier as B_i

that is, iff the two rules above are the same.

             . . .

For any two implicit tree domain denoting expressions:

$$(A_1 \ A_2 \ \ldots \ A_m)$$
$$(B_1 \ B_2 \ \ldots \ B_n)$$

objects:

$$mk(a_1, a_2, \ldots, a_m)$$
$$mk(b_1, b_2, \ldots, b_n)$$

or, which is the same:

$$(a_1, a_2, \ldots, a_m)$$
$$(b_1, b_2, \ldots, b_n)$$

are identical iff:

$m = n$, $a_i = b_i$ and

A_i is the same identifier as B_i for all i.

Example 35-36:

The abstract syntax rules:

$$CTLG \quad = \quad Fid \underset{m}{\to} (Ktp \ Dtp)$$
$$Define \quad :: \quad Fid \ (Ktp \ Dtp)$$

are intended to define the semantic domain of file description
CaTaLoGues, respectively the syntactic domain of file definition

commands. To each file, identified by its name (in *Fid*) is associated,
in the catalogue, its description -- namely a 'pair' consisting of a
Key type-, and a *Data type-* indication, i.e. an object in *(Ktp Dtp)*.
A file definition command names, say *fid*, the file to be defined
(fid ∈ Fid), and gives the *Key type-*, and *Data type* indication, i.e.
an object likewise in *(Ktp Dtp)*. In particular a catalog, *ctlg*, may
look like:

$$[\; fid_1 \rightarrow mk(ktp_1,dtp_1),$$
$$...$$
$$fid_n \rightarrow mk(ktp_n,dtp_n) \;],$$

with a define command looking like:

$$mk\text{-}Define(fid,mk(ktp,dtp)).$$

Dropping the somewhat superfluous mentioning of the otherwise nameless *mk* (prefixing *(...)*), we get that *ctlg*, upon execution of the
define command, is augmented to:

$$ctlg \cup [fid \rightarrow (ktp,dtp)]$$

provided, of course *fid* ~∈ <u>*dom*</u> *ctlg!*

$$...$$

As another example of nameless tree constructions let us abstract
the syntactic domain of procedures of some source language :

$$Proc \quad :: \quad (Id \; Tp)^* \; Block$$

The form *(Id Tp)** could be written *Parm**, i.e.:

$$Proc \quad :: \quad Parm^* \; Block$$

provided:

$$Parm \quad :: \quad Id \; Tp$$

In the former case the parameter list is abstracted as a possibly zero-length tuple of parameters, these being abstracted as nameless trees, themselves being 'pairs' of formal parameter *Identifiers* and their *Types* (not being further specified). In the latter case these parameters are abstracted as named (*Parm*) trees. Given that suitably decorated *id*'s, *tp*'s and *b*'s denote objects in *Id*, *Tp* and *Block*, respectively, we get, in the two cases, that:

$$mk\text{-}Proc(<(id_1,tp_1),(id_2,tp_2),\ldots,(id_n,tp_n)>,b)$$

respectively:

$$mk\text{-}Proc(<mk\text{-}Parm(id_1,tp_1),\ldots,mk\text{-}Parm(id_n,tp_n)>,b)$$

display instances of procedures according to either abstraction. Thus observe that the (*,*)'s in *(Id Tp)** serve the double function of constructing a domain of anonymous trees, as well as indicating the scope of the tuple domain building * operator.

5.2 Representing Instances of TREE Objects

Given objects o_1, o_2, ..., o_n of not necessarily distinct domains, e.g.: D_1, D_2, ..., D_n, the constructor expressions:

$$(o_1,o_2,\ldots,o_n), \quad mk(o_1,o_2,\ldots o_n)$$

denote (identical) tree objects of domain:

$$(D_1\ D_2\ \ldots\ D_n)$$

i.e. an anonymous tree. Given that there exists an abstract syntax rule of the form:

$$D\ ::\ D_1\ D_2\ \ldots\ D_n$$

the constructor expression:

$$mk\text{-}D(o_1,o_2,\ldots,o_n)$$

denotes a tree object of domain D, i.e. a root labelled tree.

5.3   *TREE* Operations: Selector Functions

The only special operation defined on *TREE*s is the selector function.
Names of selector functions are either explicitly, or implicitly, definable.

Explicitly Defined Selector Function Names

In the named tree constructing abstract syntax rule:

$$D \quad :: \quad s\text{-}nm_1 : D_1 \; s\text{-}nm_2 : D_2 \; \ldots \; s\text{-}nm_l : D_l$$

as well as in the anonymous tree constructing domain expression:

$$(s\text{-}nm_1 : D_1 \; s\text{-}nm_2 : D_2 \; \ldots \; s\text{-}nm_l : D_l)$$

the identifiers:

$$s\text{-}nm_1, \; s\text{-}nm_2, \; \ldots, \; s\text{-}nm_l$$

denote selector functions obeying:

$$s\text{-}nm_1(mk\text{-}D(o_1, o_2, \ldots, o_l)) \;=\; o_1$$
$$s\text{-}nm_2(mk\text{-}D(o_1, o_2, \ldots, o_l)) \;=\; o_2$$
$$\ldots$$
$$s\text{-}nm_l(mk\text{-}D(o_1, o_2, \ldots, o_l)) \;=\; o_l$$

respectively

$$s\text{-}nm_1((o_1, o_2, \ldots, o_l)) \;=\; o_1$$
$$s\text{-}nm_2((o_1, o_2, \ldots, o_l)) \;=\; o_2$$
$$\ldots$$
$$s\text{-}nm_l((o_1, o_2, \ldots, o_l)) \;=\; o_l$$

for all $o_1, o_2, \ldots, o_l$.

In the above, explicit, selector function name defining forms, it is
assumed that all identifiers $s\text{-}nm_i$ and $s\text{-}nm_j$ are distinct. You may
wish to omit any subset of these, including all, as we have done in the
past.

Implicitly Defined Selector Function Names

Assuming uniqueness of D_i , for some or all i in $\{1:l\}$ in:

$$D \quad :: \quad D_1\, D_2\, \ldots\, D_l$$

respectively:

$$(D_1\, D_2\, \ldots\, D_l),$$

and in particular, assuming that D_i is an identifier, the above two tree domain constructing forms define the selector function:

$$s\text{-}D_i \,.$$

Example 37:

In the source language *Statement* syntax rules:

$$
\begin{array}{lll}
Stmt & = & Asgn \mid While \\
Asgn & :: & Id\ Expr \\
While & :: & Expr\ Stmt
\end{array}
$$

$s\text{-}Id$ applies to *Asgn* objects and yields the *Id* component; $s\text{-}Expr$ applies to *Asgn* and *While* objects and yield the *Expr* component; and $s\text{-}Stmt$ applies to *While* objects and yield the proper *Stmt* component. We emphasize: 'proper component' since any *While* object, by the first abstract syntax rule, is itself a *Stmt* object.

Non-Unique Selector Function Name Convention

For the common case where two or more identifiers, D_i and D_j, of either:

$$D \quad :: \quad D_1\, D_2\, \ldots\, D_l$$

or:

$$(D_1\, D_2\, \ldots\, D_l)$$

are the same, the following convention is adopted:

In the form $D_1 D_2 \ldots D_l$ let there be k distinct occurrences of the same identifier, say C, then:

$$s-C-1, \ s-C-2, \ \ldots, \ s-C-k$$

are the selector functions which select the 1st, the 2nd,..., respectively the kth proper C component -- from left-to-right.

Example 38:

In the source language Statement syntax rules:

> Stmt = ... | For | If
>
> For :: Id Expr Expr Expr Stmt*
>
> If :: Expr Stmt Stmt

the selector function s-Expr-1, s-Expr-2 and s-Expr-3 select the same For object components as would s-init, s-step and s-limit in:

> For :: Id s-init:Expr s-step:Expr s-limit:Expr Stmt*;

and s-Stmt-1 and s-Stmt-2 selects the same If object components as would s-then and s-else in:

> If :: Expr s-then:Stmt s-else:Stmt.

Programming Notes

The meta-language leaves unexplained the names of the implicitly defined selector functions in such forms as:

> Block :: Id-set (Id $\underset{m}{\to}$ Prc) Stmt*

and: For :: s-cv:Id (s-i:Expr s-b:Expr s-t:Expr)$^+$ Stmt*

In the latter form there are only two implicitly defined selector functions, namely the two selecting the (Expr Expr Expr)$^+$ and Stmt* tuple objects of For objects.

The reason for introducing explicit selector function names is mostly pragmatic. That is: there is, in most cases, no technical need for inventing names. To see 'this, recall that the technical purpose of selector functions is to select proper (sub-)components of trees. But this could as well be done by a 'reverse' use of the mk function! Let e.g. t be an object of

$$(D_1 \ D_2 \ \dots \ D_n),$$

then: the $\underline{let}$ clause:

$$\underline{let} \ (o_1, o_2, \dots, o_n) = t$$

so-to-speak decomposes t into its n subcomponents. So would:

$$\underline{let} \ o_1 = s\text{-}D_1(t),$$
$$o_2 = s\text{-}D_2(t),$$
$$\dots$$
$$o_n = s\text{-}D_n(t)$$

provided, of course, all D_i were distinct (and) identifiers! Similar for D objects t, where:

$$D \ :: \ D_1 \ D_2 \ \dots \ D_n$$

leading to:

$$\underline{let} \ mk\text{-}D(o_1, o_2, \dots, o_n) = t$$

etc. .

6 FUNCTIONs

By a function, we shall -- in a somewhat circular fashion -- understand an operation which, when applied to something, which we shall
call its argument yields a certain thing as the value of the function
for that argument.

The object to which the function is applicable, i.e. for which it is
guaranteed to yield a value (defined result), constitutes the domain
of the function. The yielded values constitute the range (or: co-
domain) of the function.

Two functions are identical iff they (1) have the same domain, (2)
the same range, and (3) for each argument in the domain the same value. *FunCT*ion equality is, however, not a defined operation.

To denote the value of a *function* for a given *argument* we write a
name of the function, say *f*, followed by a name of the argument, say
a; the latter, the former or both possibly enclosed between parentheses:

$$fa, \quad f(a), \quad (f)(a), \quad (fa), \quad (f)a$$

Many functions can more easily be described algorithmically, i.e. by
a recipe for how to compute the result value given an argument value,
than by explicit or implicit enumeration. Moreover, some, if not most
such, functions, which we wish to manipulate (create, pass and apply),
have an infinite domain -- and by the pragmatics of *MAP*s could not be
constructed as such. Finally: many functions can best be described in
an implicit, or even recursive, way, which certainly does not conjure
the image, or thought, of its graph being computed at the time of definitions. (By the graph of a function we understand the set of all
argument result 'pairs'.)

For maps this graph is indeed being computed at "time" of definition,
whereas we may think of this graph never being computed in connection
with the kind of function definitions we are interested in in this
section.

<u>Examples 39-40</u>:

The following is a block-expression of the meta-language; its value
is that of the denotation of f, which is the factorial function:

  $(\underline{let}\ f(n) = \underline{if}\ n=0\ \underline{then}\ 1\ \underline{else}\ n \times f(n-1)\ \underline{in}$
  $f)$

    ...

Let, as another example, the procedure header -- exclusive of procedure name -- and procedure body, of some source language be abstract syntactically describable as:

  $Prc\ ::\ Id^*\ Block$

Here Prc is the name of the domain of procedure definienses (header + body, - name), Id of the domain of formal parameter names, and
$Block$ of blocks -- as e.g. statement blocks.

The meaning of a procedure, i.e. the denotation of a procedure name,
may, according to the school of mathematical semantics, be taken as
a function from argument lists to the denotation of blocks. If the
denotation of these latter are functions from states (Σ) to states
then:

  $Prc:\ ARG^*\ \tilde{\to}\ (\Sigma\ \tilde{\to}\ \Sigma)$

Given a Prc object, prc, i.e. one of the form $mk\text{-}Prc(idl,bl)$, we now
give the function which itself yields the denotation of prc. Let, as
a last preparation, procedure denotations be functions of the defining
rather than calling environment.

  $V\text{-}Prc(mk\text{-}Prc(idl,bl))(\rho)(\sigma)=$
   $(\underline{let}\ fct(al)(\xi)=$
     $(\underline{let}\ \rho' = [\ idl[i] \to al[i]\ |\ 1 \leq i \leq l\ al\ ]\ \underline{in}$
     $I\text{-}Blk(bl)(\rho + \rho')(\xi))$ $\underline{in}$
   $fct)$

Observe the following: eValuation of a $Procedure$ denotation takes
place in a defining environment, ρ, and state, σ. The state is ignored, and need thus not have been shown. The result of $Procedure$

e𝒱aluation is a function, *fct*. This function is completely described in the three-line *let* clause. The definition given there can be read as follows: *fct* is that function which when applied to some argument list, *al*, and in some state, ξ, will yield a new state. This new state results from Interpreting the *Block bl* in the defining environment ('slightly') extended -- by the bindings of formal parameter identifiers, *idl[i]*, to actual, call time, arguments, *al[i]* -- and in the calling state, ξ. We do not here display the *I-Block* elaboration function, but see section 6.3.

6.1 Defining Domains of FunCTion Objects

Let *A* and *B* denote Domains. To define the class of implicitly λ-defined objects which are partial, respectively total functions from *A* into *B*, we use the domain expression operators $\overset{\sim}{\rightarrow}$, respectively $\rightarrow$:

$$A \overset{\sim}{\rightarrow} B, \qquad A \rightarrow B \quad .$$

Example 41:

Applying the ability to describe function spaces to the built-in operations of the meta-language itself, we can now list the logical type of these:

Sets:	*type:*				
	∪:	SET	SET	→	SET
	∩:	SET	SET	→	SET
	∖:	SET	SET	→	SET
	⊆:	SET	SET	→	BOOL
	⊂:	SET	SET	→	BOOL
	power:		SET	→	SET
	union:		SET	$\overset{\sim}{\rightarrow}$	SET
	∈	OBJ	SET	→	BOOL
	card		SET	→	N_0

Tuples: *type*: $\frown$:   TUPLE TUPLE $\to$ TUPLE

    h, *hd*:   TUPLE $\xrightarrow{\sim}$ OBJ

    t, *tl*:   TUPLE $\xrightarrow{\sim}$ TUPLE

    l, *len*:   TUPLE $\to$ N_0

    [.]:   TUPLE N_1 $\xrightarrow{\sim}$ OBJ

    elems: TUPLE $\to$ SET

    ind: TUPLE $\to$ N_1-set

    conc: TUPLE $\xrightarrow{\sim}$ TUPLE

    +:   TUPLE MAP $\xrightarrow{\sim}$ TUPLE

    \:   TUPLE N_1-set $\xrightarrow{\sim}$ TUPLE

Maps: *type*: U: MAP MAP $\xrightarrow{\sim}$ MAP

    +:   MAP MAP $\to$ MAP

    \:   MAP SET $\to$ MAP

    |:   MAP SET $\to$ MAP

    (.):   MAP OBJ $\xrightarrow{\sim}$ OBJ

    dom: MAP $\to$ SET

    rng: MAP $\to$ SET

    •:   MAP MAP $\xrightarrow{\sim}$ MAP

The reason why certain of these operations are partial functions will now be explained. The *union* operation applies to sets of sets, SET just expresses: sets of objects. We could get around this by writing SET-*set* whereby: *type*: *union*:   SET-*set* $\to$ SET, i.e. *union* is total over SET-*set*. *hd* and *tl* applies to non-zero length tuples, i.e.:

type: *hd*: $OBJ^+ \to OBJ$, *tl*: $OBJ^+ \to OBJ^*$ -- note totality. Indexing, [*i*], must have *i* lie in the *ind*ex set of the tuple, otherwise *unde-fined*. *conc* is to tuples what *union* is to sets, i.e.

type: *conc*: $TUPLE^* \to TUPLE$. Updating (+) tuple elements must have MAP in ($N_1 \xrightarrow{m} OBJ$) with domain elements be in *ind*ex set of tuple. So not even: *type*: +: TUPLE ($N_1 \xrightarrow{m} OBJ$) $\xrightarrow{\sim}$ TUPLE would make + total over defined domain.

6.2 Representing Instances of Fun*CT*ion Objects

This section is somewhat differently organized than were otherwise comparable earlier sections (i.2 for i=2,3,4,5). In a number of subsections we recount basic aspects of so-called λ-expressions.

We shall shortly, in a sequence of eight small steps, arrive at an understanding of functional abstraction. The idea being to write forms which denote functions. One such class of forms were the map expressions covered in section 4. Another such form is that of λ-expressions. Map expressions are used to define functions whose argument-value association is known (i.e. being fixed) at the instance of definition, and whose domain-range sets are individually known and finite.

Functional Abstraction

(0)   There are simple and composite proper names.

(1)   Simple names are either arbitrarily assigned to denote something, or their denotation has been assigned an arbitrary name. Composite names express through their structure some analysis of the way in which they denote.

(2)   A constant is a proper name having a fixed, or single denotation.

(3)   A variable is a proper name whose denotation may range over a set of values.

(4)   An expression is a name containing other names as proper constituents.

      Composite names are expressions.

(5)   A form is either a variable or an expression in which one or more proper names have been replaced by variables.

(6)   In order to speak about the function of a free variable that a form is we abstract the form by prefixing it with a sequence of three symbols: a λ, the free *variable* and a *dot*.

      $\lambda y.3+y$ is the function of y that $3+y$ is; i.e. which increments any number by *three*.

(7)   The passage from a form to an associated function is called functional abstraction.

Functionally abstracting the forms: $3+y$, $x+y$ and $\lambda y.x$ into e.g. $\lambda y.3+y, \lambda x.\lambda y.x+y$ respectively $\lambda x.\lambda y.x$ results in the increment-by-3 function, the addition (of two numbers) function and the function from (say) integers (x) to constant functions from (say) booleans (y) to that integer x.

In the above we have employed a rather restricted and not completely detailed use of the concepts: names, expressions and forms. The term expression shall imply the inclusion of simple constants and variable (identifier)s. Forms are henceforth expressions.

λ-expressions

Any clause (expression or statement), *clause*, of the meta-language can be functionally abstracted, whether containing free variables or not (for free/bound variables, see below).

Functional abstraction in zero variables is written:

$\lambda()$. *clause*

Writing, in the meta-language, the definition:

let $f = \lambda()$. *clause*

or :

let $f() = clause$

-- which is equivalent -- thus identifies f as a name for the function of no variables that *clause* is. Any subsequent occurrence in the scope of the definition, i.e. *use* in contrast to *definition*, of f without $()$ shall then denote the function, whereas any subsequent occurrence in the scope of the definition of f of $f()$ shall denote the elaboration of *clause*.

If the valuation of *clause* is dependent on a state -- not shown -- then repeated occurrences of $f()$, elaborated in different states, may result in distinct $f()$, i.e. *clause*, 'values'. These remarks also apply to functions of several variables

Functional abstraction in two or more variables is written either:

$$\lambda id_1 \cdot \lambda id_2 \cdot \ldots \cdot \lambda id_n \cdot clause$$

or :

$$\lambda(id_1, id_2, \ldots, id_n) \cdot clause$$

where $n \geq 2$, all id's distinct and ... is a shortening ellipsis extraneous to the meta-language. Let id_i range over D_i and the values of (for suitable substitutions of actual for formal parameters, see below) over D, then the denoted function is in the space:

$$D_1 \rightarrow (D_2 \rightarrow (\ldots \rightarrow (D_n \rightarrow D) \ldots))$$

respectively:

$$D_1 \; D_2 \; \ldots \; D_n \rightarrow D$$

The former form corresponds to a so-called "currying" or "schön-finckeling" of the more familiar, latter, form. The former form also permits the application of (strictly) less than, as here, n arguments, namely the first (from left-to-right, say) k $(k<n)$ arguments.

Such an application then denotes a function in the space:

$$D_{k+1} \rightarrow (D_{k+2} \rightarrow (\ldots \rightarrow (D_n \rightarrow D) \ldots))$$

where $k+1 \leq n$. [Of course, if D is a itself a functional space, say $D' \rightarrow D''$, then application of n arguments will also yield a function.]

m-ary functions, for $m \geq 0$, can be identified:

$$\underline{let} \; f(id_1, id_2, \ldots, id_m) = clause$$

or:

$$\underline{let} \; f = \lambda(id_1, id_2, \ldots, id_m) \cdot clause$$

where no two id_i and id_j are the same. If f occurs free (see below) in *clause* then the denoted function is the so-called minimal fix-point solution to the (recursive) equation:

$$f(id_1, id_2, \ldots, id_m) = clause$$

etc. The minimal fix-point finding operation, γ, will be explained subsequently. We could have indicated any such intended recursion by instead defining f by:

$$\underline{letrec}\ f(id_1, id_2, \ldots, id_m) = clause$$

respectively:

$$\underline{let}\ f = \gamma\lambda g.\lambda(id_1, id_2, \ldots, id_m) \cdot clause'$$

where *clause'* arises from *clause* by substituting all free occurrences in *clause* of f by g.

[Using g instead of f on the right-hand side is strictly speaking not necessary, since -- under the *letrec* versus *let* convention -- the left hand f is not bound to any of the right-hand f's.]

We shall, however, always force the user of the meta-language to mean recursion when using the defined function identifier in *clause*. Hence we choose to omit the *rec* suffix on *let*'s and never to use the γ recursion maker. Consequently the only style in which a function can be recursively defined (inside a conventional function definition, see section 5) is by means of a *let* definition which also gives name to the function, a name whose denotation is known within the scope of the meta-language block in which the *let* occurred. This is in contrast to the form :

$$\gamma\lambda f.\lambda(id_1, id_2, \ldots, id_m) \cdot clause$$

which otherwise defines the same function, but does not further identify it!

Free and Bound Variables, Scope

For the purpose of the definition of the concepts of *free* and *bound*
variables we consider the meta-language programs (or: function definitions) as made up from the following three expression constructs:

      (1) Variables
      (2) Function Applications
      (3) Function Abstractions

(1) x is *free* in x.

(2) x is *free* in $f(a)$ if it is *free* in either f, or a, or both.

(3) x is *free* in $\lambda y.clause$ if $x \neq y$ (i.e. if x is an identifier dis-
       tinct from y) and x is *free* in *clause*.

(4)   Since the non-recursive *let* definition block:

$$(let\ y = expr\ \ in$$
$$se)$$

    where *se* is either a meta-language *statement* or expression, can
    be understood to be a syntactic sugaring of:

$$(\lambda y.se)(expr)$$

    provided *call-by-value* is used, we see that *freeness* of x in a
    let definition block follows the rules for *freeness* of x in an
    application.

(5)   Similar for statement composition:

$$(stmt1;$$
$$stmt2)$$

    only makes sense if *stmt1* and *stmt2* both denote functions from
    states, σ, to states, σ', (stores to stores), hence:

$$(stmt1;\ stmt2)\sigma$$

    is really to be understood as:

$$(\underline{let}\ \sigma' = stmt1(\sigma)\ \underline{in}$$
$$stmt2(\sigma'))$$

which then reduces to:

$$(\lambda\sigma'.(stmt2(\sigma')))(stmt1(\sigma))$$

A variable is bound in some expression if it occurs in the expression but is not free.

It follows then that the formal parameter variables (identifiers) bind all of the free occurrences of such identifiers in the body, i.e. *clause*, of a λ-expression:

$$\lambda(id_1, id_2, \ldots, id_m).clause$$

The id_i's are called bound variables.

The scope of a bound variable is the entire body-part of the λ-expression to which it belongs, with the specific exception of each properly contained λ-expression of the body-part having that same bound variable identifier.

Application

Applying a λ-defined function:

$$\lambda var.clause$$

to an argument, *arg*:

$$(\lambda var.clause)(arg)$$

then means to evaluate the expression *clause'* which arises from *clause* by substituting all free occurrences of (the syntactic object) the identifier *var* in *clause* by the (semantic) object denoted by *arg*.

Hence the meta-language only has call-by-value.

The above application rule extends to functions of several arguments.

Definition versus Application

To write:

$$(\underline{let}\ f(a) = clause\ \underline{in}$$
$$C(f))$$

means: let f denote the function which satisfies the above equation and evaluate or interpret $C(f)$ in such an environment where f is bound to that function. It does, e.g., not mean: evaluate $clause$ before proceeding to elaboration of $C(f)$. $clause$ is evaluated iff f is applied and then the suitable substituted $clause'$ is evaluated everytime, afresh, whenever f is so applied!

The γ Operator

For the benefit of those who are not familiar with the γ operator of the λ-Calculus we now present a development leading up to this operator and its purpose.

Let :

$$(\underline{let}\ f(x) = F(x,f)\ \underline{in}$$
$$...)$$

define f recursively -- i.e.: the right-hand side occurrence(s) of f in $F(...)$ denotes the same as does the left-hand side f.

Since, in the λ-Calculus:

$$G = (\lambda x.G)(x)$$

provided x does not occur (free) in G, and since $\underline{let}\ f(x) = F(x,f)$ is the same as $\underline{let}\ f = \lambda x.F(x,f)$ we get:

$$(\underline{let}\ f = (\lambda g.\lambda x.F(x,g))(f)\ \underline{in}$$
$$...)$$

where g does not occur (free) in $F(x,f)$. If we ascribe the name F to $\lambda g.\lambda x.F(x,g)$, i.e. if we let:

$$F = \lambda g. \lambda x. F(x,g)$$

then the previous can be written:

$$(\underline{let} \ f = F(f) \ \underline{in}$$
$$\ldots)$$

Now: F is a function, in fact it is a functional. And objects, say w, satisfying:

$$w = Hw$$

where H is any function, are said to be <u>fixed-points</u> of H. The f we are looking for, i.e. defining by the <u>let</u> clause, thus is a fixed-point of F. It turns out that there may be many fixed-points of any given functional -- so, following good practice, we select one which is in some way unique; in particular, we choose to let such f's denote the so-called <u>minimal</u> fixed-point. This means: that solution, f, (to the equation) whose <u>graph</u> is included ($\subseteq$) in any other solution. It then turns out that, under suitable and always reasonable constraints (monotonicity, etc.), there exists a functional, let us name it γ, which when applied to objects, like F, produce their minimal fixed-point!

This is the γ we are referring to. It is the so-called <u>minimal fixed-point finding operator</u>. Observe the sequence, repeated from above:

$$\underline{let} \ f(x) = F(x,f)$$
$$\underline{let} \ f \quad = \lambda x. F(x,f)$$
$$\underline{let} \ f \quad = (\lambda g. \lambda x. F(x,g))(f)$$
$$\underline{let} \ f \quad = F(f)$$
$$\underline{let} \ f \quad = \gamma F \qquad \left.\right\} \text{where} : F = \lambda g. \lambda x. F(x,g)$$
$$\underline{let} \ f \quad = \gamma \lambda g. \lambda x. F(x,g)$$
$$\underline{let} \ f \quad = \gamma \lambda f. \lambda x. F(x,f)$$

That is: writing $\lambda g. \lambda x. F(x,g)$ or writing $\lambda f. \lambda x. F(x,f)$ produces identical meanings, since the λ's shield the right-hand side f from the left-hand side f -- they are now, formally speaking, not the same, although they denote the same object!

6.3 FunCTion Operations

There is only defined one operation on FunCTion objects:

$$(\ldots) \quad \text{apply}.$$

Example 42:

In the introductory example we illustrated the 'concoction' of procedure denotations. In the following example we show their application.
Let:

1         $Block \quad :: \quad Var\text{-}set \quad (Id \xrightarrow{m} Prc) \quad Stmt^*$

be an abstract syntax (::-) rule. $Block$ abstracts the domain of the
blocks of some goto-free source language. They consist of three parts:
$Variable$ declarations, uniquely named (Id) $Procedures$, and a $Statement$
list. Their semantics is:

$$\underline{type}\text{: } I\text{-}Block\text{: } Block \xrightarrow{\sim} (ENV \xrightarrow{\sim} (\Sigma \xrightarrow{\sim} \Sigma))$$

where:

2        $\Sigma \quad = \quad LOC \xrightarrow{m} VAL$

3        $ENV \quad = \quad Id \xrightarrow{m} DEN$

4        $DEN \quad = \quad LOC \quad | \quad (ARG^* \xrightarrow{\sim} (\Sigma \xrightarrow{\sim} \Sigma))$

and :

5.0 $I\text{-}Block(mk\text{-}Block(vars,procm,stl))(\rho)(\sigma)=$

.1 $(\underline{let} \ (\sigma',map) = allocate(vars)(\sigma)$ $\underline{in}$

.2 $\underline{let} \ \rho' = \rho + map$

.3 $+ \ [id \rightarrow V\text{-}Prc(procm(id))(\rho')(\sigma')$

.4 $| \ id \in \underline{dom} \ procm \ ]$ $\underline{in}$

.5 $\underline{let} \ \sigma'' = I\text{-}Stmt\text{-}list(stl)(\rho')(\sigma')$ $\underline{in}$

.6 $\sigma'' \diagdown \underline{rng} \ map)$

Lines .1-.4 constitute the block activation prologue, line .6 the matching epilogue. The function allocate is given variable names and states
and produces a new state in which is allocated all the cells corresponding to the variables, their cell locations is recorded in map which

binds variable names to these locations:

```
6.0     allocate(vars)(σ)=
 .1         if vars={}
 .2         then (σ,[])
 .3         else (let id ∈ vars                                    in
 .4               let (σ',map) = allocate(vars∖{id})(σ)           in
 .5               let l ∈ LOC be s.t. l ~∈ dom σ'                 in
 .6               (σ' ∪ [l→undefined],map ∪ [id→l]))
```

$$\textit{type: allocate: } \textit{Var-set} \rightarrow (\Sigma \overset{\sim}{\rightarrow} (\Sigma \; (Var \underset{m}{\rightarrow} LOC)))$$

and:

$$\textit{type: I-Stmt-list: } \textit{Stmt}^* \overset{\sim}{\rightarrow} (ENV \overset{\sim}{\rightarrow} (\Sigma \overset{\sim}{\rightarrow} \Sigma)).$$

Now a statement could be a *call* of a procedure:

```
7       Stmt   =   Call  |  ...
8       Call   ::  Id Expr*
```

and with:

```
9.0     I-Stmt-list(stl)(ρ)(σ)=
 .1         if stl=<>
 .2         then σ
 .3         else (let σ' = I-Stmt(h stl)(ρ)(σ)  in
 .4               I-Stmt-list(t stl)(ρ)(σ'))
```

we end up having to explain:

```
10.0    I-Stmt(stmt)(ρ)(σ)=
 .1         cases stmt:
 .2         (mk-Call(id,el) →
 .3             (let argl = < V-Arg(el[i])(ρ)(σ) | i ∈ ind el >,
 .4                  fct  = ρ(id)                                    in
 .5              fct(argl)),
              ...)
```

where it is assumed that:

$$\textit{type: V-Arg: } \textit{Expr} \overset{\sim}{\rightarrow} (ENV \overset{\sim}{\rightarrow} (\Sigma \overset{\sim}{\rightarrow} ARG))$$

in other words, that evaluation of the *arg*ument *l*ist does not create side-effects by changing the state (σ).

Observe now, how the procedure denotation, which is a *FunCT*ion, $(ARG^* \overset{\sim}{\to} (\Sigma \overset{\sim}{\to} \Sigma))$, "packed" in the environment ρ' set up at prologue "time", is retrieved (10.4) and applied (10.5) at "calling" time.

We have completed our task of showing the construction of *FunCT*ion objects, the second of the introductory examples of this section; and the application of such objects to their arguments.

Observe that the apply operator of line .4 above, retrieving *fct* from the *MAP* object ρ, is a *MAP* operation; whereas the apply operator of line .5 above, applying the *FunCT*ion object, *fct*, to its *arg*ument *l*ist, is the *FunCT*ion operation of apply.

7. ABSTRACT SYNTAX

Example 43:

Program	=	*Stmt*
Stmt	=	*Block* | *If* | *For* | *Call* | *Goto* |
		Assign | *In* | *Out* | <u>NULL</u>
Block	::	*(Id $\xrightarrow[m]{}$ Type) Proc-set Named-Stmt**
Type	::	*Scalar-type* [*(Expr* | <u>*</u>*)*$^+$]
Proc	::	*Id Parm** *Stmt*
Parm	::	*Id (Type* | <u>PROC</u>*)*
Named-Stmt	::	[*Id*] *Stmt*
If	::	*Expr Stmt Stmt*
For	::	*Id Expr Expr Expr Stmt*
Call	::	*Id (Var-ref* | *Id)**
Goto	::	*Id*
Assign	::	*Var-ref Expr*
In	::	*Var-ref*
Out	::	*Expr*
Expr	=	*Infix-expr* | *Rhs-ref* | *Con-var-ref* | *Const*

The above is an example of an incomplete(d) abstract syntax. It is intended to define fragments of the syntactic domains of some source language. Before commenting on its use of = and :: rules; and of domain operators: |, $\xrightarrow[m]{}$,*, -*set* and [...], let us, for the sake of instruction, annotate the above syntax in the way we believe a formal model should render itself more open to inspection by casual readers:

-- annotation

A program is a statement .

A statement is either a block, or an if, or a for, or a call, or a goto, or an assign, or an in, or an out, or a null.

A block has a variable declaration part which to variable identifiers uniquely associates the type of the values that can be stored in the variable, a set of procedures, and a list of named statements. Thus a block has three parts. And either, some, or all, of these may be void.

A variable type is either a scalar or an array type. In this model the scalar type is modeled whenever the optional $[(Expr|*)^+]$ object is 'absent', i.e. _nil_. An array type has all array elements being of the same scalar type. The dimension of the array is given by the length of the present $(Expr \mid *)^+$ list.

A procedure has an identifying name, a parameter specification list, and a body which is a statement.

A parameter specification has an identifying formal parameter name and an argument type description. The type of an argument is either that of a scalar-, an array- or, a procedure.

A named statement has two parts: an optional label, which is an identifier, and a statement.

Etcetera.

Comments

From the above annotations it transpires that the domain expression "|" operator stands for "either", the paired operators "[...]" for optionality, and "(...)" delimits the scope of the infix $\underset{m}{\rightarrow}$ in rule 3, the suffix $^+$ in rule 4, the infix | in rule 6, and the suffix * in rule 10.

Next we observe that the above syntax defines e.g. the domain _Stmt_ recursively. For example: a statement is (=) an if-then-else statement (2); and an if-then-else statement contains both a (then) consequence and an (else) alternative (8), both of which are statements.

Finally we conclude that the domains denoted by the rule left-hand sides must constitute some kind of solution to the mutually recursive set of equations, whether the definition symbol be "=" or "::".

7.1 Domains of Abstract Objects

In the following we shall rely on your returning yourself to the above example, as well as to some of the abstract syntax examples previously shown .

The aim of section 7 is to teach you how to decompose the more general
task of defining recursive classes of abstract objects. Sections
2-3-4-5-6 already taught you the more isolated construction of set,
tuple, map, tree and function domains.

Motivation:

The reason why we in general, wish to define arbitrarily compounded
classes is the following.

The meta-language is used, primarily, to describe complex software
architectures: programming languages, data bases, operating system
command & control language interfaces; and their stepwise realization:
language processors, etcetera. Just like we ordinarily describe the
concrete text strings, making up e.g. programs, queries and commands,
in terms of e.g. BNF grammars -- so we now desire to give abstractions
of these classes of objects. Likewise: just as we, when coding a higher-
level language program, a data base data definition, etcetera, define,
normally as part of variable declarations, the structure of our internal, stored objects -- so we now desire to give storage layout-indepen-
dent abstractions of the more intrinsic of these value classes.

Syntactic & Semantic Domains:

In the motivation above, two kinds of abstract object classes were
singled out. The ones input to the software systems being defined,
viz.: program texts, data base query & update commands, operating
system job control language commands, etc. And the ones manipulated,
and, as we shall take it in general, denoted by these inputs, viz.:
internal data structures; catalogues, files & records; processes, resources, ercetera. We shall generally refer to the former object classes as being of syntactic nature, and the latter as being semantic.
Syntactic and semantic domains will, in the meta-language be defined
using the programming construct of abstract syntax.

Analogies:

The "programming construct" of BNF grammars or some extended variant
thereof is usually applied when defining sets of concrete text strings

-- i.e. context-free "languages". And the <u>type</u> and <u>mode</u>, definition
facility of PASCAL, respectively ALGOL 68, is the corresponding programming construct for the internal data structures. In the meta-language the same tool will be applied in the construction of potentially,
and usually, infinite classes, or as we shall prefer to call them,
domains of abstract objects.

Motivation:

The reason why we apply the same tool and why this tool is neither that
of e.g. BNF, the PASCAL <u>type</u> definition nor the ALGOL 68 <u>mode</u> definition facility, is that we, on one hand, neither want to deal with text
strings (or corresponding parse trees), nor, on the other hand, are
concerned about storage space and access-efficient layout of objects.
Instead we desire to provide what we believe to be appropriate & fitting representational abstractions.

Representational Abstractions:

By representational abstraction is meant the target system (e.g. input/
output terminal-, or machine-storage device) independent specification
of software function concepts, especially objects, emphasizing the
choice of such abstractions whose, usually composite, (logical) type
most directly expresses intrinsic, i.e. to our understanding relevant,
properties of the notions being specified.

Domain Definitions & Compositions

In order:

>   (1)   to decompose the task of constructing domains, i.e. of
>   composing them from constituent domains, and in order

>   (2)   to permit the constructions of reflexive domains, i.e.
>   composite domains whose objects contain properly em-
>   bedded objects of the same kind (-- or domain)

the meta-language provides the conventional notion of definitions.

Definitions / Rules

A domain definition consists, as does any definition, of two parts. A left- and a right hand side. Other words are lhs, respectively rhs; and definiendum ("that which is being defined"), respectively definiens ("that which defines it"). We shall use the words abstract syntax rule synonymously with the concept of a domain definition.

Abstract syntax rules all have their lhs's being simple names, i.e. identifiers. The rhs's are usually compound expressions henceforth referred to as logical type, or domain expressions.

The first point, above, about decomposing the task of defining domains is achieved by the ability to use, in the rhs's of some rules, the lhs identifier of some other rule. The second point, then, is achieved by permitting the use, in the rhs of any rule, of the lhs identifier of that (or those) rule(s).

Compositions / Domain Expressions

In order:

(3) to model notions of software systems representationally abstract, and in order

(4) to provide a reasonably fitting variety of choices for abstracting objects

the meta-language centers its abstract compound objects around the mathematically tractable concepts of sets, tuples, functions and trees together with associated, primitive operations.

Domain Operators:

As a consequence the meta-language provides a number of operations which apply to arbitrary (constituent, elementary &/or composite) domains to denote set-, tuple-, map-, function- and abstract tree domains.

These operators have already been introduced, and are:

$$-set; \; ^*, \; ^+ \; ; \; \underset{m}{\rightarrow}, \; \overset{\sim}{\rightarrow}, \; \rightarrow \; ; \; (...)$$

the latter ((...)) denoting (implicit or anonymous) tree construction.

In the compounding, usually signalled by the implicit, or anonymous, tree constructor $(...)$, of more than one domain:

$$(D_1 \quad D_2 \quad ... \quad D_n) \qquad\qquad n \geq 2$$

there is an invisible "cartesian product-like" operator, $\times$. That is, you might read the above as:

$$(D_1 \times D_2 \times ... \times D_n).$$

The point about the use in this meta-language of the cartesian operation is that it is only used when domains of trees of two or more subcomponents are denoted. Not, e.g., when tuple domains are to be constructed. These can only be constructed, in this meta-language, using the $*$ or $+$ operations. Thus, where context permits, we may drop implicit tree constructors, as in:

$$A \rightarrow B\ C$$

which is taken to be identical to:

$$A \rightarrow (B\ C)$$

That is: the precedence of $\times$ is higher than any other infix operator, but lower than any suffix operator. We usually omit writing the $\times$ operator.

The following domain operators assemble not necessarily disjoint domains into 'unions' of these:

$$\mid \qquad \underline{U}$$

-- the latter applicable only in connection with map domains, as explained in section 4.1. The $\mid$ operator will be further defined below.

Finally the operators:

$$[...] \qquad\qquad \text{-- optionality}$$
$$(...) \qquad\qquad \text{-- grouping/delimiting}$$

enables shortness of descriptions. The former:

$$[A] \quad = \quad A \mid nil.$$

The Scope Delimiting (...) Operator

The latter can easily be confused with the tree construction operator. Therefore: when (...) surrounds two or more domain expressions with no infix domain operator, other than the cartesian operator, separating them, e.g. as in:

$$(A^* \; B\text{-}set \; C),$$

then (...) denotes tree domain construction; otherwise (...) as in :

$$(A^* \mid (B\text{-}set \underset{m}{\to} C))^*,$$

serves to indicate, i.e. delimit, the scope of infix or suffix domain operators. The corresponding scope rules are the conventional ones.

Infix Operator Commutativity and Associativity

With infix operators the question of their commutativity and associativity arises:

$$\mid \; , \; \underline{\cup} \qquad \text{are commutative}$$
$$\underset{m}{\to} \; , \; \overset{\sim}{\to} \; , \; \to \qquad \text{associates to the right.}$$

The cartesian product operator, ×, does not associate!

Examples 44-45-46:

(1) The domains denoted by:

$$A \mid B \qquad \text{and} \qquad B \mid A$$

are identically the same, and so are:

$$(A \underset{m}{\to} B) \; \underline{\cup} \; (C \underset{m}{\to} D) \; , \quad \text{and} :$$
$$(C \underset{m}{\to} D) \; \underline{\cup} \; (A \underset{m}{\to} B).$$

(2) The domains:

$$A \to (B \to (C \to D)) \; , \quad \text{and} :$$
$$A \to B \to C \to D$$

are identically the same. Writing the former is a clarification of the latter, should you have forgotten the rules of associativity. Thus the domain:

$$((A \to B) \to C) \to D$$

is distinct from the domain denoted by the former expressions.

(3) The tree domains:

$$(A \times B \times C), \quad ((A \times B) \times C), \quad \text{and} \quad (A \times (B \times C))$$

are all distinct (in fact, disjoint). Only in this, the 3rd example, was (...) used for tree domain construction.

Semantics of the | Operator

Of the new domain expression operators ([...], (...), |) introduced in section 7 only the meaning of | remains to be explained.

Let A and B be domain expressions, denoting A, respectively B. Then:

$$A \mid B$$

denotes:

$$A \cup B$$

where U is the (potentially infinite set) union operator; i.e.:

$$A \mid B \quad \triangleq \quad \{ o \mid o \in A \lor o \in B \}$$

Comment:

Thus | does **not** denote the discriminated or disjoint union operation.

In Scott 76 the disjoint union operator is represented by +, and:

$$A + B \quad \triangleq \quad \{ (\underline{A}, a) \mid a \in A \} \cup$$
$$\{ (\underline{B}, b) \mid \quad \in B \}$$

The "tagging" of the $A+B$ domain elements, with a "label" indicating the originating domain, is useful whenever (1) domains A and B overlap, and (2) the need arises for testing, say in some function, whether an $A+B$ object comes from A or from B.

Since the $|$ operator does not separate the operand domains it is the task of the definer to see to it that $|$ operand domains are disjoint whenever some functions applicable to the union domain need ascertain originating domain.

Constructing Disjoint Domains

Let us assume that a union domain, roughly of the type:

$$D_1 \mid D_2 \mid \ldots \mid D_n$$

is required. Let us further assume that for some, or all, $i \neq j$:

$$D_i \text{ is } \underline{\text{not}} \text{ disjoint from } D_j$$

Since D_i and D_j overlap there is no direct way of separating (some) D_i objects from D_j.

Introducing the abstract syntax tree domain constructing rules:

$$A_1 :: D_1$$
$$A_2 :: D_2$$
$$\ldots$$
$$A_n :: D_n$$

and :

$$A_1 \mid A_2 \mid \ldots \mid A_n$$

(in lieu of $D_1 \mid D_2 \mid \ldots \mid D_n$), effectively corresponds to a distinct marking $(mk\text{-}A_1, mk\text{-}A_2, \ldots, mk\text{-}A_n)$ of respective $D_1, D_2, \ldots, D_n$ objects in the union domain $A_1 \mid A_2 \mid \ldots \mid A_n$. Distinctness is solely achieved by distinctness of left-hand side (A_i, A_j) names.

Thus we introduce $::$ abstract syntax rules whenever disjointness is desired.

7.2 Abstract Syntaxes & Rules

Abstract Syntaxes

$$
\text{Abstract-Syntax} \quad ::= \quad \begin{array}{l} \text{Rule}_1 \\ \text{Rule}_2 \\ \cdots \\ \text{Rule}_r \end{array}
$$

is an informal "extended" BNF, or BNF-like, syntactical description
defining an abstract syntax as consisting of a number of rules. Each
rule:

$$
\text{Rule} \quad \begin{array}{l} ::= \quad \text{Identifier} = \text{Domain-Expression} \\ ::= \quad \text{Identifier} :: \text{Domain-Expression} \end{array}
$$

basically consists of two parts: a left-hand side definiendum, which
is an identifier; and a right-hand side definiens, which is a domain
expression. The two rule parts are separated either by an equality $(=)$
operator or by the so-called tree domain constructor $(::)$ operator.
Both the $=$ and the $::$ operators are definition symbols (like: ▲
or $\overset{=}{\text{def}}$). The latter, in addition, 'constructs' trees. Its use in:

$$
A \quad :: \quad B_1 \ B_2 \ \cdots \ B_n
$$

could be taken as an abbreviation for the (intended, reflexive) use of
$::$ in:

$$
A \quad = \quad ::(B_1 \ B_2 \ \cdots \ B_n) \, .
$$

Context Constraint

In a complete meta-language program there must be no two rules of any
one or pair of abstract syntaxes with identical definienda, i.e. lhs
identifiers.

is-Function:

Any abstract syntax rule implicitly introduces, i.e. defines, a predicate function *is*-Identifier:

$$\underline{type:} \quad is\text{-Identifier:} \quad OBJ \to BOOL$$

which applies to any object and yields _true_ if it is an object in the domain denoted by Identifier, otherwise _false_.

Note:

We could have chosen to write:

$$obj \in \text{Identifier}$$

instead of:

$$is\text{-Identifier}(obj)$$

but, except for a few cases, we reserve the former form for set membership tests where the set is not one defined as a Domain as defined by some abstract syntax. The exceptions are those illustrated by the following descriptor and quantified expressions (see sections 1.5 & 1.4.1):

$$(\Delta x \in \text{Identifier})(P(x))$$
$$(\forall x \in \text{Identifier})(P(x))$$
$$(\exists x \in \text{Identifier})(P(x))$$
$$(\exists! x \in \text{Identifier})(P(x))$$

Example 47:

Given the introductory abstract syntax example, and given: _is-Stmt(s)_, _is-ID(id)_, _is-Scalar Type(st)_, _is-Named-Stmt(ns1)_, _is-Named-Stmt(ns2)_, _is-Stmt(s1)_, _is-Stmt(s2)_, and _is-Expr(e)_ we are able to construct:

mk-Program(s)	_pr_
mk-Block([id→mk-Type(st,nil)],{},<ns1,ns2>)	_bl_
mk-Named-Stmt(nil,s)	_ns_
_mk-If(e,s1,s2)_	_if_

etc.. Let us call these four objects _pr_, _bl_, _ns_ and _if_. Now:

$is\text{-}Program(pr)$	$\sim is\text{-}Program(bl)$
$\sim is\text{-}Stmt(pr)$	$is\text{-}Stmt(bl)$
$\sim is\text{-}Block(pr)$	$is\text{-}Block(bl)$
$\sim is\text{-}Named\text{-}Stmt(pr)$	$\sim is\text{-}Named\text{-}Stmt(bl)$
$\sim is\text{-}If(pr)$	$\sim is\text{-}If(bl)$
$\sim is\text{-}Program(ns)$	$\sim is\text{-}Program(if)$
$\sim is\text{-}Stmt(ns)$	$is\text{-}Stmt(if)$
$\sim is\text{-}Block(ns)$	$\sim is\text{-}Block(if)$
$is\text{-}Named\text{-}Stmt(ns)$	$\sim is\text{-}Named\text{-}Stmt(if)$
$\sim is\text{-}If(ns)$	$is\text{-}If(if)$

etc..

Further Context Constraint

A =-rule, when expressible in the form:

$$Identifier \quad = \quad D_1\ D_2\ \ldots\ D_n \quad (n \geq 2)$$

is identical to the rule:

$$Identifier \quad :: \quad D_1\ D_2\ \ldots\ D_n \quad (n \geq 2)$$

Semantics of Abstract Syntaxes

The prescription for computing most of the domains designated by compound domain expressions has already been given. Allowing now for domain definitions, i.e. rules, in fact for several such, and, in addition, for potentially mutually recursive rules, we require a more comprehensive prescription for computing the domains given an arbitrary abstract syntax. We shall only do that informally here, relying in general on the formal foundations laid by Scott. [Scott 1976].

An abstract syntax can, speaking rather formally, be viewed syntactically as an equation set. Its meaning is a family of named sets of mathematical objects being the minimal, fix-point solution to the equation set. That is: to each lhs there corresponds a potentially infinite class of finite objects, the domain. These domains are the smallest such classes which, when substituted in lieu of their identifying names

in the equation lhs and rhs's will, satisfy the equations. The bit
about the fix-point comes into the picture since our equations may be
mutually recursive.

Example 48:

The equation:

$$D = D \xrightarrow{m} D$$

has the following solution:

$$D: \quad \{[], [[] \rightarrow []], [[] \rightarrow [[] \rightarrow []]], [[[] \rightarrow []] \rightarrow []], \ldots \};$$

with :

$$D = (D \xrightarrow{m} D) \mid A$$

"adding":

$$\{[a_1 \rightarrow []], \ldots$$
$$[[] \rightarrow a_1], \ldots$$
$$[a_1 \rightarrow a_1], \ldots$$
$$[a_1 \rightarrow a_1, a_2 \rightarrow a_2, \ldots, a_n \rightarrow a_n], \ldots$$
$$\ldots \}$$

to the above solution.

7.3 Abstract Syntax oriented Combinators

The meta-language (structured-) expression and statement combinators specifically complementing the (abstract syntax) domain expression alternative operator, |, are:

The McCarthy Conditional Clause:

$$(pe_1 \to c_1,$$
$$pe_2 \to c_2,$$
$$\dots$$
$$pe_n \to c_n)$$

The Cases Conditional Clause:

$$cases \; e_0:$$
$$(e_1 \to c_1,$$
$$e_1 \to c_2,$$
$$\dots$$
$$e_n \to c_n)$$

Here pe_i stand for predicate expressions, c_j for either expressions or statement, and e_k for expressions. A clause is either a statement or an expression. If either of the above conditional clauses is (intended to be) of the expression type, then all c_j are (to be) expressions. Similarly they are all to be statements if the above clauses are to be conditional statements. We refer to the e_k expressions as follows: e_0 as the root expression and e_k, for $1 \leq k \leq n$, as the branch expressions.

Example 49:

Given the abstract syntax for expressions of some source language:

1	*Expr*	=	*Infix | Rhs-ref | Con-var-ref | Const*
2	*Infix*	::	*Expr Op Expr*
3	*Rhs-ref*	::	*Var-ref*
4	*Con-var-ref*	::	*Id*
5	*Const*	=	*INTG | BOOL*
6	*Var-ref*	::	*Id [Expr$^+$]*
7	*Op*	=	*Int-Op | Bool-Op | Rel-Op*

We can define a function, *ex-tp*, which given a dictionary:

8	*DICT*	=	*Id $\xrightarrow{m}$ (Type | PROC | ...)*
9	*Type*	::	*Scalar-type [(Expr | *)$^+$]*
10	*Scalar-type*	=	*INT | BOOL*

computes the *Scalar-type* of an expression, *e*:

```
11.0    ex-tp(e,dict)=
  .1        cases e
  .2          (mk-Infix( ,op, ) →
  .3                (is-Int-Op(op )    →   INT,
  .4                 is-Bool-Op(op)    →   BOOL,
  .5                 is-Rel-Op(op)     →   BOOL),
  .6          mk-Rhs-ref(mk-Var-ref(id, )) →
  .7                s-Scalar-type(dict(id)),
  .8          mk-Con-var-ref( ) →
  .9                INT,
  .10         T   →  (is-INTG(e)      →   INT,
  .11                 is-BOOL(e)       →   BOOL))
```

        type: Expr DICT → Scalar-type

Observe how, in this case, we nested the Cases and the McCarthy constructs. Relate the structures of the abstract syntax and the *ex-tp* function, and observe how they "match". Observe next the use of *mk-*constructs in the cases branch expressions. Observe finally that we only name those arguments of the *mk-* functions which we explicitly require.

-- annotations:

An expression is either an infix expression, a right-hand-side reference, a controlled variable reference or a constant.

An infix expression has three parts: two operand expressions and an operator.

A right-hand-side variable reference is a variable reference.

A controlled variable reference is an identifier.

A constant is either an integer or a boolean.

A variable reference has an identifier and, if this identifier denotes an array location, then an index list, which is a non-zero, finite length expression list, else nil.

An operator is either an integer (arithmetic) operator, a boolean operator, or a relational operator.

-- comments:

An expression either denotes an integer or a boolean. Hence the type of an expression is (said) either (to be) INT or (to be) $BOOL$. The type of an expression -- which is otherwise well-formed -- can be statically ascertained. Given that the type with which a variable or formal parameter is declared:

12      $Block :: (Id \underset{m}{\to} Type) \ Proc\text{-}set \ Named\text{-}Stmt^*$

13      $Proc :: Id \ Parm^* \ Stmt$

14      $Parm :: Id \ (Type \mid PROC)$

is recorded in some (compile-time) dictionary, also called static environment, the function ex-tp computes (at compile-time) the type of any expression.

-- annotations, continued:

$ex\text{-}tp$ is given an expression, e, and a dictionary, $dict$.

If e (.1) is an infix expression (.2), i.e. if e can be expressed as some $mk\text{-}Infix(e1,op,e2)$, where $e1,op$ and $e2$ become the names of those $Expr$, Op, respectively $Expr$ objects of which e is made up, then the type of e is ascertainable from the kind of operator that op is. If op is .3) an integer operator, then the type of e is INT; if op instead is either (.4) a boolean or (.5) a relational (or comparison) operator, then the type of e is $BOOL$.

If e (.1) is a right-hand side reference (.6), i.e. if e can be expressed as some $mk\text{-}Rhs\text{-}ref(vr)$, where vr is a variable reference (meta-)expressible as some $mk\text{-}Var\text{-}ref(id,el)$, where id and el become the names of the Id, respectively $[Expr^+]$ objects of which e can be made up, then the type of e can be looked up in the dictionary as that of the *Scalar-type* component of the *Type* object with which *id* is associated.

PART III   COMBINATORS

In part II, i.e. in sections 2-7 inclusive, we dealt with all aspects of constructing domains of objects, constructing objects and performing primitive, i.e. language-defined operations on objects.

Certain desired transformations on objects are, however, of a complexity which cannot easily be described by some such operator/operand expression, regardless of its composition. To that end, and as is quite customary in programming, the meta-language provides a number of constructs which facilitate the gradual composition of transformations and processes on objects. We call these constructs for combinators. They are:

        Variables: Declarations, Assignment & the State
        Structured Clauses
        Blocks: Let & Return
        Exits

So far we have officially dealt only with the applicative aspects of the meta-language. Introducing variables implies introducing imperative constructs, i.e. statements. The applicative part of the language, however, includes the *let* constructs of, and hence also, blocks, as well as most of the structured clauses. We say, in general, that the applicative constructs of the language permit the expression of composite transformations on objects. The imperative constructs correspondingly enable the decomposed, stepwise statement of processes on objects.

8. VARIABLES

Example 50:

The following four function definitions all define f_i to denote the factorial function:

1     $f_0(n)$ = *if* $n=0$ *then* 1 *else* $n*f_0(n-1)$

2     $f_1(n)$ =   (*dcl* $\underset{\sim}{v}$:= 1 *type* N_1;
.1   *for* $i=1$ *to* n *do*
.2 $\underset{\sim}{v}$:= ($\underline{c}\,\underset{\sim}{v}$)*$i$;
.3   *return*($\underline{c}\, v$))

3     $f_2(n)$ =   (*dcl* $\underset{\sim}{v}$:= 1 *type* N_1;
.1   *for* *all* $i \in \{1:n\}$ *do*
.2 $\underset{\sim}{v}$:= ($\underline{c}\,\underset{\sim}{v}$)*$i$;
.3   *return*($\underline{c}\,\underset{\sim}{v}$))

4     $f_3(n)$ =   (*dcl* $\underset{\sim}{v}$:= 1 *type* N_1,
.1 $\underset{\sim}{i}$:= n *type* N_0;
.2   *while* ($\underline{c}\,\underset{\sim}{i}$ $\neq$ 0) *do*
.3   ($\underset{\sim}{v}$:= ($\underline{c}\,\underset{\sim}{v}$)*($\underline{c}\,\underset{\sim}{i}$);
.4 $\underset{\sim}{i}$:= ($\underline{c}\,\underset{\sim}{i}$) $-$ 1);
.5   *return*($\underline{c}\,\underset{\sim}{v}$))

The first defines f_i applicatively; the remaining three, imperatively.

We say that the parenthesized constructs: (*dcl* ... *return*(...)) are blocks. $\underset{\sim}{v}$ and, only in the last definition, $\underset{\sim}{i}$ are (assignable) variables. They form part or all of the state current in these blocks. If no other (externally declared) variables 'exist', then they form all of the state. The logical type of the four f's are:

       type: f_0: $N_0 \rightarrow N_1$

$$\underline{type}: \quad f_1, f_2, f_3: \quad N_0 \rightarrow (\Sigma \rightarrow (\Sigma \; N_1))$$

where Σ denotes the state space. The contributions of $\underset{\sim}{v}$ and $\underset{\sim}{i}$, inside the blocks, to this space is:

$$\Sigma = \quad \ldots \; \underline{\cup} \; (\underset{\sim}{v} \underset{m}{\rightarrow} N_1) \; \underline{\cup} \; (\underset{\sim}{i} \underset{m}{\rightarrow} N_0)$$

where the ... ellipsis refers to possibly externally declared variables. Since none of the f_1, f_2 nor f_3 assign to any such global variables it is easy to see that they do not alter any global state, and hence that the potential state transformation indicated by:

$$\Sigma \rightarrow \Sigma$$

is in fact the identity change. Thus the four functions can indeed be shown 'equivalent' even when considering a global state.

8.1 Declarations & The State

Although the examples above featured block local declarations we shall normally not find a need for other than global variables in abstract models of higher-level software.

The meaning of a declaration:

$$\underline{dcl} \; \underset{\sim}{Var} := \ldots \underline{type} \; D$$

-- in which we may omit the $\underline{type}$ D clause -- is that of joining to our state, σ, a contribution:

$$\sigma \; \cup \; [\underset{\sim}{Var} \rightarrow obj]$$

It is understood that $\underset{\sim}{Var}$ is not already declared, i.e. that $\underset{\sim}{Var} \; \underline{\sim \in dom} \; \sigma$. In general, the state space, Σ, given a collection of (global) declarations:

$$\underline{dcl} \; \underset{\sim 1}{V} := \ldots \underline{type} \; D_1,$$
$$\underset{\sim 2}{V} := \ldots \underline{type} \; D_2,$$
$$\ldots$$
$$\underset{\sim n}{V} := \ldots \underline{type} \; D_n;$$

can be defined as:

$$\Sigma = (\underset{\sim}{V}_1 \underset{m}{\rightarrow} D_1) \; \underline{\cup} \; (\underset{\sim}{V}_2 \underset{m}{\rightarrow} D_2) \; \underline{\cup} \; \cdots \; \underline{\cup} \; (\underset{\sim}{V}_n \underset{m}{\rightarrow} D_n)$$

The domain expressions:

$$(\underset{\sim}{V}_i \underset{m}{\rightarrow} D_i)$$

are degenerate in that the denoted map domains are singular, i.e. consist of just one element, the (quotation-like) object $\underset{\sim}{V}_i$ which can be regarded as denoting itself.

Example 51:

Our source language example features the ability to input data from an (one) external device, to output data to an (one) external device -- distinct from the input device, and to declare variables in any (nested) block. The relevant syntactic domains, continuing example 31, are:

$$
\begin{array}{lll}
Block & :: & (Id \underset{m}{\rightarrow} Type) \; \ldots \; Stmt^* \\
Stmt & = & In \mid Out \mid Assign \mid \ldots \\
In & :: & Var\text{-}ref \\
Out & :: & Expr \\
Assign & :: & Var\text{-}ref \; Expr
\end{array}
$$

The semantic functions ascribing meaning to these source constructs will be based on the following three (global) variables:

$$
\begin{array}{lll}
\underline{dcl} \; \underset{\sim\sim\sim}{Input} & := \; <\ldots> & \underline{type} \; (INTG \mid BOOL)^*, \\
\underset{\sim\sim\sim}{Output} & := \; <> & \underline{type} \; (INTG \mid BOOL)^*, \\
\underline{STG} & := \; [\,] & \underline{type} \; STG;
\end{array}
$$

where STG was defined in the last example of section 4.4.

The state space, Σ, of the elaboration functions, is:

$$
\begin{array}{ll}
\Sigma = (\underset{\sim\sim\sim}{Input} \underset{m}{\rightarrow} & (INTG \mid BOOL)^*) \; \underline{\cup} \\
\quad (\underset{\sim\sim\sim}{Output} \underset{m}{\rightarrow} & (INTG \mid BOOL)^*) \; \underline{\cup} \\
\quad (\underline{STG} \underset{m}{\rightarrow} & STG)
\end{array}
$$

8.2 Variable References

Prelude

Recall the introductory examples of section 8. Variable identifiers (V) occurred in two contexts:

$$V := \ldots \underline{c} \, V \ldots$$

The left-hand side occurrence denotes itself, i.e. the meta-storage (state) location. The right-hand side occurrence of V likewise denotes itself ! But here we traditionally expect the value kept in the V location. The meta-language breaks with this tradition. If you need the content, then you are required to perform the $\underline{c}$ operation to V.

end-of-Prelude

If V is the name of a declared variable:

$$\underline{dcl} \; V := \ldots \underline{type} \; D$$

then V is said to denote itself, or if need arises for more precision, to denote a $\underline{ref} \, D$ object, i.e. a reference to an object of type D.

To get at the value 'stored' in V apply the contents-of operation denoted by $\underline{c}$:

$$\underline{c} \, V$$

V and $\underline{c} \, V$ are meta-language expressions. Given the state, σ:

$$\sigma = [V \rightarrow obj, \ldots \,]$$

$\underline{c} \, V$ is explained as :

$$\sigma(V).$$

If V is of type $\underline{ref} \, D$, then $\underline{c} \, V$ is of type D. That is: $\underline{c}$ de-references V. Thus $\underline{c}$ denotes a function from state variables and states to objects; which we generalize to a function from state-variable and states to states 'paired' with objects:

$$\underline{c} \quad \sim \quad \lambda v.\lambda\sigma.(\sigma,\sigma(v))$$

$$\underline{c} \quad \in \quad (V \to (\Sigma \overset{\sim}{\to} (\Sigma\ OBJ)))$$

8.3 Assignment

Assignment is a meta-language statement:

$$\underline{V} := expr$$

If $\underline{V}$ is of type $\underline{ref}\,D$ then $expr$ must be of a type D', included in D, i.e. $D'\subseteq D$, e.g. $D\equiv D'$

The meaning of assignment is as you think it. Formally, however:

$$:= \quad \sim \quad \lambda v.\lambda obj.\lambda\sigma.(\sigma+[v\to obj])$$

i.e.: $\quad := \quad \in \quad (V \to (OBJ \to (\Sigma \overset{\sim}{\to} \Sigma)))$

Example 52:

We now conclude the examples of sections 4.4, 6.3 and 8.1. Recall in particular the last example of section 4.4.

The elaboration functions ascribing meaning to the source language In, Out and $Assign$ statements will themselves employ, but now, meta-language assignments. Since the basic source language means of referring to a variable is through:

$$Var\text{-}ref \quad :: \quad Id\ [Expr^+]$$

we define a set of auxiliary functions:

$\underline{type}$: $eval\text{-}Var\text{-}ref$: $Var\text{-}ref \overset{\sim}{\to} (ENV \overset{\sim}{\to} (\Sigma \overset{\sim}{\to} (\Sigma\ Scalar\text{-}loc))$

$contents$: $\quad Scalar\text{-}loc \overset{\sim}{\to} (\Sigma \overset{\sim}{\to} (\Sigma\ (INTG|BOOL)))$

$assign$: $\quad Scalar\text{-}loc\ (INTG|BOOL) \overset{\sim}{\to} (\Sigma \overset{\sim}{\to} \Sigma)$

$eval\text{-}Var\text{-}ref$ takes a variable reference, an environment and a state, and produces the same state and the scalar location denoted by the variable reference. The need for accessing the state arises as a result

of potentially evaluating array variable subscripts. Whereas
eval-Var-ref applies to a syntactic object (*Var-ref*), and hence needs
the environment; *contents* and *assign* apply only to semantic objects,
and hence do not require the environment. Finally: objects assigned
to storage locations must have their type match the type of the location. Recall that the storage model of the last example of section 4.4
distinguished between integer- and boolean locations:

```
0          v-tp-match(v, sloc)=
 .1            (is-INTG(v) → is-Intg-loc(sloc),
 .2            is-BOOL(v) → is-Bool-loc(sloc))
              type:  (INTG|BOOL) (Intg-loc|Bool-loc) → BOOL
```

Now:

```
1.  int-In(mk-In(vr))(ρ)=
 .1    if c Input = <>
 .2    then error
 .3    else (let sloc : eval-Var-ref(vr)(ρ),
 .4              iv   : hd c Input;
 .5          if v-tp-match(iv,sloc)
 .6          then (Input := tl c Input;
 .7                assign(sloc,iv))
 .8          else error)
       type: In →̃ (ENV →̃ (Σ →̃ Σ))


2.  int-Out(mk-Out(e))(ρ)=
 .1    (let ov : eval-Expr(e)(ρ);
 .2    Output := (c Output)⌢<ov>)
       type:  Out →̃ (ENV →̃ (Σ →̃ Σ))


3.  int-Assign(mk-Assign(vr,e))(ρ)=
 .1    (let sloc : eval-Var-ref(vr)(ρ),
 .2         val  : eval-Expr(e)(ρ);
 .3    assign(sloc,val))
       type: Assign →̃ (ENV →̃ (Σ →̃ Σ))
```

The auxiliary functions:

4. *eval-Var-ref(mk-Var-ref(id,ssl))(ρ)=*
   .1 *if* ssl=nil
   .2   *then* *return(ρ(id))*
   .3   *else* (*let* arrloc = ρ(id) *in*
   .4   *let* il   : < eval-Expr(ssl[i])(ρ) | 1 ≤ i ≤ len ssl >;
   .5   *if* il ~∈ *dom* arrloc
   .6   *then* *error*
   .7   *else* *return(arrloc(il)))*

5. *contents(l)=*
   .1 (*let* v : (*c* STG)(l);
   .2 *if* v=undefined
   .3   *then* *error*
   .4   *else* *return(v))*

6. *assign(l,v)=*
   .1 STG := *c* STG + [l→v]

-- annotations

1. *Interpreting* an *Input* statement proceeds as follows: (.1) If there
   is no more *Input*, then (.2) interpretation halts, otherwise (.3-.8)
   we *evaluate* (.3) the scalar *location* denoted by the *variable* reference constituting the *Input* statement and (.4) retrieve the front
   input stream *value*. If (.5) the *type* of this *value* *matches* that of
   the scalar location then (.6-.7) we proceed to (.6) 'shorten' the
   Input stream by the element value just retrieved, and (.7) to *assign*
   this *value* to the scalar storage *location*; otherwise interpretation
   halts.

2. *Interpreting* an *Output* statement consists, rather more simply, of
   (.1) *evaluating* the *expression* it is composed of and (.2) of append-
   ing the resulting output *value* to the *Output* stream.

Etc. for 3., *int-Assign*.

4. *Evaluating a variable reference* which consists of a possibly void
    array subscript list and the variable *identifier* proceeds as fol-
    lows: (.1) If the subscript list is absent, then (.2) the *identi-
    fier* is guaranteed, by well-formedness context conditions not
    shown, to denote a scalar variable, whose location can be obtained
    from the environment directly. (.3-.7) If instead the subscript
    list is present, then (.3) the *identifier* denotes an *array* variable
    whose *location* is kept in the environment. The subscript list is
    guaranteed to consist of proper *expressions* all yielding integer
    values. Well-formedness context conditions for this are not shown,
    but see [Jones 1978a]. We therefore (.4) *evaluate* all the subscript
    expressions to obtain an *index* list. (.5) If this *index* list is
    not one of the array, then (.6) interpretation fails, otherwise
    the denoted scalar location is obtained by applying the *array*
    location, which is a map from index lists to scalar locations, to
    the computed *index* list.

Comments

In the above definitions certain 'pairs' of evaluations proceeded in
"parallel": 1.3-1.4, 3.1-3.2. In [Jones 1978a] the same evaluations
proceed sequentially, in the order listed. This gives rise to two distinct semantics!

8.4 Derived References

Section 8.2 dealt only with simple variable references. That is: references denoting the location of an 'entire' variable. In the design and
use, since 1973, of the meta-language, a need, when abstracting software, has not been registered for easily denoting references to proper
components of store composite objects.

When applying the meta-language to lower-level abstractions, i.e. to
rather more implementation-biased specifications, such a need may arise.
The following notation is therefore offered.

Sub-References to *TUPLE* Elements

Given:

(0) $\underline{dcl}$ $\underset{\sim}{Tuple}$:= <...> $\underline{type}$ D^*

Retrieving the i'th component of $\underline{c}$ $\underset{\sim}{Tuple}$ is basically expressible as:

(1) $(\underline{c}\,\underset{\sim}{Tuple})[i]$

with the selective update of that tuple position basically expressible as:

(2) $\underset{\sim}{Tuple}$:= $\underline{c}\,\underset{\sim}{Tuple}$ + $[i{\rightarrow}d]$;

It is now suggested to let:

(3) $\underset{\sim}{Tuple}\,^{\cdot}[i]$

denote the reference to the i'th position of $\underline{c}\,\underset{\sim}{Tuple}$, permitting (1) to be rewritten:

(1') $\underline{c}(\underset{\sim}{Tuple}\,^{\cdot}[i])$

and (2) as:

(2') $\underset{\sim}{Tuple}\,^{\cdot}[i]$:= d

Sub-References to *MAP* Range Elements

The forms corresponding to (1,2,3,1',2') above, but for variables of type map:

(0) $\underline{dcl}$ $\underset{\sim}{Map}$:= $[...]$ $\underline{type}$ $A\underset{m}{\rightarrow}D$;

are:

(1) $(\underline{c}\,\underset{\sim}{Map})(a)$

(2) $\underset{\sim}{Map}$:= $\underline{c}\,\underset{\sim}{Map}$ + $[a{\rightarrow}b]$

(3) $\underset{\sim}{Map}\,^{\cdot}(a)$

(1') $\underline{c}(\underset{\sim}{Map}\,^{\cdot}(a))$

-- where $a \in \underline{dom}\,c$ Map prior to (2).

<u>Sub-References to Sub-"*TREE*"s.</u>

Given:

$$D \quad :: \quad s\text{-}nm_1\!:\!D_1 \quad s\text{-}nm_2\!:\!D_2 \quad \ldots \quad s\text{-}nm_l\!:\!D_l$$

and:

(0) $\underline{dcl}$ $Tree$ $:= mk\text{-}D(\ldots)$ $\underline{type}$ D.

The forms corresponding to (1,2,3,1',2') above are now:

(1) $s\text{-}nm_i(c\;Tree)$ $1 \leq i \leq l$

(2) $(\underline{let}\;mk\text{-}D(d_1,\ldots,d_i,\ldots,d_l) := c\;Tree;$
      $Tree := mk\text{-}D(d_1,\ldots,d_i',\ldots,d_l))$

where all d_j for $j \neq i$ are unchanged, i.e. where (2) only 'changes' the $s\text{-}nm_i$ sub-"tree". Now:

(3) $s\text{-}nm_i \cdot Tree$

(1') $c(s\text{-}nm_i \cdot Tree)$

(2') $s\text{-}nm_i \cdot Tree := d_i'$

<u>Discussion</u>

The reader may verify that a similar need for variables containing sets does not arise.

Also: the benefit of the derived reference operation, denoted by $\cdot$, is higher in forms (2') than (1') -- cf. forms (2) and (1), respectively.

Finally: the semantics of the derived reference operator, $\cdot$, is fully explained by the equivalence of forms (1) and (1'), (2) and (2'), respectively.

9 STRUCTURED CLAUSES

As used in this section a clause is either a statement or an expression.

It turns out that to each structured statement, and block, see next section, there corresponds a structured expression. The conditional form of such clauses syntactically looks very much alike, whereas this is not the case for the iterative clauses.

9.1 Overview

Let in the following s and $S(...)$ stand for statements, $E(...)$ and suitably decorated e's for expressions, suitably decorated pe's for predicate expressions, and suitably decorated c's for clauses. It is further assumed that the c's of a given conditional structure are either all statements, or all expressions, leading to this conditional in turn being a statement, respectively an expression.

The following presents the various structured clauses in a schematic way:

Conditional Clauses

(1)   *if* pe *then* c_1 *else* c_2

(2) $(pe_1 \rightarrow c_1,$ and (2') $(pe_1 \rightarrow c_1,$
        $pe_2 \rightarrow c_2,$ $pe_2 \rightarrow c_2,$
        $...$ $...$
        $pe_n \rightarrow c_n)$ $T \;\;\; \rightarrow c_n)$

(3)   *cases* e_0:   and (3') *cases* e_0:
        $(e_1 \rightarrow c_1,$ $(e_1 \rightarrow c_1,$
        $e_2 \rightarrow c_2,$ $e_2 \rightarrow c_2,$
        $..$ $..$
        $e_n \rightarrow c_n)$ $T \;\;\; \rightarrow c_n)$

<u>Iterative</u> <u>Clauses</u>:

(4)   <u>for</u> $i = m$ <u>to</u> n <u>do</u> $S(i)$ (4') $<E(i) \mid m \leq i \leq n>$

(5)   <u>for</u> <u>all</u> $id \in set$ <u>do</u> $S(id)$ $\begin{cases} (5') & \{E(id) \mid id \in set\} \\ (5'') & [id \rightarrow E(map(id)) \mid id \in \underline{dom}\, map] \end{cases}$

(6)   <u>while</u> pe <u>do</u> s (6') $\begin{cases} f(obj)= \\ \quad \underline{if}\ P(obj) \\ \quad\quad \underline{then}\ F(obj) \\ \quad\quad \underline{else}\ G(obj,f(H(obj))) \end{cases}$

where in the last schema ((6')) P, F, G and H are appropriate functions, P being a predicate. (4, 5, 6) are statements; (4', 5', 5") are expressions, and so is an application of f.

<u>Examples</u> -- <u>53</u>:

Illustrations of the duality between clauses (4) and (4'), respectively (5) and (5'), (5"), have already been given -- see sections 3.4, respectively 2.4, 4.4.

The duality of the conditional statements and conditional expressions need not be further discussed.

The following examples illustrate the duality of forms (6) and (6').

To sum the elements of a tuple, t, of integers:

$$
\begin{aligned}
&(\underline{dcl}\ q\ := t\ \underline{type}\ INTG^*, \qquad\quad sum(t)= \\
&\quad\quad sum := 0\ \underline{type}\ INTG; \qquad\quad \underline{if}\ t = <> \\
&\quad \underline{while}\ (c\,q) \neq <>\ \underline{do} \qquad\qquad \underline{then} \\
&\quad\quad (sum := (c\,sum) + hd\,c\,q; \qquad \underline{else}\ hd\,t + sum(tl\,t) \\
&\quad\quad\ q\ := tl\,c\,q) \\
&\quad \underline{return}(c\,sum))
\end{aligned}
$$

Subsequent elaboration functions will illustrate the power and neatness of recursive definitions centered around a simple <u>if-then-else</u> clause.

9.2 Detailed Syntax & Semantics

9.2.1 If-then-else Conditional

Schema:

    if expr   predicate-expression
      then clause   consequent
      else clause   alternative

Meaning:

Elaboration of an if-then-else clause proceeds as follows: first the premiss- (or test-) predicate expression is evaluated. If it does not yield a truth value an *error* has occurred -- and the meta-language program is in error! If the premiss yields truth then the consequent clause is elaborated. Otherwise the alternative clause. Any elaboration of either the consequent- or the alternative clause strictly succeeds the evaluation of the premiss.

Programming Notes:

1.   Observe that the form :

    if expr *then* stmt

  is not provided. Instead the programmer, if so forced, is adviced to use:

    if expr *then* stmt *else* *I*

  for *I* see section 1.2. Note that the converse is possible:

    if ~expr *then* *I* *else* stmt

  and that the 'similar' problem is not relevant for if-then-... expressions!

2.   The premiss sometimes relates as follows to either the consequent or alternative clause:

$\underline{if}$ $(\exists x...)(P(x))$
   $\underline{then}$ $(\underline{let}$ x $\underline{be}$ $s.\underline{t}.$ $P(x);$
       $cC(x))$
   $\underline{else}$ ...

or, e.g.:

$\underline{if}{\sim}(\exists!y...)(P(y))$
   $\underline{then}$ ...
   $\underline{else}$ $(\underline{let}$ $z = (\Delta x)(P(x));$
       $aC(z))$

Whereever the 'connection' is so obvious, then we informally, but strictly speaking erroneously, write:

$\underline{if}$ $(\exists x...)(P(x))$
   $\underline{then}$ $cC(x)$
   $\underline{else}$ ...

respectively:

$\underline{if}{\sim}(\exists!x...)(P(x))$
   $\underline{then}$ ...
   $\underline{else}$ $aC(x)$

etcetera. The 'shifts' in identifier naming is, of course, immaterial. Thus the x of the latter two premisses (informally) bind as far as the entire consequent and alternative clauses.

9.2.2 McCarthy Conditional

Schema:

$(e_1 \rightarrow es_1,$
$e_2 \rightarrow es_2,$
$\qquad ...$
$e_n \rightarrow es_n)$ $\qquad\qquad\qquad n \leq 2$

and:

$$
\begin{aligned}
(e_1 &\rightarrow es_1, \\
e_2 &\rightarrow es_2, \\
\dots& \\
T &\rightarrow es_n) \qquad\qquad n \geq 2
\end{aligned}
$$

where the T of the latter form is a meta-language keyword only used in McCarthy and Cases constructs in the e_n 'position', i.e. in lieu of e_n. All e_i $(1 \leq i \leq n)$ are predicate (or propositional) expressions.

Meaning:

We give the semantics of the above in terms of their transcription into the if-then-else form:

$$
\begin{aligned}
(\underline{if}\; e_1\; &\underline{then}\; es_1 \\
&\underline{else} \\
(\underline{if}\; e_2\; &\underline{then}\; es_2 \\
&\underline{else} \\
(\quad &\dots \\
&\underline{else} \\
(\underline{if}\; e_n\; &\underline{then}\; es_n \\
&\underline{else}\; \underline{error})\dots)))
\end{aligned}
$$

respectively:

$$
\begin{aligned}
(\underline{if}\; e_1\; &\underline{then}\; es_1 \\
&\underline{else} \\
(\underline{if}\; e_2\; &\underline{then} \\
(\quad &\dots \\
&\dots \\
&\underline{else}\; es_n\dots)))
\end{aligned}
$$

Programming Note

The same remarks concerning informal name binding and scope as for the *if-then-else* construct apply with the constraint of the scope of an identifier defined in some e_i $(1 \leq i \leq n)$ restricted to the corresponding es_i:

$$(\ldots \qquad \ldots$$
$$\ldots$$
$$(\exists \ldots x \ldots)(P(x)) \quad \to \quad ES(x),$$
$$\ldots$$
$$\ldots \qquad \ldots)$$

9.2.3 The Cases Conditional

Schema:

$$\text{\textit{cases}} \; e_0:$$
$$(e_1 \;\; \to \;\; es_1,$$
$$e_2 \;\; \to \;\; es_2,$$
$$\ldots$$
$$e_n \;\; \to \;\; es_n)$$

and:

$$\text{\textit{cases}} \; e_0:$$
$$(e_1 \;\; \to \;\; es_1,$$
$$e_2 \;\; \to \;\; es_2,$$
$$\ldots$$
$$T \;\; \to \;\; es_n)$$

with T as defined above. The form of e_i $(1 \le i \le n)$ is either an ordinary expression, i.e. one all of whose free identifiers are bound by/in the surrounding context, or it is one of the so-called defining expression forms:

$$\{d_1, d_2, \ldots, d_k\}$$
$$<d_1, d_2, \ldots, d_k>$$
$$mk\text{-}Nm(d_1, d_2, \ldots, d_k)$$
$$id, cst$$

where the d_j's $(1 \le j \le k)$ are of either of these five forms. id represents identifiers, cst constants.

Programming Note:

Usually the d_j's of an immediate defining expression are identifiers.

Some of these may be bound in the containing scope. If all are bound or constants, then we have an ordinary expression.

Meaning:

We first assume ordinary, i.e. bound expressions, and explicate through reduction to earlier understood forms:

$$(\underline{let}\ v_0 : e_0;$$
$$\underline{if}\ v_0=e_1\ \underline{then}\ es_1$$
$$\underline{else}$$
$$(\underline{if}\ v_0=e_2\ \underline{then}\ es_2$$
$$\underline{else}$$
$$(\qquad \ldots$$
$$\underline{else}$$
$$(\underline{if}\ v_0=e_n\ \underline{then}\ es_n$$
$$\underline{else}\ \underline{error})\ldots)))$$

respectively:

$$(\underline{let}\ v_0 : e_0;$$
$$\underline{if}\ v_0=e_1\ \underline{then}\ es_1$$
$$\underline{else}$$
$$(\underline{if}\ v_0=e_2\ \underline{then}\ es_2$$
$$\underline{else}$$
$$(\qquad \ldots$$
$$\underline{else}\ es_n\ldots)))$$

Name Binding & Scope:

We explain the free identifier, defining expression variants by specifically presenting an atypical combination and then transcribing it to an if-then-else form combined with *let* blocks. The example assumes all branch defining expressions identifiers free and rather casually mixes sets, tuples and trees!

$$\underline{cases}\ e_0:$$
$$(\{id_1, id_2, \ldots, id_k\} \quad \rightarrow es_1,$$
$$<id_1, id_2, \ldots, id_k> \quad \rightarrow es_2,$$
$$mk\text{-}Nm(id_1, \ldots, if_k) \quad \rightarrow es_3,$$
$$id \qquad\qquad\qquad \rightarrow es_4,$$
$$\ldots \qquad\qquad\qquad \ldots)$$

e.g. transcribes into:

$$(\underline{let}\ v_0:\ e_0;$$
$$\underline{if}\ is\text{-}SET(v_0) \wedge \underline{card}\ v_0 = k$$
$$\quad \underline{then}\ (\underline{let}\ \{id_1, id_2, \ldots, id_k\} = v_0\ \underline{in}$$
$$\qquad\qquad es_1)$$

$$\quad \underline{else}$$
$$(\underline{if}\ is\text{-}TUPLE(v_0) \wedge \underline{l}\ v_0 = k$$
$$\quad \underline{then}\ (\underline{let}\ <id_1, id_2, \ldots, id_k> = v_0\ \underline{in}$$
$$\qquad\qquad es_2)$$

$$\quad \underline{else}$$
$$(\underline{if}\ is\text{-}Nm(v_0)$$
$$\quad \underline{then}\ (\underline{let}\ mk\text{-}Nm(id_1, id_2, \ldots, id_k) = v_0\ \underline{in}$$
$$\qquad\qquad es_3)$$
$$\quad \underline{else}\ (\underline{let}\ id = v_0\ \underline{in}$$
$$\qquad\qquad es_4))))$$

This latter form is now annotated (i.e. commented) referring alternatively to the former form:

First the base expression, e_0, is evaluated. The name v_0 identifies the evaluated object. Following the listing given in the cases form we now elaborate, in turn, successive branches until a match is found. Specifically: we first ask whether v_0 is a set and, if so, of cardinality k. If a fit is thus found we dissolve the set v_0 into its k elements naming these $id_1, id_2, \ldots, id_k$, whereupon the expression- or statement clause, es_1, is elaborated. This terminates elaboration of the cases clause. If v_0 is not a set it is then asked whether it is a tuple, and if so, of length k. If a fit is thus found..., etc. If v_0 is not a set, tuple, nor a tree of type N_m then v_0 is renamed id and es_4 is elaborated Thus a free name, as here: id, 'corresponds' to a T-clause -- leading to no elaboration ever of succeeding branches.

The scope of the free identifiers of the branch-expressions is that of
the corresponding expression, or statement, clause.

···

And so on: many variations, combinations and permutations (e.g. order-
ings of free- & bound variables). The above 'schematic' examples have
attempted to convey the general idea of defining expressions, their
possible mixture of free- & bound variables and even constants. The
reader should, from this, be able to extrapolate. The basic point is
this: since it is an abstraction, i.e. meta-language and since there
is generally not to be an interpreter for it, anything sensible and
context-wise obvious is to be allowed.

Example 54:

We shall use the meta-language conditional expressions and recursion
to exemplify simpler versions of the conditional statements. That is:
we applicatively define imperative constructs!

Abstract Syntax:

The syntactic domains:

$$
\begin{array}{lll}
Cond = & If \mid McC \mid Case \\
If & :: & Expr \;\; Stmt \; Stmt \\
McC & :: & ExSt^{+} \; [Stmt] \\
Case & :: & Expr \; ExSt^{+} \; [Stmt] \\
ExSt & :: & Expr \; Stmt
\end{array}
$$

where $Expr$ and $Stmt$ are the meta-language expression and statement domains:

The semantic domains; first the textual, then the temporal:

$$
\begin{array}{lll}
\rho \in ENV & = & Id \underset{m}{\to} (LOC \;...) \\
\sigma, \xi \in STG & = & LOC \underset{m}{\to} OBJ
\end{array}
$$

where Id is the syntactic domain of identifiers, LOC the further un-
analyzed domain of locations.

Semantic Functions:

Let I and V be names of the generic functions elaborating meta-language
statements, respectively expressions, i.e.:

$$\textit{type: } I: \quad Stmt \xrightarrow{\sim} (ENV \xrightarrow{\sim} (\Sigma \xrightarrow{\sim} \Sigma))$$
$$\textit{type: } V: \quad Expr \xrightarrow{\sim} (ENV \xrightarrow{\sim} (\Sigma \xrightarrow{\sim} \Sigma \; OBJ))$$

$I(stmt)(\rho)(\sigma)=$

  cases $stmt:$

    $(mk\text{-}If(p,c,a)$

    → $(\underline{let}\ (\sigma',b) = V(p)(\rho)(\sigma)\ \underline{in}$

       $\underline{if}\ b$

         $\underline{then}\ I(c)(\rho)(\sigma')$

         $\underline{else}\ I(a)(\rho)(\sigma')),$

    $mk\text{-}McC(esl,t)$

    → $(\underline{let}\ mcc(les)(\xi)=$

          $((lse \neq <>)$

            → $(\underline{let}\ (\xi',b) = V(s\text{-}Expr(\underline{h}\ lse))(\rho)(\xi)\ \underline{in}$

              $\underline{if}\ b$

                $\underline{then}\ I(s\text{-}Stmt(\underline{h}\ lse))(\rho)(\xi')$

                $\underline{else}\ mcc(\underline{t}\ lse)(\xi')),$

         $(t \neq \underline{nil})$

           → $I(t)(\rho)(\xi),$

        $T →\ \underline{error})\ \underline{in}$

      $mcc(esl)(\sigma)),$

    $mk\text{-}Cases(e,esl,t)$

    → $(\underline{let}\ (\sigma',v) = V(e)(\rho)(\sigma)\ \underline{in}$

      $\underline{let}\ case(lse)(\xi)=$

          $((lse \neq <>)$

            → $(\underline{let}\ (\xi',v') = V(s\text{-}Expr(\underline{h}\ lse))(\rho)(\xi)\ \underline{in}$

              $\underline{if}\ v=v'$

                $\underline{then}\ I(s\text{-}Stmt(\underline{h}\ lse))(\rho)(\xi')$

                $\underline{else}\ case(\underline{t}\ lse)(\xi')),$

         $(t \neq \underline{nil})$

           → $I(t)(\xi),$

        $T →\ \underline{error})\ \underline{in}$

      $case(esl)(\sigma')),$

   $...)$

9.2.4 The Ordered, Iterative For-To-Do Statement

Schema:

>   *for* id = $expr_m$ *to* $expr_n$ *do* $stmt$

id must be free in the surrounding context. $expr_m$ and $expr_n$ must be integer valued expressions. All occurrences of id in $stmt$ are free in $stmt$.

Programming Note

We usually constrain $expr_m$ and $expr_n$ to be so-called static expressions. These are expressions whose value can be ascertained statically, without reference to any computation (e.g. state). As such, static expressions are usually either constants (viz.: $expr_m$ = 1) or simple operator/operand expressions involving only textual, i.e. syntactic domain objects.

The Controlled Variable

id is called a, or the, controlled variable. It is not a variable in the sense of denoting a REFerence, and thus it cannot be changed in $stmt$. id denotes an integer.

Name Binding & Scope:

The first occurrence of id in *"for* id =..." is the defining occurrence. It binds all (free) occurrences of id in $stmt$. The scope of this controlled variable is the for statement in which it is defined.

Meaning:

We first explicate the primarily intended usages of the for statement: namely the ones which have $expr_m$ and $expr_n$ being static expressions evaluating to m, respectively n. Let $S(id)$ be another way of alluding to $stmt$. Then:

>   *for* id = m *to* n *do* $S(id)$
>
>   ■
>
> $S(m);S(m+1);...;S(n-1);S(n)$

Thus if $m<n$ then: *"for* $id = m$ *to* n *do* $S(id) = $ *"I"*. Given $S(id)$, $S(k)$ means the substitution of all id in S by k.

We then explain the meaning of for statement whose from and to expressions, $expr_m$ & $expr_n$ are expressions of any kind. To this end we apply the meta-language itself!

Example 55:

Let the for statement syntactic domain specification be:

> *For* $::$ *Id Expr Expr Stmt*

where $Id \subset TOKEN$, and *Expr* & *Stmt* denote the class of respectively source-language expressions and statements.

Let the semantic domains pertaining to the interpretation of *For* Statements be the temporal store:

> $\sigma \in STG$ $=$ $LOC \underset{m}{\rightarrow} OBJ$

which maps *LOC*ations to *OBJ*ects, and the simplified textual environment:

> $\rho \in ENV$ $=$ $Id \underset{m}{\rightarrow} (LOC \mid INTG \mid \ldots)$

which maps source-language text *Id*entifiers into either *LOC*ations, if they are names of declared variables, or to *INTeG*ers, if they are e.g. controlled variable names, or... .

Let V denote the generic expression evaluation function which applies to source -language expressions, environments & states/stores and yields state changes & objects -- in this case *INTeG*ers. I denotes the generic statement interpretation which applies to source-language statements, environments & states/stores and yields state changes.

$I(mk\text{-}For(id,fe,te,s))(\rho)(\sigma)=$

.1 $\quad (\underline{let}\ (\sigma',f)\ =\ V(fe)(\rho)(\sigma),$

.2 $\qquad\qquad (\sigma'',t)\ =\ V(te)(\rho)(\sigma)\ \underline{in}$

.3 $\quad \underline{let}\ \sigma'''\in\{\sigma',\sigma''\}\ \underline{in}$

.4 $\quad \underline{let}\ for\ (\rho')(\xi)=$

.5 $\qquad\qquad \underline{if}\ \rho'(id)>t$

.6 $\qquad\qquad\quad \underline{then}\ \xi$

.7 $\qquad\qquad\quad \underline{else}\ (\underline{let}\ \xi'\ =\ I(s)(\rho')(\xi)\ \underline{in}$

.8 $\qquad\qquad\qquad\qquad for(\rho'+[id\rightarrow(\rho'(id))+1])(\xi'));$

.9 $\quad for(\rho\cup[id\rightarrow i])(\sigma'''))$

Annotations:

.1-.2   Both specification expressions, the *from* expression and the *to* expression, are eValuated in parallel "," (or in any order), and both may lead to implicit state changes (σ', respectively σ'') and to the explicitly desired from, f, and to, t, values.

.3   This line illustrates the problem: which new (or next) state, σ' or σ'', to choose. In this case the problem has been brought upon us by our insistance on parallel evaluation of all specification expressions. Had our pragmatics' lead us to choose sequentiality of *from*- and *to* expressions evaluation there would have been no need for a non-deterministic choice.

.4   A local function, *for*, is recursively (.4 vs. .8) defined which if applied:

.5   will test whether the controlled variable value ($\rho'(id)$) has gone beyond the limit (t),

.6   if so, the final state is the one current when the last invocation (.8 or .9) of *for* was made, i.e. at the end of last iteration, respectively when *for* was first called (initialized);

.7   otherwise the value of the controlled variable is still within bounds, and the 'body', s, of the *for* statement shall be Interpreted, leading to a new state, ξ'.

.8   With this state, and the 'updated' environment which binds the (textual) name of the controlled variable to its incremented value the *for* loop is invoked (recursively).

This completes the definition of the auxiliary *for* function,

.9   which is first activated with the 'initial' state, σ''', and an environment which binds the controlled variable to its *initial* value, i.

10   Note that the environments are simply extended versions of the environment in which the for statement is interpreted.

In summary: the meta-language for loop was conceived of as a means for iterating through syntactic tuple structures, tl. Hence the standard requirement that $expr_m$ and $expr_n$ be static expressions, the former usually 1, the latter usually $\underline{l}\ tl$.

Further Examples 56 & 57:

We now illustrate imperative and applicative definitions of the *Compound Statement* source language construct:

$Cmpd \quad :: \quad Stmt^*$

The *imperative* version is basically based on a state:

$\Sigma_i \; = \; (\underset{\sim}{STG} \rightarrow STG)\; \underline{U} \ldots$

$Int\text{-}Cmpd(mk\text{-}Cmpd(stl))(\rho)=$
    $\underline{for}\ i=1\ \underline{to}\ \underline{l}\ stl\ \underline{do}\ int\text{-}Stmt(stl[i])(\rho)$
$\underline{type}: \quad Cmpd \overset{\sim}{\rightarrow} (ENV_i \overset{\sim}{\rightarrow} (\Sigma_i \overset{\sim}{\rightarrow} \Sigma_i))$

$\ldots$

The *applicative* version is similarly based on a state:

$\Sigma_a \quad :: \quad STG \ldots$

$I\text{-}Cmpd(mk\text{-}Cmpd(stl))(\rho)(\sigma)=$
    $\underline{if}\ stl=<>$
        $\underline{then}$
        $\underline{else}\ (\underline{let}\ \sigma' = I\text{-}Stmt(\underline{h}\ stl)(\rho)(\sigma)\ \underline{in}$
            $I\text{-}Cmpd(mk\text{-}Cmpd(\underline{t}\ stl))(\rho)(\sigma'))$
    $\underline{type}: \quad Cmpd \overset{\sim}{\rightarrow} (ENV_a \overset{\sim}{\rightarrow} (\Sigma_a \overset{\sim}{\rightarrow} \Sigma_a))$

where correspondingly:

$$type: \quad int\text{-}Stmt: \quad Stmt \overset{\sim}{\to} (ENV_i \overset{\sim}{\to} (\Sigma_i \overset{\sim}{\to} \Sigma_i))$$

$$type: \quad 1\text{-}Stmt: \quad Stmt \overset{\sim}{\to} (ENV_a \overset{\sim}{\to} (\Sigma_a \overset{\sim}{\to} \Sigma_a))$$

9.2.5 The unordered For-All & Parallel Statements

The For-All Statement

Schema:

> $for\ all\ def \in set\ do\ stmt$

where def and stmt pairwise are of the forms:

$$id \qquad\qquad\qquad\qquad\qquad \sim S(id)$$

$$\{cd_1, cd_2, \ldots, cd_n\}$$
$$<cd_1, cd_2, \ldots, cd_n> \qquad\qquad \sim S(id_1, id_2, \ldots, id_m)$$
$$mk\text{-}Nm(cd_1, \ldots, cd_n)$$

where a proper subset of cd_1, cd_2, ..., cd_n may be constants, otherwise of either of the above four listed forms, usually identifiers, id! These must all be distinct. And where id_1, id_2, ..., id_m are the identifiers of def free in the containing context. All such must be free in S. It must be statically decidable that set denotes a set. And if either of the latter three def forms are used, then it must be statically decidable that set is of a logical type, Y, such that either some $X\text{-}set$, X^* or Nm is contained in Y; viz.: $X\text{-}set \subseteq Y$, $X^* \subseteq Y$ or: $Nm \subseteq Y$!

The Controlled Variables

The identifiers of def free in the containing context are the controlled variables. Again, as in section 9.2.4 they are not assignable but directly denotes non-REFerence OBJects.

Name Binding & Scope

The identifier occurrences in def free in the containing context are defining occurrences. They bind all their (free) occurrences in $Stmt$ (S). The scope of these controlled variables is the for statement in which they are defined.

Meaning:

In this section we only explicate the semantics of the for-all statement for the simple case of static *set* expressions and simple identifier *def*'s -- this is also the most common case. Let *set* denote a set
of k objects, and name these $id_1, id_2, \ldots, id_k$. That is $set \sim \{id_1, id_2, \ldots, id_k\}$:

$$\underline{for} \; \underline{all} \; id \in \{id_1, id_2, \ldots, id_k\} \; \underline{do} \; S(id)$$

$$\sim$$

$$// \{S(id_1), S(id_2), \ldots, S(id_k)\}$$

The Parallel Statement

Schema:

$$//\{stmt1, stmt2, \ldots, stmtn\} \qquad n \geq 2$$

Meaning:

Elaboration of the statements $stmt1$, $stmt2$, $\ldots$, $stmt_n$ proceeds in
parallel, "independently" of each other. Elaboration of this collateral
clause terminates as a result of all statements having been elaborated.

Examples 58-59:

We now illustrate the semantics of a source language statement similar
to the parallel statement. Instead of elaborating the statements in
parallel, they are just executed in any, arbitrary order:

$$All \;\; :: \;\; Stmt\text{-}set$$

is the syntactic domain specification. The definition is kept applicative

$$\Sigma \;\; :: \;\; \ldots$$

```
I-All(mk-All(stmts))(ρ)(σ)=
    if stmts={}
        then σ
        else (let s ∈ stmts in
              let σ' = I-Stmt(s)(ρ)(σ) in
              I-All(mk-All(stmts∖{s}))(ρ)(σ'))
type: All ⇾ (ENV ⇾ (Σ ⇾ Σ))
```

...

A for-all source language construct could be given the following definition:

```
ForAll  ::  Id Expr Stmt

Σ        ::  ...

I-ForAll(mk-ForAll(id,e,s))(ρ)(σ)=
    (let (σ',set) = V-Expr(e)(ρ)(σ) in
     let all(coll)(ξ)=
              if coll={}
                 then ξ
                 else (let obj ∈ coll in
                       let ξ' = I-Stmt(s)(ρ+[id→obj])(ξ) in
                       all(coll∖{obj})(ξ'))                      in
     all(set)(σ'))
type: ForAll ⇾ (ENV ⇾ (Σ ⇾ Σ))
```

where it is assumed that the eValuation function, which elaborates *id*,
finds the meaning of *id* just by looking up in the environment!

```
type: I-Stmt:  Stmt ⇾ (ENV ⇾ (Σ ⇾ Σ))
type: V-Expr:  Expr ⇾ (ENV ⇾ (Σ ⇾ (Σ OBJ)))
```

9.2.6 The While-Do Statement

Schema:

    while *expr* do *stmt*

where it is statically decidable that *expr* is a truth-valued expression.

Programming Note:

expr is usually an impure expression, i.e. one whose value depends on the current state. The state is, of course, potentially being changed by *stmt*..

Meaning:

As you might expect it -- but here is an applicatively expressed formalization of the imperative while construct.

Example 60:

Abstract Syntax:

> *Wh*   ::   *Expr Stmt*

for the syntactic domain. And:

$$\sigma \in STG = LOC \xrightarrow{m} OBJ$$
$$\rho \in ENV = Id \xrightarrow{m} (LOC|...)$$

for the semantic domains.

Semantic Functions:

$$I\ (mk\text{-}Wh(e,s))(\rho)(\sigma)=$$
$$\quad (\underline{let}\ wh(\xi)=$$
$$\qquad\qquad (\underline{let}\ (\xi',b) = V(e)(\rho)(\xi)\ \underline{in}$$
$$\qquad\qquad \underline{if}\ b$$
$$\qquad\qquad\quad \underline{then}\ (\underline{let}\ \xi'' = I(s)(\rho)(\xi')\ \underline{in}$$
$$\qquad\qquad\qquad\qquad wh(\xi''))$$
$$\qquad\qquad\quad \underline{else}\ \xi') \qquad\qquad\qquad \underline{in}$$
$$\quad wh(\sigma))$$

$\underline{type}:\ I:\ Wh \xrightarrow{\sim} (ENV \xrightarrow{\sim} (\Sigma \xrightarrow{\sim} \Sigma))$

$\underline{type}:\ wh:\ \Sigma \xrightarrow{\sim} \Sigma$

Example 61:

Dijkstra's Guarded, Repetitive Construct [Dijkstra 75]:

$rg \in RepGuard \quad :: \quad (Expr \quad Stmt)\text{-}set$

with *STG* and *ENV* as above, has the following 'informal' semantics:
Execute *rg* as long as evaluation of at least one expression in the un=
ordered set of pairs of *Expression-Statements* yields *true*:

$I(mk\text{-}RepGuard(ess))(\rho)(\sigma)=$
.1   ($\underline{let}$ $gwh(ses)(\xi) =$
.2 $\underline{if}$ $ses=\{\}$
.3 $\underline{then}$ ξ
.4 $\underline{else}$ ($\underline{let}$ $(e,s) \in ses$ $\underline{in}$
.5 $\underline{let}$ $(\xi',b) = V(e)(\rho)(\xi)$ $\underline{in}$
.6 $\underline{if}$ b
.7 $\underline{then}$ ($\underline{let}$ $\xi'' = I(s)(\rho)(\xi')$ $\underline{in}$
.8 $gwh(ess)(\xi''))$
.9 $\underline{else}$ $gwh(ses\setminus\{(e,s)\})(\xi))$ $\underline{in}$
.10 $gwh(ess)(\sigma))$

        $\underline{type}$: $RepGuard \overset{\sim}{\to} (ENV \overset{\sim}{\to} (\Sigma \overset{\sim}{\to} \Sigma))$

In this definition, evaluation of guards (*e*) may cause side-effects,
i.e.: ξ goes to ξ'. Thus repeated evaluations of some (one) guard, in=
itially yielding falsity, might eventually produce truth -- had we not
passed the initial state (σ, subsequently ξ) onto alternative evalua=
tions (.9). Doing so also secures Dijkstra's requirement that if some
guard is chosen, then it was *true* in the 'initial' state (σ, subse=
quently ξ).

The non-deterministic aspect of this construct is exhibited by the ar=
bitrary set element selection of line .4.

The reader may verify that this command is a (sledge-hammer ?) general=
ization of the *while* *do* construct above!

10. BLOCKS

A compound statement:

$$(stmt_1; \ stmt_2; \ \dots \ ; \ stmt_n)$$

is a sequence of two or more statements. The semicolon, ";", acts as the combinator here.

A block:

$$(\underline{let} \ id = expr_d \ \underline{in} \ expr_b) \qquad (\underline{let} \ id = expr \ \underline{in} \ stmt)$$

$$(\underline{let} \ id : expr_d; \ expr_b) \qquad (\underline{let} \ id : expr; \ stmt)$$

$$(\underline{dcl} \ vr := expr_d; \ expr_b) \qquad (\underline{dcl} \ vr := expr; \ stmt)$$

consists of a ($\underline{let}$) definition of a constant, non-$\underline{ref}$erence object, or a ($\underline{dcl}$) declaration (of a variable) -- on one hand --, compounded with an expression, or a statement (-sequence) -- on the other hand. The com= binators here are either the semicolon, ";", or the "$\underline{in}$" symbol.

This section will not bring very many examples. Previous sections abound with examples of blocks. We leave it to the reader to look these up for re-confirmation:

Reference to block-examples:

Parenthesized numerals refer to example numbers, the i.j-k trailing these refer to formulae (i) and line number (j-k) sequences.

Applicative expression blocks:

    (0)11.3-8, (0)11.6-8, (0)16.1-6, (0)17.3-7, (0)18.3-21, (0)18.8-21, (0)20.3-11, ...

Imperative expression blocks:

    (31)14.3-6, (31)14.12-17, (50)2.0-3, (50)3.0-3, (52)4.3-7, (52)5.1-4, ...

Statement blocks:

    (31)13.1-8, (52)1.3-8, (52)2.1-2, (52)3.1-3, ...

The Block Concept

The block concept of the meta-language essentially deals with the notion of scope. Blocks are of the forms:

> (*let* id = *expr* *in*
> *clause*)

and:

> (*let* id : *expr*;
> *clause*).

We have, however, in past examples, also permitted ourselves to introduce local variables:

> (*dcl* id := *expr* *type* D;
> *clause*).

In all three cases id stands for a locally, i.e. a block, defined, constant quantity. We say that the scope of id is the block: (...) in which it is defined. Only in this textual part, may it be referred to. In the first two blocks id denotes the value of *expr* upon block entry. In the last case id denotes the location of a meta-storage cell, i.e. an object in the domain of Σ:

$$\Sigma = \dots \underline{\cup} (Id \xrightarrow[m]{} D)$$

In particular:

$$\sigma = \dots \cup [\underset{\sim}{id} \to obj]$$

where $\underset{\sim}{id}$ is the denotation of id, and obj is the value of *expr* upon block entry.

The *let* (or *dcl*) definitions of id are said to **bind** any free occurrences of id in *clause*. Thus the scope of id extends to inner, nested blocks in which id is not redefined.

clause may be a meta-language expression or a sequence of one or more statements.

10.1 Let Constructs

Observe the two distinct cases of *let* constructs:

The syntactic, or applicative *let* construct:

> (*let* id = expr *in*
>   clause)

If *expr* is a pure expression, i.e. an expression whose evaluation does not require access to any state components, then we use "=" and "*in*" as delimiters.

The semantic, or imperative *let* construct:

> (*let* id : expr;
>   clause)

If, on the other hand, evaluation of *expr* requires access to the state, i.e. if *expr* is an imperative, or impure, expression , then we use ":" and ";" as delimiters.

Assume *id* to occur free in *clause*, i.e. think of *clause* as C(*id*). Then the meaning of the syntactic *let* clause block is C(*expr*), i.e. can be obtained by substituting *expr* for all free occurrences of *id* in *clause*. Note that the substitution could be done on the syntactic level, i.e. by replacing texts. The meaning, however, of the semantic *let* clause block is C(*val*), where *val* is the value of *expr* upon block entry. That is: the meaning can be obtained by substituting values of *expr* for all free occurrences of *id* in *clause*.

Let Construct Variants

A very useful *let* variant is:

> (*let* obj ∈ D *be* s.t. P(obj);
>   clause)

which we understand as: let *obj* <u>be</u> an object in the domain or set D such <u>that</u> it satisfies the predicate P. Other variants, which are simple cases of the above are:

> (<u>*let*</u> *obj* $\in$ *Set*;
> *clause*)

and:

> (<u>*let*</u> *obj* <u>*be*</u> <u>*s.t.*</u> $P(obj)$;
> *clause*)

The above three variants were indicated, by the ";" separating the <u>*let*</u> construct from the block body *clause*, to be of the semantic type. Similar, but syntactic constructs would instead of the infix ";" use an infix "<u>*in*</u>".

Composite Object Let Decomposition

The following are useful, so-called composite <u>*let*</u> constructs:

> (<u>*let*</u> $mk\text{-}D(d_1,d_2,\ldots,d_n) = expr_d$ <u>*in*</u>
> *clause*)

> (<u>*let*</u> $<d_1,d_2,\ldots,d_n> = expr_t$ <u>*in*</u>
> *clause*)

and:

> (<u>*let*</u> $\{d_1,d_2,\ldots,d_n\} = expr_s$ <u>*in*</u>
> *clause*)

Their respective meanings are:

$expr_d$ must evaluate to a D tree object, with:

> $D \quad :: \quad D_1 \; D_2 \; \ldots \; D_n$

then the above is equivalent to:

$$(\underline{let}\ tree = expr_d\ \underline{in}$$
$$(\underline{let}\ d_1\ = s\text{-}D_1(tree),$$
$$d_2\ = s\text{-}D_2(tree),$$
$$..$$
$$d_n\ = s\text{-}D_n(tree)\ \underline{in}$$
$$clause)).$$

$expr_t$ must evaluate to an n-tuple:

$$(\underline{let}\ tuple = expr_t\ \underline{in}$$
$$(\underline{let}\ d_1\ = tuple[1],$$
$$d_2\ = tuple[2],$$
$$..$$
$$d_n\ = tuple[n]\ \underline{in}$$
$$clause)).$$

$expr_s$ must evaluate to a set of cardinality n. The 'assignment' of set objects to d_i is arbitrary:

$$(\underline{let}\ set = expr_s\ \underline{in}$$
$$(\underline{let}\ d_1 \in set\ \underline{in}$$
$$(\underline{let}\ d_2 \in set\diagdown\{d_1\}\ \underline{in}$$
$$(\underline{let}\ d_3 \in set\diagdown\{d_1,d_2\}\ \underline{in}$$
$$...$$
$$(\underline{let}\ d_n \in set\diagdown\{d_1,d_2,...,d_{n-1}\}\ \underline{in}$$
$$clause)...))))$$

Simultaneous & Recursive Let Definitions

The form:

$$(\underline{let}\ d_1 = e_1,$$
$$d_2 = e_2,$$
$$...$$
$$d_n = e_n\ \underline{in} \qquad\qquad (n \geq 1)$$
$$clause)$$

simultaneously defines the objects $d_1,d_2,...,d_n$. They are, in general, to be the ("smallest" such) objects which satisfy the (above set of simultaneous) equations. This description permits d_j's to occur recursively in the equation set. The d_j's might be composite constructs, introduced in the previous subsection, in which case we mean that the constituent (free) identifiers (ultimately occurring in d_j) may occur recursively in the equation set.

For the story on recursive definitions of functions we refer to section 6.2.

Notational Conventions

The form:

$$(\underline{let}\ d_1 = e_1\ \underline{in}$$
$$\underline{let}\ d_2 = e_2\ \underline{in}$$
$$\dots$$
$$\underline{let}\ d_n = e_n\ \underline{in}$$
$$clause)$$

is a short-hand for:

$$(\underline{let}\ d_1 = e_1\ \underline{in}$$
$$(\underline{let}\ d_2 = e_2\ \underline{in}$$
$$(\dots$$
$$(\underline{let}\ d_n = e_n\ \underline{in}$$
$$clause)\dots)))$$

The form :

$$(\underline{let}\ mk\text{-}A(\ ,c,\ ) = e_a\ \underline{in}$$
$$clause)$$

where e.g.:

$$A\ ::\ B\ C\ D,$$

is a short-hand for:

$$(\underline{let}\ mk\text{-}A(b,c,d) = e_a\ \underline{in}$$
$$clause)$$

It is used to alert the reader to the non-use of the B and D components of the A tree denoted by e_a.

Similarly for anonymous trees; and:

$$(\underline{let} <x, \ ,z, \ > = e_t \ \underline{in}$$
$$clause)$$

which is the same as:

$$(\underline{let} \ t = e_t \ \underline{in}$$
$$\underline{let} \ x = t[1],$$
$$z = t[3] \ \underline{in}$$
$$clause).$$

10.2 Pure & Impure Expressions

A pure (or applicative) expression is one whose evaluation never requires access to the state.

An impure (or imperative) expression is one whose evaluation potentially requires access to the state.

Given that Σ_i denotes the state space of an imperative (global variable only) model we can say that the type of the denotation of an impure expression is either of the form:

$$\Sigma_i \overset{\sim}{\to} (\Sigma_i \ OBJ)$$

or of the form:

$$\Sigma_i \overset{\sim}{\to} OBJ$$

The former type hints that evaluation of the meta-language expression potentially leads to a (side-effect) state-change, whereas the latter type only expresses that the state is accessed in order to compose the resulting OBJect value.

. . .

The choice of forming an expression either as a pure-, or as an impure, expression, is solely determined by the kind of object to be denoted. That is: even though some abstract model is primarily centered around global state variables, some objects may still be denotable by pure expressions.

If at least one target expressions of a conditional expression is impure, then all such target expressions are to be impure. This requirement is further motivated in [Jones 1978a]. To render an otherwise pure expression impure prefix it with the operator *return*. See section 10.6.

10.3 The ";" Combinator

The ";" is a combinator. Its use can be explained in two ways: syntactically, and semantically. Syntactically speaking, ";" separates imperative clauses: statements; semantic *let* clauses; a semantic *let* clause from a statement; and a statement from an impure expression:

$$(\ldots\ stmt_1;\ stmt_2\ \ldots)$$

$$(\ldots\ \underline{let}\ x_1\ :\ expr_1;\ \underline{let}\ x_2:\ expr_2;\ \ldots)$$

$$(\ldots\ \underline{let}\ x:\ expr;\ iexpr)$$

$$(\ldots\ stmt;\ iexpr)$$

Semantically speaking ";" denotes functional composition. Since the type of the denotation of a meta-language semantic *let* clause, let, or statement, stmt, is:

$$let,\ stmt:\ \Sigma_i\ \tilde{\rightarrow}\ \Sigma_i$$

The construct:

$$(c1;c2)$$

where $(c1,c2)$ are either (semantic lets, statements) or (statements, statements), means:

$$\lambda\sigma.(c2(c1(\sigma)))$$

where ci is the meaning of ci (i=1,2). Thus:

$$; \quad \sim \quad \lambda c1.\lambda c2.\lambda\sigma.(c2(c1(\sigma)))$$

i.e. $\quad ; \quad \in \quad (\Sigma \overset{\sim}{\rightarrow} \Sigma) \rightarrow ((\Sigma \overset{\sim}{\rightarrow} \Sigma) \rightarrow (\Sigma \overset{\sim}{\rightarrow} \Sigma))$

10.4 Compound Statements & Statement Sequences

The meta-language permits any statement to be a compound statement:

$$(stmt_1;\ stmt_2;\ \ldots;\ stmt_n)$$

The body of a (statement-) block, i.e. the syntactic construct referred to as *clause* in e.g. section 10.1, may be a statement sequence:

$$stmt_1;\ stmt_2;\ \ldots;\ stmt_n$$

There is no semantic difference between these two constructs. We omit parenthesizing the latter since it is always superfluous.

The formal meaning is:

$$\lambda\sigma.stmt_n(stmt_{n-1}(\ldots(stmt_2(stmt_1(\sigma)))\ldots))$$

where $stmt_i$ is the meaning of $stmt_i$.

We refer to [Jones 1978a] for a further λ-definition of the meanings of the basic statements.

The informal meaning is as you would expect it to be.

10.5 Statement- & Expression Blocks

A statement-block is a statement. The block, when interpreted, effects a state-change. An expression-block is an expression. The block, when evaluated, may effect a state-change, but always, in addition, delivers a value:

$$stmt\text{-block:} \quad \Sigma_i \overset{\sim}{\rightarrow} \Sigma_i$$
$$expr\text{-block:} \quad \Sigma_i \overset{\sim}{\rightarrow} (\Sigma_i\ OBJ)$$

A statement block consists of a sequence of one or more syntactic and/or semantic *let* clauses followed by a sequence of one or more statements.

An expression block is either a pure- or an impure- (i.e. an applicative-, respectively an imperative-) expression. A pure expression block consists of one or more syntactic *let* clauses followed by a pure expression. An impure expression block consists of a non-zero length sequence of zero, one or more syntactic- or semantic *let* clauses followed either by an impure expression or a statement all of whose syntactically possible execution paths end with an impure expression. Since only well-structured statements are permitted the test for this latter is quite simple.

10.6 Return

From the explanation of ";" it follows that if a statement sequence, of an expression block, is to be followed by an expression, then the type of this expression must be:

$$\Sigma \to (\Sigma \; OBJ)$$

i.e. impure.

In general, if the context determines that an expression be impure, and the value to be yielded can be denoted by a pure expression, *e*, then we need to render *e* impure. This is the purpose of the monadic expression operator *return*.

$$return \quad \sim \quad \lambda obj.\lambda\sigma.(\sigma,obj)$$
$$return \quad \in \quad (OBJ \to (\Sigma \to (\Sigma \; OBJ)))$$

Examples

See examples: (31) 14.6, (31) 14.17, (50) 2.3, (50) 3.3, (50) 4.5.

11. EXITs

Even though the meta-language has imperative constructs, it lacks the conventional GOTO construct. Hence it lacks labels.

The exit mechanisms, in many ways, replace the GOTO construct. You may say, without being grossly wrong, that _exit_ provides a structured GOTO, albeit, in general, to a dynamically determined, and -- in any case -- unlabelled, program point.

Example 62:

We use the exit mechanism when modeling the GOTO concept of our running example source language! Therefore: in the following read carefully. Observe the distinction between _source_- and meta-language constructs, in particular the block constructs.

```
1     Block        ::  (Id → Type) ... Named-Stmt*
                           m
2     Named-Stmt   ::  [Lbl] Stmt

3     Stmt         =   Block | Goto | ...
```

In this source language _Gotos_ may not go into phrase structures. That is _Gotos_ may e.g. go from one statement of a _Named-Statement_ list to another statement of the same list, or out of the containing _Block_ to a statement of the _Named-Statement_ list of the next embracing _Block_, in fact it may go out of any such number of nested levels. Each time a _Block_ activation is left, whether through (normal) epilogue due to all statements having been executed, or whether due to a global _Goto_, the same 'clean-up' epilogue actions -- as were illustrated in e.g. example 31, section 4.5 -- must first take place:

```
4  int-Block(mk-Block(dcls,procs,nstl))(ρ,ca)=
  .1  (let aid ∈ AID be s.t. aid ~∈ ca in
  .2   let ρ' : ρ+[ lbl → mk-LAB(aid,lbl) | lbl ∈ Labels(nstl) ]
  .3            +[ v → get-loc(dcls(v))(ρ) | v ∈ dom dcls ]
  .4            +[ s-ID(p) → eval-Proc(p)(ρ') | p ∈ procs ];
  .5   always
  .6     (let locs  = {ρ'(v) | v ∈ dom dcls}          in
  .7      let slocs = { ... see example 31 ... }      in
  .8      STG := c STG~slocs)
  .9   in int-Named-Stmt-list(nstl)(ρ,ca∪{aid},aid))

       type:  Block ⥲ ((ENV AID) ⥲ (Σ ⥲ Σ))
```

.4 *eval-Proc* is the imperative version of example 40's *V-Prc*, as used
in example 42 (section 6, respectively 6.3).

.2 The denotation of a label is in the domain:

$$LAB :: AID\ Lbl$$

The *AID* component serves to keep track of active source language
block activations.

.1 The prologue action of a *Block* selects an *activation identifier* not
in the set of (identifiers selected by all) *current activations*.

.2 The block environment associates all *Labels* of its *named statement*
list with this (unique) activation (identifier).

.4 Since procedures may be recursive, and -- independently thereof --
since *gotos* may occur from within a procedure (activation) to the
named statement lists of any of its embracing, including defining,
blocks, the environment passed to *eval-Proc* is the environment being
(thus recursively) defined.

We shall return to lines .5-,9, which -- on the whole -- resemble
lines .4-.8 & .3 of *int-Block* of example 31, section 4.5.

5 *int-Named-Stmt-list(nstl)(ρ,ca,aid)=*
.1 (*tixe* [*mk-LAB(aid,l) → cue-int-Named-Stmt-list(i,nstl)(ρ,ca)*
.2 | *1 ≤ i ≤ len nstl ∧ s-Lbl(nstl[i] = l ≠ nil*]
.3 *in cue-int-Named-Stmt-list(1,nstl)(ρ,ca))*

6 *cue-int-Named-Stmt-list(i,nstl)(ρ,ca))=*
.1 *for j=i to len nstl do int-Stmt(s-Stmt(nstl[j]))(ρ,ca)*

7 *int-Stmt(stmt)(ρ,ca)=*
.1 *cases stmt:*
.2   (*mk-Goto(lbl) → exit(ρ(lbl)),*
.3   *mk-Block(...) → int-Block(stmt)(ρ,ca),*
..   ...)

-- annotations:

5.0 *Interpreting a named statement list is the same as:*

5.3   *interpreting that list as from its 1st statement.*

That is: the *tixe* (*exit* spelled in Polish) clause of lines 5.1-5.2 is not 'executed' by the meta-language elaborator when first entering the *int-Named-Stmt-list* functions. We shall subsequently 'discover' the purpose of the *tixe* clause.

6.0   Having *cued* this function with *i*, i.e. having given it the start-word *i*, *interpretation of the statements of the (named) statement list*

6.1   proceeds linearly, as from the *cued, i*th, statement until the last -- provided, of course, meta-elaboration is not re-directed.

When & how this occurs will presently be uncovered.

7.1   **If** the *interpreted statement is*

7.2   a *Goto*, **then** an *exit* is performed. It is given an argument. This argument is the *LAB*el denotation, *mk-LAB(aid,lbl)*, by which this label is known in the environment.

Meta-elaboration of an *exit* dynamically 'unravels' the meta-language block invocations. That is: we retrace our steps, back to (here) the most recent meta-language block having a *tixe* clause. We say that the *tixe* clause stops the *exit*.

5.1   The *tixe* clause we backtrack to, is the one associated with the *named statement list* of which the 'offending' *Goto* was an immediate statement.

The *tixe* clause is to be understood as follows: **if** the argument passed back with the *exit* (7.2) is equal to some *mk-LAB(aid,l)* of the "map" component of the *tixe* clause, **then** the corresponding *cue-int-Named-Stmt-list,* with the appropriate *cue* position (*i*), is invoked; otherwise the despatching *exit* is not stopped here, but passed out to the next embracing *tixe* clause -- i.e. the *Goto* is to an embracing *Block*.

6-7   In now (re-)*interpreting the (same) named statement list*, but, possibly, as from another, *cued*, position, new *Goto*s may occur.

5.1   These are stopped, thus recursively, by the 'same' *tixe* clause.

7.1 *If* the *interpreted* *statement* is instead, in contrast to annotations
     7.1-7.3 above,

7.3 a *Block*, *then* that, nested, *Block* is *interpreted*.

And so on. *exit*s are always stopped by an *always* clause before being
passed on (4.5-4.8).

Comments

The "maps" of *tixe* clauses may, as we have done in the above annotations,
be considered *not* to be "computed" when the meta-language elaborator en-
ters a meta-language block having a *tixe* clause. The domains of such
"maps" are constrained to be statically determinable, and finite. Since,
in the *cue-int-*... elaboration function, *nstl* is a static (i.e. fixed)
object, this constraint is satisfied.

You may in fact view the domain of the "map" of the *tixe* clause as being
'computed' upon entry to the meta-language block of which it is part.
Now, for this source language, the test for whether the "returned" argument of an *exit* belongs to such a "map" is likewise 'statically' decidable since only *Goto*s with constant *Label* designators were permitted.

11.1 The Exit Mechanisms

In the following the language constructs, dealt with and mentioned, are
those of the meta-language, and not constructs of a *source* language
being modeled.

Variables presuppose declarations, and declarations define a state.
Statements are requests for state changes, and denote state transfor-
mers, i.e. functions from states to states. The serial statement composition operator ";" (semicolon) thus denotes functional composition .

In compound expressions all component sub-expressions are (usually)
completely evaluated before any result value is yielded.

In this section we shall describe the only statement- and expression
construct available for changing the meta-language statement interpre-

tation-, respectively controlling the expression evaluation-, part.

The *exit* mechanism now to be explained offers -- in the context of statements -- in one sense a restricted form of, or alternative to conventional *goto*s. In particular: instead of providing, in the meta-language, *goto*s to (arbitrary or phrase-structure constrained) labelled statements *exit*s provide such *goto*s to statement-block or block-expression "*ends*".

In the context of an applicative language it is an altogether new construct.

The meta-language provides two kinds of *exit* designators:

1,2   *exit*,   *exit(expr)*

and three kinds of *exit* stopping constructs:

3.0   *(always* F(...)
 .1   *in* C(...))

4.0   *(trap exit(def) with* F(def)
 .1   *in* C(...))

5.0   *(tixe* [G(def) → F(def) | P(def)]
 .1   *in* C(...))

Lines 3.0, 4.0 and 5.0 schematize the stopping clauses. Any clause, C(...), prefixed by a stopping construct becomes a block.

Clauses 1 or 2 can occur where meta-language statements or expressions may occur. Thus the *exit* mechanism is an imperative, as well as an applicative construct -- see [Bjørner 77e]. The use of the *always* stopping clause, as will be seen, is, however, restricted to imperative blocks.

The forms *def* can be of either of the forms:

$$\{ d_1, d_2, \ldots, d_n \}$$
$$< d_1, d_2, \ldots, d_n >$$
$$mk\text{-}D(d_1, d_2, \ldots, d_n), \quad (d_1, d_2, \ldots, d_n),$$
id,   or
cst

where *id* stand for (free or bound) *identifiers*, *cst* for *constants* (literals), d_i for forms of the above kind, and where the *def* form need not contain any free identifiers.

11.2 Pragmatics & Semantics of the Exit Mechanism

The *exit* concept is based on the following four principles:

(I) The first basic principle of *exit* is to permit *goto*-like transfer of elaboration (statement interpretation, respectively expression evaluation) control to block boundaries -- i.e. to just outside their terminating part.

In particular: elaboration of any *exit* not definitively stopped in a block properly contained in $C(...)$ will result in immediate termination of any further parts of $C(...)$, this to be followed by elaboration of some $F(...)$.

(II) The second basic principle of *exit* is to permit the user to (implicitly) specify which (dynamically enclosing) block end the *exit*s go to!

A block with no stopping clause is said to not definitively stop any *exit*. A *trap exit* unit whose elaboration may result in an *exit* is likewise said to not definitively stop an arbitrary *exit*. Finally: if an elaboration of $F(...)$ is completed with no *exit* then the *exit* is said to be definitively trapped. In that case elaboration of the block consists of elaboration of the part of $C(...)$ up to the *exit* followed by elaboration of the $F(...)$. The potential state transformation yielded by an imperative block is in this case the serial composition of the two net effects. For the case the block is a block-expression $F(...)$ must in this case, namely that of definitive entrapment, yield a value.

(III) The third basic principle of *exit* is to permit the meta-language programmer to specify that certain actions be taken at any stopping block end.

The stop clauses serves this purpose. *exit*s from multiply nested blocks may cause successive stopping actions, one per block (inside-out), and each being terminated by an *exit* to the next enclosing block.

An *exit* not definitively stopped by a stop clause of the (outer-most) block of a function definition is dynamically passed to the immediately embracing block in which the actual reference to the function, i.e. "to this function definition", occurred.

The *always* stop clause unconditionally filters any *exit*, its F(...) is elaborated, and the *exit* passed on to outer blocks.

In consequence: *exit*s of one function definition may, depending on dynamic calling patterns, be trapped by a multitude of stop clauses of blocks contained in various (other) function defini-tions. An *exit* of an activation of a recursively defined function may thus be stopped by a prior, temporarily suspended activation of that "same" function.

(IV) The fourth basic principle of the *exit* mechanism, i.e. the joint use of *exit*s and stopping clauses is finally to communicate infor-mation from the (usually only dynamically determinable) point of *exit* to *trap exit* and *tixe* stop clauses' F(...). The idea being to let the elaboration of F(...) depend on *exit* "returned" data.

In particular: the value, *v*, of the *expr* of *exit(expr)* is obtained; the proper stop clause is found; and *v* is substituted for all free occurrences of that unit's formal parameter *def* in that unit's F(...) resulting in F'(...). Then F'(...) is elaborated.

Scope Rules

An alternative way of describing some of the linguistic properties (of the exit mechanism) is now presented.

Two scope aspects are important: A syntactic (or static), and a seman-tic (or dynamic).

The syntactic scope rule is concerned with the scope of identifiers occurring in the *def* form of the *trap exit* clause. Identifiers of *def*, free in the embracing context, bind free occurrences of these identi-fiers in the corresponding F(*def*). The static scope rules of the *tixe* "map" are the same as those of any implicit map (set or tuple) construc-tion.

The semantic scope rule is concerned with the scope of the *always*, *trap exit* and *tixe* clauses.

The dynamic scope rules of the *always* and *trap exit* clauses is the text
C(...); whereas the dynamic scope rule of the *tixe* clause includes both
the *tixe* "map" and the text C(...)!

Thus: an *exit* 'occurring' as a result of elaborating F(def), of 3.0 or
4.0, if not stopped in F(...), is not stopped by this (3.0, respectively
4.0) instance of the *always*, respectively *trap exit* clause. Instead it
is passed out to possibly embracing meta-blocks.

An *exit* 'occurring' as a result of elaborating some F(def) of 5.0, i.e.
of a *tixe* "map", if not trapped in F(...), is trapped by this *tixe*
clause (5.0). Thus the *tixe* clause is said to apply recursively!

Some Equivalence Transformations

The *always* stop clause in:

    (always F(...)
     in C(...))

is semantically equivalent to:

    (trap exit(id) with (F(...); exit(id))
     in C(...))

In general a block with no stopping clause:

    (let x : E(...);
     C(...))

is identical to a block with the simple gate:

    (trap exit(id) with exit(id)
     in (let : E(...);
         C(...))).

When no block termination actions are needed in an imperative block,
then we write:

    (trap exit with I
     in C(...))

Correspondingly, when the value passed back (by the _exit_) unconditionally is to become the result of the block, we write:

$$(\underline{trap}\ \underline{exit}(id)\ \underline{with}\ id$$
$$\underline{in}\ C(\ldots))$$

or:

$$(\underline{trap}\ \underline{exit}(id)\ \underline{with}\ \underline{return}(id)$$
$$\underline{in}\ C(\ldots))$$

dependent on whether the block (-expression) is pure or impure.

Finally: 'mixed', nested uses of _exit(e)_ and _exit_, and thus e.g.
$(\underline{trap}\ \underline{exit}\ \underline{with}\ V(\ldots)\ \underline{in}\ C(\ldots))$ and $(\underline{trap}\ \underline{exit}(id)\ \underline{with}\ F(id)\ \underline{in}\ C(\ldots$
do not make sense:

$$(\underline{trap}\ \underline{exit}(id)\ \underline{with}\ \ F_1(id)$$
$$\underline{in}\ (\ldots)$$
$$\qquad (\underline{trap}\ \underline{exit}\ \underline{with}\ F_2(\ldots)$$
$$\qquad \underline{in}\ (\ldots$$
$$\qquad\qquad exit(expr)$$
$$\qquad\qquad \ldots))$$
$$\qquad \ldots))$$

Etcetera.

Example 63:

Continuing our directory example, from examples 19 & 29, we recall:

$$DIR\ =\ Rid\ \underset{m}{\rightarrow}\ RES$$
$$RES\ =\ VAL\ |\ DIR$$

with:

$$retrieve\text{-}res(dir,ridl)=$$
$$((ridl = <>)\ \rightarrow\ dir,$$
$$T\qquad\qquad \rightarrow\ (\underline{let}\ rid = \underline{hd}\,ridl\ \underline{in}$$
$$\qquad\qquad \underline{if}\ rid \in \underline{dom}\ dir$$
$$\qquad\qquad\qquad \underline{then}\ retrieve\text{-}res(dir(rid),\underline{tl}\,ridl)$$
$$\qquad\qquad\qquad \underline{else}\ \underline{undefined}))$$
$$type:\ DIR\ Rid*\ \overset{\sim}{\rightarrow}\ RES$$

Users of the system directory each have their qualified name, uid in $Rid*$, otherwise guaranteed to designate a DIR object:

    $is\text{-}DIR(retrieve\text{-}res(Dir,uid))$

Users issue resource names, vid in Rid^+, designating values in the glo= bal directory, Dir, as follows: let dir be the directory designated by uid :

    $\underline{let}\ dir = retrieve\text{-}res(Dir,uid)$

If vid is some $<rid>$ then either rid names an entry in dir, and we are through, the result is $dir(rid)$. Or rid does not name an entry in dir. We now chop off the last Rid element of uid-- to resume the search as from the directory designated by the resulting ('remaining') uid'.
If vid is some $<rid_1,rid_2,\ldots,rid_n>$ for $n>1$, then rid_1 either names a DIR entry in dir, and we search as from the designated directory, with resource name: $<rid_2,\ldots,rid_n>$, or rid_1 does not name a DIR entry, and we 'back' up the directory hierarchy, to a level one higher, i.e. nearer the root, than that at which we originally started , or at which the search which just failed took place. We complete the above incomplete description by giving the formal definition of the proper search algo= rithm:

```
        search(uid,vid)(updown)(Dir)=
.1          (let dir = retrieve-res(Dir,uid) in
.2          (trap exit with
.3                  if updown = DOWN
.4                      then exit
.5                      else if uid = <>
.6                              then undefined
.7                              else search(fst(uid),vid)(UP)(Dir) in
.8          if len vid = 1
.9              then if hd vid ∈ dom dir
.10                      then dir(hd vid)
.11                      else exit
.12              else if hd vid ⁓∈ dom dir
.13                      then exit
.14                      else search(uid⁓<hd vid>,tl vid)(DOWN)(Dir)))

        type: Rid* Rid⁺ ⥲ ((UP|DOWN) ⥲ (DIR ⥲ RES))
```

where:

$$fst(ridl) = <ridl[i] \mid 1 \leq i \leq (\underline{len}\,ridl) - 1 >$$

Given the global directory, Dir, which we could omit as a parameter, and a 'relative' resource name, vid, we initially invoke the above search function with the users identification and the $updown$ marker set to $\underline{UP}$.

We may tie up any loose ends in your understanding of the search algo= rithm, by the following, alternative characterization: uid designates a node, N, in the directory hierarchy (or: "tree", see example 19). There are now three possibilities for vid. Either there is a downward path, towards the leaves, from N whose sequence of edge labels is vid. Then vid designates the object 'hanging' on to the other end of this path (as seen from N). If there is no such path, starting at N, then vid might still designate an object in the hierarchy, but now as from a node N', between the root of the overall directory and N. Search starts with the node N' immediately above N.

The purpose of the updown marker is to guide the trap mechanism in backing up beyond already searched 'subtrees'.

The third possibility, for vid, is that there is no resource, relative to uid, that is named by it.

Example 64:

The Zahn Event Mechanism [Zahn 74, Knuth 74, Halås 75, Bjørner 77d] sche= matically looks like:

$$\underline{loop}\;stmtl0$$
$$\underline{until}\;eid1\;\underline{do}\;stmtl1,$$
$$eid2\;\underline{do}\;stmtl2,$$
$$\ldots$$
$$eidn\;\underline{do}\;stmtln$$
$$\underline{pool}$$

An abstract syntax is:

$$Zahn \quad :: \quad Stmt^+ \ (Eid \underset{m}{\rightarrow} Stmt^+)$$

No statement in any $stmtl_i$ $(1 \leq i \leq n)$ may name any event:

event eid

on any eid_j $(1 \leq j \leq n)$. With:

$$Event \quad :: \quad Eid$$

as a statement, i.e. with:

$$Stmt \ = \ Event \ | \ Zahn \ | \ ...$$

the static well-formedness criteria can be completely specified:

```
    is-wf-Stmt(s)(eids)=
.1      cases s:
.2         (mk-Event(eid)      → eid ∈ eids,
.3          mk-Zahn(stl0,esm) → (∀c ∈ elems stl0)
.4                                  is-wf-Stmt(c)(eids ∪ dom esm)
.5                               ∧(∀eid ∈ dom esm)
.6                                (∀c ∈ elems(esm(eid)))
.7                                   is-wf-Stmt(c)(eids∖dom esm),
.8          ...                 → ...)
```

The informal, incomplete semantics is: $stmtl0$ is repeatedly interpreted. If an event is interpreted in $stmtl0$ then interpretation of $stmtl0$ is terminated. If the event names some eid_k $(1 \leq k \leq n)$, then the corresponding $stmtl_k$ is interpreted. This terminates interpretation of the mechanism. If the event names some properly containing mechanisms' eid_ℓ, then its $stmtl_\ell$ is obeyed, ..., etc. Formally, we can capture things much more succinctly:

Assuming:

$$\Sigma = (\underset{\sim}{STG} \rightarrow STG) \underline{\cup} (... \ ...)$$

we get an imperative formulation:

type: int-Stmt: $Stmt \overset{\sim}{\rightarrow} (ENV \overset{\sim}{\rightarrow} (\Sigma \overset{\sim}{\rightarrow} \Sigma))$

```
int-Stmt(s)(env)=
  cases s:
    (mk-Event(eid)
      → exit(eid),
    mk-Zahn(stl,esm)
      → (tixe  [eid → int-Stmt-list(esm(eid))(env) | eid ∈ dom esm]
        in
        while true do int-Stmt-list(stl)(env)),
    .. → ..)


int-Stmt-list(stl)(env)=
  for i=1 to len stl do int-Stmt(stl[i])(env)
```

It is thus we observe that the *tixe* construct closely parallels the Zahn event mechanism. The reader is,however, well-adviced to study [Jones 78a,78b] in order to discover the neatness of the λ-calculus semantics given there for this meta-language combinator.

PART IV ABSTRACT MODELS

Part I exemplified a complete, abstract model. Its components were: (1) abstract syntaxes for both syntactic & semantic domains; (2) [static and dynamic] consistency constraints on objects of these domains -- called *is-wf-*... functions; (3) semantic elaboration- , and (4) auxiliary function definitions.

In part II, sections 2.1, 3.1, 4.1, 5.1, 6.1 and 7 taught the notation for, and techniques of, defining domains. Sections 2.2, 3.2, 4.2, 5.2 and 6.2 taught the notation for representing objects of these domains. Sections 2.3, 3.3, 4.3, 5.3 and 6.3 finally taught the notation for, and techniques of, expressing transformations on objects.

Part III generally taught the notation for, and techniques of, stating processes, respectively composite transformations, on objects.

Part IV finally closes the story on the meta-language. With the bits and pieces of the meta-language introduced formally, and also heavily exemplified in parts II & III, we can now formally introduce the notion of function definitions. Function definitions have, however, already been extensively exemplified. Section 12 will therefore wrap-up our tutorial on the meta-language. The section can best be understood if you frequently compare the formal information and schematized "examples" with examples 0-63! That is: we do not present comprehensive, abstract models involving function definitions, although those are its prime subjects!

12 Function Definitions & Abstract Models

In section 5 we introduced the notation for denoting domains of FunCTion objects, for representing FunCTion objects, and for operations on FunCTion objects. In a sense we are here continuing the story we started giving there.

Example

Recall the abstract models of e.g. examples 0,19,29,42,51-52,54-55,58-59-60,61. On one hand we gave abstract syntaxes for syntactic domains, on the other we gave abstract syntaxes for semantic domains. The meaning of a syntactic object was a semantic object. The meaning of a Proce-dure, i.e. an object in Prc (example 40), is an object in $ARG^* \tilde{\rightarrow} (\Sigma \tilde{\rightarrow} \Sigma)$. The "thing" which takes a Prc object and yields its denotation, i.e. an $ARG^* \tilde{\rightarrow} (\Sigma \tilde{\rightarrow} \Sigma)$ object, we call a semantic elaboration function (V-Prc). It is a function. This function, like all the FunCTion objects of section 5, is described by the meta-language construct we call a function definition.

12.1 The Syntax of Function Definitions

A function definition consists of three parts:

> a header: $fid(d_1, d_2, \ldots, d_k)(d_{k+1}) \ldots (d_n) =$
>
> a body: $C(\ldots)$
>
> a type clause: <u>type</u>: $D_1 \, D_2 \, \ldots \, D_k \rightarrow (D_{k+1} \rightarrow (\ldots \rightarrow (D_n \rightarrow D') \ldots$

The body is any statement or expression clause you choose. The d_i for $1 \leq i \leq n$ are usually formal parameter identifiers. They, or any identifiers occurring in d_i's, and the function name, fid, bind free occurrences of these identifiers in $C(\ldots)$. The D_i's and D are domain expressions.

Observe the following relations between the d_i's of the formal parameter list and the D_i's of the <u>type</u> clause.

(1) If d_i is of the form $<d_{i1}, d_{i2}, \ldots, d_{im}>$, the D_i is either an identi-fier, and is then either the name of a domain defined by some abstract syntax rule:

$$D_i \ = \ D^*, \qquad D_i \ = \ D^+ \qquad \text{or}$$
$$D_i \ \subset \ D^*;$$

or D_i is (directly) either D^* or D^+ -- for some D.

(2) If d_i is of the form $\{d_{i1}, d_{i2}, \ldots, d_{im}\}$ then:
$$D_i \ = \ D\text{-}set$$

etcetera.

(3) If d_i is of the form $mk\text{-}D_i(d_{i1}, d_{i2}, \ldots, d_{im})$, then there is an abstract syntax rule:
$$D_i \ :: \ D_{i1} \ D_{i2} \ \ldots \ D_{im}$$

(4) If d_i is of the form $(d_{i1}, d_{i2}, \ldots, d_{im})$, respectively $mk(d_{i2}, d_{i2}, \ldots, d_{im})$, then D_i is of the form:
$$(D_{i1} \ D_{i2} \ \ldots \ D_{im})$$

We do not presently see a need for writing d_i's in forms other than the above, where ultimately d_{ij}'s end up as identifiers, or letting the d_i's be identifiers. In the latter case D_i's may be any appropriate domain expression, not just an identifier. Experience shows forms (1)-(2) to rarely occur.

Example 65:

This continues example 40. Now, let:

$$PROC \ = \ ARG^* \ \tilde{\rightarrow} \ (\Sigma \ \tilde{\rightarrow} \ \Sigma)$$
$$Prc \ :: \ Id^* \ Block$$

and:

$$ENV \ = \ Id \ \underset{m}{\rightarrow} \ DEN$$
$$DEN \ = \ LOC \ | \ PROC$$

With these prerequisites we could also write the $V\text{-}Prc$ elaboration function definition in this way:

$$V\text{-}Prc(p)(\rho) =$$
$$(\underline{let}\ mk\text{-}Prc(idl,bl) = p\ \underline{in}$$
$$\underline{let}\ fct(al)(\xi) =$$
$$(\ldots$$
$$\ldots)\ \underline{in}$$
$$fct))$$

' $\underline{type}:$ $Prc \overset{\sim}{\to} (ENV \overset{\sim}{\to} PROC)$

or

     $\underline{type}:$ $Prc \overset{\sim}{\to} ((Id \underset{m}{\to} DEN) \overset{\sim}{\to} (ARG^* \overset{\sim}{\to} (\Sigma \overset{\sim}{\to} \Sigma)))$

Relating the last $\underline{type}$ clause to the formal parameter list $((p)(\rho))$ we observe that p is of type Prc, ρ of type $(Id\underset{m}{\to}DEN)$, and the result yielded by $V\text{-}Prc$ is whatever remains to the right of the arrow after the ENV specification!

end-of-Example

The form of D remains to be constrained.

(5)   If the body, $C(\ldots)$, of the function definition is a statement (-block), then D is of the form:

     $\Sigma \to \Sigma$, or: $\Sigma \overset{\sim}{\to} \Sigma$

where Σ is the state resulting from global variable declarations.

(6)   If the body, $C(\ldots)$, is instead an impure expression (-block), then D is of the form:

     $\Sigma \overset{\sim}{\to} (\Sigma\ D')$, or: $\Sigma \overset{\sim}{\to} (\Sigma\ D')$

where D' denotes the domain of results yielded by $C(\ldots)$ with Σ as in (5).

(7)   If finally $C(\ldots)$ is a pure expression, D is any domain expression (etcetera -- concerning relation to $C(\ldots)$).

Example 66:

Observe that D of e.g. the pure (applicative) $I\text{-}Block$, $I\text{-}Stmt\text{-}list$, and $I\text{-}Stmt$, definitions of example 42, were all Σ. But then the Σ was not

that of any global variable state space -- since there was none --, but
explicitly defined in example 42 formula 2!

end-of-example

Schönfinckeling/Currying

The "back-to-back" ("dos-á-dos") parentheses, ")(", of the formal parameter list, e.g. to the left of d_i, may be replaced, starting with
$i=k+1$, by commas "," -- provided we simultaneoursly delete the "$\rightarrow$ ("
in the type clause, to the left of the corresponding D_i, and delete a
(matching) right parentheses (")").

Formal Examples

$$f(a)(b)(c)(d) = C(...) \quad \underline{type}: A \rightarrow (B \rightarrow (C \rightarrow (D \rightarrow E)))$$

is one way,

$$f(a,b)(c)(d) \quad = C(...) \quad \underline{type}: A\ B \rightarrow (C \rightarrow (D \rightarrow E))$$

is another way,

$$f(a,b,c)(d) \quad = C(...) \quad \underline{type}: A\ B\ C \rightarrow (D \rightarrow E)$$

and:

$$f(a,b,c,d) \quad = C(...) \quad \underline{type}: A\ B\ C\ D \rightarrow E$$

is a final way of following the so-called de-Schönfinckeling or de-
Currying rule given above.

The form:

$$f'(a)(b,c)(d) = C(...) \quad \underline{type} \quad A \rightarrow ((B\ C) \rightarrow (D \rightarrow E))$$

is, however, not a currying of f's definition above. De-Currying f'
would lead to:

$$f'(a,(b,c),d) = C(...) \quad \underline{type} \quad A\ (B\ C)\ D \rightarrow E$$

The conclusion to be drawn from the last example is that the type clause:

$$\underline{type}:\ g':\quad (D_1\ D_2\ ...\ D_n) \rightarrow D$$

is altogether distinct from:

$$\underline{type}:\ g'':\quad D_1\ D_2\ ...\ D_n \rightarrow D$$

Although we might (sloppily) write:

$$g'(d_1, d_2, \ldots, d_n)$$

where, more correctly, we should write:

$$g'((d_1, d_2, \ldots, d_n))$$

to distinguish it from the (correct):

$$g''(d_1, d_2, \ldots, d_n)$$

end-of-formal-examples

The rule for removing ")("s etc. can be used in reverse -- and this was covered in section 6.2 (see subsection on λ-Expressions). In 6.2 we "Curry", whereas here we "de-Curry". As implied by the last, formal, example above, we must observe the dual role of parentheses: delimiting and anonymous tree domain & tree object construction! If your keyboard has an extra pair of bracket/brace/parenthesis delimiters (other than our {}, <>, (), [], then use them to distinguish!

The Currying/de-Currying Rule is one form of syntàctic transformation on function definitions. It involved the header/*type*-clause 'pair'. Semantics remained invariant!

Formal Parameter Syntactic Transformations

Another kind of syntactic transformation rule involves the header/body 'pair'. It can most simply be dealt with by listing the following semantic identities:

(1)
$$f(<d_{i1}, d_{i2}, \ldots, d_{im}>) = C(\ldots)$$
$$\equiv$$
$$f(d) = (\underline{let} <d_{i1}, d_{i2}, \ldots, d_{im}> = d \underline{in} \, C(\ldots))$$

(2)
$$f(mk\text{-}D_i(d_{i1}, d_{i2}, \ldots, d_{im})) = C(\ldots)$$
$$\equiv$$
$$f(d) = (\underline{let} \, mk\text{-}D_i(d_{i1}, d_{i2}, \ldots, d_{im}) = d \underline{in} \, C(\ldots))$$

etc.. It is here assumed that d is not free in $C(\ldots)$.

12.2 The Semantics of Function Definitions & Abstract Models

Scope & Binding

The identifiers occurring in the header of a function definition bind
all their (free) occurrences in the body! Usually there is no need to
re-define identifiers in any block.

General

An abstract model consists of a set of function definitions, a set of
abstract syntaxes, and possibly also a set of variable declarations.
All names of defined functions, domains and variables are globally known.

The function denoted by any such, global function definition headers'
first identifier, i.e. by the function identifier, fid, is the one you
would expect. Formally: it is the least fix-point solution to the equation set that the function definitions form.

Informally we observe that an abstract model is all definitions -- and
no real "action"! Nobody really invokes any of the specified functions.

An abstract model defines a class of systems.

Examples

Example 0 defined the structure and possible behavioral patterns of a
class of grocery stores.

Examples 3-8, 12-13, 17-18, 20-25, 27-28 & 35 defined fragments of
classes and manipulations of file systems.

Examples 19,29&62 defined the structure and operations on a class of
operating system directories.

Examples 30-34, 36-38,40,42-43,47,49,61,63,70 defined fragments of structures and meaning of some class of programs, i.e. a source language.

If you come with a particular grocery store, or a particular file system, or a particular directory and a corresponding action (e.g. pur-

chase, read, respectively *catalog),* then the definitions, i.e. the models, tell you what to expect happening. If you come with a particular state configuration **and** a program then the model will compute you a result.

However, you need not come with a semantic **and** a syntactic object. Come just with a syntactic object. And the model will produce the answer: this syntactic object denotes such-and-such a function from semantic objects to semantic objects.

If you are asking for the meaning of say a *Purchase,* example 0, then "stick" your *mk-Purchase(...)* object into the *Elab-Purchase* semantic function. That is: **you** decide which part of your model to concentrate on. Therefore we, the model builders, do not tell you which one semantic function is the most important, i.e. which one should always be invoked first when "starting up" a model!

end-of-example

A Note on Input/Output

Based on the discussion (of example 69) it should now be easy to understand why the meta-language has no *input/output* constructs.

A program in the meta-language defines a function. The meaning function from syntactic objects to semantic objects. The prime means for expressing this function is the set of function definitions. The abstract syntaxes describe the domain and range of this meaning function: the class of syntactic objects, and the class of semantic objects.

PART V: MISCELLANEAE

There remains only to formally introduce the elementary domains used in examples throughout this tutorial.

13 *ELEMentary* Data Types

Usually a programming language comes ready-made, equipped with a set of basic data types.

A number of such have been employed in the examples given so far. These are:

.1 Rational *NUM*bers, *INTeG*ers (...,$-2,-1,0,1,2$,...), *N*atural numbers -- with the operations: $+$, $-$, $*$, $\searrow$, $<$, $\leq$, $=$, $\neq$, $\geq$, $>$, exponentiation, *ceil*, *floor*, etc.

.2 *BOOL*eans (*true*, *false*) -- with the operations: $\sim$, $\vee$, $\wedge$, $\supset$, $\equiv$.

.3 *QUOT*ations ($\underline{A}$, $\underline{AB}$, $\underline{ABC}$, ...) -- with the operations: $=$, $\neq$.

.4 *TOKEN*s (-- for which no representation is required --) -- with the operations: $=$, $\neq$.

Other elementary data types could be considered.

(A data type is a set of objects and a set of operations. For a data type to be elementary its objects must all be considered elementary, i.e. having no structure.

The data types so far formally introduced were:

$$SET; \quad TUPLE; \quad MAP, \; FCT; \quad TREE$$

They were all *COMP*osite. Thus the *OBJ*ects of the meta-language satisfy:

$$OBJ \quad = \quad ELEM \mid COMP$$
$$COMP \quad = \quad SET \mid TUPLE \mid MAP \mid FCT \mid TREE$$

where the five sub-domains of *COMP* are all considered disjoint.

In this tutorial we take *ELEM* to be:

$$ELEM \quad = \quad NUM \mid BOOL \mid QUOT \mid TOKEN$$

The following relations apply:

$$N_1 \subset N_0 \subset INTG \subset NUM$$

Otherwise the *ELEM* sub-domains are considered disjoint.)

If you need to introduce further objects or domains of objects -- by almost all means! At least as long as they are in keeping with the principles of abstractions (exemplified), and thus of the meta-language.

13.1 Rational *NUM*bers

Useful domains are:

NUM   Rational numbers, i.e. the numbers that arise as the result of integer (non-zero) divisions.

INTG   Integers

N_0 Natural numbers, in particular the positive integers including 0.

N_1 Natural numbers larger than or equal to 1.

We only find a need to represent the integers:

$$\ldots, -3, -2, -1, 0, 1, 2, 3, \ldots$$

Useful operators/operations are:

+   addition

-           subtraction

*   multiplication

/   division: integer division leaving quotient voiding remainder, if *INTG* (N_0, or N_1) result is expected.

etc. If you would like to use:

ceil r   smallest integer larger than or equal to its only operan

floor r   largest integer smaller than or equal to its only operan

i^j the exponentiation of i by j

etc., then we see no problem in you doing so. Etcetera -- for the introduction and proper explanation of your own operators (*mod*, *ln*, *rmd*,
sgn, ...).

Programming Note

We abstract numerals by the numbers they denote. Thus in example 49 constants of expressions are *INTeGers* (and *BOOLeans*).

13.2 *BOOLeans* & Logic Expressions

We name the domain in question:

> *BOOL*   Booleans values

In this tutorial we count on it having just two objects which we represent:

> *true*, *false*

Useful operators/operations are:

> ~   negation,
> ∨   or,
> ∧, &   and (two forms provided), and
> ⊃, →   implication (two forms provided).

In order to compact formulae we take the ∧, ∨, ⊃ operators as non-commutative! Thus if in *b1∧b2 b1* is *false*, *b2* is never evaluated. Likewise
if *b1* in *b1∨b2* is *true*.

Predicate Expressions

Besides the propositional expressions which can be formed using expressions denoting booleans and the above, conventional operators, proper
use of the meta-language heavily relies on the possibility of forming
quantified expressions:

$$(\forall x)(P(x)) \qquad\qquad (\forall x \in Set)(P(x))$$

$$(\exists x)(P(x)) \qquad\qquad (\exists x \in Set)(P(x))$$

$$(\exists!x)(P(x)) \qquad\qquad (\exists!x \in Set)(P(x))$$

We 'read' the above expressions: "for all x the predicate $P(x)$ is true", "for all x in the set Set the predicate $P(x)$ is true", "there exists an x for which the predicate $P(x)$ is true", "there exists an x in the set Set for which the predicate $P(x)$ is true", "there exists a unique x for which $P(x)$ holds", and "there exists a unique x in the set Set for which $P(x)$ holds". In your reading the formulae 'aloud' you can e.g. vary as we did in the last two forms -- and you can instead of 'x' say 'objects x' or 'object x', etc.

Examples

We refer to examples 0, 9, 10, 11, 31 (10), etc.

Comments:

For the case where

$$Set = \{o_1, o_2, \ldots, o_n\}$$

the quantified expressions can be simply transliterated:

$(\forall x \in Set)(P(x))$
$\triangle \quad P(o_1) \wedge P(o_2) \wedge \ldots \wedge P(o_n)$

$(\exists x \in Set)(P(x))$
$\triangle \quad P(o_1) \vee P(o_2) \vee \ldots \vee P(o_n)$

$(\exists!x \in Set)(P(x))$
$\triangle \quad$ _if_ $(\exists x \in Set)(P(x))$
$\qquad$ _then_ ($\underline{let}$ $o \in Set$ $\underline{be}$ $\underline{s.t.}$ $P(o)$ $\underline{in}$
$\qquad\qquad (\forall x \in Set \setminus \{o\})(\sim P(x)))$
$\qquad$ _else_ _false_

Also:

$$\sim(\exists x)(P(x)) \quad \equiv \quad (\forall x)(\sim P(x))$$
$$\sim(\exists x \in Set)(P(x)) \quad \equiv \quad (\forall x \in Set)(\sim P(x))$$

13.3 *QUOT*ations

The subject domain is here named:

QUOT

Quotations are objects whose representations can be said to denote themselves. They are not to be confused with characters and characterstrings of conventional languages. We choose under-dashed sequences of (preferably) upper-case letters, and (rarely) other symbols:

$\underline{A}, \underline{B}, \ldots, \underline{Z}, \underline{AA}, \underline{AB}, \ldots, \underline{AZ}, \underline{BA}, \underline{BB}, \ldots, \underline{BZ}, \ldots, \underline{AA\ldots A}, \ldots$

The only two operations intended are:

$=$ equality

$\neq$ non-equality

(Quotations correspond to the enumerated type objects of PASCAL, but we define no ordering on them.) If you wish to use quotations to model characters then observe that $\underline{ABC}$ is indivisible; and if you wish to use these modeling strings, then make tuples of quotations!

Example 67:

The following formulae may complete the syntax of example 49:

$$Int\text{-}Op \quad = \quad \underline{ADD} \mid \underline{SUB} \mid \underline{MPY} \mid \underline{DIV}$$
$$Bool\text{-}Op \quad = \quad \underline{AND} \mid \underline{OR} \mid \underline{IMP}$$
$$Rel\text{-}Op \quad = \quad \underline{LARG} \mid \underline{LAEQ} \mid \underline{EQ} \mid \underline{NEQ} \mid \underline{SMAL} \mid \underline{SMEQ}$$

An evaluation function for the expressions of example 49 might use these quotations:

```
eval-Expr(e)(ρ)=
    cases e:
        (mk-Infix(le,op,re)
            → (let lv : eval-Expr(le)(ρ),
                   rv : eval-Expr(re)(ρ);
                cases op:
                    (ADD  → return(lv+rv),
                     SUB  → return(lv-rv),
                     ...
                     AND  → return(lv∧rv),
                     OR   → return(lv∨rv),
                     ...
                     LARG → return(lv>rv),
                     ...
                     SMEQ → return(lv≤rv))),
         ...)
    type:  Expr ⇴ (ENV ⇴ (Σ ⇴ (Σ VAL)))
```

Here it was assumed that *lv* and *rv* were of the appropriate type. Suppose the language is statically type checkable, then:

```
is-wf-Expr(e)(dict)=
    cases e:
        (mk-Infix(le,op,re)
            → (is-wf-Expr(le)∧
               is-wf-Expr(re)∧
               (let lt = e-tp(le)(dict),
                    rt = e-tp(re)(dict);
                (is-Bool-Op(op) → lt = BOOL = rt,
                 T              → lt = INT = rt))),
         ...)
    type:  Expr → (DICT → BOOL)
```

where:

```
DICT  =  Id →m (INT|BOOL)
```

13.4 TOKENs

The subject domain is named:

TOKEN

Tokens are objects for which we seek no representation.

The only two operations provided are:

=	equality
≠	in-equality

Example 68 :

When modeling the identifiers of software systems (e.g. the operating system directory, examples 19 & 29; the file system file identifiers, examples 20, 24-25, 27-28 & 36; the source language variable procedure and formal parameter identifèrs, examples 30-31-32-33, 36 etcetera), when modeling labels of a goto language (example 61), or when modeling storage addresses, or as we call them: Locations (example 30-31) we use *TOKEN*s. That is:

Rid	= *TOKEN*	(exs. 19),
Fid	= *TOKEN*	(exs. 20),
Id	= *TOKEN*	(exs. 30-33, 36,...),
Lbl	= *TOKEN*	(ex. 61),
LOC	= *TOKEN*	(ex. 30), and
Scalar-Loc	= *TOKEN*	(ex. 31).

When in e.g. examples 24-25 & 27 we write suitably decorated *fid*'s, these are meta-language identifiers naming otherwise unrepresented *Fid* objects.

When in example 31 we need to 'generate' new *Scalar-Loc*ations, then we "pull them out of the *Scalar-Loc* bag":

    (let sloc ∈ Scalar-Loc be s.t. P(sloc)
    ...)

sloc names a *TOKEN* object. We need not know "what it looks like"!

PART VI: POSTLUDE

This completes the informal introduction to the meta-language.

ACKNOWLEDGEMENTS:

The author is pleased to acknowledge all of his former colleagues of the IBM Vienna Laboratory, and Mrs.Jytte Søllested for her expert handling of eight IBM "golf ball" type-fonts!

EXAMPLE INDEX:

Number:	Subject:	Meta-Language Constructs:
0.	Grocery Store.	A Complete Model: Abstract Syntax, Domains, Objects, Operations, Func= tion Definitions.
1.	School-Class of Students.	Section Introduction: Sets, Ab= stract Syntax, Domains, Objects, Operations.
2.	Collections of Classes of Integers.	Set Domains.
3.	Files: Unordered Collec= tions of Records.	-"-
4.	Collections of Integers.	Explicit Set Constructions.
5.	Records, Files.	-"-
6.	-"-	-"-
7.	File Manipulations & Record Handling.	Primitive Set Operations.
8.	-"-	Imperative Set Operations.
9.	Equivalence Classes.	Complete Specification: Abstract Syntax, Function Definitions.
10.	Coarsest Partitionings.	-"-
11.	Pascal Triangle.	Section Introduction: Tuples, Do= mains, Objects, Applicative & Im= perative Function Definitions.
12.	Ordered Fields of Records.	Tuple Domains, Abstract Syntax.
13.	-"-	Tuple Enumerations.

214

14.	Fibonacci Numbers	Tuple Enumerations.
15.	Pascal Triangle.	Implicit Tuple Enumeration.
16.	Value Stacks.	Tuple Domain & Primitive Tuple Operations.
17.	File Handling.	Primitive Tuple Operations.
18.	-"-	Applicative & Imperative Tuple Operations.
19.	System Directory.	Section Introduction: Maps, Ab= stract Syntax, Domains, Objects, Operations, Function Definitions.
20.	File System & Files.	Map Domains.
21.	Files.	-"-
22.	-"-	-"-
23.	-"-	-"-
24.	File System & Files.	Explicit Map Constructions.
25.	-"-	Implicit Map Constructions.
26.	Conceptual Example.	Implicit Map Construction: the Scope of Identifiers, Abstract Syntax.
27.	File System & Files.	Primitive Map Operations.
28.	-"-	Imperative Map Operations.
29.	System Directory.	Function Definitions, Map Opera= tions.
30.	Progr.Lang.:States & Envi= ronments as Models of Var= iables & Scopes.	Map Domains, Primitive Operations, Abstract Syntax.

31. Prgr.Lang.:Model of Block   Abstract Syntax, Map Domains,
    Concept & Storage.   Function Definitions.

32. Prgr.Lang.:Blocks.   Trees, Syntactic Domains.

33. -"-   Trees, Abstract Syntax.

34. Prgr.Lang.:Statements.   -"-

35. System Directory & Direc=   -"-
    tory Update Commands.

36. Prgr.Lang.:Procedures.   -"-

37. Prgr.Lang.:Statements.   Selector Functions, Abstract
                                     Syntax.

38. -"-   -"-

39. Factorial Function.   Section Introduction: Functions,
                                     Function Definitions, Block Ex=
                                     pressions.

40. Prgr.Lang.:Procedures.   Function Denotations, Semantic
                                     Domains, Syntactic Domains, Ab=
                                     stract Syntax, Elaboration Func=
                                     tions.

41. Meta-Language: Type of   Function Types.
    Primitive Operations.

42. Prgr.Lang.:Blocks & Sta=   Abstract Syntax, Elaboration
    tements.   Function Definitions, Function
                                     Application.

43. Prgr.Lang.   Section Introduction: Abstract
                                     Syntax.

44-46. Conceptual Examples.   Abstract Syntax.

47. Prgr.Lang.:Syntax   *is*-functions.

48. Reflexive Domains.   Abstract Syntax, Map Domains,
                                  Map Objects.

49. Prgr.Lang.:Expressions.   Abstract Syntax, McCarthy Condi=
                                  tional Clause, Function Definition.

50. Factorial Function.   Section Introduction: Variables,
                                  Applicative & Imperative Function
                                  Definitions, Expression Blocks,
                                  The State.

51. Prgr.Lang.:Modeling   Global Variables, The State.
    Variables, Input, Output.

52. Prgr.Lang.:Assignment,   Elaboration- & Auxiliary Function
    Input, Output.   Definitions, Variables, Assign=
                                  ment.

53. Conceptual Example.   Imperative & Applicative Combi=
                                  nators.

54. Prgr.Lang.:Structured   Abstract Syntax, Semantic Domains,
    Statements.   Structured Clauses: *cases*, *if*,
                                  Applicative Definitions of Impe=
                                  rative Features.

55. Prgr.Lang.:For-To-Do   Abstract Syntax, Semantic Domains,
    Statement.   Elaboration Function Definitions.

56. Prgr.Lang.:Compound   -"- &: *for-to-do*, Imperative De=
    Statement.   finition.

57. -"-   -"-, but Applicative Definition.

58. Prgr.Lang.:Arbitrary   -"-
    Ordering.

59. -"-, For-All Statement.   -"-

60. Prgr.Lang.: While-Do   Recursive ("sledge-hammer") Defi=
                                  nition of ("egg") *while*.

1.	Prgr.Lang.:Guarded Repe= titive Command.	Elaboration Function Definition, Applicative Definition.
2.	Prgr.Lang.:<u>GOTO</u> & Block Concept Model.	*exit* and *tixe*
3.	System Directory: Hierar= chical Entry Access.	*exit* and *trap*
4.	Prgr.Lang.:Zahn's Event Mechanism.	*exit* and *tixe*
5.	Prgr.Lang.:Procedures.	Abstract Syntax, Syntactic & Se= mantic Domains, Elaboration Func= tion Definitions.
6.	Prgr.Lang.:States.	Imperative & Applicative 'States'.
7.	Prgr.Lang.:Expressions.	Quotations.
8.	Prgr.Lang.:Names & Ad= dresses.	Tokens.

THE META-LANGUAGE: A REFERENCE MANUAL

Cliff B.Jones

Abstract:

The recent work of the Vienna Laboratory on the sub=
ject of semantic definitions has used the "denotational
semantics" approach. Although this is a clear break
with the earlier abstract interpreter approach, the
newer meta-language has tried to preserve and even
improve upon the readability of the earlier "*VDL*" no=
tation. The meta-language described here has been used
in the definitions of large programming languages and
systems. This paper is not a tutorial; rather it pro=
vides a reference document for the meta-language.

CONTENTS

0. Introduction   220

1. Logic Notation   223

2. Elementary Objects   224

3. Composite Objects   225
    3.1 Sets   226
    3.2 Pairs   228
    3.3 Maps   228
    3.4 Tuples   230
    3.5 Trees   231
    3.6 Functions   232
    3.7 Implicit Definition   235

4. Object Description   236

5. The rôle of "undefined"   239

6. Defining Semantics   240
    6.1 States & State Transitions   241
    6.2 A Macro-expansion Process   243
    6.3 Simplifying Extended Expressions   251
    6.4 Basic Combinators   258
    6.5 Other Issues   258

    APPENDICES
    I   Concrete Syntax   261
    II   Conventions   265
    III Example definition   266-277

0. INTRODUCTION

This paper is intended to provide a reference document which describes
the meta-language used throughout this volume. It is equally important
to appreciate which objectives are not being aimed for here. On the
one hand this document is definitely not a tutorial, neither for denotational semantics nor for the specific meta-language used. In much
of this paper no motivation at all is provided, the reader who is not
familiar with the general ideas is recommended to read Bjørner 78b before attempting to use this paper. On the other hand this document
does not provide a formal "foundation" for the meta-language in the
style of, say, Mosses 75.

The aim of this "reference manual" is to provide a document where
readers or writers of the meta-language can find a description of
its constructs in terms of some other notation. As such, this document
does not necessarily introduce all terms and notation in a strict left-
to-right order.

The notation to be introduced is primarily intended for the purpose of
defining languages or systems using the approach known as "denotational
semantics"; although it can also be used as a sort of programming language this is not its purpose. A general "denotational" approach can
be expected to yield a definition which can be viewed in four parts:

    i)   Abstract syntax of the language to be studied
    ii)   Context Conditions
    iii) Semantic Objects
    iv)   Meaning function(s)

Before embarking on defining the meaning of a language it is obviously
essential to fix what ("object") language is to be studied: this is
the task of the first two parts of a definition. The abstract syntax
defines a class of objects which are abstractions of the actual texts
of the language. (The class of texts would be described by a concrete
syntax: this subject is widely documented and in consequence need not
occupy space here). The abstract syntax of a language is "context free"
and it is thus impossible to restrict the class of abstract texts to
those which are obviously meaningful. For example, in a programming
language it is impossible to specify that all valid programs must use
only declared identifiers. Rather than leave such checking to cloud
the meaning functions, a separate section defines predicates over the

objects of the abstract syntax. Such predicates define a sub-set of
the objects which are specified by the abstract syntax; those objects
which satisfy the context conditions are said to be "well-formed".
The meaning functions provide denotations only for well-formed objects.

The third part of a definition defines sets of semantic objects. Both
the denotations chosen for a language (e.g. continuous functions over
states) and any auxiliary objects such as environments are described.
In a sense, this part of a definition is unnecessary! The abstract
syntax is the only way in which the class of source objects is delimit-
ed (unless a translator function from concrete syntax is written); the
denotations and auxiliary objects which can be created by the meaning
functions could, in fact, be deduced from those functions. However,
the separate description of semantic objects is both an invaluable aid
to the reader of a definition and an important tool to be used during
the development of the meaning functions.

The first three parts of a definition, then, have defined a class of
well-formed abstract objects and a class of semantic objects: meaning
is defined by a function mapping the former into the latter. This mapping will be defined by a family of (recursive) functions. An objective
of a denotational definition is that the meaning of a composite object
should be created from the meanings of its components. Given this objective there will normally be one semantic function for each sub-class
of abstract objects.

Having outlined the "denotational method" in general, a few comments
can now be made on the spefic meta-language used in this volume. (The
notation was referred to within the Vienna Lab as "Meta-IV"). It is
important to appreciate that the authors do not regard the meta-language as any sort of fixed standard. Rather, it is offerred as a basis
which has been shown to be adequate for a variety of definitions, and
which can be expected to be adequate for defining other related systems.
Even for such systems the existance of a body of notation does not eli-
minate the difficulties of choosing suitable abstractions for use in
their definition. Moreover, it must be realized that an attempt to apply the ideas of denotational semantics to systems of an entirely different nature will require the invention of suitable extensions to the
notation presented here. There does, however, appear to be some virtue
in a degree of standardisation in the basic notation.

The notation used by the Oxford University group (cf. Stoy 74) for denotational semantics definitions is rather different in appearance from that presented here and it may be useful to speculate as to the cause. The Oxford group have been principally concerned with questions of foundations and have worked with relatively small languages. They have, in fact, chosen languages which illustrate the key problems with a minimum of unnecessary detail. In contrast, the Vienna group have tended to tackle larger (given) languages and systems. Furthermore, the languages have usually been defined "warts and all". For a definition of a certain size it becomes virtually impossible to remember enough conventions to permit use of single character names, type clauses given implicitly by Greek letters chosen for parameters etc. Thus, for large languages a different style is adopted to provide a readable definition. For example, a syntax is employed which is as abstract as possible, (longer) function names are used in the hope that they are suggestive to the reader etc. It is interesting to compare the relative merits of succinctness and readability on Mosses 74 and Henhapl 78.

The various topics are distributed throughout this paper as follows. Section 4 is concerned with the abstract syntax notation. The actual objects (and their operators) which have been found to be of use in earlier applications of this meta-language, are described in sections 2 and 3. Sections 1 and 5 briefly outline the logic notation used. The heart of the meta-language is the means for defining and combining meaning functions: this is described in section 6. The subject of arbitrary order or merging of operations is completely omitted from this paper for reasons given in section 6.

An outline concrete syntax for the meta-language is given in appendix I and appendix II lists some conventions which have been used in earlier definitions. Appendix III contains a definition of a small language, close study of which should provide the reader with a clear understanding of the use of the notation.

1. LOGIC NOTATION

In defining any language something has to be taken as a basis. For the description of the operators of the meta-language, the first-order predicate calculus with equality is chosen. There are two reasons for this choice. Firstly, a consistent and complete axiomatic definition can be provided (e.g. Kleene 67). Secondly, it is widely enough understood that the presentation here can be restricted to providing "readings" for the particular symbols chosen.

Fig. 1-1 displays the notation adopted throughout this paper. The constraints on bounded quantifiers are used in preference to implications (Thus:

$$(\forall x \in Nat^0)(\neg is\text{-}prime(4 \cdot x)) \qquad \text{, rather than}$$
$$(\forall x)(x \in Nat^0 \Rightarrow \neg is\text{-}prime(4 \cdot x)) \;)$$

in order to reduce the number of "undefined" operands. However, the problem of the meaning of the logical operators with undefined values must be faced and is discussed in section 5. The constraints on quantifiers may be omitted where the context makes them obvious.

The (iota) description operator yields the unique object satisfying a predicate. It is an error to use the operator if no, or more than one, value satisfies the predicate. Thus:

$$(\exists! x_0 \in X)(p(x_0)) \Rightarrow p((\iota x \in X)(p(x)))$$

Here again, the constraint may be omitted if it is clear from the context.

Symbol	Reading
TRUE	} *truth values*
FALSE	
&	*and*
v	*or*
➡	*implies*
↔	*equivalence*
¬	*not*
∀	*for all*
∃	*there exists*
∃!	*there exists exactly one*
	the unique object
(∀x∈X)(p(x))	*for all members of set X, p(x)*
(∀x|c(x))(p(x))	*for all x satisfying c, p(x)*

similarly for other quantifiers

fig. 1-1: Logic notation

2. ELEMENTARY OBJECTS

In writing a definition it will normally be necessary to use objects
which are structured (i.e. composite). Some types of composite objects,
together with their operators, are described in section 3. A definition
will, however, also have to employ certain basic objects whose structure is of no interest for the system being defined. For example, many
definitions will require natural numbers but will wish to treat them
as elementary objects.

Two standard objects, the truth values, have already been introduced:

TRUE,   *FALSE*

Another object which will be explained below (roughly, it is a place holder for an omitted branch in a tree) is:

NIL

An author may also enumerate any other objects required for his definition in a notation explained in section 4. The only property which is assumed about elementary objects is that they are distinguishable. Thus two meaningful operators are the equality operators (=,≠). Among the elementary objects to be enumerated for a definition are "references" (see section 6.1).

In addition to those objects which can be enumerated, a definition will usually also require known objects like natural numbers, integers, reals etc. With such familiar sets one may also wish to adopt some of their standard operators (e.g. $<,\leq,\sqrt{}$). Any definition should include a list of such assumed objects and their operators. Section 3.1 lists some suggested names for sets of such objects. All definitions will be assumed to use the standard propositional connectives on the truth values.

3. COMPOSITE OBJECTS

A definition will have to define a number of classes of objects, not least the texts of the language or system being defined. The style of defining classes of objects is described in section 4. This section will introduce a number of classes of objects which are useful in building abstractions appropriate for most systems. The objects given here, in distinction to those discussed in section 2, have structure. Thus operations will be introduced for manipulating (building), decomposing and interrogating the objects of each class. The test for equality is available for each class and will be defined.

The objects are defined in the first place in terms of the logic notation introduced in section 1; there is then a layer by layer construction of each more complex class of objects. Because of this construction, certain objects of different classes are formally identical:

in fact definitions will ensure that the types are not mixed.

3.1 Sets

Sets are characterized by the members they contain. Testing whether an object is a member of a set is achieved by a two place infix operator:

$e \in S$

This is a propositional expression and thus yields *TRUE* or *FALSE*.

Its converse is written:

$e \notin S \leftrightarrow \neg(e \in S)$

Fig. 3-1 uses the test for membership to define the set operators. Notice that the distributed <u>union</u> is defined only for sets of sets.

Set Operator	Definition
$S = T$	$e \in S \leftrightarrow e \in T$
$S \cup T$	$\{x \mid x \in S \lor x \in T\}$
<u>union</u> S	$\{e \mid (\exists s \in S)(e \in s)\}$
$S \cap T$	$\{x \mid x \in S \ \& \ x \in T\}$
$S - T$	$\{x \mid x \in S \ \& \ x \notin T\}$
$S \subseteq T$	$e \in S \rightarrow e \in T$
$s \subset T$	$S \subseteq T \ \& \ S \neq T$
<u>power</u>S	$\{s \mid s \subseteq S\}$

Fig. 3-1: Set operators

The basic way of constructing sets is by implicitly defining, via a predicate, those elements of some other set which are to be included:

$$x_0 \in \{x \in S \,|\, p(x)\} \iff (x_0 \in s \,\&\, p(x_0))$$

Where some set is clearly implied as the range by the context in which a formula appears, the "$\in S$" can be omitted.

It is possible to view the explicit enumeration of the elements of a (finite) set as an abbreviation:

$$\{x_1, x_2, \ldots, x_n\} \overset{\Delta}{=} \{x \,|\, x=x_1 \lor x=x_2 \lor \ldots \lor x=x_n\}$$

In particular, for the empty set:

$$\{\} \overset{\Delta}{=} \{x \,|\, x \neq x\}$$

Thus:

$$\neg(\exists x_0)(x_0 \in \{\})$$

For two integers a set of integers can be defined by the abbreviation:

$$\{i:j\} \overset{\Delta}{=} \{x \in Int \,|\, i \leq x \leq j\}$$

Where context makes clear which variable(s) is (are) to be considered bound:

$$\{f(x) \,|\, p(x)\} \overset{\Delta}{=} \{z \,|\, (\exists x)(p(x) \,\&\, z=f(x))\}$$

The number of elements in a finite set can be determined by:

$$\underline{card}\ \{\} = 0$$
$$x_0 \notin S \rightarrow \underline{card}\ (S \cup \{x_0\}) = \underline{card}\ S + 1$$

It is well known that an unconstrained view of sets will permit the possibility of paradoxical sets (e.g. $\{S \,|\, S \notin S\}$): starting from non-paradoxical sets and using the operators given here this danger does not exist.

The following standard sets will be used:

$$Bool = \{\underline{TRUE}, \underline{FALSE}\}$$
$$Nat\ \ = \{1, 2, \ldots\}$$

$$Nat^0 = \{0, 1, 2, ...\}$$
$$Int = \{..., -1, 0, 1, ...\}$$

3.2 Pairs

In building the subsequent notion of *MAP* it will be necessary to have
a notation for ordered pairs: such a notation is introduced in this
section but will not be used other than within section 3 (a general
tuple notation is developed in section 3.4.)

The objects considered here will be best understood as ordered pairs:

$$pair(e_1, e_2) \in PAIR$$

They, and their operations, are defined via sets:

$$pair(e_1, e_2) = \{e_1, \{e_1, e_2\}\}$$

Selection of elements is achieved by:

$$first(pr) = (\imath e_1)(\exists e_2)(pr = \{e_1, \{e_1, e_2\}\})$$
$$second(pr) = (\imath e_2)(\exists e_1)(pr = \{e_1, \{e_1, e_2\}\})$$

Notice that it is an immediate consequence of the definition that:

$$pair(e_1, e_2) = pair(e_1', e_2') \longleftrightarrow (e_1 = e_1' \ \& \ e_2 = e_2')$$

3.3 Maps

The *Maps* to be introduced here are a restiction of the general functions
to be covered in section 3.6. The restriction is that the domain of a
map is finite and constructable (i.e. every way of generating a map
also shows how to compute the domain). The usefulness of this restricted class of functions (along with its separate notation) comes from
their use in a definition.

The basic model is a set of pairs which pair a unique second element
with any first element:

for $m \in Map$:

$$p_1, \; p_2 \in m \; \& \; first(p_1) = first(p_2) \;\rightarrow\; p_1 = p_2$$

For some *MAP* m, the operations of domain, application and range are defined in terms of the set model:

$\underline{domm} = \{d \mid (\exists p \in m)(d = first(p))\}$

$m(d) = (\imath r)(pair(d,r) \in m)$

$\underline{rngm} = \{m(d) \mid d \in \underline{domm}\}$

The actual computation of the domain of a map can be shown for each of the map generating expressions below. (The range operation is also recursive because domain is). Notice that applying a map to an element outside its domain is undefined.

The map constructors and operators are defined in *fig. 3-2*. The basic way of constructing maps is by implicitly defining the pairs they should contain. Strictly, the set from which d is chosen should be specified but this will be assumed to be given by the context. As with sets a finite enumeration of the elements in a map is regarded as an abbreviation.

Notation	Meaning	Domain
$[d{\rightarrow}r \mid p(d,r)]$	$\{pair(d,r) \mid p(d,r)\}$	$\{d \mid (\exists r)(p(d,r))\}$
$[d_1 {\mapsto} r_1, \ldots, d_n {\rightarrow} r_n]$	$[d{\rightarrow}r \mid (d{=}d_1 \; \& \; r{=}r_1) \lor \ldots$ $(d{=}d_n \; \& \; r{=}r_n)]$	$\{d_1, \ldots, d_n\}$
for: $\underline{domm} \cap \underline{domn} = \{\}$ $\qquad m \cup n$	$\left.\right\}\; m \cup n$	$\underline{domm} \cup \underline{domn}$
$m{+}n$	$[d{\rightarrow}r \mid d \in \underline{domm} \; \& \; r{=}n(d) \lor$ $d \in (\underline{domm}{-}\underline{dom}n) \; \& \; r{=}m(d)]$	$\underline{domm} \cup \underline{domn}$
$m \mid s$	$[d{\rightarrow}m(d) \mid d \in (\underline{domm} \cap s)]$	$\underline{domm} \cap s$
$m \backslash s$	$[d{\rightarrow}m(d) \mid d \in (\underline{domm}{-}s)]$	$\underline{domm} - s$
for: $\underline{rngn} \subseteq \underline{domm}$ $\qquad m \overset{\cdot}{\cdot} n$	$\left.\right\}\; [d{\rightarrow}m(n(d)) \mid d \in \underline{domn}]$	$\underline{domn}$

fig. 3-2: Maps

Notice that the union operator is defined between maps whose domains
are disjoint. The normal (set) union symbol will be used because it
is clear that maps are being combined.

3.4 Tuples

The objects described here will be familiar as unbounded (finite) lists,
but following Reynolds 76 we yield in the face of the established use
in computing of this term. (Although the term "list" will be used in
informal discussions).

Tuples are modelled on maps and are either empty or have a head and a
tail component. The tail component of a tuple is always a tuple. Tuples
are finite, that is after a finite number of selections of the tail
component an empty tuple will be located.

$$t \in TUPLE \rightarrow (\underline{dom}t = \{\} \vee$$
$$\underline{dom}t = \{\underline{HD}, \underline{TL}\} \ \& \ t(\underline{TL}) \in TUPLE)$$

The tuple notation (including explicit enumeration) is defined in $fig.$
3-3. Unlike sets, tuples provide an ordered access to their elements
(by $\underline{hd}$ or indexing). For this reason care must be taken in the choice
of an implicit list notation. In order to ensure that an order is defined for the created list, generation is defined only for (modifica-
tion of) a sub-list of a given list. Thus:

$$<f(tup(i))|p(tup(i))>$$

Notice that the distributed concatenation ("$\underline{conc}$") is only defined for
tuples of tuples.

Notation	Definition
$<>$	$[\,]$
$<e_1,\ldots,e_n>$	$[\underline{HD}{\rightarrow}e_1,\ \underline{TL}{\rightarrow}[\ldots,\underline{TL}{\rightarrow}[\underline{HD}{\rightarrow}e_n,\underline{TL}{\rightarrow}[\,]]\ldots]]$
for $tup{\neq}<>$: $\underline{hd}tup$	$tup(\underline{HD})$
for $tup{\neq}<>$: $\underline{tl}tup$	$tup(\underline{TL})$
$\underline{len}tup$	$(\underline{HD}{\notin}\underline{dom}tup{\rightarrow}0,T{\rightarrow}\underline{len}\underline{tl}tup{+}1)$
for $1{\leq}i{\leq}\underline{len}tup{:}\ tup(i)$	$(i{=}1{\rightarrow}\underline{hd}tup,\quad T{\rightarrow}(\underline{tl}tup)(i{-}1))$
$tup1^{\wedge}tup2$	$(\iota\ tup)(\underline{len}tup = \underline{len}tup1{+}\underline{len}tup2\ \&$ $(1{\leq}i{\leq}\underline{len}tup1\ {\rightarrow}\ tup(i){=}tup1(i))\ \&$ $(1{\leq}i{\leq}\underline{len}tup2\ {\rightarrow}\ tup(i{+}\underline{len}tup1){=}tup2(i)))$
$\underline{conc}\ tt$	$(tt{=}<>\ \rightarrow\ <>,\ T{\rightarrow}\underline{hd}tt^{\wedge}\underline{conc}\underline{tl}tt)$
$\underline{elems}tup$	$\{tup(i)\,|\,1{\leq}i{\leq}\underline{len}tup\}$
$\underline{inds}tup$	$\{1{:}\underline{len}tup\}$

fig. 3-3: tuple notation

3.5 Trees

In order to define structures which correspond to (abstract forms of) programs etc., it will be necessary to have a way of combining instances of objects into new objects and these combinations must be recognisable and decomposable. Such objects will be built by " constructor functions" the only essential property of which is their uniqueness.

$$mk\text{-}a(x_1,x_2,\ldots,x_n) = mk\text{-}a'(x_1{}',x_2{}',\ldots,x_n{}')$$
$$\longleftrightarrow\ (a{=}a'\ \&\ x_1{=}x_1{}'\ \&\ x_2{=}x_2{}'\ \&\ \ldots\ \&\ x_n{=}x_n{}')$$

(The names of constructor functions are always formed by the prefix "mk-" and the name of the relevant abstract syntax rule: for the relation to abstract syntax see section 4).

One technique for decomposing a constructed object will be to define "selector functions" in the constructor:

$$mk\text{-}a(s\text{-}1{:}x_1,\ s\text{-}2{:}x_2,\ \ldots,\ s\text{-}n{:}x_n) = a$$
$$\rightarrow\ s\text{-}1(a) = x_1\ \&\ s\text{-}2(a) = x_2\ \&\ \ldots\ \&\ s\text{-}n(a) = x_n$$

Notice that, although the selector functions do not play a part in the distinction between objects, the rules about object description (see section 4) prevent any confusion. A convenient intuitive view of the result of a constructor function is a labelled tree, thus:

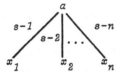

Apart from using selector functions, an object may be decomposed by writing the constructor in a defining position (e.g. parameter name, left-hand-side of a "*let*"). This achieves a complete decomposition in one step. Using the *let* construct of section 3.6:

$$\underline{let}\ mk\text{-}a(s\text{-}1{:}n_1,\ s\text{-}2{:}n_2,\ \ldots,\ s\text{-}m{:}n_m) = a \quad \underset{=}{\triangle}\ \left\{ \begin{array}{l} \underline{let}\ n_1 = s\text{-}1(a) \\ \underline{let}\ n_2 = s\text{-}2(a) \\ \quad \vdots \\ \underline{let}\ n_m = s\text{-}m(a) \end{array} \right.$$

3.6 Functions

We shall be interested in defining functions over defined domains which deliver results in defined ranges. This, so called type, information will be written:

$$f{:}\ D \rightarrow R$$

f the domain is, in fact, a cartesian product of sets, this is written
without "×" symbols):

$$f: D_1 \ D_2 \ \ldots \ D_n \rightarrow R$$

imilar extensions hold for the range. (Strictly all functions take one
rgument which is a tuple, but the actual tupling and decomposition will
e systematically omitted).

he simpler functions to be defined will define a result for any value
n their domain: they are total and the undecorated arrow will be used
o separate the domain and range. Functions which may be undefined for
ome input values are said to be partial and will use the symbol $\overset{\sim}{\rightarrow}$, for
xample:

$$Tr = \Sigma \overset{\sim}{\rightarrow} \Sigma$$

t is assumed that the reader is familiar with the standard ways of
riting and naming functions even where recursion is involved, thus:

$$f(x) = \ldots \ x \ \ldots \ f \ \ldots$$

notation will be required which enables the creation of functions
ithout having to provide names. A brief introduction to the lambda
otation is given here, for further information consult Stoy 74.

nstead of defining f by some expression in terms of its arguments
e.g.

$$f(x) = e(x) \ ),$$

he lambda notation provides a way of defining instances of functions
n the form "λ" followed by argument list followed by "." followed by
efining expression, thus:

$$\lambda x.e(x)$$

amed functions can be applied to arguments and a simple symbol sub-
titution for the parameters can be used to determine the value. In
imple cases, the same rule will provide an evaluation mechanism for
ambda expression application, thus:

$(\lambda x.5)(7) = 5$

$(\lambda x.x)(7) = 7$

$(\lambda x.(\lambda y.x+y))(7) = \lambda y.7+y$

Notice that this last application yields a function as result. We can now define the identity function:

$I = \lambda x.x$

The first operator to be considered for functions is functional composition:

$f^{\cdot}g = \lambda x.f(g(x))$

The "let" notation can now be introduced. The purpose of this notational device is to permit the introduction of local abbreviations which can then be used in an expression. Thus:

$$\text{or} \quad \left. \begin{array}{l} \underline{let}\ x = \ ... \ \underline{in}\ \acute{e}(x) \\ \underline{let}\ x = \ ... \\ \quad e\ (x) \end{array} \right\} \triangleq (\lambda x.e(x))(...)$$

i.e. "in" can be dropped if a new line is used!

Beyond this basic use, the let notation will be used to introduce recursive definitions:

$\underline{let}\ f = \ ... \ f \ ...$

with the meaning that f is to name the least fixed point (see Park 69) of the defining equation.

Several notational devices will permit the specification of different ways of computing a result. The basic conditional expression form shoul be familiar:

$\underline{if}\ p\ \underline{then}\ e_1\ \underline{else}\ e_2$

A multiple (two or greater) split can be achieved by the case construct

$$\left.\begin{array}{l} \underline{cases}\ v: \\ v_1 \rightarrow e_1 \\ v_2 \rightarrow e_2 \\ \\ \\ \\ v_{n-1} \rightarrow e_{n-1} \\ T\ \ \ \rightarrow e_n \end{array}\right\} \quad \triangleq \quad \left\{\begin{array}{l} \underline{if}\ v = v_1\ \underline{then}\ e_1 \\ \underline{else\ if}\ v = v_2\ \underline{then}\ e_2 \\ \underline{else\ if} \\ \qquad\qquad . \\ \qquad\qquad . \\ \qquad\qquad . \\ \underline{else\ if}\ v = v_{n-1}\ \underline{then}\ e_{n-1} \\ \underline{else} \qquad\qquad\qquad\qquad e_n \end{array}\right.$$

Alternatively a multiple split can be achieved by the "McMarthy conditional expression" form:

$$p_1 \rightarrow v_1, p_2 \rightarrow v_2, \ldots, p_{n-1} \rightarrow v_{n-1}, T \rightarrow v_n$$

$$\triangleq \quad \left\{\begin{array}{l} \underline{if}\ p_1\ \underline{then}\ v_1 \\ \underline{else\ if}\ p_2\ \underline{then}\ v_2 \\ \underline{else\ if} \\ \qquad\qquad . \\ \qquad\qquad . \\ \qquad\qquad . \\ \underline{else\ if}\ p_{n-1}\ \underline{then}\ v_{n-1} \\ \underline{else}\ v_n \end{array}\right.$$

In either the case construct or conditional expressions the "T" clause can be omitted if the preceding cases cover all possibilities. If, however, none of the tests are satisfied the result is undefined.

The subject functions, and their definition, is returned to in section 6.

3.7 Implicit Definition

As has been pointed out earlier, the meta-language presented here should not be considered to be closed in any way. One particular way in which it is "open-ended" is in the ability to use objects whose characterisation is implicit.

Such definitions are usually difficult (see Bekić 70b) and in languages where they can be avoided a constructive form is preferred (cf. appendix III and Henhapl 78). For general approaches to. the problem of implicit definition see Guttag   or Liskov 75.

4. OBJECT DESCRIPTION

If a definition consisted solely of functions creating objects, the
only use for describing classes of objects would be as a comment for
the reader. This is, in fact, the case for many objects and, for example, one could deduce from a definition the class of possible states
which could be generated. There is, however, another use for object
descriptions which amounts to a necessity. When a definition is to be
presented, one must have a way of defining the exact class of objects
which is to be considered. Such a definition will not normally be practical via its generation function and it is then a requirement to have
a notation for describing classes of objects.

In a simple language it would be possible to associate meaning directly with concrete forms of the object language texts. Some languages
offer a "rich" choice of representations which are semantically equivalent. An abstract syntax not only offers a way of defining some "normal form" for such expressions, it also omits the details which are
present only to ensure unambiguous parsing. Judicious choice of objects
used (e.g. sets of declarations) can also shorten the semantic descriptions.

Objects will be described by an abstract syntax. (cf. concrete syntaxes
which define a set of strings). The members of the set of rules comprising an abstract syntax will each define and name a set of objects.
Each abstract syntax class will be defined as follows:

$NAME \ \{=|::\}RULE$

By convention the first character of a *NAME* is an upper case character.
The choice between the "::" and "=" definition symbols and the form of
the *RULE* dictate the set of objects which is to be associated with *NAME*.
The majority of this section is concerned with defining the sets given
by the various possibilities. Before embarking on this we note that a
predicate which tests for membership of a particular class of objects
is implicitly defined for each *NAME*. Thus

$$is\text{-}\theta(t) \ \overset{\Delta}{=} \ t\in\Theta$$

where Θ is a *NAME* defined within an abstract syntax.

A *RULE* consists of one or more *TERMS* separated by vertical bars (i.e. "|", read as "or").

TERMS are built up by juxtaposed *ITEMS*. Unless a term contains exactly one item it is considered to be bracketed. *ITEMS* are either *NAME*s, modified *NAMES*, lists of underscored symbols, or bracketed *TERM*s.

Within a *TERM*, the meaning of a *NAME* is the set of objects defined by its rule; that of a modified *NAME* is explained later; that of a list of underscored symbols is the unit set containing an elementary object distinct from that denoted by any other string of underscored characters; a bracketed *TERM* denotes a constructed (i.e. tree-like) object. This last case requires more explanation. Section 3.5 has introduced constructor functions and the possibility to view them as trees. A bracketed term denotes the set of objects obtained by applying a constructor to elements of the cartesian product of the sets denoted by the *ITEMS* within the brackets. If the term occurs alone to the right of a "::" symbol, the name of the constructor is the *NAME*, found on the left hand side of the "::" symbol, preceded by "mk-". Thus:

$$N :: N_1 \; N_2 \; \ldots \; N_m$$

defines

$$N = \{mk\text{-}n(n_1, n_2, \ldots, n_m) \mid n_1 \in N_1 \; \& \; n_2 \in N_2 \; \& \; \ldots \; \& \; n_m \in N_m\}$$

The other contexts in which a bracketed *TERM* has been allowed above are as an option (separated by "or" form other *TERMS*) or as an *ITEM* within a *TERM*. In either of these cases the name of the constructor is "mk-α" (i.e. α is a name not used for any rule). Notice that this can introduce (sub-)classes of objects which are not distinguishable.

The set of objects denoted by an "=*rule*" (which contains zero or more "or"s) is the union of the sets denoted by the *TERMS* (which are separated by the "or"s). *Fig. 4-1* provides some examples of rules and the set of objects satisfying them.

```
Rule                      set of objects


A=B                       B
A::B                      {mk-a(b)|b∈B}
A=B|C                     B∪C
A=(BC)|D                  {mk-α(b,c)|b∈B & c∈C} ∪ D
A::C|D                    not defined
A=B|(C|D)                 erroneous
```

fig. 4-1: examples of rules

"Modified names" and the sets of objects they denote are given in *fig.* 4-2.

```
Modified Name             Set denoted


N-set                     power N
N*                        {l∈TUPLE|1≤i≤lenl ⟹ l(i)∈N}
N⁺                        {l∈N*|lenl≥1}
[B]                       B∪{NIL}
B ⇸ₘ C                    {m∈MAP|domm ⊆ B & rngm ⊆ C}
B ↔ₘ C                    {m∈(B⇸ₘC)|m(d₁)=m(d₂) ⟹ d₁=d₂}
B → C                     continuous functions
B ⇝ C                     partial functions
```

where: *N*, *B* and *C* can be *TERMS* (bracketed by implication)

fig. 4-2: Meaning of modified names

There are occasions where a class of map objects is to be defined in terms of other map types. If the new map is defined over the union of the domains a freedom is introduced which may be unwanted. This can be avoided by using:

$$M = M1 \;\underline{\cup}\; M2$$

which defines M to be a set of maps:

$$\{m\in MAP \,|\, \underline{domm} = \underline{domM1} \cup \underline{domM2} \;\&$$
$$\underline{rngm} = \underline{rngM1} \cup \underline{rngM2} \;\&$$
$$(a\in\underline{domM1} \Rightarrow m(a)\in\underline{rngM1}) \;\&$$
$$(a\in\underline{domM2} \Rightarrow m(a)\in\underline{rngM2})\}$$

A used constructor can be compared with abstract syntax rules when the syntax described is of internal (semantic) objects. Because constructors can also be used to decompose texts of the object language, a comparison is also possible between the abstract syntax of the texts being defined and their use in the semantic rules. In all cases where such a comparison is possible the used constructors, their selectors and their arguments must conform to the rules describing the class of objects.

5. THE RÔLE OF "UNDEFINED"

The treatment of logic in section 2 is somewhat over-simplified in that (in common with most text books) the possibility that expressions might be undefined has been ignored. Although the frequency has been reduced by the use of bounded quantifiers, expressions like:

$$d\in\underline{domm} \;\&\; m(d)\in c$$
$$x = 0 \;\vee\; y/x>10$$

will be found. For such expressions the "conditional expression" forms (cf. Walk 69) are assumed. For example:

$$a \;\&\; b \;\triangleq\; \underline{if}\; a \;\underline{then}\; b \;\underline{else}\; \underline{FALSE}$$

This minimizes the danger of expressions being made undefined by their operands. (Notice that Jones 72 and Dijkstra 76 adopt separate symbols for the conditional forms.)

6. DEFINING SEMANTICS

As explained in the introduction, the general approach to defining the
semantics of a language is to define a function which maps its (well-
formed) elements to some class of understood denotations. For the languages which are most commonly considered interesting these denotations
will have to be functions. Because most computer languages embody some
form of assignment operation the functions will normally be state transformations (functions from states to states). In languages which have
a procedure concept in its full generality the state transformations
will, in fact, have to be very general functions which can be applied
to functions (even themselves) and yield functions as results. If such
general functions were permitted without restriction, it would be possible to generate the sort of paradoxes which Russell observed in set
theory. However, it has been shown (cf. Scott 71) that the restriction
to monotone and continuous constructions ensures that a model can be
constructed and thus guarantees that inconsistencies are avoided. As
this result is both of considerable importance and difficulty, it would
be inappropriate to repeat that work here (for an excellent tutorial
see Stoy 74). This paper will not, then, provide a complete treatment
of the foundations of the meta-language. Rather, the approach taken
here is to accept (gratefully) that models of the lambda calculus exist
and to define meta-language expressions by specifying the closed lambda expressions into which an object program is mapped. In fact, a few
extra combinators are adopted from Stoy 74: these are discussed in
section 6.4.

The meaning function, then, is a way of mapping the object language to
lambda expressions which, in turn, denote functions. For an infinite
language (i.e. one with a recursive syntax) this function can obviously not be given extensionally. It is, indeed, very important to construct the meaning function in a way which associates (functional) denotations with parts of the constructs of the object language. Furthermore, the meaning of compound constructs of the object language should
depend only on the meaning of the components of such compounds. This
approach provides a natural way of categorising the meta-language constructs used in defining the meaning functions. Those parts of the

meta-language discussed in section 6.2 can be viewed as a macro-expansion scheme for (abstract) programs of the object language. What is
created from this expansion is an expression in an enriched ("sugared")
lambda notation. Section 6.3 explains most of the extra notation which
is used to aid readability in terms of pure lambda notation plus two
combinators which are discussed in section 6.4. The basic ideas of
states and state transition functions are reviewed in the first sub-
section below.

The whole treatment of arbitrary order has been excised from this volume. This problem had been tackled in the framework of abstract interpreters (see Walk 69) and was recognised in Bekić 74. The general problem of how to define the merging of co-operating processes using a denotational sematics approach is, however, very complex and still to
some extent "open". In view of the aim of this volume to present a
safe basis for definition work it was decided that the problems involved in merging should be dropped. There is some discussion of apparently
unordered constructs in section 6.5.

6.1 States and State Transitions

Most language definitions use a basic semantic object which is a state.
Such a state is a mapping from some class of names or their surrogates
(e.g. locations) to whatever values can be manipulated. Such a state
provides the vehicle for defining the denotations of names. Constructs
which have an assignment nature (nearly all interesting languages contain some) will naturally be granted denotations which are functions
from states to states. Such functions are usually called state transitions. Thus for some class of constructs θ:

$$m\text{-}\theta: \ \theta \rightarrow Tr$$
$$Tr = \Sigma \overset{\sim}{\rightarrow} \Sigma$$

The notation specific to states and transitions can now be introduced.

It will normally be necessary to have some structure within states (e.g.
one component for storage, one for files). This is reflected by introducing a class of elementary objects called references. References can be
explicitly enumerated by writing them as strings of underlined upper-

case characters. The only operators defined over references are the
tests for (in)equality. A state will be a mapping from such references
to any sort of objects, thus:

$$\Sigma = REF \xrightarrow[m]{} OBJECT$$

The basic way of defining a new state is by specifying a difference
from an existing state. A state transition is specified by writing a
meta-language assignment statement which uses the reference (which is
to have a different value) on the left and a value on the right. Thus
the meta-language assignment defines a transition:

$$(r := v): \Sigma \xrightarrow{\sim} \Sigma$$

and is defined as:

$$r := v \overset{\Delta}{=} \lambda\sigma.\sigma + [r \mapsto v]$$

Unlike most programming languages, a reference always denotes itself
(rather than its value) even if it is written on the right-hand-side
of an assignment. If the value is required the contents operator "$\underline{c}$"
must be used (see section 6.3 for further details).

If a semantic function maps elements of some class θ into transformations, the type will be specified as:

$$m-\theta: \theta \rightarrow$$

with the meaning:

$$m-\theta: \theta \rightarrow (\Sigma \xrightarrow{\sim} \Sigma)$$

Further, with value returning transformations (see below):

$$m-\theta: \theta \rightarrow R$$

stands for:

$$m-\theta: \theta \rightarrow (\Sigma \xrightarrow{\sim} \Sigma R)$$

Having introduced the ideas of states and state transitions, it would
be possible to build up ways of describing increasingly more complex
transitions. This is not the approach taken here. Rather, transitions
have been introduced only to provide motivation for the succeeding
three sub-sections. The treatment is now top-down in that the means of
creating extended expressions precedes the description of the extended
expressions in terms of basic combinators, so that only in section 6.4
is the treatment back to the level of lambda expressions.

6.2 A Macro-expansion Process

The assignment concept in the meta-language together with the combinators to be introduced in subsequent sub-sections provide ways of writing complex tranformations. Given some object language it is not difficult to write for any particular program a corresponding meta-language
expression which denotes the function which captures the meaning of
that particular program. Since the task in hand is defining whole languages, a way must be provided for generating the corresponding meta-
language expressions for any (well-formed) program. The generation itself, which is the subject of this sub-section, can best be understood
as a macro-expansion process. By this is meant that the parts of the
meta-language described in this section rely on the text and environment alone. This expansion is rather obvious and will be explained
with a minimum of formalism.

In a definition there will be (notionally) for each defined class of
the abstract syntax one semantic rule. This semantic rule maps objects
of the class to their denotations. The most basic part of the macro-
expansion process is the application of the relevant rules to the text
components. The qualification "notionally" has been added above for two
reasons. Partly, it would be unfortunate to apply any rule which dic-
tated a structure on the semantic functions. Thus very short semantic
functions may be better conbined with that corresponding to the syntax
class which uses them. More importantly, syntax rules which simply list
options would have corresponding semantic rules which were simply case
distinctions selecting other semantic rules. These "splitting" (or
" routing " rules) are omitted and only syntax rules which define constructors (i.e. "::rules") will normally have corresponding semantic
rules.

The syntax for an infinite language will be recursive. In consequence
the corresponding semantic rules must also be a family of mutually re-
sursive functions. However, it was pointed out in the discussion of
objects that valid tree objects will always be finite. This guarantees
that the macro-expansion process envisaged will terminate.

A trivial language can be used to illustrate this basic expansion. The
language to be considered is that of binary numerals. It is, of course,
so simple that the corresponding denotations are not transformations
but the natural numbers. The syntax of the language is:

$Bin\text{-}digit \quad = \underline{0}\,|\,\underline{1}$
$Bin\text{-}numeral = [Bin\text{-}numeral]\ Bin\text{-}digit$

Given the choice of denotations semantic functions are required of
types:

$m\text{-}d\colon\ Bin\text{-}digit \quad \to\ Nat^0$
$m\text{-}n\colon\ Bin\text{-}numeral \to\ Nat^0$

Appropriate functions might be:

$m\text{-}d(d) = \underline{if}\ d=\underline{0}\ \underline{then}\ 0\ \underline{else}\ 1$
$m\text{-}n(mk\text{-}bin\text{-}numeral(n,d)) = \underline{if}\ n=\underline{NIL}\ \underline{then}\ m\text{-}d(d)$
$\qquad\qquad\qquad\qquad\qquad\qquad \underline{else}\ 2.m\text{-}n(n)+m\text{-}d(d)$

For any element of the object language ($Bin\text{-}numeral$) the meaning function will create a finite expression. In this simple language the expression will contain only arithmetic objects and it can be simplified
by the laws of arithmetic to a natural number (the required denotation).
A number of points have, however, been illustrated. It was observed in
section 3.5 that objects can be decomposed by writing the constructor
"on the left of a let": the use of the constructor in the parameter
position of $m\text{-}n$ is a further application of this idea and is equivalent
to:

$m\text{-}n(nm) = (\underline{let}\ mk\text{-}bin\text{-}numeral(n,d) = nm$
$\qquad\qquad\ ...)$

Furthermore the conditional statement used in the definition of $m\text{-}n$ is
entirely dependent on the text being analyzed and is a part of the macro-
expansion process.

Of the three forms of conditional expression in the meta-language, *case* is always dependant on the text alone, "McCarthy" conditionals are always dependant on dynamic values and *if then else* can be used in either way. The tests which depend on dynamic values are discussed in sub-section 6.3. The meaning of the text-dependant *if then else* should be obvious: either one or the other expansion is chosen depending on the result of the test. The need for the *case* construct has been reduced somewhat by the adoption, in large definitions, of the practice of omitting semantic rules for syntax classes which are lists of options. But an artificial example can be constructed for the syntax:

$$A = B|C|D$$

$$B :: X$$
$$C :: X\ Y$$
$$D :: X\ Y\ Z$$

The definition:

$$fn\text{-}a(a) = \underline{cases}\ a:$$
$$mk\text{-}b(x) \qquad \rightarrow f(x)$$
$$mk\text{-}c(x,y) \quad \rightarrow g(x,y)$$
$$mk\text{-}d(x,y,z) \rightarrow h(x,y,z)$$

has the meaning:

$$fn\text{-}a(a) =$$
$$\underline{if}\ (\exists x)(mk\text{-}b(x)=a)\ \underline{then}\ (\underline{let}\ mk\text{-}b(x)=a\ \underline{in}\ f(x))$$
$$\underline{else}\ \underline{if}\ (\exists x,y)(mk\text{-}c(x,y)=a)\ \underline{then}\ (\underline{let}\ mk\text{-}c(x,y)=a\ \underline{in}\ g(x,y))$$
$$\underline{else}\ \underline{if}\ (\exists x,y,z)(mk\text{-}d(x,y,z)=a)\ \underline{then}\ (\underline{let}\ mk\text{-}d(x,y,z)=a\ \underline{in}\ h(x,y,z))$$

A case clause with a final "$T\rightarrow$" clause will use this last option if none of the preceding predicates were true. If no such clause is present it is an error for none of the predicates to be satisfied.

A similar static expansion from the text is given by the *for* construct. If a textual object which is a list is to be given a meaning, the semantic rule is likely to be formed from a *for* construct, thus:

$$\underline{for}\ i=1\ \underline{to}\ u\ \underline{do}\ f(list(i))$$

this can be statically expanded into:

$$f(list(l));f(list(l+1));\ldots;f(list(u))$$

where the ";" combinator between transformations is that explained in
section 6.3. Similarly a value returning transformation can be used to
define a list to be created from the list in the text by:

$$\underline{let}\ vl:\ <vt(list(i))\,|\,l\le i\le u>$$

with the meaning (again expressed in terms of combinators to be defined
in the next sub-section):

$$\underline{let}\ vll\ \ :\ vt(list(l));$$
$$\underline{let}\ vlsl\ :\ vt(list(l+1));$$
$$\ldots$$
$$\underline{let}\ vlu\ \ :\ vt(list(u));$$
$$\underline{let}\ vl\ \ \ =\ <vll,vlsl,\ldots,vlu>$$

Definitions of programming languages have universally adopted the concept of an environment to handle the problems related to block structure. Construction of explicit environments is achieved by standard
use of the meta-language; the rôle of the explicit environment in the
macro-expansion process is discussed at the end of this sub-section.
There is, however, another topic to be discussed first and that is the
exit mechanism of the meta-language.

The exit-mechanism is discussed in detail elsewhere in this volume
(Jones 78b) and a step-by-step motivation of the approach has been presented in Jones 75. Here, only a brief review of the idea is given.
For a simple language (i.e. one without constructs which cause abnormal termination) the transformations to be used as denotations will be:

$$T = \Sigma \overset{\sim}{\to} \Sigma$$

The exit approach to languages which permit abnormal termination is to
use denotations which are transformations of the type:

$$E = \Sigma \overset{\sim}{\to} \Sigma\ [Abn]$$

Here, just as Σ is chosen to fit the particular language, the class

Abn is a set of objects which can be used for the language in question to indicate what sort of abnormal termination has occured. Of importance for the meta-language is only the distinction between *NIL* (*Abn* omitted) and an actual *Abn* value. A particular element of *E* which takes an element of Σ into a pair which contains a (possibly different) element of Σ and *NIL* is a "normal" transition. In other words no abnormal situation is to be resolved. On the other hand, if the second element of the output pair is not *NIL*, it provides not only the knowledge that an abnormal situation is to be resolved, but also some information which aids resolution. In a simple language with goto statements, for example, the set *Abn* might be identical with label identifiers. An unresolved goto is then denoted by an element of *E* which yields the label as the second component of the result. It is "resolution" which is of concern in this section because it employs a sort of implicit environment. The *exit* and normal successor (i.e. ";") combinators are defined in the next sub-section; the technique for resolving exits plays a part in the macro-expansion scheme. Firstly, however, the definitions are provided.

The basic construct to be used is written:

$$\underline{tixe}\ [a{\mapsto}t_1(a)\,|\,p(a)]\ \underline{in}\ t_2$$

Intuitively this requires that the basic tranformation (in *E*) to be used is t_2; if for a particular $\sigma\epsilon\Sigma$ this results in a *NIL* *Abn* component then that element of t_2 is also an element of the overall transformation; if, however, an abnormal component is returned which satisfies the predicate *p* then transformation t_1 is used to attempt to resolve the abnormality; if an abnormal result is delivered by t_2, but this value does not satisfy *p*, then the same abnormal result is delivered by the overall construct. To define this formally the types are given first, suppose:

$$t_1\ :\ Abn \rightarrow E$$
$$t_2\ :\ E$$
$$p\ :\ [Abn] \rightarrow Bool$$
$$E\ =\ \Sigma \overset{\sim}{\rightarrow} \Sigma\ [Abn]$$

then the type of the construct is:

$$(\underline{tixe}\ [a{\mapsto}t_1(a)\,|\,p(a)]\ \underline{in}\ t_2):\ E$$

and the definition is:

$$(\underline{tixe} \; [a \mapsto t_1(a)|p(a)] \; \underline{in} \; t_2)$$
$$\underset{\triangle}{=} \; (\underline{let} \; e = [a \mapsto t_1(a)|p(a)]$$
$$\underline{let} \; r(\sigma,a) = (a \in \underline{dome} \mapsto r^{\cdot}e(a)(\sigma), T \mapsto <\sigma,a>)$$
$$r^{\cdot}t_2)$$

Notice that r in the above expansion is used recursively. Thus if a-
nother abnormal situation results which still satisfies p, the effect
defined in e will again be used. This recursive form fits the problem
of goto handling (see the definition in appendix III) very well. In
earlier definitions a non-recursive "$\underline{trap}$" was used with which it was
then necessary to construct the required recursion in the semantic
functions. For:

$$t_1 \; : \; Abn \; \to \; E$$
$$t_2 \; : \; E$$

the type of the $trap$ construct is:

$$(\underline{trap}(a) \; \underline{with} \; t_1(a);t_2): \; E$$

and the definition is:

$$\underline{trap}(a) \; \underline{with} \; t_1(a);t_2$$
$$\underset{\triangle}{=} \; (\underline{let} \; h(\sigma,a) = (a \neq NIL \mapsto t_1(a)(\sigma), T \mapsto <\sigma,NIL>)$$
$$h^{\cdot}t_2)$$

Returning to the "$\underline{tixe}$" construct, it is necessary to explain its role
in the macro-expansion. Firstly, it could be argued that, for a concept
which is used very few times in a definition (cf. Henhapl 78 in this
volume), it is not worth providing a special meta-language construct.
The justification for so doing is precisely to provide a framework for
the resolution of exits which does fit with a macro-expansion view of
the text. The key point is the use of a mapping in the $\underline{tixe}$ construct.
The finiteness criteria of mappings is met because, for finite texts,
the predicate p must yield a finite number of abnormal conditions to
be resolved. In order for the overall $\underline{tixe}$ construct to yield a denotation for a text, both the t_1 and t_2 semantic functions should only
be used on sub-parts of the overall text being defined. Referring to
the semantic function "$i\text{-}named\text{-}stmt\text{-}list$" in the definition in appendix III, it will be seen that the rôle of the $\underline{tixe}$ construct is essen-

tially to generate a static environment the elements of which are mutually dependant on one another. (The discussion of this sort of recursion is given under the general topic of environments).

The remaining topic to be explained with regard to the macro-expansion is the rôle of the environment object (*Env*). In a language without block structure it would be possible to write semantic functions for each class (θ) of abstract syntax objects.

$$m\text{-}\theta\colon \Theta \to (\Sigma \overset{\sim}{\to} \Sigma)$$

In a language which permits redefinition of identifiers at different levels of the block structure, an environment is introduced, so that most semantic functions are of type:

$$m\text{-}\theta\colon \Theta \ Env \to (\Sigma \overset{\sim}{\to} \Sigma)$$

The highest (program) construct of the language has a corresponding semantic rule which creates an empty environment and this semantic rule is thus still of type:

$$m\text{-}program\colon Program \to (\Sigma \overset{\sim}{\to} \Sigma)$$

If the language to be defined permits recursion (e.g. recursive procedures in Algol 60) the equations for creating environments will themselves be recursive. This recursion must, of course, be understood for the whole definition to be sound.

If the definition were in fact to be treated as though it were an abstract interpreter, it would be fairly easy to clarify the recursive equations on environments by adopting an appropriate mode for parameter passing. One way of ensuring that a denotational view was sound would be to set up an ordering over environments. Such an ordering could be defined pointwise over the transformations to be held as values in the environments. Here an alternative view is taken. Essentially the environment is viewed as a way of avoiding a name creation process for the denotations to be stored therein. The motivation for introducing this "linguistic level" can best be given by, initially, restricting the discussion to a language which only has local variables (i.e. no procedures). For any particular program in the language, it is easy to write an associated extended lambda expression. Thus:

begin *integer* *a,b;* ... *end*

might have a denotation like:

(*let* l_a:*get-loc(a);* *let* l_b:*get-loc(b);* ...)

As has been stated repeatedly, the problem that must be solved is to provide a way of generating denotations for any program. The possibility of using an elipses notation was excluded, but the environment can be seen precisely as a way of taking away the need for such a notation for the creation of names for the location. Thus for a program:

begin *integer* *c,d;* ... *c:=d+c;* ... *end*

the environment might be such that the denotation of the body is created by:

i-*body*((...*c:=d+c;*...), [$c{\mapsto}l_c$, $d{\mapsto}l_d$])

The definition of i-*body* will be such that this expands to:

...
let *vd* : *contents*(l_d);
let *vc* : *contents*(l_c);
assign (l_c,(vd+vc));
...

In other words, the environment itself disappears entirely during the macro-expansion process. The functions defining the meaning of blocks will create new locations for locally declared identifiers. For block structured languages the outer environment is updated with a pairing of the local names with the new locations. This modified environment has two uses: for local uses of identifiers the location is obtained from the environment; for nested blocks it is the basis for generating further environments. In order to exhibit the denoted expression, it is necessary to create (arbitrary) names for the locations.

It is now necessary to show how such an explanation can be extended to cover the more interesting case of languages which permit recursive procedures. For a program:

begin p1:<u>proc</u> ... p2 ...;

     p2:<u>proc</u> ... p1 ... p2 ...;

     ...

     p1

     ...

end

the definition will generate a denotation for the block via:

let $nenv = env+[p1\mapsto e\text{-}proc\text{-}den((...p1...),nenv),$

                 $p2\mapsto e\text{-}proc\text{-}den((...p1...p2...),nenv)]$

$i\text{-}body((...p1...),nenv)$

Introducing names for the procedure denotations, this expands to:

let $pden1 = ... pden2 ...$

let $pden2 = ... pden1 ... pden2 ...$

$... pden1 ...$

This time the disappearance of *nenv* is doubly welcome: with it has gone the recursion whose least fixed point could only be discussed in terms of an ordering. A different recursion (that in terms of procedure denotations) has become visible but for one thing it was there anyway and for another it is precisely the recursion over transformations which has to be explained below.

This section, then, has shown how a definition can be viewed as a series of macros which expand objects of the language to be defined into expressions in an extended lambda notation. At the expense of introducing the concept of names for locations and procedure denotations, the explanation of these extended expressions below will not be burdened with the concept of environments.

6.3 Simplifying Extended Expressions

The previous sub-section has shown how a definition of the type given in appendix III can be used to create (by macro-expansion) an expression which is the denotation of the given object language text. This expression itself denotes a transformation. However, the expression will be to explain those combinators which can be regarded simply as "syntactic sugar" for making the generated result more readable.

It will be easier to comprehend the full combinator definitions if the idea is first explained with a simplified problem. Suppose the denotation of some compound object:

$$a \in A \quad \text{where}$$
$$A = B \ C$$

is sought. Given two functions:

$$m\text{-}b \ : \ B \to (\Sigma \overset{\sim}{\to} \Sigma)$$
$$m\text{-}c \ : \ C \to (\Sigma \overset{\sim}{\to} \Sigma)$$

there are many possible ways of combining them to create a transformation. Given the objective that the denotations of compound objects should depend only on the denotations of their components, one of the most pleasing combinations is a composition of the two created functions. Thus:

$$m\text{-}a(mk\text{-}a(b,c)) = m\text{-}c(c)^{\bullet}m\text{-}b(b)$$
$$= \lambda\sigma.(m\text{-}c(c)(m\text{-}b(b)(\sigma)))$$

One objective of introducing combinators (like composition) is to avoid having to write out many "λ"'s and "σ"'s. In addition to a "σ-free$" style, a much more natural definition can be achieved by the use of well chosen combinators. In this case we can define a "semicolon" combinator:

for: $\qquad\qquad\qquad t_1 \qquad : \ \Sigma \overset{\sim}{\to} \Sigma$
$\qquad\qquad\qquad\qquad\quad t_2 \qquad : \ \Sigma \overset{\sim}{\to} \Sigma$

the type is: $\qquad\qquad (t_1;t_2) \ : \ \Sigma \overset{\sim}{\to} \Sigma$

and the definition: $\quad t_1;t_2 \quad \overset{\Delta}{=} \ t_2^{\bullet}t_1$

and then rewrite the above example:

$$m\text{-}a(mk\text{-}a(b,c)) = m\text{-}b(b);$$
$$m\text{-}c(c)$$

In a simple language definition, the meaning of a sequence of statements is likely to be the composition of the meanings of the single
statements. Since, in the concrete syntax of such an object language,
the elements of the sequence are likely to be separated by ";", a
pleasing symmetry has been created. Notice, however, that the meta-
language semicolon operator has been formally defined and there is no
element of circularity in such a link between object and meta-language.
It would be useful to define a few other combinators (e.g. *if*, *while*)
on these simple transformations. This is not done here since the languages which are of general interest require slightly more complex denotations. Since the combinators given below can be specialized very
easily to those for the simple transformations, attention is now turned
to the more general versions.

The object language features which demand richer denotations are those
which manifest an "abnormal *exit*" behaviour. The archetypal statement
is "*goto*", but also much error handling can best be dealt with in the
same way. One approach to this problem is to use transformations which
create states and optional abnormal indications.

The type of a transformation now becomes:

$$E = \Sigma \overset{\sim}{\to} \Sigma \; [Abn]$$

where *Abn* is chosen for a particular definition. The intuitive meaning
of such a (partial) function is that it maps state values into pairs
whose first element is always a (possibly different) state value; in
the case that the computation was "normal", the second component will
be the elementary object $\underline{NIL}$; if termination was abnormal, the second
component will be other than $\underline{NIL}$ and its actual value will provide information about the encountered exception.

The notation introduced for type clauses must now be extended. Rather
than write:

$$m\text{-}\theta: \; \Theta \; Env \to (\Sigma \overset{\sim}{\to} \Sigma \; [Abn])$$

such function types will be written:

$$m\text{-}\theta: \; \Theta \; Env \Rightarrow$$

and for value returning transformations:

$$m-\theta: \; \Theta \; Env \; \to \; (\Sigma \; \overset{\sim}{\to} \; \Sigma \; \{Abn\} \; Val)$$

is written:

$$m-\theta: \; \Theta \; Env \; \Rightarrow \; Val$$

It is now necessary to define the combinators which are used to combine transformations of type E. Firstly if a simple transformation

$$t \; : \; \Sigma \; \overset{\sim}{\to} \; \Sigma$$

is written in a context where a transformation of type E is required, it is interpreted as:

$$t \; \overset{\Delta}{=} \; \lambda\sigma.<t(\sigma),\underline{NIL}>$$

that is, viewing

$$t \; : \; E$$

it is ensured that it always has a normal termination. Notice, in particular "I" the identity over Σ gives:

$$I \; \overset{\Delta}{=} \; \lambda\sigma.<\sigma,\underline{NIL}>$$

The full semicolon combinator can now be introduced. Intuitively its purpose is to avoid applying the second transformation if the first results in abnormal termination. Formally, given transformations with types:

$$t_1 \; : \; E$$
$$t_2 \; : \; E$$

then the type of the result is:

$$(t_1;t_2) \; : \; E$$

and its definition:

$$(t_1;t_2) \; \overset{\Delta}{=} \; (\lambda\sigma,a.\,a=\underline{NIL}\to t_2(\sigma),T\to<\sigma,a>)\overset{\cdot}{} t_1$$

In order to signal, with some given value v (in Abn), that an abnormal exit is to occur, the *exit* combinator is used, its type is:

$(\underline{exit}(v))$: E

and its definition:

$(\underline{exit}(v)) \overset{\Delta}{=} \lambda\sigma.<\sigma,v>$

The *error* construct of the meta-language is used to indicate that no defined result is given. Thus the value of *error* anywhere in the denotation is to show an abnormal result for the whole text. To achieve this, the *exit* can be used with the rule that no *tixe* covers the *ERROR* case; thus:

$\underline{error} \overset{\Delta}{=} \underline{exit} (ERROR)$

The *tixe* combinator, which was explained as part of the macro-scheme, and the semicolon combinator have provided two ways of conditionally applying subsequent transformations. A combinator which causes application of a second transformation in both normal and abnormal cases is "*always*". Given:

t : $\Sigma \overset{\sim}{\to} \Sigma$
e : E

then the type is:

$(\underline{always}\ t\ \underline{in}\ e)$: E

and the definition:

$(\underline{always}\ t\ \underline{in}\ e)$
$\overset{\Delta}{=} (\lambda\sigma,a.<t(\sigma),a>)\dot{}\ e$

If t is, in fact, of type E then it is an *error* if a non-*NIL* second component is ever returned.

There are occasions where an *exit* or *error* construct is required also with pure functions. It is straightforward to redefine composition in a way analogous to the semicolon combinator. Having done so, of course, semicolon is defined in terms of (the revised) composition).

This concludes the combinators which are especially designed for building up expressions from (expressions denoting) transformations of type E. Attention is now turned to value returning transformations of type:

$$R = \Sigma \overset{\sim}{\rightarrow} \Sigma \; [Abn] \; V$$

The most basic way of generating such a transformation is by the _return_ combinator. Thus:

$$for \; v \in V, \; (\underline{return}(v)) : R$$

is defined:

$$(\underline{return}(v)) \overset{\Delta}{=} \lambda\sigma.<\sigma,\underline{NIL},v>$$

A transformation of type R may be placed after one of type E (separated by ";") and make the whole of type R. Thus given:

$$t \; : \; E$$
$$r \; : \; R$$

then:

$$(t;r) \; : \; R$$

is defined:

$$(t;r) \overset{\Delta}{=} (\lambda\sigma,a.(a=\underline{NIL}\rightarrow r(\sigma),T\rightarrow<\sigma,a,\underline{?}>))\overset{\bullet}{} t$$

Notice that as a consequence of this definition abnormal _exit_ results in returning an undefined (here ?) result.

The value generated by a value returning transformation can be used in a following transformation in a way which is analogous to the simple _let_ shown below. Given:

$$r \; : \; R$$
$$t \; : \; V \rightarrow E$$

then:

$$(\underline{let} \; v:r;t(v)) \; : \; E$$

is defined:

$$(\underline{let}\ v:r;t(v))$$
$$\overset{\Delta}{=}\ (\lambda\sigma,a,v.(a=\underline{NIL}\to t(v)(\sigma),T\to<\sigma,a>))\cdot r$$

To reduce the number of separate cases to be distinguished, the contents operator ($\underline{c}$) is considered to be a value returning transformation. Thus:

$$\underline{c}\ :\ REF\ \to\ R$$

and:

$$\underline{c}r\ \overset{\Delta}{=}\ \lambda\sigma.<\sigma,\sigma(r)>$$

The contents operator, or any other value returning transformation, can occur in contexts where the construct is defined only for values. The meaning is:

$$\ldots\ r\ \ldots\ \overset{\Delta}{=}\ (\underline{let}\ v:r;\ \ldots\ v\ \ldots)$$

In the case of the $\underline{while}$ combinator this rule must be interpreted as:

$$(\underline{while}\ r\ \underline{do}\ t)\ \overset{\Delta}{=}\ (\underline{let}\ w\ =\ (\underline{let}\ v:r;\ \underline{if}\ v\ \underline{then}\ (t;w)\ \underline{else}\ I)\ \underline{in}\ w)$$

The recursive $\underline{let}$ on the right hand side defines that w should be the minimal fixed-point of the equation.

The remaining items of syntactic sugar to be defined are more basic (i.e. are not specialized to particular sorts of transformations.) In its simplest form $\underline{let}$ provides an abbreviation:

$$(\underline{let}\ v\ =\ e1\ \underline{in}\ e2(v))\ \overset{\Delta}{=}\ (\lambda v.e2(v))(e1)$$

The recursive form of $\underline{let}$:

$$(\underline{let}\ v\ =\ e1\ \underline{in}\ e2(v))\ \overset{\Delta}{=}\ (\lambda v'.e2(v'))(Y\lambda v.e1(v))$$

defines v to be be the minimal fixed point of expression $e1$.

Functional composition is straightforward:

$$(f \overset{\cdot}{} g) = (\lambda x. f(g(x)))$$

The dynamic conditional is defined in terms of a combinator discussed in the next section:

$$(\underline{if}\ v\ \underline{then}\ t_1\ \underline{else}\ t_2) \overset{\Delta}{=} cond(t_1, t_2)(v)$$

6.4 Basic Combinators

A definition as viewed in section 6.2 is a way of generating, for any object text whose meaning is sought, an expression in an extended lambda notation. The length of such expressions is reduced and the readability much increased by the use of various combinators. Section 6.3 has shown how these can be eliminated in a way which yields a much longer expression whose structure corresponds much less closely to that of the original text. The advantage of this expression is however, that it is almost in pure lambda notation and it is now only necessary to discuss the meaning of two remaining combinators.

In fact all that is done at this point is to rely on the work of others. Thus along with the models of the lambda calculus in Stoy 74, the minimal fixed point operator (Y) and the "doubly strict" conditional are adopted:

$$
\begin{aligned}
cond(t_1, t_2)(\mathsf{T}) &= \mathsf{T} \\
cond(t_1, t_2)(\underline{TRUE}) &= t_1 \\
cond(t_1, t_2)(\underline{FALSE}) &= t_2 . \\
cond(t_1, t_2)(\bot) &= \bot
\end{aligned}
$$

The adequacy of the doubly strict functions comes from the explicit treatment of errors in the meta-language.

6.5 Other Issues

The question of how to define arbitrary order of evaluation in a language has been omitted for reasons explained elsewhere. There are, however, some points where it appears to occur in the definitions given in this volume. Consider the use of:

> *let* $l \in Sc\text{-}loc$ *be* *s.t.* $l \notin dom$ c $R\text{-}STG$
> $R\text{-}STG$:= c $R\text{-}STG$ ∪ [$l \to ?$]

Clearly, this intends to show a freedom of choice which would be lost by pre-defining an order over elements of $Sc\text{-}loc$ and always choosing the "next" free location. Equally clearly, it would be unnecessarily complex to use some general treatment for non-determinism (e.g. all functions are $\Sigma \to \Sigma\text{-}set$) in order to provide a formal definition of this construct. Essentially, it is clear that the particular choice makes no difference and it is no more worthwhile to prove this claim than it is to over-define (see Jones 77c) and then prove what properties of the definition are irrelevant.

It must, however, be clear that the "*let be s.t.*" construct could be used unwisely and each use should really be accompanied by its own argument of well-foundedness.

Similarly, the simple rule that value returning transformations can be written in positions where values are required presents a danger. The expansion given in section 6.3 that they should be extracted and formed into a preceding *let* is only clear if either there is only one such value returning transformation or if their order will have no effect on the result. This latter is the case in:

> *let* $nenv$: $env + ([id \to e\text{-}type(dclm(id),env) \mid id \in domdclm]$ ∪ ...)

Finally the topic of errors in the definition should be mentioned. At a number of points it has been indicated that something is simply considered to be a wrong use of the meta-language (e.g. an incomplete case construct). In such a case, just as with:

> $(\iota i)(7 < i < 3)$ or $\sqrt{'ABC'}$

nothing is defined. This is in distinction to the use of *error* which shows that the object text is defined by the definition to be in *error*. In this case it is permitted for a (valid) implementation to produce any result (although a diagnostic is, of course, the most useful result!)

ACKNOWLEDGEMENTS

The basis of the work on formal definition was laid in the Vienna Laboratory during the 1960's; Bekic 70a already showed a dissatisfaction with the "abstract interpreter" approach; the actual meta-language described in this paper was developed at that Laboratory during the period 1973/75. This author would like to acknowledge the stimulus and enjoyment he has derived from his years in Vienna. In particular the co-operation with Hans Bekić both in writing the notation section of Bekić 74 and in discussing a draft of this paper, have been invaluable.

APPENDIX I: Concrete Syntax of the Meta-language

The rules given below are an outline of a concrete syntax in the notation of Walk 69. Basically, the rules are context-free, but sub-classes
of expressions are used in order to indicate the types of permitted arguments to operators.

Written definitions use a number of relaxations on this syntax which
are not formally defined.

a) Brackets around blocks and *cond-stmts* as well as commas and "*in*" are
   omitted where indentation or line breaks make the result unambiguous.

b) Comments, enclosed in "/**/" may be used freely.

c) Where an expression occurs at the end of an *expr-ld*, "*result is*"
   can be used.

d) The order of precedence of operators (standard) is modified by use
   of blanks and line-breaks in order to avoid excessive bracketing.

defn	::=	{·{*fn-defn*│*tr-defn*}...}
tr-defn	::	*tr-id*{(*defs*)}... = *block*
tr-id		usually begins with "*i-*" or "*e-*"
defs	::=	[,·*def*...]
def	::=	*v-id*│*constructor*
construcor		"*mk-*" followed by name of abstract syntax class
		(possibly followed by *defs* in parenthesis)
block	::=	([*exit-spec*][*let-cl*]{;·*stmt*...})
exit-spec	::=	*tixe* map-*expr* *in*
let-cl	::=	*let* *def*:*expr*;
expr-block		as *block* but is value returning
stmt	::=	*stmt-block*│*cond-stmt*│*iter-stmt*│*stmt-ld*│*assign-stmt*│
		int-stmt│*return-stmt*│I│*exit-stmt*│*error*

```
cond-stmt   ::= if expr then stmt [else stmt]|
                ({,·{expr→stmt}...}[,T→stmt]|
                (cases expr: {,·{expr→stmt}...}[,T→stmt])

iter-stmt   ::= for v-id=expr to expr do stmt |
                while expr do stmt

stmt-ld     ::= (ldl;stmt)
assign-stmt ::= v-id:=expr
int-stmt    ::= tr-id{(args)}...
return-stmt ::= return(expr)
exit-stmt   ::= exit(args)

fn-defn     ::= fn-id(defs) = pure-expr

expr        ::= prefix-expr|infix-expr|quant-expr|const|fn-ref|eval-stmt|
                var-ref|(expr)|cond-expr|expr-block|expr-ld

fn-ref      ::= fn-id(args)
eval-stmt   ::= eval-id{(args)}...
args        ::= [,·expr···]

var-ref     ::= [c] v-id[(args)]
cond-expr   ::= if expr then expr else expr |
                ({,·{expr→expr}...}[,T→expr])|
                (cases expr:{,·{expr→expr}...}[,T→expr])
expr-ld     ::= (ldl;expr)
ldl         ::= {;·ld...}
ld          ::= let {def|fn-id(defs)} = expr in

pure-expr   as expr but does not (directly) contain:
            expr-block, c, eval-stmt
```

general expressions

```
prefix-expr ::= hd tuple-expr
descr-expr  :: (ιdef[∈set-expr])(log-expr)
```

see also selectors and constructors of abstract syntax.

arith-expr

$prefix\text{-}expr$ ::= <u>len</u> $tuple\text{-}expr\,|$ <u>card</u> $set\text{-}expr$

See also operators on any standard sets.

log-expr

$prefix\text{-}expr$ ::= $\neg log\text{-}expr$

$infix\text{-}expr$ ::= $log\text{-}expr\ \{\&|\vee|\rightarrow|\leftrightarrow\}log\text{-}expr\,|$
$\qquad\qquad expr\in set\text{-}expr\,|$
$\qquad\qquad set\text{-}expr\ \{\subset|\subseteq\}set\text{-}expr$
$\qquad\qquad expr\ \{=|\ne\}expr$

$quant\text{-}expr$ ::= $(\{\forall|\exists|\exists!\}def[\in set\text{-}expr])(log\text{-}expr)$

$const$ ::= <u>TRUE</u> $|$ <u>FALSE</u>

See also operators (e.g. relational) on standard sets and "is-" pre-fixed to abstract syntax class names.

set-expr

$prefix\text{-}expr$ ::= $\{$<u>union</u>$|$<u>power</u>$\}set\text{-}expr\,|$
$\qquad\qquad \{$<u>dom</u>$|$<u>rng</u>$\}map\text{-}expr\,|$
$\qquad\qquad \{$<u>inds</u>$|$<u>elems</u>$\}tuple\text{-}expr$

$infix\text{-}expr$ ::= $set\text{-}expr\{\cup|\cap|-\}set\text{-}expr$

$const$ ::= $\{[,\cdot expr\cdots]\}|$
$\qquad\qquad \{expr\rfloor log\text{-}expr\}|$
$\qquad\qquad \{arith\text{-}expr:arith\text{-}expr\}$

See also standard set names: $Bool,\ Nat,\ Nat^{\bullet},\ Int$

tuple-expr

prefix-expr ::= {$\underline{tl}$ | $\underline{conc}$}*tuple-expr*

infix-expr ::= *tuple-expr*^*tuple-expr*

const ::= <[, · *expr*···]>|
         <*tuple-expr*⌊*log-expr*>

map-expr

infix-expr ::= *map-expr*{+ | U | $\overset{\cdot}{}$}*map-expr*|
         map-expr{\ | ⌊}*set-expr*

const ::= ⌊{, · {*expr*→*expr*}···}⌋|
         ⌊*expr*→*expr*⌊*log-expr*⌋

APPENDIX II: Conventions

Apart from notation which is strictly part of the described meta-language, a number of conventions have developed in its use. While changes to the notation should be reflected in a revised definition of the meta-language, the conventions can be ignored with impunity.

This appendix lists some possible naming conventions:

usage	example	convention
keyword	_for_	underlined sequence
operators	_dom_	of lower case (_l.c._)
variables	_val_	sequence of _l.c._
of list type	_intl_	last letter "_l_"
of set type	_cas_	last letter "_s_"
of map type	_dclm_	last .letter "_m_"
class names	_Program_	first _u.c._, rest _l.c._
elementary objects	_INT_	underlined sequence of _u.c._
references	_R-STG_	first letter "_R_"
context conditions	_is-wf-expr_	predicate names begins "_is-wf-_"
selector names	_s-bdl_	begins "_s-_"

APPENDIX III: Example Definition

This appendix presents an example whose study will considerably increase the reader's understanding of the meta-language. The definition
itself is divided into abstract syntax, context conditions, semantic
objects and semantic function parts. Before these are presented a few
points of explanation will be offered. (In addition Bjørner 78b has
taken examples from this definition and thus provided a useful introduction).

The abstract syntax should present no difficulties.

The context conditions are also straightforward, but note that in addition to the convention for dropping formulae corresponding to "splitting rules", an obvious extension permits equations for rules of the
form:

$A :: B \ C \ D$

to be omitted if they are of exactly the form:

$is\text{-}wf\text{-}a(mk\text{-}a(b,c,d),env) =$
    $is\text{-}wf\text{-}b(b,env) \ \& \ is\text{-}wf\text{-}c(c,env) \ \& \ is\text{-}wf\text{-}d(d,env)$

Notice that the context condition $is\text{-}wf\text{-}block$ shows that recursive
calls of procedures are allowed while references to locally declared
identifiers within the definitions of variables (i.e. bound lists) are
prohibited. It can also be observed that $is\text{-}wf\text{-}for$ shows that the control variable of a for construct is strictly local to the body of the
for.

The description of the semantic objects yields most insight into the
language. The state is divided into three components of which the most
important is storage; this is defined as a disjoint union of two types
of mapping. The environment auxiliary object provides denotations for
the identifiers. In the simple case for variables, these denotations
are locations; for arrays the locations are themselves (one-one) mappings. For control variable identifiers the denotation is simply an
integer because no assignment to such variable is allowed (cf. $i\text{-}for$,
$e\text{-}con\text{-}var\text{-}ref$). Procedure denotations are functions from argument lists
(and $Aid\text{-}set$) to transformations (cf. $e\text{-}proc\text{-}den$, which is a function

rather than a transformation, and *i-call*). The basic model for goto definition is discussed in Jones 78b. Here, because procedures can be passed as arguments, there is an additional problem of locating the proper generation of a label. This problem is handled by activation identifiers. For a more detailed description of this approach see Jones 75.

Given an understanding of the semantic objects an examination of the "type" clauses of the semantic functions should give an overview of the whole definition. Notice that *i-program* is the only function which does not create a (value returning) transformation. The function *i-block* defines *nenv* recursively to create the appropriate procedure denotations (see section 6.2). The handling of exits is simplified in this language (cf. *i-named-stmt-list*) since no compound statement is available.

ABSTRACT SYNTAX

```
Program      :: Stmt
Stmt         =  Block|If|For|Call|Goto|Assign|In|Out|NULL
Block        :: s-dcls:(Id→Type) Proc-set Named-stmt*
Type         :: s-sc-type: Scalar-type s-bds:[(Expr|*)⁺]
Proc         :: s-nm: Id Parm* Stmt
Parm         :: s-id: Id s-attr:(Type|PROC)
Named-stmt   :: s-nm:[Id] s-stmt: Stmt
If           :: s-b: Expr s-th: Stmt s-el: Stmt
For          :: s-con-var: Id s-init: Expr s-step: Expr s-limit: Expr Stmt
Call         :: s-pn: Id s-args:(Var-ref|Id)*
Goto         :: Id
Assign       :: s-lhs: Var-ref s-rhs: Expr
In           :: Var-ref
Out          :: Expr
Expr         =  Infix-expr|Rhs-ref|Con-var-ref|Const
Infix-expr   :: Expr Op Expr
Rhs-ref      :: Var-ref
Var-ref      :: Id s-sscs:[Expr⁺]
Con-var-ref  :: Id
Const        =  Int-const|Bool-const        disjoint
Op           =  Int-op|Bool-op|Comp-op      disjoint
Scalar-type  =  INT|BOOL
```

CONTEXT CONDITIONS

$Env\text{-}static = Id \rightarrow (Type \mid \underline{PROC} \mid \underline{LABEL} \mid \underline{CON\text{-}VAR})$

$is\text{-}wf\text{-}program(mk\text{-}program(t)) = is\text{-}wf\text{-}stmt(t,[\,])$

$is\text{-}wf\text{-}block(mk\text{-}block(dclm,procs,nsl),env) =$
  $\underline{let}\ ll = <s\text{-}nm(nsl(i)) \mid 1\underline{\le}i\underline{\le}\underline{len}\ nsl\ \&\ is\text{-}id(s\text{-}nm(nsl(i)))>$
  $\underline{let}\ pnms = \{s\text{-}nm(p) \mid p\epsilon procs\}$
  $is\text{-}unique\text{-}ids(ll)\ \&$
  $(p1\epsilon procs\ \&\ p2\epsilon procs\ \&\ p1\neq p2 \rightarrow s\text{-}nm(p1)\neq s\text{-}nm(p2))\ \&$
  $is\text{-}disjoint(<\underline{dom}\ dclm,\ pnms,\ \underline{elems}\ ll>)\ \&$
  $(\underline{let}\ renv = env \setminus (\underline{dom}\ dclm \cup pnms \cup \underline{elems}\,ll)$
  $\underline{let}\ nenv = renv \cup$
           $[id \mapsto star(dclm(id)) \mid id \in \underline{dom}\ dclm] \cup$
           $[id \mapsto \underline{PROC} \mid id \in pnms] \cup$
           $[id \mapsto \underline{LABEL} \mid id \in \underline{elems}\ ll]$
  $(dcl\epsilon\underline{rng}\ dclm \rightarrow is\text{-}wf\text{-}type\text{-}dcl(dcl,renv))\ \&$
  $(pr\epsilon procs \rightarrow is\text{-}wf\text{-}proc(pr,nenv))\ \&$
  $(1\underline{\le}i\underline{\le}\underline{len}\ nsl \rightarrow is\text{-}wf\text{-}stmt(s\text{-}stmt(nsl(i)),nenv))$
  $)$

$is\text{-}wf\text{-}type\text{-}dcl(mk\text{-}type(sctp,bdl),env) =$
  $is\text{-}wf\text{-}type(mk\text{-}type(sctp,bdl),env)\ \&$
  $(bdl=\underline{NIL}\ \vee$
   $is\text{-}expr\text{-}list(bdl)\ \&\ (1\underline{\le}i\underline{\le}\underline{len}bdl \rightarrow ex\text{-}tp(bdl(i),env)=\underline{INT}))$

$is\text{-}wf\text{-}proc(mk\text{-}proc(nm,parml,st),env) =$
  $is\text{-}unique\text{-}ids(<s\text{-}id(parml(i)) \mid 1\underline{\le}i\underline{\le}\underline{len}\ parml>)\ \&$
  $(\underline{let}\ nenv = env +$
           $[s\text{-}id(parml(i)) \mapsto s\text{-}attr(parml(i)) \mid i\in\{1:\underline{len}\ parml\}]$
   $is\text{-}wf\text{-}stmt(st,nenv)\ )$

$is-wf-parm(mk-parm(id,attr),env) =$
    $attr=\underline{PROC} \lor s-bds(attr)=\underline{NIL} \lor is-*-list(s-bds(attr))$

$is-wf-if(mk-if(b, ,),env) = ex-tp(b,env)=\underline{BOOL}$

$is-wf-for(mk-for(id,init,step,limit,st),env) =$
    $\underline{let}\ nenv = env + [id \mapsto \underline{CON-VAR}]$
    $ex-tp(init,env) = ex-tp(step,env) = ex-tp(limit,env) = \underline{INT}\ \&$
    $is-wf-stmt(st,nenv)$

$is-wf-call(mk-call(pn,al),env) =$
    $pn \in \underline{dom}\ env\ \&\ env(pn)=\underline{PROC}\ \&$
    $(1 \leq i \leq \underline{len}\ al \rightarrow is-wf-var-ref(al(i),env) \lor env(al(i))=\underline{PROC})$

$is-wf-goto(mk-goto(id),env) = id \in \underline{dom}\ env\ \&\ env(id)=\underline{LABEL}$

$is-wf-assign(mk-assign(lhs,rhs),env) =$
    $is-scalar(lhs,env)\ \&$
    $ex-tp(rhs,env) = var-ref-tp(lhs,env)$

$is-wf-in(mk-in(vr),env) = is-scalar(vr,env)$

$is-wf-infix-expr(mk-infix-expr(e1,op,e2),env) =$
    $is-int-op(op)\ \&\ ex-tp(e1,env)=ex-tp(e2,env)=\underline{INT}\ \lor$
    $is-bool-op(op)\ \&\ ex-tp(e1,env)=ex-tp(e2,env)=\underline{BOOL}\ \lor$
    $is-comp-op(op)\ \&\ ex-tp(e1,env)=ex-tp(e2,env)=\underline{INT}$

$s-wf-rhs-ref(mk-rhs-ref(r),env) = is-scalar(r,env)$

```
is-wf-var-ref(mk-var-ref(id,el),env) =
    id∈dom env & is-type(env(id)) &
    (el=NIL v (s-bds(env(id))≠NIL &
            len el = len s-bds(env(id)) &
            (1≤i≤len el → ex-tp(el(i),env)=INT)))
```

```
is-scalar(mk-var-ref(id,sscl),env) =
    sscl=NIL → s-bds(env(id))=NIL
```

```
is-wf-con-var-ref(mk-con-var-ref(id),env) =
    id∈dom env & env(id)=CON-VAR
```

```
ex-tp(e,env) =
    cases e:
    mk-infix-expr(e1,op,e2) →
        (is-int-op(op) → INT
         is-bool-op(op) → BOOL
         is-comp-op(op) → BOOL)
    mk-rhs-ref(vr) → var-ref-tp(vr,env)
    mk-con-var-ref(id) → INT.
    T                  → (is-int-const(e) → INT
                          is-bool-const(e) → BOOL)
```

```
var-ref-tp(mk-var-ref(id, ),env) = s-sc-type(env(id))
```

```
is-unique-ids(idl) = /* true iff no duplicates */
type: Id* → Bool
```

```
star(t) = /* all bounds changed to * */
type: Type → Type
```

```
is-disjoint(sl) = /* tests sets pairwise disjoint */
type: Set* → Bool
```

$is\text{-}scalar\text{-}type(t) = is\text{-}type(t)$ & $s\text{-}bds(t)=\underline{NIL}$

$is\text{-}array\text{-}type(t) = id\text{-}type(t)$ & $s\text{-}bds(t)\neq\underline{NIL}$

SEMANTIC OBJECTS

$$
\begin{aligned}
State &= (R\text{-}STG \to Storage) \underline{\cup} (R\text{-}IN \to Value\text{*}) \underline{\cup} (R\text{-}OUT \to Value\text{*}) \\
Storage &= (Bool\text{-}loc \to (Bool \mid \underline{?})) \underline{\cup} (Int\text{-}loc \to (Int \mid \underline{?})) \\
Value &= Int \mid Bool \\
Env &= Id \to (Loc \mid Con\text{-}var\text{-}den \mid Label\text{-}den \mid Proc\text{-}den) \\
Loc &= Array\text{-}loc \mid Scalar\text{-}loc \\
Array\text{-}loc &= (Int^{+} \leftrightarrow Bool\text{-}loc) \mid (Int^{+} \leftrightarrow Int\text{-}loc) \\
&\quad constraint:\ l \in Array\text{-}loc \Rightarrow (\exists il \in Nat^{+})(\underline{dom}\ l = rect(il)) \\
Scalar\text{-}loc &= Bool\text{-}loc \mid Int\text{-}loc \\
Con\text{-}var\text{-}den &= Int \\
Label\text{-}den &:: Aid\ Id \\
Aid &\quad \text{is an infinite set} \\
Proc\text{-}den &:: ((Loc \mid Proc\text{-}den)\text{*}\ Aid\text{-}set \to Tr) \\
Tr &= State \overset{\sim}{\to} State\ Abn \\
Abn &= [Label\text{-}den] \\
\left.\begin{array}{l} Int\text{-}loc \\ Bool\text{-}loc \end{array}\right\} &\quad \text{infinite sets } s.t.\ Bool\text{-}loc \cap Int\text{-}loc = \{\}
\end{aligned}
$$

FUNCTIONS

$i\text{-}program(mk\text{-}program(t))(inl) =$
   $(\underline{let}\ in\text{-}state =$
               $[\underline{R\text{-}STG}\mapsto[], \underline{R\text{-}IN}\mapsto inl, \underline{R\text{-}OUT}\mapsto <>]$
    $\underline{let}\ fin\text{-}state = i\text{-}stmt(t,[],\{\})(in\text{-}state)$
    $fin\text{-}state(\underline{R\text{-}OUT})$
   $)$

type: $Program \to (Value\text{*} \to Value\text{*})$

$i\text{-}stmt:\ Stmt\ Env\ Aid\text{-}set \Rightarrow$

```
i-block(mk-block(dclm,procs,nsl),env,cas) =
    (let aid∈Aid be s.t. aid∉cas
     let nenv: env +
            ([id ↦ mk-label-den(aid,id) | is-cont(id,nsl)] ∪
             [id ↦ e-type(dclm(id),env) | id∈domdclm] ∪
             [s-nm(p) ↦ e-proc(p,nenv) | p∈procs]);
     always
            (let locs = {nenv(id) | id∈domdclm}
             let sclocs = {l∈locs | is-scalar-loc(l)} ∪
                            union{rgnl | l∈locs & ¬is-scalar-loc(l)}
             R-STG := c R-STG \ sclocs
             )
     in i-named-stmt-list(nsl,nenv,cas∪{aid},aid)
     )


e-type(mk-type(sctp,bdl),env) =
    if bdl=NIL then
        (let l∈Scalar-loc be s.t.
                            is-tp-scalar-loc(sctp,l) & l∉dom c R-STG
         R-STG := c R-STG ∪ [l ↦ ?];
         return(l)
         )
    else
        (let ebdl: <e-expr(bdl(i),env) | 1≤i≤lenbdl>;
         if (∃i∈{1:lenbdl})(ebdl(i)<1) then error;
         let l∈Array-loc be s.t.
                scl∈rng l ↦ is-tp-scalar-loc(sctp,scl) &
                dom l = rect(ebdl) &
                rng l ∩ dom c R-STG = {}
         R-STG := c R-STG∪[scl↦? | scl∈rng l];
         return(l)
         )

type: Type Env ↦ Loc
```

```
e-proc(mk-proc( ,parml,st),env) =
    let f(denl,cas) =
        (if lendenl≠lenparml ∨
            (∃i∈{1:lenparml})(¬is-pmatch(denl(i),s-attr(parml(i)))
                then error;
        let lenv = env +
            [s-id(parml(i)) ↦ denl(i) | i ∈ {1:len parml}]
        i-stmt(st,lenv,cas)
        )
    mk-proc-den(f)

type: Proc Env → Proc-den


-named-stmt-list(nsl,env,cas,aid) =
    tixe [mk-label-den(aid,tid)↦it-named-stmt-list(tno,nsl,env,cas)
                        | 1≤tno≤lennsl & s-nm(nsl(tno))=tid≠NIL]
    in it-named-stmt-list(1,nsl,env,cas)

ype: Named-stmt* Env Aid-set Aid →


t-named-stmt-list(i,nsl,env,cas) =
    for j = i to len nsl do i-stmt(s-stmt(nsl(j)),env,cas)

ype: Nat Named-stmt* Env Aid-set →


-if(mk-if(be,th,el),env,cas) =
    (let bv: e-expr(be,env);
    if bv then i-stmt(th,env,cas)
    else        i-stmt(el,env,cas)
    )
```

```
i-for(mk-for(cv,ie,se,le,st),env,cas) =
   (let i: e-expr(ie,env);
    let s: e-expr(se,env);
    let l: e-expr(le,env);
    let f(x) = if (s>0 → x≤l, s<0 → x≥l, s=0 → TRUE)
                    then (i-stmt(st,env+[cv→x],cas);f(x+s))
    f(i)
   )



i-call(mk-call(pid,al),env,cas) =
   (let mk-proc-den(f) = env(pid)
    let dl: <is-var-ref(al(i)) → e-var-ref(al(i),env),
             T                  → env(al(i))    | 1≤i≤len al>;
    f(dl,cas)
   )



i-goto(mk-goto(id),env) =
   exit(env(id))



i-assign(mk-assign(vr,e),env) =
   (let l: e-var-ref(vr,env);
    let v: e-expr(e,env);
    assign(l,v)
   )



i-in(mk-in(vr),env) =
   (if c R-IN = <> then error;
    let l: e-var-ref(vr,env);
    let v: hd c R-IN;
    if ┐is-vmatch(v,var-ref-tp(vr)) then error
    else
        (R-IN := tl c R-IN;
         assign(l,v)
        )
   )
```

```
i-out(mk-out(e),env) =
   (let v: e-expr(e,env);
   R-OUT := c R-OUT ^ <v>
   )


e-expr: Expr Env ⟼ Value ·


e-infix-expr(mk-infix-expr(e1,op,e2),env) =
   (let v1: e-expr(e1,env);
    let v2: e-expr(e2,env);
    let v: apply-op(v1,op,v2);
    return(v)
   )


e-rhs-ref(mk-rhs-ref(vr),env) =
   (let l: e-var-ref(vr,env);
    contents(l)
   )


e-var-ref(mk-var-ref(id,sscl),env) =
   if sscl=NIL then return(env(id))
   else
       (let aloc = env(id)
        let esscl: <e-expr(sscl(i),env) | 1≤i≤lensscl>;
        if esscl∉dom aloc then error;
        return(aloc(esscl)))

ype: Var-ref Env ⟼ Loc


-con-var-ref(mk-con-var-ref(id),env) = return(env(id))


-const(e,) = /* return a Value corresponding to the Constant */
```

```
apply-op(v1,op,v2) = /* Returns an appropriate Value */
type: Value Op Value ⟶ Value


assign(l,v) =
    R-STG := c R-STG + [l ↦ v]


type: Scalar-loc Value ⟶
pre:  l∈dom c R-STG, is-lmatch(l,v)


contents(l) =
    let v: c R-STG(l);
    if v=? then error;
    else return(v)

type: Scalar-loc ⟶ Value
pre:  l∈dom c R-STG


rect(il) = /* generates a dense rectangle of integers */
type: Int⁺ → (Int⁺)-set
pre:  1≤i≤ len il ⟶ il(i)≥1


is-lmatch(l,v) = /* checks location and value are of same scalar type */
type: Scalar-loc Value → Bool


is-vmatch(v,t) = /* checks value is of scalar type */
type: Value Scalar-type → Bool


is-pmatch(d,s) = /* checks the argument matchs parameter specification */
type: (Loc | Proc-den) (Type | PROC) → Bool
```

s-tp-$scalar$-$loc(tp,l)$ =

   $tp=\underline{BOOL} \rightarrow is$-$bool$-$loc(l)$

   $tp=\underline{INT} \rightarrow is$-$int$-$loc(l)$

$ype:$ $Scalar$-$type$ $Scalar$-$loc \rightarrow Bool$

s-$cont(id,nsl)$ = $(\exists i \in \{1:\underline{lennsl}\})(id=s$-$nm(nsl(i)))$

$ype:$ Id $Named$-$stmt^* \rightarrow Bool$

DENOTATIONAL SEMANTICS OF GOTO:

AN EXIT FORMULATION AND ITS RELATION TO CONTINUATIONS

Cliff B.Jones

Abstract:

This paper discusses the problem of providing a defini=
tion for the "GOTO" statement within the framework of
denotational semantics. The accepted approach to the
problem is to use "Continuations". An alternative "Exit
Formulation" is described in this paper. A small language
is introduced which illustrates the difficulties caused
by statements which terminate abnormally. For this lan=
guage definitions based on both approaches are provided.
A proof of equivalence of the two definitions is then
given. In a closing discussion it is pointed out that
continuations can define a wider class of languages than
exits, although the latter have been shown to be adequate
to define languages as complex as PL/I.

CONTENTS

1. Introduction   280

2. Notation   281

3. A Small Language   282

4. Definition By Exit   285

5. Definition By Continuations   289

6. Equivalence of the Two Definitions   292

7. Discussion   302-304

Figures:

Fig.1: The Language to be Defined   283

Fig.2: Definition Using Exit Combinators   286

Fig.3: Definition by Exit Mechanism with Combinators Expanded 289

Fig.4: Definition Using Continuations   291

Fig.5: Definition Using Continuations --
        with Merge of $c-c$ and $c-l$ 293

Fig.6: Definition Using Continuations --
        Recomputed at Each Compound Statement   296

Fig.7: Definition Using (E) Continuations --
        Without Environments   300

1. INTRODUCTION

There exists by now a considerable body of work on the formal definition of programming languages (see Lucas 78, in this volume, for a historical review). Most of the work can be categorised as either "abstract interpreters", "denotational semantics" or "axiomatic". This
paper attempts to make a contribution to the understanding of denotational semantics. This approach is particularly associated with the
Programming Research Group at Oxford University. Evolving from the
earlier work on abstract interpreters (see Lucas 69) the more recent
work of the Vienna Laboratory has also used the denotational style
(see Bekić 74).

A language can be given by the set of its texts. To define the semantics of a language one must associate a meaning or denotation with
each text in the set. Since the set of texts will, for interesting
languages, be of infinite cardinality, this link will be shown by defining a function from the set of texts to a set of denotations. For
such a definition of a large language to be comprehensible, it is required that the denotation of a compound text should depend solely on
the denotations of its component parts. (Clearly, this rule must be applied only to a sensible level: ascribing meaning to single characters
and then trying to construct the meaning of identifiers and keywords
is unlikely to prove illuminating. The limit of sensible decomposition
is usually indicated by the abstract synta of a language.) In order
for a function from texts to denotations to define the semantics of the
texts, it is obviously a pre-requisite that the denotations themselves
should be objects with known meanings. One characteristic of denotational semantics is the use of mathematical objects (especially functions)
as the denotations. This accounts for the alternative name of "mathematical semantics". In fact the functions chosen as denotations are
of a very general form and it has been a considerable task to show
that such functions do indeed have a consistent meaning (see Scott 71).

There is, within the "denotational school", agreement as to the concepts required to provide definitions of simple languages. (However,
a number of notational differences lead to differences in the appearanc
of conceptually similar definitions, see next section). Remembering the
"denotational rule" that denotations of composite objects should be
built from the denotations of their components, the following observations can be made. For a purely functional language it is easy to a-
gree a definition; for a language which includes an assignment construc

the concept of a store (i.e. a mapping from identifiers to values) permits denotations to be defined which are functions from stores to stores; the generally accepted approach to block structured languages is to introduce locations and environments. Whilst refs Mosses 74 and Bekič 74 build from this basic list of agreements and tackle similar large languages, an important difference can be found.

The important difference between the Oxford and Vienna groups can be found in their approach to problems of abnormal termination. The archetypal problem in this category is the "goto" statement. A definition conforming to the denotational rule is difficult to construct for languages which include goto statements precisely because their effect is to transfer control across the structure over which the denotations are being constructed. (This power of goto statements has led to a movement for their elimination. This controversy is not entered into here. Rather, models are explained which are general enough to model goto. On such models one can then compare alternative language constructs which might offer the desirable features, without the danger, of goto statements. Of course, a language feature may eventually be selected for which simpler models are possible. What the models here offer is a basis from which to work.) The Oxford group use "continuations" (see Strachey 74) to define goto-like constructs: the definition in section 5 below is in this style. The same small example language is defined using the Vienna "exit" approach in section 4. The language itself is introduced informally in section 3 after some comments on notation. Given two definitions of the same language, the question of their relationship can be posed: equivalence is proved in section 6. Whilst both continuations and exits have been shown to be powerful enough to define commonly used programming languages, the two approaches are not of equivalent power, section 7 contains some concluding comments on this point.

2. NOTATION

The basis of the notation to be used in this paper is taken from logic and lambda calculus and will probably be familiar from the literature. The items of special interest within this paper are introduced below as required. A more complete explanation is available elsewhere in this volume (Jones 78a); Jones 75 provides a stepwise development of the exit concept.

One of the most dangerous traps when comparing two languages is to
let the superficial syntactic differences confuse the real issue which
is that of meaning. The difference in appearance between the Oxford
and Vienna definitions is very striking. The former group has achieved succinctness in order to facilitate formal reasoning about smaller
definitions, whilst the tasks tackled by the Vienna group have led
them to strive for readability. This paper, being based on a very small
language, compromises a little for the sake of compactness. Thus short
names are used for the syntactic classes and "<>" is used instead of a
named (tree) constructor where context makes the choice clear (the convention for dropping semantic rules for syntax classes defined to be
a list of alternatives is also followed). Other than this the definitions, even that by continuations, are given in a Vienna-style. The
issue to be reviewed is the differences between the domains and function types. Choices like the use of different bracket symbols, explicit versus implicit typing of functions and the degree of abstractness
for the syntax might influence the number of characters in a definition
but would, if used on one of the definitions, serve only to cloud the
main distinction.

3. A SMALL LANGUAGE

This section introduces the language which will be used as the basis
for the remainder of the paper. The basic statements of the language
are "goto" and an unanalyzed class of elementary statements. About
these latter all necessary knowledge is given by the function "el-sem"
which associates a state-transformation (i.e. a function over the
class Σ) with each member of El-stmt. Statements can be optionally
named and lists thereof can be formed into compound statements. Such
compound statements are also statements and thus can be named and used
as elements of other lists. The abstract syntax of the language is
given, along with a full name for each class of objects to aid comprehension, in *fig. 1*. The structure of the classes Id and El-stmt is not
further defined.

Note: In this paper a superscript ^{0} is to be read as the functional
      composition operator. It is elsewhere represented by the fat
      dot: •.

Full name	Abstract syntax
Program	P :: C
Compound statement	C :: $s\text{-}b:Ns*$
Named statement	Ns :: $s\text{-}n:[Id]\ s\text{-}b:S$
Statement	S = $C\ \|\ G\ \|\ E$
Goto statement	G :: Id
Elementary statement	El :: $El\text{-}stmt$
Identifiers	Id

Fig. 1: The Language to be Defined

n order to facilitate discussion of the identifier prefixes of statements, two predicates which check for the (direct and indirect) con-
tainment of identifiers and a function yielding the index of that
statement which contains an identifier (under the assumption that it is
contained somewhere) are introduced:

$$is\text{-}dcont(id,nsl) \Leftrightarrow (\exists i \in \{1:\underline{lenn}sl\})(s\text{-}n^0 nsl(i) = id)$$
$$type:\ Id\ Ns* \to Bool$$

$$is\text{-}cont(id,nsl) \Leftrightarrow (is\text{-}dcont(id,nsl) \lor$$
$$(\exists i \in \{1:\underline{lenn}sl\})(s\text{-}b^0\text{-}nsl(i) \in C\ \&\ is\text{-}cont(id,s\text{-}b^0 s\text{-}b^0 nsl(i))))$$
$$type:\ Id\ Ns* \to Bool$$

$$ind(id,nsl) =$$
$$\quad is\text{-}dcont(id,nsl)\ \to\ (\imath i)(s\text{-}n^0 nsl(i) = id)$$
$$\quad T\ \to\ (\imath i)(s\text{-}b^0 nsl(i) \in C\ \&\ is\text{-}cont(id,s\text{-}b^0 s\text{-}b^0 nsl(i)))$$
$$type:\ Id\ Ns* \to Nat$$
$$pre:\ is\text{-}cont(id,nsl)$$

It is assumed that well-formed programs satisfy the context condition
that all label identifiers used in goto statements are contained exactly once within the program. With respect to the statement list within
which the goto is placed, the target statement may be within the same
list, within a containing list or within a compound statement which
is a member of the same list, The local "hop" and the abnormal exit
from a list should require no comment. The ability to jump into a
phrase structure is allowed, because it is included in many programming languages (cf. Algol 60 "goto" into branches of conditional statements.)

The choice of features in this language has been made with some care
in order to exhibit most of the complexity of large languages in a
framework of reasonable size. Thus the ability to hop between elements
of a list has been supplemented by permitting goto statements to enter
and leave syntactic units. In fact if the reader compares this language
to Algol 60 (see Henhapl 78 in this volume) only the ability to pass
labels and procedures as parameters forces an extension of the ideas
used here. Abnormal termination of a block via a goto statement is a
straightforward extension and the problems associated with redefinition of names in a block-structured language can be solved in a uni-
form way for variable and label identifiers (see Bekić 74 for a discussion of label variables).

The elementary statements of the language are assumed to cause changes
to a class of states (Σ):

el-sem: El-stmt $\rightarrow$ ($\Sigma \rightarrow \Sigma$)

Were it not for the inclusion of the "goto" construct, it would be
straightforward to provide a definition which associated a transformation with any elements of S. (The denotation of a list of statements
being the composition of the denotations of the elements of the list.)
Whilst as a result of the context condition given above, the denotation
of a whole program will be such a transformation, it is not possible
to ascribe such a simple denotation to "goto" statements. The next two
sections offer different solutions to this problem.

4. <u>DEFINITION</u> <u>BY</u> <u>EXIT</u>

The difficulty of finding a suitable definition for a language which includes goto statements is that its ability to cut across syntactic units forces changes on the semantics of all such units. A motivation of the exit approach to be defined in this section was to minimize the effect of these changes on the overall appearance of a definition. The key to achieving the desired effect without writing it into all of the semantic equations is to define appropriate combinators. Thus in a simple language (i.e. one without goto statements) a combinator denoting functional composition might be written ";". If this same symbol is reinterpreted as the more complex combinator used below, a definition for a language with goto statements can preserve a simpler appearance except, of course, for those semantic equations which deal specifically with goto statements.

The basic idea of definition by exit is to associate a denotation with each statement which is a function of type:

$$E = \Sigma \rightarrow \Sigma \ A$$

where:

$$A = Id \mid \underline{NIL}$$

Thus the denotation of a statement is a function from states to pairs: the first element is a state and the second is either an identifier or $\underline{NIL}$. In the case that applying the denotation of a statement to a state results in no "goto", the respective range element will be the result state paired with $\underline{NIL}$. If, however, a "goto" is encountered to a label not contained within the statement, the range element will pair the state reflecting state transition up to the time of the "goto" with the target label.

The definition, using combinators whose meaning is made precise below, is given in *fig 2*. The function names all begin with "x-" to signify that they are part of the exit-style definition. It is not difficult to provide an intuitive understanding of this definition. The function x-g which defines the semantics of goto statements uses the "$\underline{exit}$" combinator which simply pairs the argument state with the given identifier) value. Wherever a simple ($\Sigma \rightarrow \Sigma$) function is shown it is interpreted as yielding $\underline{NIL}$ paired with whatever the output state

```
x-p(<cp>)  =  x-c(cp)


x-c(cp)  =  x-cp(NIL,cp)


x-cp(ido,<nsl>) =
    tixe [ id→x-l(id,nsl) | is-cont(id,nsl) ]
    in  x-l(ido,nsl)


x-l(ido,nsl) =
    ido=NIL              →   x-nsl(nsl,1)
    is-dcont(ido,nsl)→   x-nsl(nsl,ind(ido,nsl))
    T                    →   (let i = ind(ido,nsl)
                              x-cp(ido,s-b(nsl(i)));
                              x-nsl(nsl,i+1)
                             )


x-nsl(nsl,i) =
    i<lennsl  →  (x-s(s-b(nsl(i)));x-nsl(nsl,i+1))
    T         →  I


x-g(<id>)  =  exit(id)


x-el(<el>)  =  el-sem(el)



    fig 2: Definition using exit combinators
```

would have been. This explains x-el and the second case of x-nsl (I is the identity on Σ). The fact that these denotations, and thus that of the excised x-s, are of type E force their combination with one another to be more complex. The ";" combinator applies the second E

transformation only if the second component of the first result is *NIL*,
otherwise the result of the two composed transformations is exactly
that of the first. It remains only to explain *x-cp*. Here the combinator "*tixe*" (spell back-to-front!) is for the converse situation from
";". If a normal pair (i.e. *NIL* second component) is the result of the
in transformation nothing more is done; the first mapping defines, for
some restricted set of exit values, the action to be taken if the *in*
transformation returns a non-*NIL* result. It is important to realize
that this mapping covers a finite number of cases which can be determined from the text being defined.

The types of the semantic functions can be given:

$$x\text{-}p: \quad P \rightarrow E$$
$$x\text{-}c: \quad C \rightarrow E$$
$$x\text{-}cp: \quad [Id]\ C \ \rightarrow\ E$$
$$x\text{-}l: \quad [Id]\ Ns^* \ \rightarrow\ E$$
$$x\text{-}nsl: \quad Ns^*\ Nat \ \rightarrow\ E$$
$$x\text{-}s: \quad S \rightarrow E \qquad \text{(assumed)}$$
$$x\text{-}g: \quad G \rightarrow E$$
$$x\text{-}el: \quad El \rightarrow E$$

The formal meanings of the combinators is now given. The format used
for these definitions is first to list any assumptions, then show the
type of the combinator expression (after a ":") and finally to provide
the definition (after "$\triangleq$").

Firstly the *exit* combinator:

for $id \in Id$
$$\underline{exit(id)}\ :\ E$$
$$\underline{exit(id)}\ \triangleq\ \lambda\sigma.<\sigma, id>$$

The promotion of a simple transformation to one of type E is governed
by context:

for $t\ :\ \Sigma\rightarrow\Sigma$ in a context requiring E
$$t\ :\ E$$
$$t\ \triangleq\ \lambda\sigma.<t(\sigma),\underline{NIL}>$$

In particular:

$$I \stackrel{\Delta}{=} \lambda\sigma.<\sigma,\underline{NIL}>$$

The semicolon combinator is defined as:

for t_1 and t_2 : E

$$(t_1;t_2) : E$$
$$(t_1;t_2) \stackrel{\Delta}{=} (\lambda\sigma,ido.(ido=\underline{NIL} \rightarrow t_2(\sigma),T \rightarrow <\sigma,ido>))^0 t_1$$

The most interesting of the combinators is "*tixe*":

for t_1 : $Id \rightarrow E$, t_2 : E, p : $[Id] \rightarrow Bool$
$$(\underline{tixe}\ [a \rightarrow t_1(a)|p(a)]\ \underline{in}\ t_2) : E$$
$$\underline{(\underline{tixe}\ [a \rightarrow t_1(a)|p(a)]\ \underline{in}\ t_2)}$$
$$\stackrel{\Delta}{=}\quad (\underline{let}\ e = [a \rightarrow t_1(a)|p(a)]$$
$$\underline{let}\ r(\sigma,ido) = (ido \in dome \rightarrow r^0 e(ido)(\sigma),T \rightarrow <\sigma,ido>)$$
$$r^0 t_2)$$

Notice that r is used recursively, thus the effort to resolve an abnormal exit with t_1 continues until p is not satisfied.

Fig 3 provides a rewriting of the exit definition with the above combinator definitions applied to provide a definition in almost-pure lambda notation. Although this is more convenient for the proofs of section 6, the combinators have considerable value in providing a shorter and more intuitive definition of a large language (compare refs Bekić 74 and Allen 72).

Notice that the only labels which are returned from (non-*NIL* second components of the function) "*x-1*" are those which are not contained in the text argument. Thus it can be proved:

$$pre\text{-}x\text{-}l(ido,nsl) \quad <\Rightarrow> \quad (ido=\underline{NIL} \lor is\text{-}cont(ido,nsl))$$
$$post\text{-}x\text{-}l(ido,nsl,\sigma,\sigma',ido') \quad <\Rightarrow> \quad (ido'=\underline{NIL} \lor \neg is\text{-}cont(ido',nsl))$$

and because of the context condition it is possible to show that $x\text{-}p$ is of type:

$$\Sigma \rightarrow \Sigma\ \underline{NIL}$$

and from this extract a denotation of type: $\Sigma \rightarrow \Sigma$

$x\text{-}cp(ido,<nsl>) =$

 $\underline{let}\ e = [id \to x\text{-}l(id,nsl) \mid is\text{-}cont(id,nsl)]$

 $\underline{let}\ r(\sigma,ido') = (ido' \in \underline{dom}e \to r^0 e(ido')(\sigma),\ T \to <\sigma,ido'>)$

 $r^0 x\text{-}l(ido,nsl)$

$x\text{-}l(ido,nsl) =$

 $ido=\underline{NIL}$ $\to x\text{-}nsl(nsl,1)$

 $is\text{-}dcont(ido,nsl) \to x\text{-}nsl(nsl,ind(ido,nsl))$

 T $\to (\underline{let}\ i = ind(ido,nsl)$

          $(\lambda\sigma,ido'.(ido'=\underline{NIL} \to x\text{-}nsl(nsl,i+1)(\sigma),$

              $T \to <\sigma,ido'>))^0 x\text{-}cp(ido,s\text{-}b^0 nsl(i))$

$x\text{-}nsl(nsl,i) =$

 $i \leq \underline{len}nsl \to ((\lambda\sigma,ido'.(ido'=\underline{NIL} \to x\text{-}nsl(nsl,i+1),\ T \to <\sigma,ido'>))^0$

        $x\text{-}s(s\text{-}b(nsl(i))))$

 T $\to \lambda\alpha.<\sigma,\underline{NIL}>$

$x\text{-}g(<id>)\ =\ \lambda\sigma.<\sigma,id>$

$x\text{-}el(<el>)\ =\ \lambda\sigma.<el\text{-}sem(el)(\sigma),\underline{NIL}>$

$x\text{-}p,\ x\text{-}c$ $unchanged$

 Fig 3: Definition by exit mechanism with combinators expanded

. DEFINITION BY CONTINUATIONS

'his section introduces the more widely used continuation approach for
he definition of languages which include goto statements. As with
xits, this approach recognises that denotations of type $\Sigma \to \Sigma$ will not

suffice. While continuations themselves are:

$$T = \Sigma \to \Sigma$$

the denotations of statement-like constructs become:

$$T \to T$$

The question of the meaning of goto statements is handled by associating continuations with identifiers. The denotation of a goto statement for any continuation is then the continuation associated with the
contained identifier. In a complex language definition, block structure would anyway force the use of an explicit environment argument to
the semantic functions and this can be used to record the associated
continuation for labels. Thus, in the current case:

$$Env = Id \to T$$

Intuitively, one can consider statement denotations as yielding, for
a given subsequent computation (i.e. continuation), the overall computation starting at this statement. Notice that this is not simply the
composition of two functions of type $\Sigma \to \Sigma$ because of the possibility of
"goto". The label denotations are the transitions resulting from starting execution at that label and executing to the end of the program.
Thus a function of type $\Sigma \to \Sigma$ is associated with a text given a particular environment and continuation. A more complete description of the
method of continuations is given in *Strachey 74*. The definition by continuations is given in *fig 4*. (The use of braces to bracket arguments
which are continuations is adopted for the benefit of the reader.)

Since there are no combinators to be explained in this definition, no
intuitive explanation is offered. The reader who is unfamiliar with
this style of definition is, however, advised to study this definition
carefully (possibly with the aid of an example) to be sure he has
grasped the rather back-to-front construction of denotations. The
types of these semantic functions are:

$$
\begin{aligned}
c\text{-}p: &\quad P &&\to T \\
c\text{-}c: &\quad C &&\to (Env \to (T \to T)) \\
c\text{-}nsl: &\quad Ns^* \; Nat &&\to (Env \to (T \to T)) \\
c\text{-}s: &\quad S &&\to (Env \to (T \to T)) \qquad \text{(assumed)}
\end{aligned}
$$

$$c\text{-}p(<cp>)=$$
$$\quad \underline{let}\ env_0 = [id \rightarrow c\text{-}l(id,s\text{-}b(cp))(env_0)\{I\} \mid is\text{-}cont(id,s\text{-}b(cp))]$$
$$\quad c\text{-}c(cp)(env_0)\{I\}$$

$$c\text{-}c(<nsl>)\ =\ c\text{-}nsl(nsl,1)$$

$$c\text{-}nsl(nsl,i)(env)\{c\}=$$
$$\quad i<\underline{len}nsl \rightarrow c\text{-}s(s\text{-}b(nsl(i)))(env)\{c\text{-}nsl(nsl,i+1)(env)\{c\}\}$$
$$\quad T \qquad\ \rightarrow c$$

$$c\text{-}g(<id>)(env)\{c\}\ =\ env(id)$$

$$c\text{-}el(<el>)(env)\{c\}\ =\ c^0el\text{-}sem(el)$$

$$c\text{-}l(id,nsl)(env)\{c\}=$$
$$\quad is\text{-}dcont(id,nsl) \rightarrow c\text{-}nsl(nsl,ind(id,nsl))(env)\{c\}$$
$$\quad T \qquad\qquad\ \rightarrow (\underline{let}\ i = ind(ido,nsl)$$
$$\qquad\qquad\qquad\qquad c\text{-}l(id,s\text{-}b^0s\text{-}b^0nsl(i))(env)\{c\text{-}nsl(nsl,i+1)(env)\{c\}\}$$
$$\qquad\qquad\qquad\quad)$$

fig 4: Definition using continuations

$$c\text{-}g: \quad G \qquad \rightarrow \ (Env \ \rightarrow \ (T \ \rightarrow \ T))$$
$$c\text{-}el: \quad EL \qquad \rightarrow \ (Env \ \rightarrow \ (T \ \rightarrow \ T))$$
$$c\text{-}l: \quad Id \ Ns* \quad \rightarrow \ (Env \ \rightarrow \ (T \ \rightarrow \ T))$$

6. EQUIVALENCE OF THE TWO DEFINITIONS

Sections 4 and 5 have both provided mappings from programs to functions
$(\Sigma\rightarrow\Sigma)$: the aim of this section is to show that the definitions are e-
quivalent in the sense that they associate the same transformation with
any well-formed program. It is possible to discern three important
differences between the exit and continuation definitions:

(i) The continuation definition associates with each label identifier
a denotation (i.e. continuation) which reflects the effect of starting
execution at that label and continuing to the end of the entire program. On the other hand, the exit definition provides (see point *(ii)*)
different denotations for label identifiers at each nested compound
statement: in each case the denotation captures the meaning of execution from any contained label to the end of the current compound statement.

(ii) Whereas the continuation definition passes the denotations of
label identifiers to semantic functions explicitly in the environment,
the meaning of labels (an E) in exit definitions is used (by the *tixe*
combinator) at the level of the containing compound statement.

(iii) The mode of generation of the respective denotations in the two
approaches differs: in the exit-style the denotation of a label is
derived by starting at that label and "composing" forwards (via the
semicolon combinator); continuations are built up from the final transformation composing backwards.

The proof style adopted below is to show a sequence of definitions
(each with different prefixes for the function names) and show that
each is equivalent to its predecessor. Since the point of departure
is the "c-" definition of section 5 and the last step shows the equivalence of the "f-" definition to the (expanded form of the) "x-" definition of section 4 a complete proof of equivalence is given. A good
overview of the reasoning can be obtained by understanding the intermediate definitions without following the details of the individual

equivalence proofs.

The first step (i.e. the "d-" definition) is purely preparatory, as, in a sense, is the second ("e-") although this relates specifically to difference *(i)*. The step to the "f-" definition completes the resolution of differences *(i)* and *(ii)*. The final step from the "f-" to the "x-" functions resolves difference *(iii)*.

The first step in our equivalence is trivial. Looking at the "c-" functions, it is obvious that c-c and c-l are both special cases of a more general function which takes an <u>optional</u> identifier as its first argument.

$d-l:$ $[Id]$ $Ns*$ $\rightarrow$ $(Env$ $\rightarrow$ $(T$ $\rightarrow$ $T))$

Since a combination of these two tasks has been employed in the "x-" definition the difference must be resolved somewhere and early resolution will shorten some of the inductive arguments to be used below. In fact the definition given in *fig 5* could have been presented in section 5: equivalence with that actually given follows from:

$is-cont(id,nsl)$ $\rightarrow$ $d-l(id,nsl) = c-l(id,nsl)$
$d-l(\underline{NIL},nsl)$ $=$ $c-c(<nsl>)$

$d-c(<nsl>)=d-l(\underline{NIL},nsl)$

$d-l(ido,nsl)(env)\{c\}=$
    $ido=\underline{NIL}$ $\rightarrow$ $d-nsl(nsl,1)(env)\{c\}$
    $is-dcont(ido,nsl)\rightarrow$ $d-nsl(nsl,ind(ido,nsl))(env)\{c\}$
    T $\rightarrow$ $(\underline{let}\ i = ind(ido,nsl)$
                                 $d-l(ido,s-b^0s-b^0nsl(i))(env)\{d-nsl(nsl,i+1)(env)\{c\}\}$
                              $)$

$d-p,d-nsl,d-g,d-el:$ models of respective "c-" functions

    fig 5: Definition using continuations with merge of c-c and c-l.

The next step in the proof also changes very little. The types of the
"e-" functions are the same as those of the "d-" functions. The difference is that some elements of the environment (i.e. contained label
denotations) are recomputed at each compound statement level. What has
to be proved is that the recomputed values are exactly the same as
those already stored (the usefulness of this step will become apparent later). A good intuitive confirmation of this claim can be obtained by viewing the "e-" functions as a macro-expansion and observ-
ing that the continuation argument of $e\text{-}cp(\underline{NIL},<nsl>)$ is identical
with that used to generate the denotations (in env_0 of $d\text{-}p$) of all
labels contained in nsl.

Proceeding more formally, from the substitutivity of equal values it
is obvious that:

$(is\text{-}cont(id,nsl) \;\rightarrow\; env(id)=d\text{-}l(id,nsl)(env)\{c\}) \quad \&$
$(ido=\underline{NIL} \;\lor\; is\text{-}cont(ido,nsl))$
$\quad\rightarrow\; d\text{-}l(ido,nsl)(env+[id\text{-}d\text{-}l(id,nsl)(env)\{c\}|is\text{-}cont(id,nsl)])\{c\}$
$\qquad =\quad d\text{-}l(ido,nsl)(env)\{c\}$

It is now necessary to show that for all

$d\text{-}l(ido,nsl)(env)\{c\}$

it is true that:

$is\text{-}cont(id,nsl) \;\rightarrow\; env(id) = d\text{-}l(id,nsl)(env)\{c\}$

Observe that this is true for the reference to $d\text{-}l$ from $d\text{-}p$. For recursive calls of $d\text{-}l$ consider:

id_n such that $is\text{-}cont(id_n,nsl)$ & $\neg is\text{-}dcont(id_n,nsl)$

its denotation is given by:

$env(id_n) \;=\; d\text{-}l(id_n,s\text{-}b^0 \, s\text{-}b^0 nsl(i_n))(env)\{d\text{-}nsl(nsl,i_n+1)(env)\{c\}\}$
where $i_n = ind(id_n,nsl)$

but for recursive references to $d\text{-}l$ in $d\text{-}nsl(nsl,i_n)(env)\{c\}$

$$d\text{-}nsl(nsl,i_n)(env)\{c\}$$
$$= d\text{-}s(s\text{-}b^0 nsl(i_n))(env)\{d\text{-}nsl(nsl,i_n+1)(env)\{c\}\}$$
$$= d\text{-}l(\underline{NIL},s\text{-}b^0 s\text{-}b^0 nsl(i_n))(env)\{d\text{-}nsl(nsl,i_n+1)(env)\{c\}\}$$

o for:

$$is\text{-}cont(id_n,s\text{-}b^0 s\text{-}b^0 nsl(i_n))$$

he required property still holds since the continuations match.
his concludes the argument and the definition in *fig 6* can be seen
o be equivalent to the "*d-*" functions because *e-cp* is introduced
ust to "recompute" some label denotations; other functions are changed
ccordingly including the fact that *e-p* need no longer generate an en-
ironment:

$$e\text{-}cp \; : \; [Id] \; C \to (Env \to (T \to T))$$

he next stage of the proof is the most interesting. Before coming to
he "*f-*" functions a useful lemma on continuations will be given. In-
uitively this lemma states that in order to achieve the same effect
s composing some function with the denotation of a statement, that
unction must be composed with both the contination and each label de-
otation used in deriving the given denotation.

```
e-p(<cp>)  =  e-c(cp)([]){I}



e-c(cp)  =  e-cp(NIL,cp)



e-cp(ido,<nsl>)(env){c}=
  let env' = env+[id→e-l(id,nsl)(env'){c}|is-cont(id,nsl)]
  e-l(ido,nsl)(env'){c}



e-l(ido,nsl)(env){c}=
  ido=NIL                →  e-nsl(nsl,1)(env){c}
  is-dcont(ido,nsl)      →  e-nsl(nsl,ind(ido,nsl))(env){c}
  T                      →  (let i = ind(ido,nsl)
                               e-cp(ido,s-b⁰nsl(i))(env){e-nsl(nsl,i+1)(env){c}}
                           )
```

`e-nsl,e-g,e-el:` **models of respective "c-" functions**

`fig 6:` **Definition using continuations recomputed**
       at each compound statement

Lemma I

define: $me(c,env) = [id \rightarrow c^0 env(id) \mid id \in domenv]$

show for: et is $e\text{-}s(s), e\text{-}nsl(nsl,i), e\text{-}l(ido,nsl)$ or $e\text{-}cp(ido,cp)$

that: $c_2{}^0 et(env)\{c_1\} = et(me(c_2,env))\{c_2{}^0 c_1\}$

Proof:

The argument is by induction on the structure of the text, as a basis consider statements of G and E:

$$c_2{}^0 e\text{-}g(<id>)(env)\{c\} = c_2{}^0 env(id)$$
$$e\text{-}g(<id>)(me(c_2,env))\{c_2{}^0 c_1\} = me(c_2,env)(id)$$
$$= c_2{}^0 env(id)$$

$$c_2{}^0 e\text{-}el(<el>)(env)\{c_1\} = c_2{}^0 c_1{}^0 el\text{-}sem(el)$$
$$e\text{-}el(<el>)(me(c_2,env))\{c_2{}^0 c_1\} = c_2{}^0 c_1{}^0 el\text{-}sem(el)$$

next in the basis consider elements of $Ns*$ where no element contains a C, here a subsidiary inductive proof (on $lennsl\text{-}i$) is made. For the basis, consider $i > lennsl$:

$$c_2{}^0 e\text{-}nsl(nsl,i)(env)\{c_1\} = c_2{}^0 c_1$$
$$e\text{-}nsl(nsl,i)(me(c_2,env))\{c_2{}^0 c_1\} = c_2{}^0 c_1$$

for the inductive step $i \leq lennsl$:

$$c_2{}^0 e\text{-}nsl(nsl,i)(env)\{c_1\}$$
$$= c_2{}^0 e\text{-}s(s\text{-}b(nsl(i)))(env)\{e\text{-}nsl(nsl,i+1)(env)\{c_1\}\}$$
$$= e\text{-}s(s\text{-}b(nsl(i)))(me(c_2,env))\{c_2{}^0 e\text{-}nsl(nsl,i+1)(env)\{c_1\}\} \qquad \text{I.H.on } S$$
$$= e\text{-}s(s\text{-}b(nsl(i)))(me(c_2,env))\{e\text{-}nsl(nsl,i+1)(me(c_2,env))\{c_2{}^0 c_1\}\} \qquad \text{I.H.on } Ns*$$

$$e\text{-}nsl(nsl,i)(me(c_2,env))\{c_2{}^0 c_1\}\}$$
$$= e\text{-}s(s\text{-}b(nsl(i)))(me(c_2,env))\{e\text{-}nsl(nsl,i+1)(me(c_2,env)\{c_2{}^0 c_1\}\}$$

For elements of $Ns*$ where no element contains a compound statement, the results for $e\text{-}l(ido,nsl)$ and $e\text{-}cp(ido,cp)$ are immediate from the above.

For the inductive step, the only additional case to be considered is the construction of elements of C, thus:

$$c_2{}^0 e\text{-}c(cp)(env)\{c_1\} = c_2{}^0 e\text{-}cp(s\text{-}b(cp))(env)\{c_1\}$$
$$e\text{-}c(cp)(me(c_2,env))\{c_2{}^0 c_1\} = e\text{-}cp(s\text{-}b(cp))(me(c_2,env))\{c_2{}^0 c_1\}$$

which are equal by induction hypothesis.

This concludes the proof of Lemma I.

Lemma I will now be used to justify change from passing in label denotations in environments to composing them with the revised meaning of the basic statement list. The revision to the meaning of a statement list changes it to type E and makes any goto statement cause a label to be returned as the second component of the result. The composition of the label denotations is now (recursively) applied only if this indication of abnormal exit is present. Intuitively the proof which follows shows that any environment is equivalent to a composition of a test and a constant environment, and any continuation is equivalent to a composition of a test and a constant function. Since both of these tests are the same, lemma I can be used to factor out the test.

Proceeding more formally, it is observed that though the used types of the "e-" functions are:

$$e\text{-}\theta: \quad \theta \rightarrow ((Id \rightarrow T) \rightarrow (T \rightarrow T))$$

they are perfectly general in that they also fit:

$$e\text{-}\theta: \quad \theta \rightarrow ((Id \rightarrow (\Sigma \rightarrow \Omega)) \rightarrow ((\Sigma \rightarrow \Omega) \rightarrow (\Sigma \rightarrow \Omega)))$$

Writing:

$$xe(nsl) = [id \rightarrow \lambda\sigma.<\sigma,id> | is\text{-}cont(id,nsl)]$$
$$xt(env,c) = \lambda\sigma,a.(a=\underline{NIL}\rightarrow c(\sigma),T\rightarrow env(a)(\sigma))$$

it is immediate that:

$$\underline{domenv} = \{id | is\text{-}cont(id,nsl)\}$$
$$\Rightarrow \quad [id \rightarrow xt(env,c)^0 xe(nsl) | id \in \underline{domenv}] = env$$

and:

$$xt(env,c)^0 \lambda\sigma.<\sigma,NIL> = c$$

ut then:

$$e\text{-}l(ido,nsl)(env')\{c\} = e\text{-}l(ido,nsl)([id \rightarrow xt(env',c)^0 xe(nsl) \mid id \in dom\,env'])$$
$$\{xt(env',c)^0 \lambda\sigma.<\sigma,\underline{NIL}>\}$$
$$= xt(env',c)^0 e\text{-}l(ido,nsl)(xe(nsl))\{\lambda\sigma.<\sigma,\underline{NIL}>\}$$

o:

$$e\text{-}op(ido,<nsl>)(env)\{c\}$$
$$= (\underline{let} \; env'=env+$$
$$[id \rightarrow (\lambda\sigma,a.(a=\underline{NIL} \rightarrow c(\sigma),T \rightarrow env'(a)(\sigma)))^0$$
$$e\text{-}l(id\,,nsl)(xe(nsl))\{\lambda\sigma.<\sigma,\underline{NIL}>\} \mid is\text{-}cont(id,nsl)]$$
$$(\lambda\sigma,a.(a=\underline{NIL} \rightarrow c(\sigma),T \rightarrow env'(a)(\sigma)))^0$$
$$e\text{-}l(ido,nsl)(xe(nsl))\{\lambda\sigma.<\sigma,\underline{NIL}>\})$$
$$= (\underline{let} \; e=[id \rightarrow e\text{-}l(id,nsl)(xe(nsl))\{\lambda\sigma.<\sigma,\underline{NIL}>\} \mid is\text{-}cont(id,nsl)]$$
$$\underline{let} \; r(\sigma,a) = (a \in dom\,e \rightarrow r^0 e(a)(\sigma),T \rightarrow env(a)(\sigma))$$
$$r^0 e\text{-}l(ido,nsl)(xe(nsl))\{\lambda\sigma.<\sigma,\underline{NIL}>\})$$

trictly, the whole definition has now become:

$$e\text{-}p: \quad P \rightarrow (\Sigma \rightarrow \Sigma \; [Id])$$

and this was why it was necessary to observe above that T could be re-
laced by $\Sigma \rightarrow \Omega$. But, as with the exit definition in section 4, it can
e shown that only non-contained labels can be returned. Thus at the
rogram level it can be shown for well-formed programs that the second
lement of the result must be $\underline{NIL}$.

t all *env* arguments now give constant denotations for labels! Be-
tuse the definition only considers well-formed programs these con-
ant functions can be moved into the semantic definition of goto.
rthermore, since the environment argument is now used nowhere, it
n be omitted. This results in the definition in *fig 7*.

$$f\text{-}p(<cp>) = f\text{-}c(cp)\{\lambda\sigma.<\sigma,\underline{NIL}>\}$$

$$f\text{-}c(cp) = f\text{-}cp(\underline{NIL},cp)$$

$$f\text{-}cp(ido,<nsl>)\{c\}=$$
$$\quad \underline{let}\ e = [id{\to}f\text{-}l(id,nsl)\{\lambda\sigma.<\sigma,\underline{NIL}>\}\,|\,is\text{-}cont(id,nsl)]$$
$$\quad \underline{let}\ r(\sigma,a) = (a{\in}\underline{dome}{\to}r^0 e(a)(\sigma),T{\to}\lambda\sigma.<\sigma,a>)$$
$$\quad r^0 f\text{-}l(ido,nsl)\{\lambda\sigma.<\sigma,\underline{NIL}>\}$$

$$f\text{-}l(ido,nsl)\{c\}=$$
$$\quad ido{=}\underline{NIL} \qquad\qquad\qquad \to\ f\text{-}nsl(nsl,1)\{c\}$$
$$\quad is\text{-}dcont(ido,nsl) \to\ f\text{-}nsl(nsl,ind(ido,nsl))\{c\}$$
$$\quad T \qquad\qquad\qquad\qquad \to\ (\underline{let}\ i = ind(ido,nsl)$$
$$\qquad\qquad\qquad\qquad\qquad f\text{-}cp(ido,s\text{-}b^0 nsl(i))\{f\text{-}nsl(nsl,i+1)\{c\}\}$$
$$\qquad\qquad\qquad\qquad\qquad)$$

$$f\text{-}nsl(nsl,i)\{c\}=$$
$$\quad i{\leq}\underline{lennsl} \to\ f\text{-}s(s\text{-}b^0 nsl(i))\{f\text{-}nsl(nsl,i+1)\{c\}\}$$
$$\quad T \qquad\quad \to\ c$$

$$f\text{-}g(<id>)\{c\} = \lambda\sigma.<\sigma,id>$$

$$f\text{-}el(<el>)\{c\} = c^0 el\text{-}sem(el)$$

fig 7: Definition using (E) continuations without environments.

The "$f\text{-}$" functions have the types:

$$
\begin{array}{llll}
f\text{-}p\text{:} & P & \to E \\
f\text{-}c\text{:} & C & \to (E \to E) \\
f\text{-}cp\text{:} & [Id]\ C & \to (E \to E) \\
e\text{:} & Id & \to E
\end{array}
$$

$$r: \quad \Sigma \; [Id] \quad \to E$$
$$f\text{-}l: \quad [Id] \; Ns* \to (E \to E)$$
$$f\text{-}nsl: \; Ns* \; Nat \quad \to (E \to E)$$
$$f\text{-}s: \quad S \qquad \to (E \to E) \qquad \qquad \text{(assumed)}$$

This definition presents one in which the earlier differences (i) and (ii) have been eliminated and which only requires the equivalence of the alternative directions for computing denotations to be established to complete the equivalence proof to the "x-" functions of section 4.

The approach to this last difference is similar to that taken at the previous stage. Firstly a lemma is introduced which shows that the "f-" functions are equivalent to a composition of a test and the corresponding "x-" function. Whereas in the previous stage the test was a simulation of the "$tixe$" combinator, this stage is simulating the "$;$" combinator. Applying this lemma generates a set of functions (which could be written out as "g-" functions) which pass the same constant "continuation" of $\lambda\sigma.<\sigma,\underline{NIL}>$ to all functions. Once again this constant can be dropped and written directly in the two places where the argument had previously been used. We then have precisely the expanded form of the "x-" functions from section 4.

Formally, the lemma is

Lemma II

define: $t(c) = \lambda\sigma,a.(a=\underline{NIL} \to c(\sigma),T \to <\sigma,a>)$

show for: $ft(xt)$ is $f\text{-}s(x\text{-}s),f\text{-}nsl(x\text{-}nsl)$ or $f\text{-}l(x\text{-}l)$ respectively

that: $t(c)^0 xt(s) = ft(s)\{c\}$

The proof (not given here) is by a similar induction to that of Lemma I.

Using Lemma II:

$$f\text{-}nsl(nsl,i)\{c\}=$$
$$i\underline{\le}lennsl \to t(f\text{-}nsl(nsl,i+1)\{c\})^0 x\text{-}s(s\text{-}b^0nsl(i))$$
$$T \qquad\qquad \to c$$

and:

$$f\text{-}l(ido,nsl)\{c\}=$$

$$\ldots$$

$$T \to (let \; i = ind(ido,nsl)$$
$$t(f\text{-}nsl(nsl,i+1)\{c\})^0 x\text{-}cp(ido,s\text{-}b^0 nsl(i)))$$

rewriting the second case of $f\text{-}nsl$ as:

$$\lambda\sigma.<\sigma,\underline{NIL}>$$

and the definition of $f\text{-}el$ as

$$\lambda\sigma.<el\text{-}sem(el)(\sigma),\underline{NIL}>$$

the continuation arguments to all functions can be dropped and the "$x\text{-}$" functions remain.

7. DISCUSSION

Two different definitions of a language have been given and proved e-
quivalent. It is important to realize that this is a limited proof in
the sense that nothing has been established about the power of the two
mechanisms in general. In fact continuations can be stored and passed
in a way which cannot be simulated by exit. Thus, co-routines or like
features can be defined using continuations but not exits (see Reynolds 74). However, both approaches have been used to define major programming languages (cf. Mosses 74, Bekić 74, Henhapl 78) and there is
experience from the work on abstract interpreter definitions to argue
that where a more powerful construct is not necessary, its use should
be avoided.

The choice of which technique is most appropriate might well depend
on the intended use of a definition. For general clarity it could be
that the ability of the exit combinators to hide the effect of a goto
in most parts of a language definition is valuable. On the other hand,
proofs about the meaning of programs will anyway have to expose the
combinators and a continuation definition may be more directly usable.
Even here there is one important advantage of the exit approach and

that is the ability to localize the effect of goto statements within
the syntactic unit containing the goto and the label. Thus in:

begin
  .
  .
  .
  begin
    .
    .
    .
    begin
      .
      .
      .
      goto ℓ,
      .
      .
      .
    end;
    .
    .
    .
    ℓ: ... ;
    .
    .
    .
  end
  .
  .
  .
end

the second nested block will have a denotation of type:

$$\Sigma \rightarrow \Sigma \ \underline{NIL}$$

This closing-off of the semantic effects of goto cannot be simulated
with continuations.

Both the Oxford and Vienna groups have made experiments with using definitions to provide a starting point for systematic (justified) compiler development (see Milne 76, Jones 76a). It is in this area that
more meaningful comparison of continuations and exits should be
sought.

Hopefully the proof in section 6 has been presented in an intuitively clear style. For more interesting approaches to such proofs see Reynolds 74, Reynolds 75.

ACKNOWLEDGEMENTS

An earlier draft of this paper was submitted to, and eventually accepted by the IBM Journal of Research and Development. Two of the referees provided very valuable comments for which the author would like to express his gratitude. (The paper was subsequently withdrawn with the argreement of the editor of that journal in order to place it in the current volume.)

FORMAL DEFINITION OF ALGOL 60 AS DESCRIBED IN THE 1975 MODIFIED REPORT

Wolfgang Henhapl & Cliff B.Jones

Abstract:

This paper provides a formal definition of a version of the ALGOL 60 programming language. In particular the definition uses the denotational approach and the meta-language presented in this volume (-- known with= in the Vienna Laboratory as "*META-IV*"). As well as ex= emplifying the meta-language, (yet) another definition of ALGOL 60 is justified by the recent revision of the language which resolved most of the open points in the earlier "Revised Report".

CONTENTS

0. Introduction   307

1. Abstract syntax   310
    1.1 Definitions   310
    1.2 Translator notes   312

2. Context Conditions   313
    2.1 "is-wf" Rules   314
    2.2 "tp" Determining Rules   318
    2.3 Auxiliary Functions   319

3. Semantic Objects   319

4. Meaning Functions   320
    4.1 Functions from Object Language   320
    4.2 Auxiliary Functions   334-336

0. INTRODUCTION

For many years the official description of ALGOL 60 has been the "Revised Report" (Naur 63). Not only the language, but also its extremely precise description have been seen as a reference point. There were, however, a number of known unresolved problems and most of these have been eliminated by the recent modifications given in De Morgan 75. A number of formal definitions exist for the language of the revised report: this paper presents a denotational definition of the language as understood from the modified report (MAR).

Before making some introductory remarks on the definition, three points will be made about the language itself (as in De Morgan 75). Firstly the modifications have followed the earlier "*ECMA subset*" by making the language (almost) statically typed. Although all parameters must now be specified, there is still no way of fixing the dimensions of array parameters nor the required parameter types of procedure or function parameters (cf. ALGOL 68). In connection with this it could be observed that the parameter matching rules of section 4.7.5.5 are somewhat difficult. In particular the definition given below assumes that, for "*by name*" passing of arithmetic expressions, the types must match exactly!

The third observation is simply one of surprise. The decision to restrict the control variable of a <*for statement*> to be a <*variable identifier*> (i.e. not a subscripted variable) may or may not be wise: but the argument that <*for statement*> can now be defined by expansion within ALGOL is surely dangerous. The definition given here would have had no difficulty treating the more general case because the concept of location has anyway to be introduced for other purposes.

Two of the major points resolved by the modifications are the meaning of "*own*" variables and the provision of a basic set of input-output functions: particular attention has been given to these points in the formal definition below. In fact, the treatment of own given here is more detailed than that for PL/I static variables in Walk 69. Rather than perform name changes and generate dummy declarations in the outermost block, an extra environment component is used here to retain a mapping from (additional) unique names to their locations. This "*Own-env*" is used in generating the denotations for own variables for insertion in the local "*Env*". The input-output functions are defined to change the "Channel" components of the state (Σ).

Much of the definition which follows should be easy to read after a study of the example given in Jones 78a. The treatment of goto is similar to that given there (for discussion see Jones 75) except that the use of the "*tixe*" combinator has been held here to a minimum. Instead of the use in *i-block*, an argument can be made for localizing the effects of goto at the level of *comp-stmt*, *cond-stmt* and *stmt*. In a version which used "*tixe*" at all three levels it was found advantageous to merge the "*cue*" and "*i*" functions (cf. Jones 78b).

As has been discussed elsewhere in this volume, the definition of arbitrary order of evaluation has not been addressed: had it been, one would, for example, have to show that the elements of an expression can be evaluated in any order.

With the aid of the list of abbreviations given at the end of this introduction, the abstract syntax and context conditions should be straight forward. Notice that, although the abstract syntax itself is a "*context-free*" production system, context dependant typing (e.g. Array-name) is used and secured by the context conditions. (Notice by-value variables are, in fact, non-by-name - i.e. by-value includes non-parameters).

The semantic objects are the key to the definition. States contain two components, one of which stores scalar values for each current scalar location (the division to the sub-types of *Sc-loc* is not necessary, it is only made to fit the implementation viewpoint), the other of which contains an abstraction of the objects which can be accessed by the input-output statements. State transformations are of the type required by the "*exit treatment*" of goto.

The composite objects *Stmt-env* and *Expr-env* are introduced solely as abbreviations; *Own-env* has been mentioned above; the real interest lies in the denotations which can be stored in *Env*. *Type-dens* are obviously scalar locations. A function procedure which is activated sets up a value to be returned by assigning to the *Atv-proc-id*: again a scalar location is the appropriate denotation. Array denotations store the (one-one) mapping from all possible subscript values to scalar locations; notice that the constraint requires that the domain of an array denotation is "*dense*". Procedure denotations are functions which, for given arguments and a current set of activations, yield transformations. Notice that the *Act-parm-dens* carry type information with them for checking within the *Proc-den*. Switch denotations are similar.

The very general parameter passing "by name" permitted in ALGOL requires that the *By-name-dens* are rather like procedure denotations. Because formal parameter names can occur as Destinations for assignment statements it is also necessary to know whether a by-name parameter can be evaluated to a location or not (cf. *e-parm-expr, e-var-ref, e-var*). Furthermore, the question whether a parameter is to be passed by-name or by-value is not decidable at the point of call. Thus all parameters are passed by-name and the *Proc-den* has the task of creating the locations to store by-value parameters (cf. *e-proc-decl, e-val-parm*).

The classes *Loc* and *Val* are auxiliary and are used only in type clauses.

Given an understanding of the semantic objects the reader should be able to tackle section 4. Remember that for "splitting" rules only a type clause is given.

ACKNOWLEDGEMENT.

Returning the compliment to Peter Mosses, one of the authors would like to acknowledge that a part of the incentive to write this definition was the hope to provide an equally abstract but more readable definition than that in Mosses 74!

ABBREVIATIONS.

Abnormal component	constant	operator
actual	declaration	parameter
activation identifier	denotation	procedure
activated	designator	reference
arithmetic	descriptor	scalar
assignment	destination	specification
by-name	element	statement
Boolean	environment	subscripted
by-value	expression	transformation
character	function	unlabelled
compound	identifier	value
conditional	integer	variable

1. ABSTRACT SYNTAX

1.1 Definitions

```
Program    :: Block
Block      :: s-dp:Decl-set  s-sl:Stmt*
Stmt       :: s-lp:Id-set  s-sp:Unlab-stmt
Unlab-stmt = Comp-stmt | Block | Assign-stmt | Goto-stmt |
             Dummy-stmt | Cond-stmt | For-stmt | Proc-stmt
```

```
Comp-stmt        :: Stmt*
Assign-stmt      :: s-lpl:Destin⁺  s-rp:Expr
```

$$Assign\text{-}stmt \quad :: \quad s\text{-}lpl\text{:}Destin^{+} \quad s\text{-}rp\text{:}Expr$$

```
Destin           :: s-tg:Left-part  s-tp:Type
Left-part        = Var | Atv-proc-id
Atv-proc-id      :: Id
Goto-stmt        :: Expr
Dummy-stmt       :: DUMMY
Cond-stmt        :: s-dec:Expr  s-th:Stmt  s-el:Stmt
For-stmt         :: s-cv:Var  s-cvtp:Type  s-fl:For-list-elem⁺  s-b:Bloc
For-list-elem    = Expr-elem | While-elem | Step-until-elem
Expr-elem        :: Expr
While-elem       :: s-in:Expr  s-wh:Expr
Step-until-elem  :: s-in:Expr  s-st:Expr  s-un:Expr
Proc-stmt        :: (Proc-des | Funct-des)
Proc-des         :: s-pn:Id  s-app:Act-parm*
```

```
Expr           = Type-const | Var-ref | Label-const | Switch-des | Funct-de
                 Prefix-expr | Infix-expr | Cond-expr
Type-const     = Bool-const | Arithm-const
Bool-const     :: Bool
Arithm-const   = Real-const | Int-const
Real-const     :: Real
Int-const      :: Int
Var-ref        :: Var
Var            = Simple-var | Subscr-var
Simple-var     = Simple-var-bn | Simple-var-bv
Simple-var-bn  :: s-nm:Id
Simple-var-bv  :: s-nm:Id
Subscr-var     = Subscr-var-bn | Subscr-var-bv
Subscr-var-bn  :: s-nm:Id  s-sscl:Expr⁺
Subscr-var-bv  :: s-nm:id  s-sscl:Expr⁺
```

```
Label-const     :: Id
Switch-des      :: s-id:Id   s-ssc:Expr

Funct-des       :: s-nm:Id   s-app:Act-parm*
Act-parm        :: s-v:Act-parmv   s-tp:Specifier
Act-parmv       =  Parm-expr | Array-name | Switch-name | Proc-name | String
Parm-expr       :: Expr
Array-name      :: Id
Switch-name     :: Id
Proc-name       :: Id
String          =  Char*
Char            =  Implementation defined set

Prefix-expr     :: s-opr:Prefix-opr   s-op:Expr
Prefix-opr      =  REAL-PLUS | REAL-MINUS |
                   INT-PLUS | INT-MINUS | NOT
Infix-expr      :: s-op1:Expr   s-opr:Infix-opr   s-op2:Expr
Infix-opr       =  REAL-ADD | REAL-SUB | REAL-MULT | REAL-DIV |
                   INT-ADD | INT-SUB | INT-MULT | INT-DIV |
                   REAL-EXP | REAL-INT-EXP | INT-EXP |
                   LT | LE | EQ | NE | GE | GT | IMPL | EQU | AND | OR
Cond-expr       :: s-dec:Expr   s-th:Expr   s-el:Expr
Decl            =  Type-decl | Array-decl | Switch-decl | Proc-decl
Type-decl       :: s-id:Id   s-oid:[Own-id]   s-desc:Type
Array-decl      :: s-id:Id   s-oid:[Own-id]   s-tp:Type   s-bdl:Bound-pair⁺
Bound-pair      :: s-lbd:Expr   s-ubd:Expr
Switch-decl     :: s-id:Id   s-el:Expr⁺
Proc-decl       :: s-id:Id
                   s-tp:(Type | PROC)
                   s-fpl:Id*
                   s-vids:Id-set
                   s-spm:(Id→Specifier)
                   s-body:(Block | Code)
Specifier       =  Type | Type-array | Type-proc | PROC | LABEL | STRING | SWITCH
Type-array      :: Type
Type-proc       :: Type
Type            =  Arithm | BOOL
Arithm          =  INT | REAL
Code            :: Tr
Tr                 see "semantic objects"
```

Own-id	infinite set
Id	infinite set

Real	=	the set of rational numbers with the usual arithmetic
Int	=	the set of integers (embedded in *Real*)
Bool	=	*TRUE* | *FALSE*

Standard-proc-names = *Real-funct-names* \| *Int-funct-names* \| *Proc-names*

Real-funct-names = *"abs"* \| *"sqrt"* \| *"sin"* \| *"cos"* \| *"arctan"* \| *"ln"* \| *"exp"* \| *"maxreal"* \| *"minreal"* \| *"epsilon"*

Int-funct-names = *"iabs"* \| *"sign"* \| *"entier"* \| *"length"* \| *"maxint"* \|

Proc-names = *"inchar"* \| *"outchar"* \| *"outstring"* \| *"outterminator"* *"stop"* \| *"fault"* \| *"ininteger"* \| *"outinteger"* \| *"inreal"* \| *"outreal"*

Comment: The quotes around the standard-procedure names indicate the translated version of the identifiers.

1.2 Translator Notes.

Although neither the concrete syntax of ALGOL 60, nor its translation to objects of the abstract form are formally specified, a number of points should be borne in mind:

- Concrete delimiters, comments etc. are dropped.

- Within expressions, brackets and rules of operator precedence are used to choose the appropriate tree form of *"expr"*.

- If the (concrete) outer block was labelled, the translator embeds it in another (unlabelled) block.

- The body of a procedure (which is not code) is always a block in the abstract form; the translator generates this block if it is not present in the concrete form.

- The body of a procedure which is code is translated into the appropriate state transformation.

- Constants are, similarly, translated to (abstract) values.

- The outermost block (a created one, if necessary) contains the standard functions and procedures: where these cannot be expressed in ALGOL 60, meta-language descriptions of the transformations are given.

- The body of the abstract form of a for statement is always a block; if not present in the concrete form it is generated by the translator.

- The use of one <bound pair list> to define several <array identifiers> is expanded by the translator. Notice that this can <u>not</u> be jusified from MAR and, with side-effect producing function references in the bound pair list, is strictly wrong.

2. <u>CONTEXT CONDITIONS</u>.

An environment is used to record statically known type information:

$$Static\text{-}env = Id \xrightarrow{m} Specifier$$

With the exception of $is\text{-}wf\text{-}program$, all context conditions are, for a phrase class Θ, of type:

$$is\text{-}wf\text{-}\Theta: \Theta \quad Static\text{-}env \rightarrow Bool$$

As well as the splitting ("routing") rules, certain other obvious steps have been taken to shorten the functions given below, e.g. if

$$\Theta :: \Theta_1 \Theta_2 \ldots \Theta_n$$

then a rule (or part thereof) of the form:

$$
\begin{aligned}
if\text{-}wf\text{-}&\Theta(mk\text{-}\Theta(\Theta_1,\Theta_2,\ldots,\Theta_n),env) = \\
&is\text{-}wf\text{-}\Theta_1(\Theta_1,env) \,\& \\
&is\text{-}wf\text{-}\Theta_2(\Theta_2,env) \,\& \ldots \\
&is\text{-}wf\text{-}\Theta_n(\Theta_n,env)
\end{aligned}
$$

will be omitted.

2.1 *is-wf* Rules.

is-wf-program(mk-program(b)) =
  /* for all type-decl, array-decl's within b, their s-oid is unique */ &
  (*let* oads={d|within(d,b) & is-array-decl(d) & s-oid(d) ≠ *NIL*}
  /* all expressions in s-bdl of elements of oads are integer constants */) &
  (*let* env = [n→mk-type-proc(*INT*)|n∈Int-funct-names] ∪
            [n→mk-type-proc(*REAL*)|n∈Real-funct-names] ∪
            [n→*PROC*|n∈Proc-names]
   is-wf-block(b,env))
type: Program→Bool

is-wf-block(mk-block(dcls,stl),env) =
  let labl = /* list of all labels contained in stl without an intervening
                                                    block */
  is-uniquel(labl) &
  is-disjoint(<elems labl,{s-id(d)|d∈dcls}>) &
  (*let* renv = env\{s-id(d)|d∈dcls}
   let lenv = [s-id(d)→(cases d:*
                    mk-type-decl(,,tp)   → tp
                    mk-array-decl(,,tp,)   → mk-type-array(tp)
                    mk-switch-decl(,)   → *SWITCH*
                    mk-proc-decl(,PROC,,,,)→ *PROC*
                    mk-proc-decl(,tp,,,,) → mk-type-proc(tp))
                              |d∈dcls] ∪
              [lab→*LABEL*|lab∈elems labl]
   let nenv = renv ∪ lenv
    d∈dcls →
             ((is-array-decl(d) → is-wf-array-decl(d,renv)) &
              (is-proc-decl(d) → is-wf-proc-decl(d,nenv)) &
              (is-switch-decl(d) → is-wf-switch-decl(d,nenv))) &
      (1≤i≤len stl → is-wf-unlab-stmt(s-sp(stl(i)),nenv)))

```
is-wf-assign-stmt(mk-assign-stmt(dl,e),env) =
  1≤i≤len dl ➙
     (let mk-destin(lp,tp)=dl(i)
      compat-tps(tp,expr-tp(e,env)) &
      (is-var(lp) ➙ (is-scalar(lp,env) &
                      tp=var-tp(lp,env))) &
      (is-atv-proc-id(lp) ➙ tp=s-type(env(lp))))


is-wf-goto-stmt(mk-goto-stmt(e),env) = expr-tp(e,env) = LABEL


is-wf-cond-stmt(mk-cond-stmt(dec,th,el),env) = expr-tp(dec,env) = BOOL


is-wf-for-stmt(mk-for-stmt(cv,cvtp,flel,b),env) =
  is-simple-var(cv) & is-scalar(cv,env) &
  is-arithm(cvtp) & cvtp=var-tp(cv,env)


is-wf-expr-elem(mk-expr-elem(e),env) = is-arithm(expr-tp(e,env))


is-wf-while-elem(mk-while-elem(in,wh),env) =
  is-arithm(expr-tp(in,env)) & is-BOOL(expr-tp(wh,env))


is-wf-step-until-elem(mk-step-until-elem(in,st,un),env) =
  is-arithm(expr-tp(in,env)) &
  is-arithm(expr-tp(st,env)) &
  is-arithm(expr-tp(un,env))


is-wf-proc-des(mk-proc-des(id,apl),env) =
  is-PROC(env(id)) &
  (1≤i≤len apl ➙ s-tp(apl(i))=act-parm-tp(s-v(apl(i)),env)


is-wf-var(v,env) =
  if is-simple-var(v) then is-type(env(s-nm(v)))
  else is-type-array(env(s-nm(v))) &
       (1≤i≤len s-sscl(v) ➙ is-arithm(expr-tp(s-sscl(v)(i),env)))
```

is-wf-simple-var-bn/bv
is-wf-subscr-var-bn/bv }   **former iff refers to by name formal parameter**

is-wf-label-const(mk-label-const(id),env) = env(id) = <u>LABEL</u>

is-wf-switch-des(mk-switch-des(id,e),env) =
  env(id) = <u>SWITCH</u> &
  is-arithm(expr-tp(e,env))

is-wf-funct-des(mk-funct-des(id,apl),env) =
  is-type-proc(env(id)) &
  (1≤i≤<u>len</u> apl → s-tp(apl(i))=act-parmv-tp(s-v(apl(i)),env))

is-wf-array-name(mk-array-name(id),env) = is-type-array(env(id))

is-wf-switch-name(mk-switch-name(id),env) = env(id) = <u>SWITCH</u>

is-wf-proc-name(mk-proc-name(id),env) = is-type-proc(env(id)) ∨ env(id) = <u>PROC</u>

is-wf-prefix-expr(mk-prefix-expr(opr,expr),env) =
  <u>let</u> tp = expr-tp(expr,env)
  (cases opr:
    <u>NOT</u>   → tp = <u>BOOL</u>
    <u>REAL-PLUS</u>, <u>REAL-MINUS</u> → tp = <u>REAL</u>
    <u>INT-PLUS</u>, <u>INT-MINUS</u>   → tp = <u>INT</u>)

s-wf-$infix$-$expr(mk$-$infix$-$expr(e1,opr,e2),env) =$
$\quad \underline{let}\ tp1 = expr\text{-}tp(e1,env)$
$\quad \underline{let}\ tp2 = expr\text{-}tp(e2,env)$
$\quad (\underline{cases}\ opr:$

$\underline{REAL\text{-}ADD},\ \underline{REAL\text{-}SUB},\ \underline{REAL\text{-}MULT} \rightarrow$	$(tp1=\underline{REAL}\ \vee\ tp2=\underline{REAL})\ \&$
	$is\text{-}arith(tp1)\ \&\ is\text{-}arith(tp2)$
$\underline{REAL\text{-}DIV}$	$\rightarrow\ is\text{-}arith(tp1)\ \&\ is\text{-}arith(tp2)$
$\underline{REAL\text{-}EXP}$	$\rightarrow\ is\text{-}arith(tp1)\ \&\ tp2=\underline{REAL}$
$\underline{REAL\text{-}INT\text{-}EXP}$	$\rightarrow\ tp1=\underline{REAL}\ \&\ tp2=\underline{INT}$
$\underline{INT\text{-}ADD},\ \underline{INT\text{-}SUB},\ \underline{INT\text{-}MULT}$	
$\underline{INT\text{-}DIV},\ \underline{INT\text{-}EXP}$	$\rightarrow\ tp1=\underline{INT}\ \&\ tp2=\underline{INT}$
$\underline{LT},\ \underline{LE},\ \underline{EQ},\ \underline{NE},\ \underline{GE},\ \underline{GT}$	$\rightarrow\ is\text{-}arith(tp1)\ \&\ is\text{-}arith(tp2)$
$\underline{IMPL},\ \underline{EQU},\ \underline{AND},\ \underline{OR}$	$\rightarrow\ tp1=\underline{BOOL}\ \&\ tp2=\underline{BOOL})$

s-wf-$cond$-$expr(mk$-$cond$-$exp(b,t,e),env) =$
$\quad expr\text{-}tp(b,env) = \underline{BOOL}\ \&$
$\quad (\underline{let}\ tp1 = expr\text{-}tp(t,env)$
$\quad\ \underline{let}\ tp2 = expr\text{-}tp(e,env)$
$\quad\quad compat\text{-}tps(tp1,tp2))$

s-wf-$array$-$decl(mk$-$array$-$decl(,,tp,bdl),env) =$
$\quad 1\leq i\leq \underline{len}\ bdl\ \rightarrow\ is\text{-}arith(expr\text{-}tp(s\text{-}lbd(bdl(i)),env)\ \&$
$\quad\quad\quad\quad is\text{-}arith(expr\text{-}tp(s\text{-}ubd(bdl(i)),env)$

s-wf-$switch$-$decl(mk$-$switch$-$decl(exl),env) =$
$\quad 1\leq i\leq \underline{len}\ exl\ \rightarrow\ expr\text{-}tp(exl(i),env) = \underline{LABEL}$

s-wf-$proc$-$decl(mk$-$proc$-$decl(id,tp,fpl,vids,spm,b),env) =$
$\quad is\text{-}uniquel(fpl)\ \&$
$\quad id \notin \underline{elems}\ fpl\ \&$
$\quad vids \subseteq \underline{elems}\ fpl\ \&$
$\quad \underline{dom}\ spm = \underline{elems}\ fpl\ \&$
$\quad (id\in vids\ \rightarrow\ spm(id)\in(Type\cup\{\underline{LABEL}\}\cup Type\text{-}array))\ \&$
$\quad\ is\text{-}wf\text{-}block(b,env+spm)$

2.2 *tp* Determining Rules.

expr-tp(expr,env) =
   cases expr:
     mk-bool-const()   → *BOOL*
     mk-int-const()   → *INT*
     mk-real-const()   → *REAL*
     mk-label-const()   → *LABEL*
     mk-var-ref(mk-var(var))   → *env (s-nm(var))*
     mk-funct-des(id,)   → *s-type (env(id))*
     mk-switch-des()   → *LABEL*
     mk-prefix-expr(opr,)
       cases opr:
        INT-PLUS, INT-MINUS   → *INT*
        REAL-PLUS, REAL-MINUS   → *REAL*
        NOT   → *BOOL*
     mk-infix-expr(,opr,)
       cases opr:
        INT-ADD, INT-SUB, INT-MULT,
        INT-DIV, INT-EXP   → *INT*
        REAL-ADD, REAL-SUB, REAL-MULT,
        REAL-DIV, REAL-EXP, REAL-INT-EXP → *REAL*
        LT, LE, EQ, NE, GE, GT,
        AND, OR, IMPL, EQU   → *BOOL*
     mk-cond-expr(,t,e)
       let tp1 = expr-tp(t,env)
       let tp2 = expr-tp(e,env)
       tp1 = tp2   → *tp1*
       is-arith(tp1) & is-arith(tp2) → *REAL*

var-tp(v,envs) =
   cases v:
     mk-simple-var(id,)   → *envs(id)*
     mk-subscr-var(id,,sscl) → *s-type(envs(id))*

act-parmv-tp similar to *expr-tp*

.3 Auxiliary Functions.

$compat\text{-}tps(tp1,tp2) =$
   $tp1 = tp2 \lor$
   $is\text{-}arithm(tp1) \ \& \ is\text{-}arithm(tp2)$

$type: (Type \mid \underline{LABEL}) \ (Type \mid \underline{LABEL}) \to BOOL$

$is\text{-}scalar(v,env) =$
   $is\text{-}type(env(s\text{-}nm(v))) \lor$
   $is\text{-}array\text{-}type(env(s\text{-}nm(v))) \ \& \ is\text{-}subscr\text{-}var(v)$

. SEMANTIC OBJECTS.

Tr	$=$	$\Sigma \overset{\sim}{\to} \Sigma \ Abn$
Σ	$=$	$(\underline{R\text{-}STG} \underset{m}{\to} Storage) \ \underline{\cup} \ (\underline{R\text{-}CHANS} \underset{m}{\to} Channels)$
$Storage$	$=$	$Sc\text{-}loc \underset{m}{\to} Sc\text{-}val$
$Sc\text{-}loc$	$=$	$Bool\text{-}loc \mid Real\text{-}loc \mid Int\text{-}loc$
$Bool\text{-}loc, Real\text{-}loc, Int\text{-}loc$		**are disjoint, infinite, sets**
$Sc\text{-}val$	$=$	$Int \mid Real \mid Bool$
$Channels$	$=$	$Int \underset{m}{\to} Char*$
Abn	$=$	$[Label\text{-}den]$
$Stmt\text{-}env$	$=$	$(Own\text{-}env \ Env \ Aid\text{-}set)$
$Expr\text{-}env$	$=$	$(Env \ Aid\text{-}set)$
$Own\text{-}env$	$=$	$Own\text{-}id \underset{m}{\to} (Type\text{-}den \mid Array\text{-}den)$
Env	$=$	$Id \underset{m}{\to} Den$
Den	$=$	$Type\text{-}den \mid Atv\text{-}proc\text{-}id\text{-}den \mid Array\text{-}den \mid Proc\text{-}den \mid Label\text{-}den \mid$
		$Switch\text{-}den \mid By\text{-}name\text{-}den \mid String$
$Type\text{-}den$	$=$	$Sc\text{-}loc$
$Atv\text{-}proc\text{-}id\text{-}den$	$=$	$Sc\text{-}loc$
$Array\text{-}den$	$=$	$Int^{+} \underset{m}{\leftrightarrow} Sc\text{-}loc$
$Constraint$	$:$	$(\exists ipl \in (Int \ Int)^{+})(\underline{dom} \ a \ loc = rect(ipl))$
$Proc\text{-}den$	$=$	$Act\text{-}parm\text{-}den* \ Aid\text{-}set \to (\Sigma \overset{\sim}{\to} \Sigma \ Abn \ [Sc\text{-}val])$
$Act\text{-}parm\text{-}den$	$::$	$s\text{-}v:Den \ \ s\text{-}tp:Specifier$
$Label\text{-}den$	$::$	$Id \ Aid$
$Switch\text{-}den$	$=$	$Int \ Aid\text{-}set \to (\Sigma \overset{\sim}{\to} \Sigma \ Abn \ Label\text{-}den)$
Aid		**infinite set**

$$By\text{-}name\text{-}den \qquad = \; By\text{-}name\text{-}loc\text{-}den \mid By\text{-}name\text{-}expr\text{-}den$$

$$By\text{-}name\text{-}loc\text{-}den \;\; :: \; Aid\text{-}set \to (\Sigma \overset{\sim}{\to} \Sigma \; Loc)$$

$$By\text{-}name\text{-}expr\text{-}den \;\; :: \; Aid\text{-}set \to (\Sigma \overset{\sim}{\to} \Sigma \; Sc\text{-}val)$$

$$Loc \qquad\qquad = \; Type\text{-}den \mid Array\text{-}den$$

$$Abn \qquad\qquad = \; [Label\text{-}den]$$

$$Val \qquad\qquad = \; Sc\text{-}val \mid Label\text{-}den$$

$$Implementation\text{-}defined\text{-}const = \underline{MAXINT} \mid \underline{MINREAL} \mid \underline{MAXREAL} \mid \underline{EPSILON}$$

Comment: The constants are *Sc-vals*, but no check is made as to whether they are machine representable.

4. MEANING FUNCTIONS

4.1 Functions from Object Language

$i\text{-}program(p)(chans) =$
  $\underline{let}\; state_s = \{\underline{R\text{-}STG} \mapsto [\,], \underline{R\text{-}CHANS} \mapsto chans\,]$
  $\underline{let}\; state_f = i\text{-}program1(p)(state_s)$
  $state_f(\underline{R\text{-}CHANS})$

type: *Program* → *(Channels* → *Channels)*

$i\text{-}program1(mk\text{-}program(b)) =$
  $\underline{let}\; own\text{-}decls = \{d \mid within(d,b) \;\&\; (is\text{-}type\text{-}decl(d) \lor is\text{-}array\text{-}decl(d)) \;\&$
  $\qquad\qquad\qquad s\text{-}oid(d) \neq \underline{NIL}\}$
  $\underline{let}\; oenv: ([s\text{-}oid(d) \mapsto e\text{-}own\text{-}type\text{-}decl(d) \mid d{\in}own\text{-}decls \;\&\; is\text{-}type\text{-}decl(d)] \; \cup$
  $\qquad\qquad [s\text{-}oid(d) \mapsto e\text{-}own\text{-}array\text{-}decl(d) \mid d{\in}own\text{-}decls \;\&\; is\text{-}array\text{-}decl(d)]);$
  $(\underline{tixe}[\underline{RET} \mapsto I]$
  $\underline{in}\; i\text{-}block(b,<oenv,env,\{\}>));$
  $epilogue(\{s\text{-}id(d) \mid d{\in}own\text{-}decls\},oenv)$

type: *Program* →

```
e-own-type-decl(d) =
   let l:e-type-decl(d);
   if s-desc(d)=BOOL then assign(FALSE,l)
   else                   assign(0,l);
   return (l)
```

type: Type-decl → Type-den


```
e-own-array-decl(d) =
   let l:e-array-decl(d,<[],{}>);
   if s-tp(d)=BOOL then
           for all scl∈rngl do assign(FALSE,scl)
   else
           for all scl∈rngl do assign(0,scl);
   return (l)
```

type: Array-decl → Array-den

Standard Functions and Transput

It is assumed that the translation of the standard functions and pro-cedures are contained in the ("fictitious") outer block. The interpre-ation of their *proc-decl* follows the normal interpretation rules (*e-roc-decl*) except in the cases where the body cannot be expressed in Algol. In these cases the state transition of the non-Algol part is explicitly listed below.

Note: Referencing the translated identifiers we use quotes (e.g. "*inreal*" for the translation of the identifier inreal).

n procedure *stop*:

   "*goto* Ω" → *exit(RET)*

In <u>procedure</u> *inchar*:   <body> →

    <u>let</u> channel : contents(env("chännel"));
    <u>let</u> str   = env("str")
    <u>let</u> int   : e-left-part(mk-simple-var-bn("int"),exenv)
    <u>if</u> channel∉<u>dom</u> <u>c</u> <u>R-CHANS</u>
      <u>then</u> <u>error</u>
      <u>else</u> (<u>let</u> chan: (<u>c</u> <u>R-CHANS</u>)(channel);
          <u>if</u> chan = <> <u>then</u> <u>error</u>;
          <u>let</u> char: hdchan
          <u>let</u> ind = <u>if</u> (∃i∈{1:<u>len</u>str})(str(i)=char)
                  <u>then</u> (ιi∈{1:<u>len</u>str})(str(i)=char &
                          (∀k∈{1:i-1})(str(k)≠char))
                  <u>else</u> 0;
          <u>R-CHANS</u> := <u>c</u> <u>R-CHANS</u> +
                [channel↦tlchan];
        assign(ind,int))

In <u>procedure</u> *outchar*:   <statement> →

    <u>let</u> channel : contents(env("channel"));
    <u>let</u> str   = env("str")
    <u>let</u> int   : contents(env("int"));
    <u>let</u> char   = str(int)
    <u>if</u> channel∉<u>dom</u> <u>c</u> <u>R-CHANS</u> <u>then</u> <u>error</u>;
    <u>R-CHANS</u>   := <u>c</u> <u>R-CHANS</u> +
              [channel↦(<u>c</u> <u>R-CHANS</u>)(channel)^<char>]

In <u>procedure</u> *outterminator*:   <body> →

    <u>let</u> channel : contents(env("channel"));
    <u>if</u> channel∉<u>dom</u> <u>c</u> <u>R-CHANS</u> <u>then</u> <u>error</u>;
    <u>R-CHANS</u>   := (<u>c</u> <u>R-CHANS</u>) +
              [channel↦(<u>c</u> <u>R-CHANS</u>)(channel)^<implementation
                    defined symbol depending on the current
                    state of the channel>]

Procedures "*maxint*", "*minreal*", "*maxreal*" and "*epsilon*" have bodies
which return the appropriate *Implementation-defined-const*.

```
i-block(mk-block(dcls,stl),<oenv,env,cas>) =
    let aid∈Aid be s.t. aid∉cas
    let nenv : env +
                ([s-id(d)↦oenv(s-oid(d))|d∈dcls & (is-type-decl(d) ∨
                                is-array-decl(d)) & s-oid(d) ≠ NIL] ∪
                [s-id(d)↦e-type-decl(d)|d∈dcls & is-type-decl(d) &
                                s-oid(d) = NIL] ∪
                [s-id(d)↦e-array-decl(d,<env,cas>)|d∈dcls & is-array-decl(d) &
                                s-oid(d) = NIL] ∪
                [s-id(d)↦e-switch-decl(d,nenv)|d∈dcls & is-switch-decl(d)] ∪
                [s-id(d)↦e-proc-decl(d,oenv,nenv)|d∈dcls & is-proc-decl(d)] ∪
                [lab↦mk-label-den(lab,aid)|is-contnd(lab,stl)]);
    let stenv = <oenv,nenv,cas∪{aid}>
    always epilogue({s-id(d)|d∈dcls & (is-type-decl(d) ∨ is-array-decl(d)) &
                                s-oid(d) = NIL},nenv)
    in (tixe[mk-label-den(tlab,aid)→
                    cue-i-stmt-list(tlab,stl,st-env) |
                    is-contndl(tlab,stl)]
        in for i=1 to lenstl do i-unlab-stmt(s-sp(stl(i)),stenv)
    )

type:   Block Stmt-env ⇒


epilogue(ids,env) =
    let sclocs = {env(id)|id∈ids & is-sc-loc(env(id))} ∪
                union{rng(env(id))|id∈ids & is-array-den(env(id))}
    R-STG      := R-STG\sclocs

type:   Id-set Env ⇒


cue-i-stmt-list(lab,stl,stenv) =
    let i = index(lab,stl)
    cue-i-stmt(lab,stl(i),stenv);
    for j = i+1 to lenstl do i-unlab-stmt(s-sp(stl(i)),stenv)

type:   Id Stmt* Stmt-env ⇒
pre:    is-contndl(lab,stl)
```

```
cue-i-stmt(lab,mk-stmt(labs,sp),stenv) =
    if lab∈labs then i-unlab-stmt(sp,stenv)
    else cue-i-unlab-stmt(lab,sp,stenv)

type:  Id Stmt Stmt-env ➡
pre:   is-contnd(lab,mk-stmt(labs,sp))


cue-i-unlab-stmt: Id Unlab-stmt Stmt-env ➡


cue-i-cond-stmt(lab,mk-cond-stmt(,th,el),stenv) =
    if is-contnd(lab,th) then cue-i-stmt(lab,th,stenv)
    else                      cue-i-stmt(lab,el,stenv)

pre:   is-contnd(lab,th) ∨ is-contnd(lab,el)


cue-i-comp-stmt(lab,mk-comp-stmt(stl),stenv) =
    cue-i-stmt-list(lab,stl,stenv)


i-unlab-stmt: Unlab-stmt Stmt-env ➡

i-comp-stmt(mk-comp-stmt(stl),stenv) =
    for i=1 to lenstl do i-unlab-stmt(s-sp(stl(i)),stenv)


i-assign-stmt(mk-assign-stmt(dl,e),<,env,cas>) =
    let dl:<e-left-part(s-tg(dl(i)),<env,cas>)|1≤i≤lendl>;
    let v:  e-expr(e,<env,cas>);
    for i=1 to lendl do
        (let vc:conv(v,s-tp(dl(i)));
         assign(vc,dl(i)))


e-left-part: Left-part Expr-env ➡ Sc-loc


e-atv-proc-id(mk-atv-proc-id(id),<env,>) = env(id)
```

```
-goto-stmt(mk-goto-stmt(e),<,env,cas>) =
   let ld:e-expr(e,<env,cas>);
   exit(ld)


-dummy-stmt(t,stenv) = I


-cond-stmt(mk-cond-stmt(dec,th,el),stenv) =
   let <,env,cas> = st-env
   let b:e-expr(dec,<env,cas>);
   if b then i-unlab-stmt(s-sp(th),stenv)
   else       i-unlab-stmt(s-sp(el),stenv)


-for-stmt(mk-for-stmt(cv,cvtp,flel,b),stenv) =
   for i=1 to lenflel do i-for-list-elem(flel(i),cv,cvtp,b,stenv)


-for-list-elem: For-list-elem Var Type Block Stmt-env →


-expr-elem(mk-expr-elem(e),cv,cvtp,b,stenv) =
   let <,env,cas> = stenv
   let v:e-expr(e,<env,cas>);
   let vc:conv(v,cvtp);
   let l:e-var(cv,<env,cas>);
   assign(vc,l);
   i-block(b,stenv)


-while-elem(mk-while-elem(in,wh),cv,cvtp,b,stenv) =
   let <,env,cas> = stenv
   while (let v:e-expr(in,<env,cas>);
          let vc:conc(v,cvtp);
          let l:e-var(cv,<env,cas>);
          assign(vc,l);
          let b:e-expr(wh,<env,cas>);
          b  ) do    i-block(b,stenv)
```

```
i-step-until-elem(mk-step-until-elem(in,st,un),cv,cvtp,b,stenv) =
    let <,env,cas> = stenv
    let exenv = <env,cas>
    let vin:e-expr(in,exenv);
    let vinc:conv(vin,cvtp);
    let l:e-var(cv,exenv);
    assign(vinc,l);
    while (let vst:e-expr(st,exenv);
            let b:e-expr(untest,exenv);
            b ) do (i-block(b,stenv);
                    let vcur:contents(l)+vst;
                    let vcurc:conv(vcur,cvtp);
                    assign(vcurc,l))
```

note: "untest" is an *Expr* corresponding to $\lceil (cv-un) \times \underline{signn}vst \leq 0 \rceil$

```
i-proc-stmt(mk-proc-stmt(des),<,env,cas>) =
    cases des:
      mk-proc-des(id,apl) →
          (let denl = <e-act-parm(apl(i),env)|1≤i≤lenapl>
          let f = env(id)
          f(denl,cas))
      T → (let v:e-funct-des(des,<env,cas>);
          I)
```

```
e-expr: Expr Expr-env → Val
```

```
e-bool-const(mk-bool-const(b),) = return(b)
```

```
e-real-const(mk-real-const(r),) = represent(r)
```

```
e-int-const(mk-int-const(i),)    = test(i)
```

```
e-var-ref(mk-var-ref(v),<env,cas>) =
    if is-simple-var-bv(v) ∨ is-subscr-var-bv(v) ∨ is-by-name-loc-den(env(s-nm(v)))
    then (let l:e-var(v,<env,cas>);
          contents(l))
    else (let bned = env(s-nm(v))
          bned(cas))


e-var: Var Expr-env → Sc-loc


e-simple-var-bn(mk-simple-var-bn(id),<env,cas>) =
    let bnd = env(id)
    if is-by-name-loc-den(bnd) then bnd(cas)
    else error


e-simple-var-bv(mk-simple-var-bv(id),<env,>) = env(id)


e-subscr-var-bn(mk-subscr-var-bn(id,sscl),<env,cas>) =
    let esscl:e-subscrl(sscl,<env,cas>);
    let bnd = env(id)
    if is-by-name-loc-den(bnd) then
            (let aloc:bnd(cas);
             if esscl∈domaloc then return (aloc(esscl))
             else error)
    else error


e-subscr-var-bv(mk-subscr-var-bv(id,sscl),<env,cas>) =
    let esscl:e-subscrl(sscl,<env,cas>);
    let aloc = env(id)
    if esscl∈domaloc then return (aloc(esscl))
    else error
```

```
e-subscrl(sscl,exenv) =
   let esscl:<(let essc:e-expr(sscl(i),exenv);
               let i:conv(essc,INT);
               i                    )|1≤i≤lensscl>;
   return (esscl)


type:  Expr* Expr-env ➡ Int*



e-label-const(mk-label-const(id),<env,>) = return(env(id))



e-switch-des(mk-switch-des(id,ssc),<env,cas>) =
   let ess:e-expr(ssc,<env,cas>);
   let i:conv(ess,INT);
   let f = env(id)
   let ld:f(i,cas);
   return (ld)



e-funct-des(mk-funct-des(id,apl),<env,cas>) =
   let denl = <e-act-parm(apl(i),env)|1≤i≤lenapl>
   let f    = env(id)
   let v:f(denl,cas);
   return (v)



e-act-parm(mk-act-parm(e,tp),env) =
   let d = e-act-parmv(e,env)
   mk-act-parm-den(d,tp)


type: Act-parm Env ➡ Act-parm-den



e-act-parmv: Act-parmv Env ➡ Den
```

```
e-parm-expr(mk-parm-expr(e),env) =
    if is-var-ref(e) then
        (let f(dcas) = e-var-ref(e,<env,dcas>)
         mk-by-name-loc-den(f)
        )
    else
        (let f(dcas) = e-expr(e,<env,dcas>)
         mk-by-name-expr-den(f)
        )


e-array-name(mk-array-name(id),env) = env(id)


e-switch-name(mk-switch-name(id),env) = env(id)


e-proc-name(mk-proc-name(id),env) = env(id)


e-string(s,env) = s


e-prefix-expr(mk-prefix-expr(opr,e),exenv) =
    let v:e-expr(e,exenv);
    apply-prefix-opr(opr,v)


e-infix-expr(mk-infix-expr(e1,opr,e2),exenv) =
    let v1:e-expr(e1,exenv);
    let v2:e-expr(e2,exenv);
    apply-infix-opr(opr,v1,v2)


e-cond-expr(mk-cond-expr(b,t,e),exenv) =
    if e-expr(b,exenv)
        then e-expr(t,exenv)
        else e-expr(e,exenv)
```

Comment: The evaluation of infix expressions is from left to right.
Since $Int \subseteq Real$ no explicit conversion from integer to real
is necessary in infix and conditional expressions.

$represent(r) =$
  <u>*if*</u> $-\underline{MAXREAL}<r<-\underline{MINREAL}$ ∨
      $\underline{MINREAL}<r< \underline{MAXREAL}$ ∨
            $r=0$
    <u>*then*</u> <u>*return*</u> *(an implementation defined*
                    approximation of r)
    <u>*else*</u> <u>*error*</u>

type: Real ⟶ *Real*

$test(i) =$
  <u>*if*</u> $-\underline{MAXINT}<r<\underline{MAXINT}$
    <u>*then*</u> <u>*return*</u>(i)
    <u>*else*</u> <u>*error*</u>

type: Int ⟶ *Int*

$apply\text{-}prefix\text{-}opr(opr,v) =$
  <u>*cases*</u> *opr:*
    <u>*NOT*</u>   ⟶ <u>*return*</u>$(\neg v)$
    <u>*REAL-PLUS*</u>, <u>*INT-PLUS*</u>   ⟶ <u>*return*</u>(v)
    <u>*REAL-MINUS*</u>, <u>*INT-MINUS*</u>   ⟶ <u>*return*</u>$(-v)$

type: Prefix-opr Sc-val ⟶ *Sc-val*

```
apply-infix-opr(opr,v,w) =

  cases opr:
    REAL-ADD      → represent(v+w)
    REAL-SUB      → represent(v-w)
    REAL-MULT     → represent(v*w)
    REAL-DIV      → if w=0
                       then fault1
                       else represent(v*represent(1/w))
    REAL-EXP      → if v>0
                       then value of the standard function exp
                            applied on represent(v*value of the
                                                  standard function
                                                  ln applied on w)
                       else fault2
    REAL-INT-EXP  → if v=0 & w=0
                       then fault3
                       else (let expn(n) = if n=0
                                              then 1
                                              else represent(expn(n-1)*n)
                             if w≥0
                                then expn(w)
                                else represent(1/expn(-w))
    INT-ADD       → test(v+w)
    INT-SUB       → test(v-w)
    INT-MULT      → test(v*w)
    INT-DIV       → if w=0
                       then fault1
                       else test(v/w)
    INT-EXP       → if w<0 & v=0  ∨ w=0
                       then fault4
                       else (let expi(n) = if n=0
                                              then 1
                                              else test(expi(n-1)*v)
                             return(expi(w))
    LT            → return(v<w)
    LE            → return(v≤w)
    EQ            → return(v=w)
    NE            → return(v≠w)
    GE            → return(v≥w)
    GT            → return(v>w)
    IMPL          → return(v⇒w)
```

$$\underline{EQU} \qquad \rightarrow \underline{return}(v \leftrightarrow w)$$
$$\underline{AND} \qquad \rightarrow \underline{return}(v \& w)$$
$$\underline{OR} \qquad \rightarrow \underline{return}(v \lor w)$$

type: Infix-opr Sc-val Sc-val ⟹ Sc-val

Comment: *fault1* represents the state transition, which corresponds
  to the call: *fault('div by zero',v)*
fault2 ~ fault('expr undefined',v)
fault3 ~ fault('expn undefined',v)
fault4 ~ fault('expi undefined',w)

e-type-decl(mk-type-decl(,,tp)) = gen-sc-den(tp)

type: Type-decl ⟹ Sc-loc

e-array-decl(mk-array-decl(,,tp,bdl),exenv) =
  let ebds:<(let v:e-expr(s-lbd(bdl(i)),exenv);
        let lbd:conv(v,INT);
        let w:e-expr(s-ubd(bdl(i)),exenv);
        let ubd:conv(w,INT);
        if v>w then error;
          <lbd,ubd>)|1≤i≤lenbdl>;
  let indes = rect(ebds)
  let array-den:gen-array-den(indes,tp);
  return(array-den)

type: Array-decl Expr-Env ⟹ Array-den

Comment: It is assumed that the generation of an array without elements is erroueous, rather than the access to such an array.

```
e-switch-decl(mk-switch-decl(,exl),env) =
   let f(ind,cas) =
       (if 1≤ind≤lenexl then e-expr(exl(i),<env,cas>)
        else error
        )
   f
```

type: Switch-decl Env → Switch-den


```
e-proc-decl(mk-proc-decl(id,tp,fpl,vids,spm,b),oenv,env) =
   let f(denl,cas) =
       (if lendenl ≠ lenfpl ∨
           (∃i∈{1:lenfpl})(¬is-parm-ok(denl(i),spm(fpl(i)),fpl(i)∈vids))
        then error
        else (let nenv:env+
                      ([fpl(i)↦s-v(denl(i))|1≤i≤lenfpl & fpl(i)∈vids))] ∪
                      [fpl(i)↦e-val-parm(s-v(denl(i)),spm(fpl(i)),cas) |
                              1≤i≤lenfpl & fpl(i)∈vids] ∪
                   (if tp=NIL then []
                    else [id↦gen-sc-den(tp)]));
              cases b:
                mk-code(tr) → tr
                T           → i-block(b,<oenv,nenv,cas>);
                epilogue({fpl(i)|1≤i≤lenfpl & fpl(i)∈vids &
                                  spm(fpl(i))∈Type∪Type-array})
              let rv: if tp=NIL then NIL else contents(env(id));
              if tp≠NIL then epilogue(id,nenv);
              return(rv)))
   f
```

type: Proc-decl Own-env Env → Proc-den

```
is-parm-ok(<v,spa>,spf,bv) =
    if bv then
            ( spa=spf ∨ is-arithm(spf) & is-arithm(spa) ∨
                is-type-array(spf) & is-type-array(spa) & is-arithm(s-type(spa))
                                                        & is-arithm(s-type(spf)))

        else
            ( spa=spf ∨ spf=PROC & is-type-proc(spa) ∨
                is-type-proc(spf) & is-type-proc(spa) & is-arithm(s-type(spa))
                                                        & is-arithm(s-type(spf)))


type:  Act-parm-den Specifier Bool → Bool



e-val-parm(den,sp,cas) =
    cases sp:
      mk-type-array(tp) →
          (let aloc:gen-array-den(domden,tp);
           for esscl∈domden do
               (let v:contents(den(esscl));
                assign(v,aloc(esscl)));
           return(aloc))
      LABEL → den(cas)
      T    →
          (let v:(if is-by-name-expr-den(den) then den(cas)
                  else (let l:den(cas);
                        contents(l)));
           let vc:conv(v,sp);
           let l:gen-sc-den(sp);
           assign(vc,l);
           return(l))

    type:  Den Specifier Aid-set → Den
```

4.2 Auxiliary Functions

```
    is-contnd:  Id Stmt  → Bool
    is-contndl: Id Stmt* → Bool
```

Comment: Two obvious functions for checking whether the given identi-
          fier is contained in the label part of a (contained) statement
          which is not contained in an intervening block.

$index:$ Id $Stmt*$ $\overset{\sim}{\to}$ Nat

comment: For identifiers which satisfy "$is\text{-}contndl$" this function
finds the index such that the indexed element of the statement list also contains the identifier.

$within(so,o) =$
    /* checks if so is a sub-part of o */

type: $Object$ $Object$ $\to$ $Bool$

$is\text{-}uniquel:$ $Object*$ $\to$ $Bool$

comment: True iff no duplicates

$is\text{-}disjoint:$ $(Object\text{-}set)*$ $\to$ $Bool$

comment: True iff sets are pairwise disjoint

$rect(ipl) =$
    $\{il \mid \underline{lenil}=\underline{lenipl}$ & $(1\underline{\leq}i\underline{\leq}lenipl \Rightarrow ipl(i)(1)\underline{\leq}il(i)\underline{\leq}ipl(i)(2))\}$

type: $(Int^2)^+$ $\to$ $(Int^+)\text{-}set$
pre: $1\underline{\leq}i\underline{\leq}lenipl \Rightarrow ipl(i)(1) \leq ipl(i)(2)$

$assign(v,l) =$
    $\underline{R\text{-}STG} := \underline{c} \, \underline{R\text{-}STG} + [l \to v]$

type: $Sc\text{-}val$ $Sc\text{-}loc$ $\Rightarrow$

$contents(l) =$
    $\underline{if} \, \underline{c} \, \underline{R\text{-}STG}(l) = \underline{?} \, \underline{then} \, \underline{error}$
    $\underline{else} \, \underline{c} \, \underline{R\text{-}STG}(l)$

type: $Sc\text{-}loc$ $\Rightarrow$ $Sc\text{-}val$

```
conv(v,tp) =
  if tp=INT
     then test(rounded value of v)
     else return(v)

pre:  is-bool(v) ⇒ tp=BOOL
      is-real(v) ⇒ is-arith(tp)


gen-array-den(indls,tp) =
  let den:[indl→gen-sc-den(tp)|indl∈indls]
  return(den)

type:  Int⁺-set Type ⇒ Array-den


gen-sc-den(tp) =
  let loc∈(cases tp:
                BOOL → Bool-loc
                REAL → Real-loc
                INT  → Int-loc) be s.t. loc∉dom c R-STG
  R-STG := c R-STG ∪ [loc↦?];
  return(loc)

type:  Type ⇒ Sc-loc
```

SOFTWARE ABSTRACTION PRINCIPLES:

TUTORIAL EXAMPLES OF AN OPERATING SYSTEM COMMAND LANGUAGE SPECIFICATION AND A PL/I-LIKE ON-CONDI= TION LANGUAGE DEFINITION

Dines Bjørner

Abstract:

Four groups of two, either complementing or contrasting
abstraction principles are isolated: REPRESENTATIONAL and
OPERATIONAL abstraction; CONFIGURATIONAL versus HIERAR=
CHICAL abstraction; STATE-MACHINE- versus REFERENTIALLY
TRANSPARENT, FUNCTIONAL- abstraction; and DENOTATIONAL
versus MECHANICAL specification. Tools, techniques and
examples are presented for, respectively of, each of the
eight principles.

CONTENTS

1. Introduction   339
   -- On Abstraction Techniques   339

2. Example I:
   An Abstract Processor for an Interactive,
   Operating System Command Language   344

   A. Syntactic Domains   344
   B. Semantic Domains   346
   C. Semantic Domain Consistency Constraints   349
   D. Dynamic Command / State Consistency Constraints   350
   E. Elaboration Function Types   353
   F. Elaboration Function Definitions   354
   G. Auxiliary Function Types   357
   H. Auxiliary Function Definitions   358

3. Example II:
   A PL/I-like On-Condition Language   360

   A. Syntactic Domains   360
   B. Static Context Condition Function Types   361
   C. Auxiliary Text Function Types   361
   D. Static (Compile-time) Domains   361
   E. Static Context Conditions   361
   F. Auxiliary Text Functions   364
   G. Semantic Domains   364
   H. Global State Initialization   365
   I. Elaboration Function Types   365
   J. Auxiliary Function Types   365
   K. Semantic Function Definitions   366

   Comment   372
   Discussion   372

Acknowledgements   374

1. INTRODUCTION

The problem to be solved by the methods outlined in this paper is ultimately the construction of correctly functioning, well-understood,
pleasing, yet complex software. It is our thesis that one way of achieving this is to use a systematic software development method which
provides a formalized structure for stepwise, increasingly more detailed arguments of correctness -- a method based on systematically deriving abstractions into concrete realizations; i.e. on a-priori, synthetic, constructive proofs rather than a-posteriori, analytic proofs.
Thus we see our methodology as starting with an abstract specification
of the desired software item. This paper then is concerned with some
of the techniques used in achieving such definitions. In [Bjørner 77c]
we cover the problems of mapping abstractions into concretizations.
We are there in particular concerned with the systematic derivation-
and proof techniques.

The objectives of an abstract software specification are basically two-
fold: that the resulting document serve as the basis from which an implementation take place formally, and with respect to which correctness
criteria be stated, and a proof given. Hence we require that the specification (or: meta-) language be formal. Also: that the document, and
it alone, be the specification from which we develop user's reference
(and other) manuals!

The objectives of the abstraction principles explicitly expounded in
this paper are several: That the specifications be precise, non-contra-
dictory and complete; that they be short, well-organized and comprehensible; that the described systems be well-conceived, free from mis-con-
ceptions, conceptually clean, lean and with an optimum of semantically
relevant notions; that their properties be well understood, possesing
desirable properties and with a minimum of ad-hoc ideas. We find [Li-
kov 75] to give a fine discussion of the above points.

n Abstraction Techniques

Before going on to exemplify uses of the meta-language let us first
also summarize the principles used in applying constructs of this language.
One thing is the notation: its syntax & semantics. Another thing is
the intent with which it was to be applied; its pragmatics. Any notation
can be used against its will, even a good one.

If you consider META-IV as an ultra-high-level programming language,
i.e. one which although it is intended only to specify software actually results in programs which can be considered implementations, albeit on a very abstract, and in most cases not mechanizable, level, then
which are the programming disciplines around which the meta-language
evolved, and whose application exploits its capabilities to the fullest?

We consider these to be the pre-dominant abstraction techniques: repre-
sentational- & operational- abstraction; configurational vs. hierarchical abstraction; referential transparency vs. abstract state machine
modeling; and mechanical- vs. denotational abstraction.

At each design step and at each specification stage we carefully review
the appropriateness of each abstraction choice: its level when consider
ing e.g. representational- & operational; and mechanical- vs. denotational abstractions; its mixture or blend of configuration and hierac-
chy, i.e. bottom-up synthetic vs. top-down analytic features; respectively of referential transparency or applicativeness vs. abstract state
machine imperativeness; and finally also its balance of explicitness
vs. implicitness.

Before going into a brief characterization of each of the eight abstrac
tion principles, an outline is first given of the basic parts that make
up our specification document. A rationale is given for their inclusion

The software 'function' to be modelled normally accepts inputs, emits
outputs, achieves the desired transformations of inputs into outputs
by means of internal data structures, and specifies transformations in
terms of function definitions (procedures, process descriptions, operations). Our model hence consists of two basically distinct parts: one
containing the descriptions of the input/output and internal domains
-- subsequently referred to as syntactic-, respectively semantic domain
Another part containing a number of elaboration- (and auxiliary-) function definitions which to combinations of input- and semantic- domain
objects ascribes their meaning, in terms of either semantic domain object transformations or these latter combined with output domain object

In the next paragraphs we now treat the abstraction principles individually.

By REPRESENTATIONAL ABSTRACTION we understand the specification of objects irrespective of their implementation, and such that the chosen abstractions as closely as possible only reflect relevant and intrinsic properties.

Representational abstraction of classes of objects is here expressed in terms of so-called abstract syntax. Individual instances of objects can be abstracted by corresponding expressions of the meta-language. Representational abstraction is applied in the definition of both syntactic- and semantic- domains and domain objects.

By OPERATIONAL ABSTRACTION we understand the specification of functions in extension. That is: we are primarily interested in the properties of the functions we define, notably in the properties of that which our defined functions define (be they functions themselves), i.e. in what they compute; less -- if at all -- interested in how results are computed, i.e. not in functions in extension.

Operational abstraction is here expressed primarily in the form of function definitions. We express these either by a pair of *pre*- and *post*-conditions on the functions sought, or by a constructive function definition. The former kind are thus usually more implicit, i.e. abstract, than the latter kind (of more explicit definitions). This latter form is normally still abstract, in that it usually internally employs operational abstraction on representationally abstract objects. Operational abstraction is used in the definition of the elaboration functions, as well as functions of our model auxiliary to these, and to ($is-wf-\theta$) well-*f*ormedness- context, static condition and dynamic constraint-, predicates 'narrowing' the ($\theta-$) domains otherwise defined by abstract syntaxes.

By CONFIGURATIONAL ABSTRACTION we understand the step-wise definition and realization of a model, or major model components, which proceeds in a synthetic manner in conceiving and documenting the desired system -- from the bottom-up -- by building layers of abstraction upon more concrete bases. From 'physical machines' we create (the illusion of) 'virtual machines': changing raw capabilities into sophisticated concepts. Configurational abstraction composes low-level abstractions (or rather 'mechanizations') into higher-level abstractions.

Configurational abstraction, in its inner, foundational steps, is usually expressed in rather concrete representational- and operational

forms. In its outer, so-called 'abstract' layers, expressional means
are normally tied to those of the procedure, module-, and class- like
'abstractions'. Configurational abstraction -- as a specification technique -- is brought into play whereever uncertainties concerning eithei
desired functions, and/or efficient realizability dominate our understanding of what system we are in fact aiming at.

The resulting design: its abstraction & implementation can usually, and
to great advantage however, be hierarchically documented.

By HIERARCHICAL ABSTRACTION we understand the stepwise definition of a
model which proceeds in conceiving and documenting, in an analytical
fashion -- from the top down -- the desired system (components) by
decomposing basic overall dominating concepts and transformations into
constituent ones.

Hierarchical abstraction techniques can fully exploit the representational and operational abstraction techniques descussed and elsewhere
illustrated in this paper. And hierarchical abstraction is applied wher
a sufficiently deep understanding of our system haş eventually trans-
pired.

Configurational abstraction have been used extensively in operating systems designs [Dijkstra 68; Hansen 73]. Hierarchical abstraction
mostly in e.g. programming language semantics [e.g. Bekić 74, Henhapl
78] and relational data base (system and query language) formalization
[Hansal 76, Nilsson 76].

Any one abstraction, and almost any actual, conventional program algorithm, usually exhibits some mixture of both. Only when the choice
between configurational- and hierarchical abstraction has been made as
the consequence of a careful study, and only when the resulting documentation (respectively program code) is clear, does the specification
appear transparent. The subject of choosing a bottom-up versus a top-
down abstract, and/or algorithmic design idea programming strategy is,
however, a seriously undeveloped one and we shall unfortunately not
contribute much to a clarification in this paper. It is our hope, thoug
to return later to a study of their duality. Step-wise refinement, i.e.
top-down, hierarchical abstraction in program algorithm and data structure design is extensively convered in [Wirth 71,73,76].

By a DENOTATIONAL SPECIFICATION [Scott 71,72; Tennent 73,76; Mosses
75; Milne 76] we understand a definition which ascribes meaning to
(composite) syntactic domain objects by functionally composing meanings of proper constituent parts. Thus denotational abstraction almost
invariably calls for 'homomorphic' programming [Burstall 69, Morris 73,
Reynolds 74, ADJ 77], i.e. referential transparency together with syntactic object 'driven' function specifications. And denotational definitions achieve their characteristics by employing semantic domain objects of high, functional order. Thus the meaning of a program (construct) is generally seen as a state transformation function, a state
transformer, independent of program (input) data.

By a MECHANICAL ABSTRACTION (which may hardly be an abstraction at all!)
we understand a description which assigns meaning to a program (construct) by explicitly prescribing computation (i.e. state-) sequences
given input data, thus computing result values. The meaning then becomes the state transition sequence, not the function from begin states
to end states. A mechanical definition is said to be so (or to be operational) since its direct realization is immediate (and programmable
in most languages).

Examples

We now illustrate some of the abstraction techniques through two examples. The software item to be specified in section 2 is a command
language for an operating system -- naturally: of hypothetical, illu-
trative nature. In section 3 we give the denotational semantics of a
non-trivial language with PL/I-like On-Conditions. The abstraction
principles examplified are these: representational- and operational
abstraction; functional, referentially transparent abstraction in section 2, and abstract machine/state programming featuring both local and
global states, and local semantic domain objects in section 3. Finally,
and almost exclusively: denotational semantics, whereby the model is
almost invariably forced to be hierarchically specified.

It is, however, an alltogether not un-important aim also to convince
you of the utility of abstractly specifying software in general, and
- to take the first choice as an example, to suggest that future,
professional paper proposals for e.g. command- and data base query languages be formally, hence precisely stated.

The presentations are both according to our basic principle: formulae
first, and then their national/natural language explication immediately subsequent. No introduction smoothly 'tricking' you into a subsequent formalism -- as if to excuse this latter!

2. EXAMPLE I: An Abstract Processor for an Interactive, Operating System Command Language

A. Syntactic Domains

```
1  Cmd   =   In | Clg | Dl
2  In    ::  (Input|Source|Link)  Id
3  Clg   =   C | CL | CLG | L | LG | G
4  C     ::  Cid  (Source|Id)  [Id]
5  CL    ::  Cid  (Source|Id)  [Id]  (Link|Id)  [Id]
6  CLG   ::  Cid  (Source|Id)  [Id]  (Link|Id)  [Id]  (Input|Id)
7  L     ::                    Id    (Link|Id)  [Id]
8  LG    ::                    Id    (Link|Id   [Id]  (Input|Id)
9  G     ::                          Id         (Input|Id)
10 Dl    ::  Id
```

Annotation

1 A job control *Command* is either a file *Input* data command, or (|)
a (partial or complete) *Compile-link-go* command, or it is a *Delete*
file command.

2 An *Input* command has two parts: the data part containing either
Input, *Source* or *Link* data itself, and the part which *Identifies*
the file name to be given to this data.

3 A *Compile-link-go* command is either a *COMPILE*, a *COMPILE-LINK*, a
COMPILE-LINK-GO, a *LINK*, a *LINK-GO* or just a *GO* command.

4 A *COMPILE* command has three parts: one part *Identifies* a *Compiler*,
another either directly contains the *Source* text or *Identifies* such
a text (in the *FILE* state component, see below), and a third, optional ([]) part *Identifies* the name to be given to the object (module)
resulting from compilation and to be optionally stored in the *FILE*.

. . .

A *CLG* command additionally has a component which is either the *Link* data itself or *Identifies* such a link data file, a component which optionally *Identifies* a file name for the linked load (module), and a component which either is the *Input* data for the executing load module, or *Identifies* such an input data file.

Comments concerning Abstraction Principles

Observe that we have attempted only to describe syntactically essential components of commands -- and then only abstractly, irrespective of their possible written forms:

"ALGOL" *compile* "SID" *with* *link* ["FID" → "PRINT"]
and *execute* *with* "DID"

Thus we have as far as possible avoided any mention of what the commands effect, i.e. their meaning. Of course, your previous technical knowledge may already have initiated some personal 'feel' for what they might stand for. This is because I have chosen suggestive mnemonics. I could as well have chosen x's, y's and z's, and still obtained exactly the same domains of mathematical objects. Only when I deal with concepts for which there either is no previous familiarity or which may be ambiguously understood when applying only an intuitive understanding, i.e. when not reading the entire model, shall I have to take extraordinary care in my annotations, and in judiciously keeping these and the discussion within purely syntactic domain, purely semantic domain, respectively purely semantic *Elab*oration function subject boundaries.

The commands have been representationally abstracted. There is no word here about positional parameters, mnemonic keywords nor of default such, no talk of delimiters or other syntactic 'sugar'. The objects denoted by this abstract syntax (for a definition of *Id*, *Cid*, *Input*, *Source* and *Link*, see below) are in fact mathematical, not characterstrings. We use the same kind of abstract syntax definitional facility for specifying both syntactic and semantic domain objects, as well as their definiens   logical type expressions are used in *type* definitions for *Elab*oration- and Auxiliary functions.

The presentational structure of this abstract syntax is basically hier-archical.

B. Semantic Domains

1	Σ	::	FILE SYS UTIL
2	FILE	=	Id $\underset{m}{\rightarrow}$ Data
3	SYS	=	Cid $\underset{m}{\rightarrow}$ Comp
4	UTIL	=	Uid $\underset{m}{\rightarrow}$ (Data | QUOT*)
5	Data	=	Input	Source	Object	Link	Load
6	Input	=	...
7	Source	=	...
8	Object	=	Link $\underset{m}{\rightarrow}$ Load
9	Link	=	Id $\underset{m}{\rightarrow}$ (Id | Const)
10	Load	=	Input $\overset{\sim}{\rightarrow}$ (Σ $\overset{\sim}{\rightarrow}$ (Σ Output))
11	Output	=	...
12	Comp	=	Source $\overset{\sim}{\rightarrow}$ (Object | Text)
13	Cid	=	FORTRAN	ALGOL	COBOL	PL/I	...
14	Uid	=	INPUT	OBJ	LINK	LOAD	OUTPUT	MSG	...
15	Text	=	...
16	Id	=	TOKEN

Annotations

1   In order to explain the meaning of our operating system job command and control language we introduce an abstract state space Σ. A state $\sigma \in \Sigma$, has three components: a FILE-, a SYStem programs-, and a UTILit object.

2   A FILE object is a finite domain (= ...) map from Identifiers (i.e. file names) to Data (-sets).

3   The SYStem object is a ... map from (here only:) Compiler identifier names to the Compilers themselves. (Subsequently we might contem-plate adding other systems programs to SYS: sort-, copy-, merge-, etc..)

4   The UTILity component is a ... map from identifications of Utilities to either Data or lists (*) of QUOTations (objects which you may wish to think of as characterstrings).

Besides *Input-*, *Source-* and *Link- Data* (which can be directly inserted into the *FILE* by the command language user) *Object-* and *Load* can be filed (as the result of successfully executing one of the commands *C*, *CL*, *CLG* respectively *CL*, *CLG*, *L*, *LG*).

. .

An *Object* (module) is a map from *Link* to *Load*. (That is: the result of a compilation is to be an object of type *Object*. The <u>free</u> *Identifiers* of the (compiled) *Source* text have not yet been <u>bound</u> to their meaning -- which are to be those of *Identified* (names of) filed *Data* or *Constants*.)

Link is a ... map from (free) *Identifiers* (of (compiler) texts) to *Identifiers* (of filed *Data*) or *Constants*.

0 A *Load* (module) is a function from *Input* to *state transforming functions* yielding *Output*.

. .

2 A(ny) *Compiler* is a (pure, i.e. not state, $\sigma \in \Sigma$, dependent) function from *Source* to the <u>union</u> (|) domain of *Object* and *Text* (-- the former are to be the result of successful compilation the latter of a syntactically, and otherwise erroneous, text (instead yielding *diagnostics Text*)).

3 Suggests possible compilers!

4 The *UTIL*ity components are here primarily intended to 'store' temporary results in/between the *C-L-G* steps; for details see the *Elab-clg*, *compile* and *bind* function definitions below.

. .

6 *Identifiers* are further unspecified *TOKEN*s.

Comments on Abstraction Principles

1 Suggests or relies on a configurative abstraction: from the more primitive components is built a more sophisticated. The user -- we conjecture -- need think only of Σ, and does, as far as conceptual understanding goes, not need to know of its decomposition.

8-10,12 Suggests not only a hierarchical decomposition, but relies on *Comp* and *Load* objects as primitives. These are representationally highly abstracted.

Discussion of Abstraction Choices

The crucial abstractions are these: *Comp* and *Object*. That of *Load* -- and to an even lesser degree that of *Link* -- we consider almost trivial Anticipating subsequent semantic *Elaboration* function descriptions -- which, of course, really were developed in 'parallel' with the above semantic domain definitions -- we hinge our model on the ability of the *Compiler* to produce exactly a function of the logical type *Object* (disregarding here diagnostic *Texts*). With the types we have ascribed to *Object*, and in particular to *Load*, it can be shown that the *Compiler* in fact is the function denoted by an appropriate mathematical- or denotational semantics definition, Ψ, of the *Source* language. Ψ is to take the *Source* text and produce a function which permits an act of *binding*. *Binding* is a function which takes an *Object* module and some *Link Data* and produces some *Load* module. Ψ creates this function by letting the free *Identifiers* of the *Source* text be mappable to a variety of *Constants* or *FILE Data Identifiers*:

Example:

$$
obj\text{-}k: \left[\begin{array}{l} \left[\begin{array}{lcl} pid1 & \to & fid\text{-}i1 \\ pid2 & \to & fid\text{-}i2 \\ \ldots \\ pidn & \to & fid\text{-}in \end{array} \right] \to load\text{-}i \\ \\ \ldots \\ \\ \left[\begin{array}{lcl} pid1 & \to & fid\text{-}j1 \\ pid1 & \to & fid\text{-}j2 \\ \ldots \\ pidn & \to & fid\text{-}jn \end{array} \right] \to load\text{-}j \end{array} \right]
$$

$obj\text{-}k \in Object$
$load\text{-}i \in Load$
$pid... \in Id$
$fid... \in Id$

end example.

In fact, we can impose varying degrees of easily formalizable, hence tersely expressible constraints on *Object*'s and *Link*'s:

2. Semantic Domain Consistency Constraints

Simple, Lax Version:

$$1.0 \quad is\text{-}wf\text{-}\Sigma(mk\text{-}\Sigma(f,s,u))=$$
$$.1 \quad (\forall o \in \underline{rng}\ f)$$
$$.2 \quad (is\text{-}Object(o) \supset (\forall l1, l2 \in \underline{dom}\ o)(\underline{dom}\ l1 = \underline{dom}\ l2))$$

Restrictive Version:

$$2.0 \quad is\text{-}wf\text{-}\Sigma(mk\text{-}\Sigma(f,s,u))=$$
$$.1 \quad (\forall o \in \underline{rng}\ f)$$
$$.2 \quad (is\text{-}Object(o) \supset (\forall l1, l2 \in \underline{dom}\ o)$$
$$.3 \quad ((\underline{dom}\ l1 = \underline{dom}\ l2)$$
$$.4 \quad \wedge(\underline{rng}\ l1 \diagdown Const \subseteq \underline{dom}\ f)))$$
$$.5 \quad \wedge(\forall l \in \underline{rng}\ f)$$
$$.6 \quad (is\text{-}Link(l) \supset (\underline{rng}\ l \diagdown Const \subseteq \underline{dom}\ f))$$

Annotations:

1.0-1.2 ≡ 2.0-2.3)

.1-2.4 For each *Object*, *o*, in *fILE* it must be the case that all of its *dom*ain *l*inks have the same *dom*ain of (free *Source* text) *Iden*tifiers -- since, naturally, that object, *o*, is the result of just one compilation of exactly one *Source* text. (But: binding these free *Identifiers* to different *fILEd Data* and *Cons*tants should certainly create distinct *Load* modules, cf. example above.)

.4 -- And range *Identifiers* of *Object* module *Link*'s must (in this restrictive version) already have been defined (i.e. *fILEd Data*.

.5-2.6 -- Similar for *fILEd Data*.

Comments on Abstraction Principles

The domain consistency (inspection) functions are operationally abstracted in terms of applicative, referentially transparent expressions
exploying quantified predicates, i.e. staying aloof of order of inspection!

D. Dynamic Command-State Consistency/Constraint Relations

```
1.0   pre-Elab-cmd(<cmd,σ>)=
 .1       (let mk-Σ(f,,) =.σ in
 .2       cases cmd:
 .3           (mk-In(,id)   →   id ~∈ dom f,
 .4           mk-Dl(id)     →   id ∈ dom f,
 .5           T             →   pre-Elab-clg(<cmd,σ>))
```

```
2.0      pre-Elab-clg(<clg,σ>)=
 .1          (let mk-Σ(file,sys,) = σ in
 .2          cases clg:
 .3             (mk-C(k,s,o)          →   ((k ∈ dom sys)                                          ∧
 .4                                        (is-Id(s) ⊃ ((s ∈ dom file)                     ∧
 .5                                                      is-Source(file(s)))))               ∧
 .6                                        ((o≠nil) ⊃ o~∈ dom file)),
 .7             mk-CL(k,s,o,l,e)      →   (pre-Elab-clg(<mk-C(k,s,o),σ>)                      ∧
 .8                                        (is-Id(l) → ((l ∈ dom file)                      ∧
 .9                                                     is-Link(file(l))               ∧
.10                                                     (rng(file(l))∖Const ⊆ dom file)),
.11                                         T       → (rng l∖Const ⊆ dom file))             ∧
.12                                        ((e≠nil) ⊃ e~∈ dom file)),
.13             mk-CLG(k,s,o,l,e,i)   →   (pre-Elab-clg(<mk-CL(k,s,o,l,e),σ>)                ∧
.14                                        (is-Id(i) ⊃ ((i ∈ dom file)                      ∧
.15                                                     is-Input(file(i))))),
.16             mk-L(o,l,e)           →   ((o ∈ dom file) ∧ is-Object(file(o))               ∧
.17                                        (is-Id(l) → (l ∈ dom file)                       ∧
.18                                                     is-Link(file(l))              ∧
.19                                                     (rng(file(l))∖Const ⊆ dom file)),
.20                                         T       → (rng l∖Const ⊆ dom file))            ∧
.21                                        ((e≠nil) ⊃ (e~∈ dom file))),
.22             mk-LG(o,l,e,i)        →   (pre-Elab-clg(<mk-L(o,l,e),σ>)                      ∧
.23                                        (is-Id(i) → ((i ∈ dom file)                      ∧
.24                                                     is-Input(file(i))))),
.25             mk-G(e,i)             →   ((e ∈ dom file) ∧ is-Load(file(e))                 ∧
.26                                        (is-Id(i) ⊃ ((i ∈ dom file)                      ∧
.27                                                     is-Input(file(i))))))))
```

Annotation:

Successful *Elaboration* of *commands* depend on basically three aspects:
(1) one is checkable without actually applying the functions implied
(e.g.: *C*ompile, *L*ink and *G*o), but depends on the relation between the
static *command* and the <u>dynamic</u> state, o∈Σ. (2) The other can only be
known by actually applying the implied (*C*,*L*,*G*) functions. In this example there are no, (0), static context conditions imposable on *commands*
only, as is e.g. the case with the definition and use of (variable,
procedure and label) identifiers in block-structured procedure-oriented
programming languages with a fixed, strong type system. *pre-Elab-cmd*
and *pre-Elab-clg* deals with (1). The Auxiliary functions *compile* and
bind invoked by the *Elab-clg* functions takes care of (2).

1.3   The *I*dentifier naming *Data* to be *f*ILEd must not already be used
         i.e. be 'defined'.

...

2.5   The *f*ILEd *Source* text *I*dentifier must identify a *Data* object
         of type *Source*.

2.6   If an identifier, *o*, is specified (for the thus implied *f*iling
         of the *Object* module to result from *C*ompilation) then *o* must
         not already be defined.

...

2.10,19 If only C.1 (not C.2) is specified, then this is the last
         'time'/opportunity to 'catch' the equivalent of C.2.4.

         (Notice that we have not checked *Input Link Data* in D.1.3!)

Comments <u>on</u> Abstraction <u>Principles</u>

Again the functions are operational abstractly specified. The structure
of the function definition follows that of the abstract syntax definition of (primarily) *C*ommands and (secondarily) Σ.

2. Elaboration Function Types

1	*type:*	$Elab\text{-}cmd$: $Cmd \overset{\sim}{\to} (\Sigma \overset{\sim}{\to} \Sigma)$
2		$Elab\text{-}clg$: $Clg \overset{\sim}{\to} (\Sigma \overset{\sim}{\to} \Sigma)$

Annotation:

Given a *command* the $Elaborate\text{-}command$ function ascribes to it, as its semantics, a state transformer, i.e. a function from (Operating System) states to states. This is the denotational semantics viewpoint. Thus, when a specific *command*, which denotes the function, say ψ, is executed in a state σ, $\sigma \in \Sigma$, then a new state σ', $\sigma' \in \Sigma$, will arise:

$$\underline{let} \ \psi = Elab\text{-}cmd(cmd)$$
$$\Psi(\sigma) = \sigma'$$

Comments on Abstraction Principle:

We choose this level of abstraction, in contrast to a mechanical semantics definition, since we have not yet decided on which machine, and/or how we specifically intend, to implement our command language.

Also the choice concerning the operational characterstics has been limited to the denotational ones since we anyway have decided not yet to consider how e.g. *Compilers* are to be realized, only that they perform some function, and the type of this function.

F. Elaboration Function Definitions

```
1.0   Elab-cmd(cmd) =
.1      if pre-Elab-cmd(cmd)σ
.2        then
.3          (let mk-Σ(f,s,u) = σ in
.4            cases cmd:
.5              (mk-Id(d,i) → mk-Σ(f∪[i→d],s,
.6                                    u + [MSG → u(MSG)⌢<FILED>]),
.7               mk-Dl(id)  → mk-Σ(f∖{id},s,
.8                                    u + [MSG → u(MSG)⌢<DELETED>]),
.9                    T       → Elab-clg(cmd)σ))
.10       else
.11         error
```

```
2.0   Elab-clg(clg)σ=
.1      (let mk-Σ(f,s,u) = σ in
.2      (trap exit(ξ) with ξ in
.3      cases clg:
.4        (mk-C(k,t,o)          → compile(k,t,o)σ,
.5         mk-CL(k,t,o,l,e)     → (let σ' = compile(k,t,o)σ in
.6                                  bind(l,e)σ'),
.7         mk-CLG(k,t,o,l,e,i)  → (let σ' = compile(k,t,o)σ in
.8                                  let σ" = bind(l,e)σ'      in
.9                                  execute(i)σ"),
.10        mk-L(o,l,e)          → (let σ' = mk-Σ(f,s,u+[OBJ→f(o)]) in
.11                                  bind(l,e)σ'),
.12        mk-LG(o,l,e,i)       → (let σ' = mk-Σ(f,s,u+[OBJ→f(o)]) in
.13                                  let σ" = bind(l,e)σ'          in
.14                                  execute(i)σ"),
.15        mk-G(e,i)            → (let σ' = mk-Σ(f,s,u+[LOAD→f(e)]) in
.16                                  execute(i)σ')))
```

Annotation:

1.1   Execution of a *cmd* depends on it satisfying the function independent, syntactic- and semantic domain dependent consistency
constraints specified by *pre-Elab-cmd* (and detailed there and
in *pre-Elab-clg*).

..6,8   *MeSsaGes* concerning successful completion states (status's) are
'posted' in the *UTILity MeSsaGe* component.

2.2   Erroneous, execution-time checkable only, execution of the *compile* or *bind* functions shall lead to <u>*exit*</u>s being <u>*trap*</u>ped here
-- aborting further execution of steps in the *CL*, *CLG*, *LG* commands.
(Abnormal termination in the *C*, *L* cases are of course also <u>*trap*</u>-
ped here with the same effect as if not abnormally terminated
through an <u>*exit*</u>!)

.4   To Compile is to *compile*.

..

.7   To Compile-Link-Go is to *compile* (in one state, σ), then (;) to
bind in the state, σ', resulting from compilation; and to *execute*
in the state, σ", resulting from binding.

.10   The *bind* operation expects the *UTILity OBJect* component to contain the named (*o*) *Object* module (from the *f*ile).

.5,7 Thus the *compile* operation deposits a successfully compiled
Object in the *UTILity OBJect* component.

.15   like 2.10 but now for *execute* and <u>*LOAD*</u>,

.8,13 -- like 2.5,7, but now for the objects mentioned above!

.7-9 These three lines could be written:

         execute(i)(bind(l,e)(compile(k,t,o)σ))

and so could lines 2.5-6 and 2.13-14, in their form.

Discussion of Abstraction Choices:

The restriction that a *CLG* command must have not only its "*C-*", but also its "*L-*" and "*G-*" (syntactic) components agreeing with certain state components in order that *Elaboration* of any part of the *CLG* command may be commenced, may seem rather limiting. We have, however, brought this semantics only for the purposes of exemplifying modelling techniques -- not in order to advocate the virtues of one particular command language over those of another. Only when we master our specification tools do we feel ready to seriously, and sensibly, embark on 'architectural' designs. Thus it is relatively easy, to 'chop' the *precondition* specfication up into separate parts, and merge these (or 'calls' thereon) with the constructive parts of the present *Elaboration* functions, thus permitting partial *Elaboration* of e.g. *CLG* commands.

Comments on Abstraction Principles:

The semantics assignment has been part implicitly-, part explicitly specified: one could replace *Elab-cmd* with a *post-Elab-cmd* specification:

```
3.0    post-Elab-cmd(<cmd,σ>,σ')=
 .1        (let mk-Σ(f,,) = σ,
 .2            mk-Σ(f',,) = σ' in
 .3        cases cmd:
 .4            (mk-In(d,i)  →  f' = f∪[i→d],
 .5             mk-Dl(id)   →  f' = f\{id},
 .6             T           →  post- lab-clg(<cmd,σ>,σ')
```

which, together with *pre-Elab-cmd*, uniquely determines *Elab-cmd*. (Provided of course we either specify *Elab-clg* accordingly through its *post-*, or imply the *post-Elab-clg* defined by 2 above!)

In general, if:

$$type:\ F:\qquad A \overset{\sim}{\to} B$$

then:

$$type:\ pre\text{-}F:\quad A \to BOOL$$
$$type:\ post\text{-}F:\ (A\ B) \to BOOL$$

with:

$$pre\text{-}F(a) \supset (\exists!b \in B)(F(a) = b)$$
$$pre\text{-}F(a) \land F(a) = b \supset post\text{-}F(a,b).$$

The definition of the *Elab-clg* proceeded on the basis of an iterative stepwise refinement: existence of *compile*, *bind* and *execute* was postulated after the crucial issue of their logical types were first settled -- see G below! The iteration from the internal specification of the first two of these functions occured as the result of first planning that there be an *exit* within them, and then actually fixing the places of these *exits* and the type of the value(s) (Σ) being "returned".

G. Auxiliary Function Types

1	*type: compile:*	*Cid (Source | Id) [Id]*	$\tilde{\rightarrow}$ $(\Sigma \overset{\sim}{\rightarrow} \Sigma)$
2	*bind:*	*(Link | Id) [Id]*	$\tilde{\rightarrow}$ $(\Sigma \overset{\sim}{\rightarrow} \Sigma)$
3	*execute:*	*(Input | Id)*	$\tilde{\rightarrow}$ $(\Sigma \overset{\sim}{\rightarrow} \Sigma)$

Discussion/Comments:

There is an unfortunate asymmetry between these functions: *compile* receives all the information it requires through its three arguments, but both *bind* and *execute* are not explicitly passed information about the *object* module to be linked, respectively the *Load* module to be executed -- instead these objects are to be looked up in the *UTILity* components: *BJ*, respectively *LOAD*; a fact which is hidden. This abstraction choice was made after some (trivial) experiments with explicit passing: the present solution was found not only to balance the needs better between on one hand the *CL* and *CLG* commands, and those of the *LG* and *G* commands on the other hand, but also to be in some accord with actual operating system practice (SYSLINK, ...).

H. Auxiliary Function Definitions

1.0 $compile(k,t,o)\sigma=$

.1   *(let* $mk\text{-}\Sigma(f,s,u) = \sigma$ *in*

.2   *let* $source = $ *if* $is\text{-}Id(t)$ *then* $f(t)$ *else* t *in*

.3   *let* $obj = (s(k))(source)$ *in*

.4   *if* $is\text{-}Text(obj)$

.5   *then* $exit(mk\text{-}\Sigma(f,s,u+[MSG \rightarrow u(MSG)^\frown <obj>]))$

.6   *else* $(let$ $u' = u+[OBJ \rightarrow obj, MSG \rightarrow u(MSG)^\frown <COMPILED>]$ *in*

.7   *if* $o=nil$

.8   *then* $mk\text{-}\Sigma(f,s,u')$

.9   *else* $mk\text{-}\Sigma(f\cup[o\rightarrow obj],s,u')))$

2.0 $bind(l,e)\sigma=$

.1   *(let* $mk\text{-}\Sigma(f,s,u\cup[OBJ\rightarrow obj]) = \sigma$ *in*

.2   *let* $lnk = $ *if* $is\text{-}Id(l)$ *then* $f(l)$ *else* l *in*

.3   *if* $lnk \in dom\ obj$

.4   *then* $(let$ $u' = u+[LOAD \rightarrow obj(lnk), MSG \rightarrow u(MSG)^\frown <LINKED>]$ *in*

.5   *if* $e=nil$

.6   *then* $mk\text{-}\Sigma(f,s,u')$

.7   *else* $mk\text{-}\Sigma(f\cup[e\rightarrow obj(lnk)],s,u'+[MSG\rightarrow u(MSG)^\frown <FILED>])$

.8   *else* $exit(mk\text{-}\Sigma(f,s,u+[MSG \rightarrow u(MSG)^\frown <ERRONEOUS\text{-}LINK>])))$

3.0 $execute(i)\sigma=$

.1   *(let* $mk\text{-}\Sigma(f,s,u\cup[LOAD \rightarrow load]) = \sigma$ *in*

.2   *let* $input = $ *if* $is\text{-}Id(i)$ *then* $f(i)$ *else* i *in*

.3   *let* $(mk\text{-}\Sigma(f',s,u'),output) = load(input)$ *in*

.4 $mk\text{-}\Sigma(f',s,u'+[OUTPUT \rightarrow output]))$

Comments on Abstraction Principles

It is especially in this specification step that the real 'power' of
our abstraction appears to yield their maximum return.

Annotations:

.3　　Recalling that the logical type of the *Compiler*, $s(k)$, is
　　　Source $\tilde{\to}$ *(Object | Text)* and that that of *source* is *Source*, we
　　　see that that of *obj* is either *Object* or *Text* -- concerning which
　　　we assume disjointness of domains, although that has not yet been
　　　imposed.

.9　　If *o* was specified, then the *Object obj* is to be *f*iled.

.6　　In any case a successfull *compile* leaves *obj* in the *UTIL*ity under
　　　OBJ.

.3　　A *bind* is only successful if the right *Link* information is pro-
　　　vided.

.3　　The logical type of *Load* is (see B.10) *Input* $\tilde{\to}$ $(\Sigma \tilde{\to} \Sigma$ *Output)*
　　　permitting executing (user) programs to access $(\Sigma \tilde{\to} ...)$ and up-
　　　date $(... \tilde{\to} \Sigma)$ e.g. *f*iles, thus changing the state.

Discussion of F & H, Functional versus Machine State Programming:

The specification of *Elab-cmd* has been kept completely functional, thus
referentially transparent. The meaning of a command is the simple functional composition of the meanings of the command components -- and the
overall meaning remains unchanged if we alter any syntactic component
to another, syntactically different one (*Id* for *Source*, or: *Id* for *Link*,
or: *Id* for *Input* H.1.2, H.2.2. respectively H.3.3) having the same con-
tituent meaning.

3. EXAMPLE II: A PL/I-like On-Condition Language

We begin by listing and annotating formulae. Then we end by discussing abstraction principles.

A. Syntactic Domains

$$
\begin{array}{lll}
Progr & = & Block \\
Block & :: & Id\text{-}set \quad (Id\underset{m}{\to}Proc) \quad Stmt^{+} \\
Proc & :: & s\text{-}pml:(s\text{-}Id:Id \ s\text{-}Tp:(\underline{LOC}|\underline{PROC}))^{*} \quad Block \\
Stmt & = & El\text{-}Stmt \mid Call \mid On\text{-}Unit \mid Signal \mid Revert \\
Call & :: & Id \quad Expr^{*} \\
On\text{-}Unit & :: & Cid \quad Proc \\
Signal & :: & Cid \quad Id^{*} \\
Revert & :: & Cid \\
Expr & = & Id \mid Const \mid Infix \\
Const & :: & INTG \\
Infix & :: & Expr \quad Op \quad Expr \\
Op & = & \underline{ADD} \mid \underline{SUB} \mid \underline{MPY} \mid \underline{DIV} \mid \underline{EQ} \mid \underline{NEQ} \\
Id & \supset & TOKEN \\
Lbl & \supset & TOKEN
\end{array}
\left.\begin{array}{l} \\ \\ \end{array}\right\} Id \cup Lbl = \{\}
$$

$$
\begin{array}{lll}
Cid & = & \underline{OFL} \mid \underline{ZERO} \mid \underline{UFL} \mid \ldots
\end{array}
$$

Annotations

A *Program* is a *Block*. A *Block* has three parts: a *set* of variable *Identifiers*, a set of uniquely *Identified Procedures* (hence abstracted as a *map*), and a list of *Statements*. A *Procedure* has a parameter *list* and a *Block*. The parameter *list* consists of pairs of formal parameter *Identifiers* and their corresponding *LOCation* or *PROCedure* type. A *Statement* is either an *Elelentary Statement*, a subroutine *Call*, an *On-Unit*, a *Signal*, or a *Revert* statement. An *Expression* is either a variable or a formal parameter *Identification*, a *Constant*, or an *Infix* expression. An *Infix* expression has three parts: a left- and a right operand *Expression*, and an *Operator*.

B. Static Context Condition Function Types

1	*type:*	*is-wf-Progr:*	*Progr*		→ BOOL
2		*is-wf-Block:*	*Block*	→ DICT	→ BOOL
3		*is-wf-Procedure:*	*Id Proc*	→ DICT	→ BOOL
4		*is-wf-Stmt:*	*Stmt*	→ DICT	→ BOOL
5		*is-wf-Expr:*	*Expr*	→ DICT	→ BOOL

C. Auxiliary Text Function Types

6	*type:*	*e-tp:*	*Expr* → DICT → Type

D. Static (Compile-time) Domains:

$$DICT = (Id \xrightarrow[m]{} Type)$$
$$Type = \underline{LOC} \mid \underline{PROC} \mid (Id (\underline{LOC}\mid\underline{PROC}))*$$

E. Static Context Conditions:

1   *is-wf-Progr(p)* =
     is-wf-Block(p)[]

Program *is* well-formed if its *Block is* well-formed.

2   *is-wf-Block(mk-Block(ids,pm,stl))dict* =
.1   (*let dict'* = *dict* + ([*id→LOC* | *id∈ids*]
.2   ∪[*id→s-pml(pm(id))* | *id∈dompm*]) *in*
3   (*ids* ∩ *dompm* = {})   ∧
4   (∀*id* ∈ *dompm*)(*is-wf-Procedure(id,pm(id))dict'*)   ∧
5   (∀*stmt* ∈ *rng stl*) (*is-wf-Stmt(stmt)idct'*))

Block is well-formed if:

.3   No *Identifier* is defined both as a variable and as a *Procedure* name, and

2.4   all *Procedures* are well-formed in the lexicographically embracing
      scope, *dict'*, defined up till now, and

2-5   all *Statements* are well-formed, also in the context so far defined.

dict' (2.1-2) is the association (*DICT*) which to any variable name
binds the fact, <u>LOC</u>, that it is a variable, and to any *Procedure* name
that it is a <u>PROC</u>edure -- in particular it then binds defined *Proce*-
dures to the formal *parameter* list with its type indications.

3   *is-wf-Procedure(id,mk-Proc(pml,bl))dict =*
.1   *(id* ⌐∈ *{pml[i,1]|i∈indpml})*   ∧
.2   *(∀i,j∈indpml)(s-Id(pml[i])=s-Id(pml[j])* ⊃ *i=j)*   ∧
.3   *(<u>let</u> dict' = dict +[s-Id(pml[i])→s-Tp(pml[i])|i∈indpml] <u>in</u>*
.4   *is-wf-Block(bl)dict')*

A *Procedure is* well-formed, in the context *dict*, if

3.1   the procedure name, *id*, is not also that of a formal *parameter*
      name, and

3.2   no two formal *parameters* have the same name, and

3.3   otherwise the body, *bl*, of the procedure *is* well-formed in the
      context, *dict'*, which to *dict* additionally binds formal *parameter*
      *Id*entifiers to their type indicator.

4   *is-wf-Stmt(s)dict =*
.1   *<u>cases</u> s:*
.2   *(mk-Call(id,el)*   → *((id ∈ <u>dom</u>dict)*   ∧
.3   *(∀e ∈ <u>rng</u>el)(is-wf-Expr(e)dict)*   ∧
.4   *((dict(id) = <u>PROC</u>)*   ∨
.5   *(<u>LOC</u> ≠ dict(id)) ⊃*
.6   *(<u>let</u> pml = dict(id);*
.7   *(<u>l</u>pml = <u>l</u>el)*   ∧
.8   *(∀i ∈ <u>ind</u>el)*
.9   *(e-tp(el[i])dict ≡ <u>LOC</u> ≡ s-Tp(pml[i]))))),*
.10 *mk-On-Unit(cid,p)*   → *is-wf-Procedure(cid,p)dict,*
.11 *mk-Signal(cid,idl)*   → *(<u>rng</u>idl ∈ <u>dom</u>dict),*
.12 *mk-Revert(cid)*   → *<u>true</u>,*
.13 *T*   → *is-wf-El-Stmt(s)dict) /* not written */*

The well-formedness of a Statement, in the context *dict*, depends on which kind of (what *case* of) Statement it is:

4.2-9   In a subroutine *Call* statement, which consists of a Procedure *identifier* and an expression *list*:

     4.2 The Procedure *identifier* must be known,

     4.4 and must be that of a *PROC*edure,

     4.3 and all expressions of the actual argument expression *list* must be well-formed.

     4.5 If the procedure *identifier* is that of an actually defined, i.e. not formal, procedure,

     4.6 then:

     4.7 the length of the formal parameter *list* and the actual argument expression *list* must be the same,

     4.8 and all corresponding (non-formal procedure)

     4.9 argument expressions and formal parameter must have assignable value types.

4.10   In an *On-Unit* statement, which consists of a condition *identifier* and a procedure body this combination, since it semantically corresponds very much to a procedure, must be a well-formed *Procedure* in the defining *dict*ionary context.

4.11   In a *Signal* statement, which consists of a condition *identifier* and an argument *list* of *identifiers*, these latter must be known in the *dict*ionary context -- it is not possible, due to the dynamic inheritance of associated *On-Units*, to check, as it was in 4.4-4.9, that the type of these arguments 'match' the type of the intended *On-Unit* 'procedure' parameter *list*!

4.12   A *Revert* on any condition *identifier* is always OK!

```
5    is-wf-Expr(e)dict =
 .1      cases:
 .2      (mk-Infix(e1,op,e2)→(is-wf-Expr(e1)dict ∧
 .3                           is-wf-Expr(e2)dict ∧
 .4                           (e-tp(e1)dict = LOC = e-tp(e2)dict)),
 .5           mk-Const(i)      →true
 .6           T                →(e ∈ domdict))
```

F. Auxiliary Text Functions

7   $e\text{-}tp(e)dict =$
.1 $\underline{cases}\ e:$
.2 $(mk\text{-}Infix(e1,op,e2)\rightarrow(op\ \in\ \{EQ,NEQ\})\ \rightarrow\ \underline{BOOL},$
.3 $\qquad\qquad\qquad\qquad\ T\qquad\qquad\qquad\rightarrow\ \underline{LOC}),$
.4 $mk\text{-}Const(i)\qquad\rightarrow\underline{LOC},$
.5 $T\qquad\qquad\rightarrow dict(e))$

G. Semantic Domains

$$STG\ =\quad LOC\ \underset{m}{\rightarrow}\ NUM$$
$$OE\ =\quad Cid\ \underset{m}{\rightarrow}\ FCT$$

$$ENV\ =\quad Id\ \underset{m}{\rightarrow}\ DEN$$
$$DEN\ =\quad LOC\ |\ FCT$$
$$FCT\ =\quad DEN*\ \rightarrow\ (OE\ \rightarrow\ (\Sigma\ \rightarrow\ \Sigma))$$

$$LOC\ \subset\quad TOKEN$$
$$VAL\ =\quad NUM\ |\ BOOL$$

$$\Sigma\ =\quad (\underset{\sim}{STG}\ \underset{m}{\rightarrow}\ STG)\ \ \underline{U}\ \ (\underline{ref}\,OE\ \underset{m}{\rightarrow}\ OE)$$

Annotations:

A *STora* G *e* is a finite domain map from *LOC*ations to assignable values, these are the retional *NUM*bers. An θ*n Establishment* is a finite domain map from *C*ondition *i*dentifiers to the *FunCT*ions they denote.

To model the concept of scope we use the *ENV*ironment abstraction. An *ENV*ironment is a finite domain from *Progr*am text *I*dentifiers to their *DENotations*. The *DEN*otation of a *Progr*am text *I*dentifier is either that of a *LOC*ation (if the *I*dentifier names a variable), or that of a *FunCT*ion (if it names a *Proce*dure). A *FunCT*ion is a (mathematical) function from a list of *DEN*otations (i.e. argument values) to functions from *On Establishments* to functions from states to states! that is: given an *On-Unit* or a *Proce*dure it denotes a function. In the case of the former the argument list is usually predefined, whereas in the latter it is programmer definable. Both denote *FunCT*ions which can be considered evaluated in the dynamic context of the <u>defining</u> *ENV*ironment,

ut the <u>calling</u> On Establishment. Since they are all subroutines, no
alues are returned, but side-effects, i.e. state transformations, are
ffected.

LOCation is an otherwise un-analyzed elementary object. The auxilia-
y category, VAL, stands for the union of rational NUMber and BOOLean
alues.

he state space, Σ, omitting input/output, is a map from one <u>ST</u>ora<u>G</u>e
eference to SToraGes, and a multitude of zero, one, or more <u>ref</u>erences
o On Establishments to On Establishments.

. Global State Initialization:

$$\underline{dcl}\ \underset{\sim}{STG} := [\ ]\quad \underline{type}\ STG$$

. Elaboration Function Types:

1	*type:*	int-Progr:	Progr	$\overset{\sim}{\to} (\Sigma \overset{\sim}{\to} \Sigma)$
2		int-Block:	Block $\overset{\sim}{\to}$ ENV $\overset{\sim}{\to}$ OE	$\overset{\sim}{\to} (\Sigma \overset{\sim}{\to} \Sigma)$
3		int-Stl:	Stmt* $\overset{\sim}{\to}$ ENV $\overset{\sim}{\to}$ (OE <u>ref</u> OE)	$\overset{\sim}{\to} (\Sigma \overset{\sim}{\to} \Sigma)$
4		int-Stmt:	Stmt $\overset{\sim}{\to}$ ENV $\overset{\sim}{\to}$ (OE <u>ref</u> OE)	$\overset{\sim}{\to} (\Sigma \overset{\sim}{\to} \Sigma)$
5		int-Call:	Call $\overset{\sim}{\to}$ ENV $\overset{\sim}{\to}$ OE	$\overset{\sim}{\to} (\Sigma \overset{\sim}{\to} \Sigma)$
6		eval-Proc:	Proc $\overset{\sim}{\to}$ ENV $\overset{\sim}{\to}$	$\overset{\sim}{\to}$ FCT
7		eval-arg:	Expr $\overset{\sim}{\to}$ ENV $\overset{\sim}{\to}$ OE	$\overset{\sim}{\to} (\Sigma \overset{\sim}{\to} \Sigma (FCT \mid LOC))$
8		eval-Expr:	Expr $\overset{\sim}{\to}$ ENV $\overset{\sim}{\to}$ OE	$\overset{\sim}{\to} (\Sigma \overset{\sim}{\to} \Sigma VAL)$

. Auxiliary Function Types

9	*type:*	get-loc:	$\to (\Sigma \to \Sigma \underline{LOC})$
10		free-locs:	Id-set ENV $\overset{\sim}{\to}(\Sigma \to \Sigma)$
11		type-chk:	DEN* (Id (LOC$\mid$PROC))* $\to$BOOL
12		free-dummy-locs:	DEN* Expr* $\to (\Sigma \to \Sigma)$

K. Semantic Elaboration Function Definitions

1 $int-Progr(p) =$
   $int-Block(p)([])([])$

To *interpret* a *Program* is the same as *interpreting* the *Block* it is in
an empty *ENV*ironment and an empty *On-Establishment*.

2 $int-Block(mk-Block(ids,pm,stl,stl))(env)(boe) =$
.1   (<u>let</u> env' : env + ([id → $get-loc()$ | $i \in ids$]
.2   ∪[id → $eval-proc(pm(id))(env')$ | $id \in \underline{dompm}$])
.3   <u>dcl</u> $loe := boe;$
.4 $int-stl(stl)(env)((boe,loe));$
.5 $free-locs(ids,env'))$

Interpreting a *Block* whose locally defined variables are represented
by *ids*, locally defined procedures by *pm*, and statement list by *stl*, is:

2.1 first to associate with each variable identifier a fresh *LOC*ation,
and

2.2 with each procedure identifier the *FunCT*ion it is, the latter in
the, thus circularly defined, defining *environment* (').

2.3 Then to establish a *local on* establishment which inherits the value
of the embracing *blocks' on* establishment,

2.4 whereupon actual execution, after these prologue actions, can take
place of the *statement list*.

2.5 Storage allocated in 2.1 is freed here.

9 $get-loc() =$
.1   (<u>let</u> $l \in \underline{LOC}$ <u>be</u> $s.t.$ $l \not\in \underline{dom}(\underline{c} \underline{STG});$
.2 $\underline{STG} := \underline{c} \underline{STG} \cup [l \rightarrow \underline{undefined}];$
.3   <u>return</u>$(l))$

This function allocates and 'initializes' to <u>undefined</u>, $\underline{STorage}$ on a
per-*location* basis.

10   *free-locs(ids,env) =*
          S̲T̲G̲ := o̲S̲T̲G̲\{env(id) | id∈ids}

This is block termination S̲Tora̲G̲e freeing epilogue action.

7 *eval-proc(mk-Proc(pml,bl))(env) =*
.1   *(l̲e̲t̲ f(al)(oe) =*
.2   *(i̲f̲ ~type-match(al,pml)*
.3   *t̲h̲e̲n̲ e̲r̲r̲o̲r̲*
.4   *e̲l̲s̲e̲ (l̲e̲t̲ env'=env+[s-Id(pml[i])→al[i]|i∈indal];*
.5   *int-block(bl)(env')(oe))) i̲n̲*
       f)

12 *type-match(al,pml) =*
.1   *((l̲al = l̲pml) ∧*
.2   *(∀i∈indal)(is-L̲O̲C̲(al[i]) ≡ s-Tp(pml[i]) = L̲O̲C̲))*

The meaning of a *Procedure* is the *f*unction it denotes. This *f*unction is implicitly defined by what happens if it is *Call*ed. Then:

7.4 the defining *environ*ment is augmented with the bindings between formal *p*arameter *l*ist *id*entifiers and the passed actual *a*rgument *l*ist *DEN*otations,

7.5 whereupon the *b*lock of the *Proc*edure (the 'body') is elaborated in the callling state, but essentially the defining *environ*ment! Since the calling state involves the *on*-establishment, and since each *Block* potentially defines its own 'copy' which may be dynamically updated, one needs to pass the v̲a̲l̲u̲e̲ of the current blocks' local *on* establishment to the invocation of the *Proc*edure denotation; hence, in line :

7.1 the functional dependency on the calling states' *on* establishment.

7.2 The type-check is statically decidable for ordinary procedures, but not for *On-Unit* procedures.

3 *int-Stl(stl)(env)(oep) =*
.1   *f̲o̲r̲ i=1 d̲o̲ l̲e̲n̲ stl d̲o̲ int-Stmt(stl[i])(env)(oep)*

To *interpret* a *list* is the same as *interpreting* each of its *Statements* in the order listed.

```
4     int-Stmt(s)(env)((boev,loer)) =
.1        cases s:
2         (mk-Call(id,el)→
3                (let al : <eval-arg(el[i])(env)(cloer)|i∈indel>;
4                 let f = env(id) in
5                 f(al)(cloer);
6                 free-dummy-locs(al,el)),
7         mk-On-Unit(cid,p)→
8                (let f = eval-proc(p)(env) in
9                 loer := cloer + [cid→f]),
10        mk-Signal(cid,idl)→
11               (let al = <env(idl[i])|i∈indidl> in
12                if cid ∈ dom(cloer)
13                  then (let f : (cloer)(cid);
14                        f(al)(cloer))
15                  else error),
16        mk-Revert(cid)→
17               if cid ~∈ domboev
18                 then loer := cloer∖{cid}
19                 else loer := cloer + [cid→boev(cid)]),
20    T        →int-El-Stmt(s)(env)(cloer))
```

4.   To *interpret* a *Statement* is a function of what *statement* it is:

4.2-6   *interpreting* a subroutine *Call* statement consists of the following sequence of actions:

4.3   Each *expression* of the *Argument* *list* is *evaluated*,

4.4   and the procedure (i.e. -*identifier*) denotation retrieved from the scope,

4.5   whereupon it is being applied to the evaluated *argument* *list* and the value (i.e. *contents*) of the current, *local* *on* establishment.

4.6   The locations allocated during *Argument* *evaluation* -- see 13 below -- are freed.

.7-9 *interpreting* an *On-Unit* results in the update of the *local* on establishment (known by *reference*) with the function denoted by the *On-Unit* procedure body in the position known as *cid*, i.e. for that on *condition identifier*.

.10-15 *interpreting* a *Signal* statement is like *Calling* a subroutine, but there are some significant differences.

4.11 First all *expressions* of the argument *list* must all be *identifiers*, whereby their denotation can be extracted right from the calling (i.e. *Signalling*) *environment*.

4.12 If the designated (*cid*) *On-Unit* has not been defined (by some *On-Unit* of the embracing scope) then

4.15 an *error* situation has arisen,

4.13 otherwise the *function* denoted by the specifically *Signal*-led (i.e. *identified*) condition *On-Unit*

4.14 is applied to the *argument list* concocted in line 4.11. Observe that no *environment* is supplied, but that the contents of the current, the *local* on establishment is. The former is 'embedded' in the *function* denotation, the latter part of its functionality.

.16-19 *interpreting* a *Revert* statement has the effect of letting the current, the *local* on establishment henceforth associate the denotation of the *condition identifier* with its value in the *on* establishment of the embracing *block*.

.. etcetera.

```
8  eval-arg(e)(env)(loev) =
.1     cases e:
.2       (mk-Infix(,,) → (let v : eval-expr(e)(env)(loev),
.3                           l ∈ LOC be s.t. l ~∈ dom(cSTG);
.4                        STG := cSTG ∪ [l→v];
.5                        return(l)),
.6       mk-Const(i) → (let l ∈ LOC be s.t. l ~∈ dom(cSTG);
.7                        STG := cSTG ∪ [l→i];
.8                        return(l)),
.9       T            → return(env(e)))
```

*eval*uating a subroutine *Call* *arg*ument proceeds according to the following basic scheme. The exemplified language has *Call*-by-*LOC*ation for objects other than procedures. Thus:

8.2.5   *Infix* argument *expr*essions are *eval*uated, a fresh $\underset{\sim}{S}$Tora$\underset{\sim}{G}$e pseudo *loc*ation is 'fetched', and $\underset{\sim}{S}$Tora$\underset{\sim}{G}$e initialized to the argument expression *value*, with the new *loc*ation being *return*ed.

8.6-8   Likewise for *Cons*tant expressions.

8.9   All other expressions, i.e. variable- and *Proc*edure *i*dentifiers result directly in their denotation being retrieved from the scope.

Thus *Proc*edure denotations is passed by-worth!

```
13 free-dummy-locs(al,el) =
.1      (let locs = {al[i] | ~is-Id(el[i]) ∧ i∈indel};
.2       STG := cSTG∖locs)
```

```
9   eval-expr(e)(env)(oe) =
.1      cases e:
.2      (mk-Infix(e1,op,e2)
.3          → (let v₁ : eval-expr(e1)(env)(oe),
.4                 v₂ : eval-expr(e2)(env)(oe);
.5             cases op:
.6             (ADD → ((v₁+v₂ ≥ 2↑64)
.7                       →  (if OFL ∈ domoe
.8                           then (dcl n := v₁+v₂;
.9                                 (oe(OFL))(n);
.10                                return(cn))
.11                          else return(2↑64)),
.12                   (v₁+v₂ < -2↑64)
.13                       →  (if UFL ∈ domoe
.14                           ...),
.15                   T  →  return(v₁+v₂)),
.16             SUB → ...
.17             ...
.18             EQ  → return(v₁=v₂)
.19             ...)),
.20      mk-Const(i)
.21          → return(i),
.22      T → (cSTG)(env(id)))
```

We concentrate on lines 9.6-9.11.

If evaluation of an arithmetic expression leads to overflow (9.6), then either of two situations occur.

Either there is defined, by the programmer, an *On-Unit*, in the current Establishment, for handling *OverFLow*, and then this unit is called (9.9) passing to it -- as a hypothetical example -- reference to a meta-variable initialized to the overflow value. The value of the expression becomes the contents of this variable (9.10) after execution of the defined *On Unit* procedure (9.9). Thus we expect the programmer to define the *OFL* on-units with one formal parameter of type *LOC*ation. We do not show a static test for this -- but could have.

Or: the programmer has not defined an appropriate *OFL* *On-Unit* in which case the SYSTEM action is to return, say the maximum arithmetic-value (9.11)!

Comment

From the definition we can informally derive the following informal,
technical english, users programming reference manual-like, description
of the On-Condition concept.

*On-Unit*s are like assignment statements. The target reference is one,
of a limited variety, of condition codes (*cid*). The right-hand side
expression is restricted to be a procedure (4.7-9).

To *Signal* is to invoke the most recently 'assigned' *On-Unit* of the name
(*cid*) signalled. Thus a *Signal* is like a *Call*.

To *Revert* is to locally re-assign   the *On-Unit* most recently 'assigned' in the immediately, dynamically containing block.

Further: To each block activation we let there correspond an association of *cid*s to *On-Unit* procedure values called an On-Establishment
(2.3). A block activation inherits the value of this association in the
invoking block (respectively calling procedure) (2.3 from 4.5 + 7.5).
'Falling' back to the interpretation of an invoking block brings us
back to the on-establishment of this latter block current when this
block invoked the block just terminated.

Finally: Procedures are elaborated in the defining environment (2.2 →
7.4-5), but in the calling on-establishment (4.5 → 7.1-5).

Discussion

We shall only discuss the local/global state modeling chosen in our
conceptualization of the source language On Condition-, respectively
Variable constructs. Our first example illustrated that model components, like the state (Σ), which are transformable by any syntactic
construct, can indeed be an explicit parameter to functions elaborating these constructs, provided, of course, that the possibly changed
state is likewise explicitly yielded as part, or all, of the result.
This is the rule followed in all of the Oxford models; many examples
in [Bjørner 78b] also exemplified this specification style. For block-
structured imperative programming languages it soon, however, becomes
rather cumbersome to write, and read, all these explicit passings and
returns of such all-pervasive, components.

nce itwas decided, as a concession to readability, as well as to engi-
eering, to permit variables in the meta-language. The point is now
o use variables sparingly, and to have their introduction, the fact
hether they are local or global, and their manipulation, reflect the
ery essence of the concept they are intended to model. Therefore:

ince $source$-$language$ variables, declared at any (source-language-)
lock- & procedure level, can be changed at any other, "inner" and
outer" level, the storage component of the state was chosen to be
odeled by a single, global meta-variable. (That sl-variables can be
pdated on levels outside their scope is due to the by-$\underline{LOC}$ation para-
eter passing capability.)

nd: since On-$Units$ correspond to assignments to variables (names in
id) of type procedure- (or, as in PL/I, entry-) value, the model com-
onent (on-establishment), keeping track of current Cid to procedure
alue associations, was also chosen to be a meta-variable. Further:
ince such 'assignments' in one block ($loen$) are not to disturb the
ssociations recorded in any containing block (boe), we introduce one
uch meta-variable, loe, per block activation. To shield the boe, which
s needed in a directly contained block due to $Reverts$, it is passed
y value, i.e. its content ($4.5 \rightarrow 7.5 \rightarrow 2.0 \rightarrow 2.4$); whereas the $local$
e is passed by $\underline{ref}$erence ($loen \in \underline{ref} OE$) ($2.3 \rightarrow 2.4 \rightarrow 4.0 \rightarrow 4.9, 4.18$,
.19).

odeling on-establishments by locally declared meta-language variables
hifts the burden of 'stacking' embracing on-establishments from the
efiner, and of understanding these usually rather mechanical descrip-
ions away from the reader, and onto the meta-language: its semantics,
espectively the readers understanding of, in this case, recursion.

ACKNOWLEDGEMENTS:

The author is very pleased to express, once more, his deep gratitude
for his former colleagues at the IBM Vienna Laboratory, and to Mrs.
Annie Rasmussen for her virtuoso juggling of eight distinct IBM "golf
ball" type fonts.

ACM 65]
ACM: Conference on: Programming Languages and Prag=
matics -- San Dimas, California, August 1965. Ex=
cerpts in: Comm.ACM, vol. 9, no. 6, 1966.

ADJ 77]
J.A.Goguen, J.W.Thatcher, E.G.Wagner & J.B.Wright:
"Initial Algebra Semantics and Continuous Algebra
Jour. ACM, vol.24, no.1, pp. 68-95, Jan. 1977.

Allen 72]
C.D.Allen, D.N.Chapman & C.B.Jones: "A Formal De=
finition of ALGOL 60", IBM (Hursley) Techn.Rept.No.
TR12.105, Hursley, Hants, UK., August 1972.

Alber 69]
K.Alber, H.Goldmann, P.Lauer, P.Lucas, P.Oliva, R.
Stigleitner, K.Walk & G.Zeisel: "Informal Intro=
duction to the Abstract Syntax and Interpretation
of PL/I", IBM (Vienna) Techn.Rept.No.TR25.099, Vien=
na, Austria, June 1969.

Backus 59]
J.W.Backus: "The Syntax and Semantics of the Pro=
posed International Algebraic Language of the Zü=
rich ACM-GAMM Conference", ICIP Proceedings, Paris
1959, Butterworth's, London, pp.125-132, 1960.

Bandat 65]
K.Bandat: "Tentative Steps Towards a Formal Defini=
tion of the Semantics of PL/I", IBM (Vienna) Techn.
Report.No.TR25.065, Vienna, Austria, July 1965.

Bekič 70a]
H.Bekič: "On the Formal Definition of Programming
Languages", (in:) Proceedings of the European ACM
Int'l.Comp.Symp.'70, Bonn, Germany, Nov.1970.

Bekič 70b]
------- & K.Walk: "Formalization of Storage Proper=
ties", in: [Engeler 71]

Bekič 71]
-------: "Towards a Mathematical Theory of Proces=
ses", IBM (Vienna) Techn.Rept.No.TR25.125, Vienna,
Austria, Dec.1971.

Bekič 74]
-------, D.Bjørner, W.Henhapl, C.B.Jones & P.Lucas:
"A Formal Definition of a PL/I Subset", IBM (Vien=
na) Techn.Rept.No.TR25.139, Vienna, Austria, Dec.
1974.

Bjørner 77a]
D.Bjørner: "Programming Languages: Formal Develop=
ment of Interpreters & Compilers", in: [Morlet 77]
pp.1-22.

Bjørner 77b]
---------: "Programming Languages: Linguistics and
Semantics", in: [Morlet 77], pp.511-536.

Bjørner 77c]
---------: "Systematic Program Derivation Techni=
ques", Dept.of Comp.Sci.,Techn.Rept.ID677, Techn.
University of Denmark, Nov.1976/April 1977.

Bjørner 77d]
---------: "The Systematic Development of a Compi=
ling Algorithm", ibid, ID681, Aug.1977.

Bjørner 77e]
---------: "Experiments in Block-Structured GOTO-
Language Modeling", ibid, ID716, July 1977.

[Bjørner 78a] --------- & C.B.Jones (eds.): "The Vienna Develop= ment Method: The Meta-Language", Springer Verlag, 'Lecture Notes in Computer Science', This Volume, } elberg - New York, 1978.

[Bjørner 78b] D.Bjørner: "Programming in the Meta-Language: A Tutorial", in: [Bjørner 78a] pp. 24-217.

[Bjørner 78c] ---------: "Software Abstraction Principles: Tutor= ial Examples of an Operating System Command Languag Specification and a PL/I-like On-Condition Language Definition", in: [Bjørner 78a] ,pp. 337-374.

[Burstall 69] R.M.Burstall & P.J.Landin: "Programs and their Proo An Algebraic Approach", in: 'Machine Intelligence', (ed.D.Michie) vol.4,pp.17-43, Edinburgh Univ.Press, 1969.

[Chomsky 59] N.Chomsky: "On Certain Formal Properties of Gram= mars", Information & Control, vol.2, no.2, pp.137- 167, 1959.

[Church 41] A.Church: "The Calculi of Lambda-Conversion", Annal of Math.Studies, no.6, Princeton University Press, 1941.

[deBakker 69] J.de Bakker: "Semantics of Programming Languages", in: 'Advances in Information Systems Sciences, vol. 2, chap.3, Plenum Press, pp. 173-227, 1969.

[deMorgan 75] R.M.de Morgan, I.D.Hill & B.A.Wichman: "Modified Re= port on the Algorithmic Language ALGOL 60", BCS Com Journal, vol.19, pp.364-379, Nov.1976.

[Dennis 75] J.B.Dennis: "Modularity", in: 'Software Engineering (ed.F.L.Bauer) Springer Verlag, 'Lecture Notes in Computer Science', vol.30, Heidelberg - New York, pp 128-182, 1975.

[Dijkstra 62] E.W.Dijkstra: "An Attempt to Unify the Constituent Concepts of Serial Program Execution", in: 'Symboli Languages in Data Processing', Proceedings ICC Symp Rome 1962, Gordon & Breach, New York, pp.237-251, 1962.

[Dijkstra 68] -------------: The Structure of THE Multiprogramming System", Comm.ACM, vol.11, no.5, pp.341-346, 1968.

[Dijkstra 75] -------------: "Guarded Commands, Non.Determinacy & Formal Program Derivation", Comm.ACM, vol.18, no. 8, pp.453-457, 1975.

[Dijkstra 76] -------------: "A Discipline of Programming", Pren- tice-Hall, 1976.

[ECMA 74] European Comp.Mfg.Assoc.: "PL/I BASIS/1" (also: A= merican National Standards Inst.) ECMA/TC10 & ANSI. X3J1, Basis/1-12, July 1974.

[Elgot 64] C.C.Elgot & A.Robinson: "Random-Access, Stored-Pro= gram Machines: an Approach to Programming Langua= ges", Jour.ACM, vol.11, no.4, pp.365-399, 1964.

[Engeler 71] "Symposium on Semantics of Algorithmic Languages", (ed.:E.Engeler), Springer Verlag: 'Lecture Notes in Mathematics', vol.188, 1971.

leck 69]   M.Fleck: "Formal Definition of the PL/I Compile
Time Facilities", IBM (Vienna) Techn.Rept.No.25.
095, Vienna, Austria, June 1965.

loyd 67]   R.W.Floyd: "Assigning Meanings to Programs", in:
'Mathematical Aspects of Comp.Sci.', Proceedings
of Symposia in Appl.Math., vol.19, (ed.J.Schwartz)
American Math.Soc., Providence, Rhode Island, pp.
19-32, 1967.

'orino 66]   Carraciolo di Forino: "Generalized Markov Algorithms
and Automata", in: 'Automata Theory', (ed.:E.R.Ca=
ianello) Academic Press, pp.115-130, 1966.

uttag 77]   J.Guttag: "Abstract Data Types and the Development
of Data Structures", Comm.ACM, vol.20, no.6, pp.
396-404, June 1977.

alås 75]   A.Halås: "Event Driven Control Statements", BIT, vol.
15, pp.259-271, 1975.

ansal 76]   A.Hansal: "A Formal Definition of a Relational Data
Base System", IBM (Peterlee) Techn.Rept.No.UKSC0080,
June 1976.

ansen 73]   P.B.Hansen: "Operating System Principles", (ref.:pg.
135 top) Prentice-Hall, 1973.

enderson 75]   D.A.Henderson: "The Binding Model: A Semantic Base
for Modular Programming Systems", MIT (project MAC)
Techn.Rept.No.TR-145, Feb.1975.

enhapl 70a]   W.Henhapl & C.B.Jones: "On the' Interpretation of GOTO
Statements in the ULD", IBM (Vienna) Lab.Note.No.LN
25.3.065, March 1970.

enhapl 78]   W.Henhapl & C.B.Jones: "A Formal Definition of ALGOL
60 as Described in the 1975 Modified Report", in:
[Bjørner 78a], pp.305-336, 1978.

oare 69]   C.A.R.Hoare: "The Axiomatic Basis of Computer Pro=
gramming", Comm.ACM, vol.12, no.10, pp.576-583, Oct.
1969.

oare 71]   -----------: "Procedures and Parameters: An Axiomatic
Approach", in: [Engeler 71] , pp. 102-116.

oare 73]   ----------- & N.Wirth: "An Axiomatic Definition of
the Programming Language PASCAL", Acta Informatica,
vol.2 ,   pp.335-355, 1973.

oare 74]   C.A.R.Hoare & P.Lauer: "Consistent and Complementary
Formal Theories of the Semantics of Programming Lan=
guages", Acta Informatica, vol.3,   pp.135-153,
1974.

Izbicki 75]   H.Izbicki: "On a Consistency Proof of a Chapter of
the Formal Definition of a PL/I Subset", IBM (Vienna)
Techn.Rept.No.TR25.142, Feb.1975.

Jones 70]   C.B.Jones: "Yet Another Proof of the Block Concept",
IBM (Vienna) Lab.Note.No.LN25.3.075, Vienna, Austria,
Aug.1975.

[Jones 71]   C.B.Jones & P.Lucas: "Proving Correctness of Im=
              plementation Techniques", in: [Engeler 71] , pp.
              178-211 .

[Jones 72]   C.B.Jones: "Formal Development of Correct Algorithm
              An Example Based on Earley's Recogniser", ACM SIGPI
              /SIGACT Symp. on 'Proving Assertions about Programs
              Las Cruces, Jan. 72, SIGPLAN NOTICES, vol.7, no.1,
              pp. 150-169, 1972.

[Jones 75]   ----------: "Formal Definition in Program Develop=
              ment", in: Springer Verlag 'Lecture Notes in Com=
              puter Science', vol.23, pp. 387- 443, 1975.

[Jones 76a]   ----------: "Formal Definition in Compiler Develop=
              ment", IBM (Vienna) Techn.Rept.No.TR25.145, Vienna,
              Austria, Feb.1976.

[Jones 77a]   ----------: "Program Specifications and Formal Devel
              ment", in [Morlet 77], pp. 537-554.

[Jones 77c]   ----------: "Implementation Bias in Constructive
              Specifications", IBM (La Hulpe) Manuscript, Sept.
              1977.

[Jones 78a]   ----------: "The Meta-Language: A Reference Manual",
              in: [Bjørner 78a] , pp. 218-277.

[Jones 78b]   ----------: "Denotational Semantics of GOTO: An Exit
              Formulation and its Relation to Continuations",
              in: [Bjørner 78a] , pp. 278-304.

[King 75]   J.C.King: "A New Approach to Program Testing", in:
              Springer Verlag, 'Lecture Notes in Computer Science
              vol.23, ("Programming Methodology") pp.278-290,1975

[Kleene 67]   S.C.Kleene: "Mathematical Logic", Wiley & Sons, 196

[Knuth 68]   D.E.Knuth: "Semantics of Context-Free Languages",
              Mathematical Systems Theory, vol.2, pp.127-145,1968

[Knuth 74]   ----------: "Structured Programming with GOTO State=
              ments", ACM Computing Surveys, vol.6, no.4, pp.261-
              302, 1974.

[Landin 64]   P.J.Landin: "The Mechanical Evaluation of Expres=
              sions", BCS Computer Journal, vol.6, no.4, pp.308-
              320, 1964.

[Landin 65]   -----------: "A Correspondance Between ALGOL 60 and
              Church's Lambda-Notation", (2 Parts) Comm.ACM, vol.
              8, nos.2-3, pp.89-101 & 158-165, Feb.-March 1965.

[Lauer 68]   P.E.Lauer: "Formal Definition of ALGOL 60", IBM
              (Vienna) Techn.Rept.No.TR25.088, Dec.1968.

[Lauer 71]   ----------: "Consistent Formal Theories of the Seman
              tics of Programming Languages",(Ph.D.Thesis) IBM
              (Vienna) Techn.Rept.No.TR25.121, Nov.1971.

[Lee 72]   J.A.N.Lee: "Computer Semantics", Van Nostrand Rein=
              hold Co., 1972.

iskov 75]   B.H.Liskov & S.N.Zilles: "Specification Techniques
                for Data Abstractions", IEEE Trans.Softw.Eng.,vol.
                SE-1,(vol.1) no.1, pp.7-19, March 1975.

ondon 70]   R.L.London: "Bibliography on Proving the Correctness
                of Computer Programs", in: 'Machine Intelligence',
                (eds.Meltzer & Michie), vol.5, Edinburgh Univ.Press,
                pp.569-580. 1969.

ucas 68]   P.Lucas: "Two Constructive Realizations of the
                Block Concept and Their Equivalence", IBM (Vienna)
                Techn.Rept.No.TR25.085, Vienna, Austria, June 1968.

ucas 69]   ------- & K.Walk: "On the Formal Description of
                PL/I", Annual Review in Automatic Programming,vol.
                6, pt.3, Pergamon Press, 1969.

ucas 73]   P.Lucas: "On Program Correctness and the Stepwise
                Development of Implementations", in: Proceedings
                'Convegno di Informatica Teorica', Univ.of Pisa,
                Italy, pp.219-251, March 1973.

Lucas 78]   -------: "On the Formalization of Programming Lan=
                guages: Early History & Main Approaches", in:
                [Bjørner 78a], pp. 1 - 23.

Madsen 77]   J.Madsen: "An Experiment in Formal Definition of
                Operating System Facilities", Inform.Proc.Letters,
                vol.6, no.6, pp. 187-189, Dec. 1977.

Manna 72]   Z.Manna & J.Vuillemin: "Fixed-Point Approach to the
                Theory of Computation", Stanford Univ., Comp.Sci.
                Dept. & Dept.of Artif.Intell.Rept.AIM 164, also:
                ACM SIGPLAN Notices, Jan.1972.

McCarthy 63]   J.McCarthy: "Towards a Mathematical Science of Com=
                putation", in: 'Information Processing', North-Hol=
                land Publ., 1963.

McCarthy 67]   ---------- & J.Painter: "Correctness of a Compiler
                for Arithmetic Expressions", Proceedings of Sympo=
                sia in Applied Mathematics, 'Mathematical Aspects
                of Computer Science', (ed.J.Schwartz), American
                Math.Soc., Rhode Island, pp. 33-41, 1967.

McCarthy 66]   J.McCarthy: "A Formal Description of a Subset of
                ALGOL", in:

Milne 74]   R.E.Milne: "The Formal Semantics of Computer Lan=
                guages and Their Implementation", Ph.D.Thesis,PRG-
                13, Techn.Microfiche TCF-2, Oxford Univ.Prgr.Res.
                Grp., 1974.

Milne 76]   --------- & C.Strachey: "A Theory of Programming
                Language Semantics", Chapman and Hall, 1976.

Milner 73]   R.Milner: "An Approach to the Semantics of Paral=
                lel Programs", in: Proceedings 'Convegno di In=
                formatica Teorica', Univ.of Pisa, Italy, pp.285 ff.,
                March 1973.

Morlet 77]   E.Morlet & D.Ribbens: 'International Computing Sym=
                posium 77', European ACM, North-Holland, 1977.

[Morris 38]   C.Morris: "Foundations of the Theory of Signs", in:
                   'International Encyclopedia of Unified Science',
                   vol.1, no.2, Univ.of Chicago Press, 1938.

[Morris 55]   --------: 'Signs, Language and Behaviour', G.Bra=
                   ziller, New York, 1955.

[Morris 73]   F.L.Morris: "Advice on Structuring Compilers and
                   Proving them Correct", in: 'Principles of Program=
                   ming Languages', ACM SIGPLAN Symp., Boston, pp.
                   144-152, Oct.1973.

[Moser 70]   E.Moser: "On a Formal Description of an Indexed
                   Sequential Dataset", IBM (Vienna) Lab.Rept.No.
                   LR25.1.010, March 1970.

[Mosses 74]   P.D.Mosses: "The Mathematical Semantics of ALGOL
                   60", Oxford Univ.Prgr.Res.Grp., PRG-12, 1974.

[Mosses 75]   ----------: The Semantics of Semantic Equations",
                   in: Springer Verlag, 'Lecture Notes in Computer
                   Science', vol.28, pp.409-422, 1975.

[Mosses 76]   ----------: "Mathematical Semantics and Compiler
                   Generation", Ph.D.Thesis, Oxford Univ., Prgr.Res.
                   Grp., April 1974.

[Mosses 77]   ----------: "Making Denotational Semantics Less
                   Concrete", Pres.Bad Honnef, Germany, March 1977.

[Naur 63]   P.Naur: "Revised Report on the Algorithmic Lan=
                   guage ALGOL 60", (editor) Comm.ACM, vol.6, no.1,
                   pp.1 ff, 1963.

[Neuhold 71]   E.Neuhold: "The Formal Description of Programming
                   Languages", IBM Systems Journal, vol.10, no.2,
                   pp.86-112, 1971.

[Nilsson 76]   J.F.Nilsson: "Relational Data Base Systems - Form=
                   alization and Realization", Ph.D.Thesis, Dept.of
                   Comp.Sci., Techn.Univ. of Denmark, Rept.ID641,
                   1976.

[Ollongren 75]   A.Ollongren: "A Definition of Programming Langu=
                   ages by Interpreting Automata", Academic Press,
                   1975.

[Park 70]   D.Park: "Fixpoint Induction and Proofs of Program
                   Properties", in: 'Machine Intelligence', (eds.
                   Meltzer and Michie) vol.5, Edinburgh Univ.Press,
                   pp.59-78, 1970.

[Reynolds 72]   J.C.Reynolds: "Definitional Interpreters for
                   Higher-Order Programming Languages", Procs.25th
                   ACM Nat'l.Conf., pp.717-740, 1972.

[Reynolds 73]   ------------: "Algebraic & Mathematical Semantics",
                   Course Notes SIS 670, Dept.of Sys.& Inf.Sci.,
                   Syracuse Univ.,N.Y., 1973.

[Reynolds 74]   ------------: "On the Relation Between Direct and
                   Continuation Semantics", Springer Verlag 'Lecture
                   Notes in Computer Science', vol.14, 1974.

Reynolds 75]   ------------: "Relational and Continuation Seman=
                tics for a Simple Imperative Language", 1975.

Reynolds 76]   ------------: "Topics in Programming Languages",
                Course Notes SIS 830, Dept.of Sys.& Inf.Sci.,
                Syracuse Univ., N.Y., 1974.

Schwartz 75]   J.Schwartz: "A Comment on Correctness Proofs",
                SETL Newsletter 159, Courant Inst.of Math., New
                York University, pp.6-15, 1975.

Scott 70]   D.Scott: "Outline of a Mathematical Theory of Com=
                putation", Oxford Univ.,Prgr.Res.Grp., PRG-2, Nov.
                1970.

Scott 71}   -------- & C.Strachey: "Towards a Mathematical Se=
                mantics for Computer Languages", in: Proceedings
                of the Symposium on 'Computers and Automata', MRI
                Symposia, vol.XXI, Polytechnic Inst.of Brooklyn,
                N.Y., 1971.

Scott 72]   D.Scott: "Mathematical Concepts in Programming
                Language Semantics", Proc.AFIPS, Spring Joint
                Computer Conference, vol.40, pp.225-234, 1972.

Scott 76]   -------: "Data Types as Lattices", SIAM Journal
                on Computer Science, vol. 5, no.3 , pp. 522-587,
                1976.

Steel 66]   T.B.Steel: 'Formal Language Description Langua=
                ges" (editor) North-Holland Publ., 1966.

Stoy 74]   J.Stoy: "The Scott-Strachey Approach to the Math=
                ematical Semantics of Programming Languages", MIT
                Lecture Notes, Course 6.791, Fall 1973, also: MIT
                Press, 1977.

Strachey 66]   C.Strachey: "Towards a Formal Semantics", in:
                [Steel 66] , pp. 198-220.

Strachey 73]   ----------: "The Varieties of Programming Langu=
                ages", Oxford Univ.,Prgr.Res.Grp., PRG-10, March
                1973.

Strachey 74]   ---------- and C.Wadsworth: "Continuations: A Math=
                ematical Semantics which can deal with Full Jumps",
                Oxford Univ., Prgr.Res.Grp., PRG-11, 1974.

Tennent 73]   R.D.Tennent: "The Mathematical Semantics of SNOBOL
                4", in: 'Principles of Programming Languages', ACM
                SIGPLAN Symp., Boston, pp. 95 -107, Oct.1973.

Tennent 76]   ----------: "The Denotational Semantics of Pro=
                gramming Languages", Comm.ACM, vol.19, no.8, Aug.
                1976.

Todd 76]   S.J.Todd: "The Peterlee Relational Test Vehicle:
                A System Overview", IBM Systems Journal, vol.15,
                no.4, 1976.

Urschler 69a]   G.Urschler: "Concrete Syntax of PL/I", IBM (Vienna)
                Techn.Rept.No. TR25.096, Vienna, Austria, June 1969.

Urschler 69b]   ----------: "Translation of PL/I into Abstract Syn=
                tax", IBM (Vienna) Techn.Rept.No.TR25.097, Vienna,

[Uzgalis 77]   J.C.Cleaveland & R.C.Uzgalis: "Grammars for Program
                    ming Languages", Elsevier Comp.Sci.Lib., Prgr.Lang.
                    Ser. vol.4, N.Y., 1977.

[Walk 69]   K.Walk, K.Alber, M.Fleck, H.Goldmann, P.Lauer,
                    E.Moser, P.Oliva, H.Stigleitner & G.Zeisel: "Ab=
                    stract Syntax and Interpretation of PL/I (ULD
                    Version III)", IBM (Vienna) Techn.Rept.No.TR25.
                    098, Vienna, Austria, Apr.1969.

[Wegner 72]   P.Wegner: "The Vienna Definition Language", ACM
                    Computing Surveys, vol.4, no.1, March 1972.

[Weissenböck 75]   F.Weissenböck: "A Formal Interface Specification"
                    IBM (Vienna) Techn.Rept.No.TR25.141, Vienna, Au=
                    stria, Feb.1975.

[van Wijngaarden 62] A.van Wijngaarden: "Generalized ALGOL", in: 'Sym=
                    bolic Languages in Data Processing', Proc. ICC
                    Symp., Rome, Gordon & Breach, N.Y., pp.409-419,
                    1962.

[Wirth 71]   N.Wirth: "Program Development by Stepwise Refine=
                    ment", Comm.ACM, vol.14, no.4, pp.221-227, 1971.

[Wirth 73]   -------: "Systematic Programming", Prentice-Hall,
                    1973.

[Wirth 76]   -------: "Algorithms + Data Structures = Programs",
                    Prentice-Hall, 1976.

[Zahn 74]   C.T.Zahn: "A Control Statement for Natural Top-
                    Down Structured Programming", in: 'Programming',
                    Springer Verlag, 'Lecture Notes in Computer Sci.',
                    vol.19, pp.170-180, 1974.

[Zemanek 66]   H.Zemanek: "Semiotics and Programming Languages",
                    Comm.ACM, pp.139-143, 1966.

[Zimmermann 69]   K.Zimmermann: "Outline of a Formal Definition of
                    FORTRAN", IBM (Vienna) Lab.Rept.No.LR25.3.053,
                    Vienna, Austria, June 1969.

49: Interactive Systems. Proceedings 1976. Edited by A. Blaser
C. Hackl. VI, 380 pages. 1976.

50: A. C. Hartmann, A Concurrent Pascal Compiler for Mini-
puters. VI, 119 pages. 1977.

51: B. S. Garbow, Matrix Eigensystem Routines – Eispack
e Extension. VIII, 343 pages. 1977.

52: Automata, Languages and Programming. Fourth Colloquium,
ersity of Turku, July 1977. Edited by A. Salomaa and M. Steinby.
39 pages. 1977.

53: Mathematical Foundations of Computer Science. Proceed-
1977. Edited by J. Gruska. XII, 608 pages. 1977.

54: Design and Implementation of Programming Languages.
eedings 1976. Edited by J. H. Williams and D. A. Fisher. X,
pages. 1977.

55: A. Gerbier, Mes premières constructions de programmes.
56 pages. 1977.

56: Fundamentals of Computation Theory. Proceedings 1977.
d by M. Karpiński. XII, 542 pages. 1977.

57: Portability of Numerical Software. Proceedings 1976. Edited
J. Cowell. VIII, 539 pages. 1977.

58: M. J. O'Donnell, Computing in Systems Described by Equa-
. XIV, 111 pages. 1977.

59: E. Hill, Jr., A Comparative Study of Very Large Data Bases.
0 pages. 1978.

60: Operating Systems, An Advanced Course. Edited by R. Bayer,
. Graham, and G. Seegmüller. X, 593 pages. 1978.

61: The Vienna Development Method: The Meta-Language.
d by D. Bjørner and C. B. Jones. XVIII, 382 pages. 1978.